MADE INTO MOVIES

MADE INTO MOVIES

From Literature to Film

Stuart Y. McDougal

UNIVERSITY OF MICHIGAN

Holt, Rinehart and Winston

New York   Chicago   San Francisco   Philadelphia
Montreal   Toronto   London   Sydney   Tokyo
Mexico City   Rio de Janeiro
Madrid

Library of Congress Cataloging in Publication Data

McDougal, Stuart Y.
  Made into movies.

  Includes index.
    1. Film adaptations—Addresses, essays, lectures.
  2. Moving-picture plays—History and criticism—Addresses, essays, lectures.   I. Title.
  PN1997.85.M33 1985   791.43'75   84-22361

ISBN 0-03-063804-6

Address correspondence to:
383 Madison Ave.
New York, NY 10017

5 6 7 8   090   9 8 7 6 5 4 3 2 1

CBS COLLEGE PUBLISHING

Holt, Rinehart and Winston
The Dryden Press
Saunders College Publishing

Portions of this book first appeared in a different form in *Literature/Film Quarterly,*
Style, and *Modern European Filmmakers and the Art of Adaptation* (eds. Joan
Magretta and Andy Horton). They are reprinted with permission.

Acknowledgments

Chapter 2
Photo, p. 12, courtesy of RKO Pictures and The Museum of Modern Art/Films Stills
Archive.
Photo, p. 18, courtesy of RKO Pictures and National Film Archive/Stills Library.

(Continued on p. 402)

For
Dyanthe, Gavin,
Angus, and Toby

Filmviewers at My Study Door

Preface

Film dominates our culture as no other art. By the time most students reach college, they have had far greater experience with film and video than with the written word. Yet, as a narrative form, film owes a great deal to novels, short stories, and plays. *Made Into Movies* enables students to investigate some of the principal elements shared by literature and film in order to achieve a better understanding of each. Adaptations provide a fertile field for such a study, since they involve the transformation of one art form into another. In deciding how to present his subject, the filmmaker is forced continually to assess the relative strengths and weaknesses of each medium. Through a study of adaptations, students are able to examine the differences between the media and thus become more knowledgeable readers of fiction as well as more perceptive viewers of film.

Made Into Movies is designed to be used in either lower- or upper-division courses in departments of English and American literature, foreign literatures, film, and comparative literature. The book begins with a general introduction to the problems of adaptation. A detailed examination of *Citizen Kane* serves as an introduction to the craft of film for students who have had little or no previous experience with the medium. The 7 chapters that comprise Part II present a series of comparative approaches to literature and film. In novels, short stories, and plays, filmmakers have found ways of telling stories and of developing characters that they have been able to apply to their own medium. Each chapter in *Made Into Movies* focuses on a specific area of similarity (for example, plot, character, point of view) and includes "case studies" of films adapted from literary works as illustrations. Each case study is purposely limited in approach, thereby encouraging discussion of the film from other perspectives as well. Production credits and a short bibliography accompany each study. Through these case studies, students develop a core of information leading to an increased understanding of both media.

Made Into Movies is envisioned as the central book in a course on literature and film. Texts for nine of the twenty-two adaptations are included, and the other texts are readily available in inexpensive paperback editions. The selection of "Additional Recommended Films" that follows each chapter gives the book even greater scope and flexibility. The book concludes with a glossary of literature and film terms.

The comparative analysis of literature and film remains relatively unsystematic and undeveloped. *Made Into Movies* provides a much needed methodology to further the study and discussion of this important subject.

Acknowledgments

Film criticism, like the making of movies, is a collaborative venture. I would like to thank my students at the University of Michigan, who have unknowingly participated in the creation of this book, as have many Graduate Graders, including Bill Grimes, Dave Holman, Paul Beavers, Pete Olson, and Paul Erb; Arthur R. Bottaro, who provided a model of how to teach which shaped the overall conception of this work; Ronald Mallis, who encouraged me to begin this project, and Anne Boynton-Trigg, who urged me to complete it; Karen Gruschow, Maria Palazzola, and Jean Jones, who cheerfully helped with the preparation of the manuscript; Caroline R. Helmuth, who provided invaluable assistance from beginning to end; the many helpful readers of this book, including Pamela Baker, Northeast Louisiana University; Jack Shadoian, University of Massachusetts at Amherst; Frederick Stern, University of Illinois at Chicago; Jim Welsh, Salisbury State College, and especially Eric S. Rabkin, A. R. Fulton, and Murray and Marian McDougal; and, most of all, my wife Nora Gunneng, who shared these films and much much more.

Ann Arbor, Michigan   S.Y.McD.
November 1984

Contents

PART ONE

Focus on Film

1

Adaptation: The Metamorphic Art

When a novel, short story, or play is made into a movie, a metamorphosis occurs. We often speak simply of "filming a book," as though the characters in a work could step off the page and perform before a camera, but this expression fails to convey the complicated processes involved. Every art form has distinctive properties resulting from its medium; a filmmaker must recognize the unique characteristics of each medium before transforming a story into a film. As the youngest of the arts, film has been able to expand her boundaries by drawing on traditions and techniques that have taken her sister arts—music, dance, painting, sculpture, and literature—centuries to develop. By providing stories to tell and ways of telling them, literature has contributed significantly to film. In novels, short stories, and plays, filmmakers have found models of plot construction, methods of delineating character, ways of presenting thought processes, and means of dealing with time and space that they have been able to apply to their own medium. Sergei Eisenstein pointed out forty years ago in his essay, "Dickens, Griffith and the Film Today," that novels contain literary equivalents to fades, dissolves, close-ups, methods of composition, and techniques of editing. The indebtedness of film to literature is considerable. By examining some of the principal elements shared by literature and narrative films, we can understand better the unique characteristics of each. Adaptations provide a fertile field for such a study since they involve the transformation of one art form into another. For the filmmaker, theoretical problems of adaptation require practical solutions; in deciding how to present a subject, the filmmaker is forced continually to assess the relative strengths and weaknesses of each medium. With a successful adaptation, the original work is transformed into something new and different, although retaining many traces of what it was formerly.

Although film is indebted to literature, it has developed its own methods of storytelling. Many early films used plays as their sources because of apparent similarities in terms of spectacle, but most of these movies were little more than mechanical reproductions of dramas. Directors now more frequently take advantage of film's limitless spatial and temporal possibilities to expand a drama. In addition, a director has the means to focus our attention on minute details (through close-ups), suggest relationships (through editing), and present thoughts (through editing, point-of-view shots, composition, and the use of color)—to cite a few of the techniques a filmmaker possesses and a dramatist lacks. A play on the other hand, has a sense of immediacy that film can never capture.

Film shares more methods of storytelling with the novel and short story. In general, novels are contracted when filmed through the deletion of characters and incidents. This contraction results in part from the dictates of time (most films run from ninety minutes to two hours) and the difficulties an audience has in following a large cast of characters, and in part from the nature of the medium. For example, a setting can be presented instantaneously in a film; in a novel the same scene may take many pages of description. Moreover, a director can tell a story while establishing the setting, whereas narration and description are generally developed separately by the novelist. Because of the literalness of the cinematic image, film has a high degree of particularization. Thus, physical details (both for settings and characters) are usually expanded in a film, and the specific, rather than the general, is emphasized. A short story uses the same methods as a novel and is much closer to a film in terms of the number of characters and incidents it presents; if anything, expansion will occur when the story is filmed.

Some of these differences can be highlighted by considering a simple example, like the opening lines of Ambrose Bierce's short story, "An Occurrence at Owl Creek Bridge":

> A man stood upon a railroad bridge in northern Alabama, looking down into the swift water twenty feet below. The man's hands were behind his back, the wrists bound with a cord. A rope loosely encircled his neck.

Bierce presents us with a frozen moment—almost as though he were describing a photograph or painting. These realistic physical details easily allow cinematic depiction, as does the omniscient third-person point of view. But there are also difficulties. This moment has already occurred: How can we indicate the pastness of the event in a single shot or even in several shots?

And how can we establish the location as quickly as Bierce does? Moreover, Bierce purposefully avoids any physical description of his protagonist until several paragraphs later: At this point he is simply "a man." In a film, however, it is extremely difficult to present anything but a very specific individual.

The opening lines of the second part of this story present problems of another sort:

> Peyton Farquhar was a well-to-do planter of an old and highly respected Alabama family. Being a slave owner and like other slave owners a politician, he was naturally an original seccessionist and ardently devoted to the Southern cause. Circumstances of an imperious nature, which it is unnecessary to relate here, had prevented him from taking service with the gallant army which had fought the disastrous campaigns ending with the fall of Corinth, and he chafed under the inglorious restraint, longing for the release of his energies, the larger life of the soldier, and the opportunity for distinction.

To begin with, the prose style is markedly different here. The language of the first selection is stark and realistic; the diction of the second is florid and conveys a definite attitude toward the "southern cause." Terms such as "ardently," "imperious," "gallant," and "inglorious restraint," which would be out of place in the first part of the story create a very definite change of tone here. Bierce also manages to convey considerable information in a highly compressed form. To present this information dramatically, a filmmaker would have to forgo Bierce's economy. And it is difficult to imagine conveying the protagonist's romanticism in as subtle a nature as Bierce does here. Even relatively simple passages such as this, then, require considerable rethinking on the part of the filmmaker.

Many factors that are extrinsic to the medium also shape the creation of any film. Unlike most forms of literature, film is generally a cooperative art, requiring in its production the efforts of many. In addition, the materials of production are very expensive. As a result, economic forces have a greater importance in the making of a film, than, say, in the writing of a poem. Financial supporters are rarely willing to take risks at the box office because such risks threaten their profits. Subjects of limited appeal or of a volatile political or social nature will not easily obtain backing. *The Grapes of Wrath* was a difficult novel to film, in part because of its negative portrayal of the financial institutions and governing classes that traditionally have provided monetary support for films. Consequently, the social and political radicalism of John Steinbeck's novel became severely muted in John Ford's film.

Censorship has affected artists of all sorts, but filmmakers in particular because of the public nature of their work. Until very recently, filmmakers have been restricted in terms of the sexual and political material they could display on the screen, and in many parts of the world, these restrictions still exist. Filmmakers have responded to the challenge of censorship by developing inventive tropes, symbols, and allegories to convey attitudes and actions obliquely. In *High Noon,* for example, Fred Zinnemann attacks the spirit of passivity and conformity in postwar American society in the guise of a western.

Casting, although also extrinsic to the medium of film, considerably shapes the process of adaptation. The contribution of an actor to a film can hardly be emphasized enough. A skillful actor makes a character his own. Once we have viewed *The Grapes of Wrath,* it is difficult to imagine Tom Joad without seeing the lanky physique and sensitive face of Henry Fonda. Fonda was cast "with type," which means that he was accustomed to playing such roles and was easily accepted in the part by his public. Similarly, his daughter, Jane Fonda, was cast with type as Nora in *A Doll's House.* When John Huston cast Audie Murphy, the most highly decorated hero of World War II, as the frightened soldier in *The Red Badge of Courage,* he was casting "against type." Obviously, any film would be radically changed if the casting were altered.

Expectations about a new film are created in part by the actors in it. As producers long ago realized, audiences attend films as much for the stars as for the story. Our responses to a new film are affected by everything we know about its actors. Similarly, with old films, our perceptions are influenced by what the actors have done or become since. When we watch *The Grapes of Wrath,* we cannot help viewing Henry Fonda in terms of the many roles he later played (including President of the United States), just as we recognize Ward Bond (the friendly policeman) and Joe Sawyer (the unfriendly deputy at the Keene Ranch) on the basis of their later television careers. It is equally difficult to view Jane Fonda in *A Doll's House* without thinking of her political and social activism.

Even in as cooperative a venture as filmmaking, strong directors, writers, or producers can create works that reflect their own visions. The extent to which an individual should be called the author (or *auteur,* to use a French term frequently applied to a film's director) depends largely on the amount of control he or she can exercise over the film. Do *auteurs* choose or even write their scripts? Do they have control over editing? Or casting? A consideration of all these factors is important in determining who receives principal credit for a film. *High Noon,* for example, clearly represents the visions of its writer, Carl Foreman, and its director, Fred Zinnemann, more than it does the vision of the author whose short story forms the basis for the film. But the understated acting of Gary Cooper also contributes to the film. *Citizen Kane* expresses the viewpoint of Orson Welles, its director, star, and coauthor, but the extent to which it should be called *his* film has been strongly questioned by Pauline Kael, among others.

Regardless of how we determine authorship, every adaptation is inevitably an interpretation of its source. Some adaptations remain closer in word or spirit to their sources than others, although any ideal of complete fidelity to a source should be dismissed. How could there be a "definitive" film of

Shakespeare's *Macbeth*, when critics have been arguing about the play for nearly four centuries? Roman Polanski and Akira Kurosawa interpret Shakespeare very differently, but both *Macbeth* and *Throne of Blood* are excellent films. The more complex a work, the more open it is to different interpretations, although even relatively simple works, like "Stage to Lordsburg" (*Stagecoach*), are shaped by the visions of their writers and directors.

Many factors, then, both intrinsic and extrinsic, enter the making of an adaptation. In *Made Into Movies*, we will focus on a series of topics intrinsic to both literature and film. These topics have been chosen to represent some of the major areas of convergence of the two media and are meant to suggest approaches to the comparative study of literature and film without by any means being exhaustive. First, however, we will review "the craft of the film" through a detailed examination of *Citizen Kane*. This analysis will provide a sufficient foundation for the study of the comparative topics that form the heart of this book.

A comparative analysis of film and literature, such as the one undertaken here, helps to define the unique properties of each medium by probing its relative strengths and weaknesses. Such an approach should succeed in making better readers and viewers of us all and may even result in making authors and filmmakers of a few.

2

The Craft of Film: Citizen Kane

On Halloween eve, 1938, Orson Welles's Mercury Theater caused a panic on the eastern seaboard with its radio production of *The War of the Worlds*. Based on H. G. Wells's story of an invasion from Mars, the program won both fame and notoriety for Orson Welles, who was already an accomplished director of theatrical and radio plays, and resulted in a contract for him with RKO Radio Pictures. To prepare for his new career, Welles spent hours at the projection facilities of the Museum of Modern Art, viewing the works of Frank Capra, René Clair, John Ford, Fritz Lang, and King Vidor—a practice he continued in Hollywood at the RKO studios. Ford, in particular, was a strong influence, and Welles later noted that "John Ford was my teacher. My own style has nothing to do with his, but *Stagecoach* was my movie textbook. I ran it over forty times."[1] Welles knew that the only way to learn his craft was by viewing and reviewing the greatest works of the past until he thoroughly familiarized himself with their techniques. His lesson should not be lost on us, and there are few better "movie textbooks" than Welles's own first film, *Citizen Kane* (1941). *Citizen Kane* is an eclectic work, drawing on

[1]Peter Cowie, "The Study of a Colossus," in *Focus on Citizen Kane*, ed. Ronald Gottesman (Englewood Cliffs, N.J.: Prentice-Hall, 1971), pp. 112–113.

those films Welles viewed repeatedly, as well as on his own experience in the theater and radio and his own assimilative genius. At the age of twenty-five, Welles produced a masterpiece, which remains one of the most important films ever made.

Citizen Kane tells the story of a fictitious American financier, Charles Foster Kane, whose life is loosely modeled on that of William Randolph Hearst. But *Citizen Kane* is not a conventional biography. The film opens with the death of the protagonist and focuses not on the story of his life but rather on the problems that the media have in capturing that story. The film becomes an examination of the difficulties of understanding such a complex life with the limited means of newspaper, radio, and film.

Orson Welles has always been fascinated with the influence of the media. The success of *The War of the Worlds* demonstrated the power of radio; people believed what they heard, no matter how improbable, particularly when, as in this case, the material was presented in the format of a news broadcast. *Citizen Kane* includes a newsreel, and Welles is relying on the fact that most viewers of newsreels believed in their authenticity. The newsreel in *Citizen Kane* is meant to supplement the newspaper obituary, which the reporters deem insufficient. But the very newsreel that purports to be a factual, objective presentation of Kane's life finally tells us very little, and what it shows is subject to question. "Don't believe everything you hear on the radio," declares Charles Foster Kane with a smile in one of the shots in the newsreel sequence, and his remark could just as easily pertain to film. The comment is also one that Welles could have made himself. In fact, one cannot help being struck by the many parallels between Kane's management of the newspaper and Welles's production of a film; both are communal efforts, and both reveal a dominant personality manipulating his medium for his own ends. As a young man, Kane writes to his financial adviser and guardian, "I think it would be fun to run a newspaper." Welles himself, when first shown the studios at RKO, is reported to have remarked, "This is the biggest electric train a boy ever had."[2] In an important sense, *Citizen Kane* is a film about the power (both historical and actual) and the expressive possibilities of the media, whether newspaper, radio, or film. For this reason, too, it is appropriate that we begin our study of the art of the film with this film, and the discussion that follows is meant to be accompanied by repeated viewings.

In the opening sequence of *Citizen Kane*, Welles purposely disorients and confuses us in order to force us into a questioning mood. Immediately following the titles, Welles fades in on a close-up of an imposing gate, displaying the sign *No Trespassing*. This sign functions realistically within the context of the film, of course, by announcing that we are viewing private property. It also suggests, however, that in entering these domains, we will be trespassing on the privacy of a man's life. In a film that attempts to unravel

[2]Roy A. Fowler, "*Citizen Kane:* Background and a Critique," *Focus,* p. 79.

the mysteries hidden by a man's public face, this beginning is unsettling. The camera then appears to crane up the fence as, with several dissolves, it rises higher and higher.[3] When the camera has scaled the fence, past the grillwork and finally past the large "K" identifying the property, Welles slowly begins to approach the castle. Through a series of establishing shots, separated by dissolves, we traverse the vast area between the fence and the castle, past several chattering monkeys, the sole occupants of an empty zoo; two gondolas floating without passenger or purpose on a large lagoon; a massive statue by a drawbridge over a moat; a marker indicating the distance to the next tee on a deserted golf course; and finally a blank expanse of water. The castle is in the identical place in the composition of each shot; a single window of the castle, being lit, compels our attention. Welles uses the principle of contrast throughout *Citizen Kane*: In a dark composition our eye is drawn to light; in a static composition we are attracted by movement, and vice versa. The choice of transitions here is significant; Welles could have cut directly from one shot to another, but the dissolve permits one scene to give way slowly to another. The transitions suggest that we are witnessing a process of disintegration caused by the destructive nature of time.

Until this moment the film has been realistic, although the extravagance of the setting slightly undercuts the realism. But the light is suddenly extinguished, and with this the conventions of the film cease to be realistic. In retrospect we realize that the sudden absence of light signifies the moment of Kane's death—a metamorphic use of light Welles uses again when Susan Alexander attempts suicide. From the dark window, Welles dissolves to a lit but unfamiliar scene. Snow is falling lightly on a small cottage, and as the camera dollies away we realize that this pastoral scene is enclosed in a glass ball, clutched by an unidentified hand. However, the snow is not only within the ball but is also falling everywhere within the room that contains the hand holding the ball. Time and space have become distorted. We are seeing the room as Kane sees it (hence, a subjective shot), and he is himself a part of what he sees. The disorientation of the viewer continues as Welles cuts to an extreme close-up of Kane's lips, which now fill the screen. They part and mutter, "Rosebud." Welles cuts to a shot of Kane dropping the ball, which rolls (in slow motion and close-up) down a flight of steps within the bedroom until it breaks. The next shot—of the nurse entering the room—is optically distorted by being filmed through a fragment of the broken glass. She covers Kane's dead body, and the sequence ends.

Although the mode of presentation of the first half of the sequence is realistic, the subject matter is not within the realm of most viewer's daily ex-

---

[3] The script identifies this as a "pan up." This is impossible; a pan is the movement of a camera on a stationary base through a horizontal plane, whereas a tilt is the movement of a camera on a stationary base through a vertical plane. But neither does the camera tilt; it first appears to be a moving camera, rising on a crane (a crane shot), but on closer examination the viewer notes that the shot is created with miniatures and that the background is moving.

perience. Thus, the subject matter provides a subtle modulation to the second half of the sequence, where the mode of presentation is unrealistic and distortion is maintained throughout. This moment is one of the most subjective in the entire film, for the world we view is seen as Kane sees it and heard as he hears it. Within the opening minutes of the film, the camera has penetrated not only the _No Trespassing_ sign, but Kane's mind as well.

The mood of the opening sequence or prologue is also developed by Bernard Herrmann's superb musical score. Two principal leitmotifs appear in this sequence. As Hermann describes them:

> One—a simple four note figure in the brass—is that of Kane's power. It is given out in the very first two bars of the film. The second motif is that of Rosebud. Heard as a solo on the vibraphone, it first appears during the death scene at the very beginning of the picture. It is heard again and again throughout the film under various guises, and if followed closely, is a clue to the ultimate identity of Rosebud itself.[4]

The combination of sound and visuals presents a complex mystery: "Who is this person," we ask, "and what is Rosebud?"

Without any warning the pace and style of the film change as the newsreel begins. Here, in capsule form, Welles presents the outlines of Kane's life. By doing so, Welles frees himself from the necessity of following a chronological development in the remainder of the film. The viewers understand the flashbacks that comprise the rest of the film because they operate within a framework that has already been established. In addition, the newsreel is a film-within-a-film and thus makes us conscious of our own role as spectators. Welles also employs this device to underline the limitations of cinematic reporting. This use of a film-within-a-film later became a hallmark of such New Wave French films as François Truffaut's _Jules and Jim_.

By carefully following the tone and pace of contemporary newsreels, Welles has created a realistic limitation. The "old" scenes of the newsreel sequence have been treated to make them appear aged so that their texture contrasts with the recent scenes. The earliest scenes have been filmed at slower speeds (silent speeds), and hence appear jerky when projected at a faster speed (sound speed). Older cinematic techniques, such as the iris, date the early parts as well.

There are other subtle visual contrasts within the newsreel. In the scenes where Kane is shown as a young man, full of vitality, the shots are frequently taken from a low camera angle, to emphasize his power and control. Those scenes where Kane is shown as an old man whose powers have failed, on the other hand, are frequently shot from above. In fact, Welles uses camera position throughout the film in this way. He and his photographer, Gregg Toland, experimented with scenes photographed and lit from below. The tra-

---

[4]Bernard Herrmann, "Score for a Film," _Focus,_ p. 70.

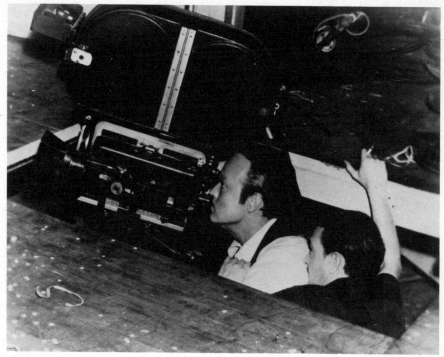

Citizen Kane. Welles at work: Preparing a low-angle shot.

ditional method of lighting scenes had been from above; therefore, most sets
had no ceilings. Toland has commented:

> The *Citizen Kane* sets have ceilings because we wanted reality, and we felt
> that it would be easier to believe a room was a room if its ceiling could
> be seen in the picture. Furthermore, lighting effects in unceilinged rooms
> generally are not realistic because the illumination comes from unnatural
> angles.
>
> We planned most of our camera setups to take advantage of the ceil-
> ings, in some cases even building the sets so as to permit shooting from
> floor level. . . . The ceilings gave us another advantage in addition to
> realism—freedom from worry about microphone shadow, the bugaboo of
> all sound filming. We were able to place our mikes above the muslin ceil-
> ing, which allowed them to pick up sound but not to throw shadows.[5]

Often, as in the scene in the newspaper offices, the ceilings seem oppressively low and hardly able to contain Kane's ebullience and dynamism. By

[5]Gregg Toland, "How I Broke the Rules in *Citizen Kane*," *Focus*, p. 75.

contrast, the higher camera position emphasizes his vulnerability and weakness. The differences between the young and old Kane are also stressed by the movement of the camera. Welles often uses dolly shots, and the movement of the camera as it follows the young Kane is rapid and steady, whereas the dollying of the aged Kane is slow and languid. Thus, Welles shapes our attitudes toward his characters by such simple means as the angle of the camera and the tracking speed.

In our discussion of the opening sequence, we spoke of the importance of the choice of the dissolve as a means of transition, and the same is true of the transitions within the newsreel. Whereas the dissolve dominated the first sequence, here the cut and the wipe are used. Early in the sequence, as the items purchased by Kane are being catalogued, a series of wipes separates one acquisition from another. The wipe emphasizes the rapidity of accumulation, as though one item were pushing another off the screen. Whereas the dissolve of the first sequence communicated dissolution and decay, the wipe suggests vitality and vigor.

Another marked contrast between this and the preceding sequence is in the rhythm. The first sequence moved very slowly. The individual shots had virtually no movement (internal rhythm), and the speed with which one shot succeeded another (external rhythm) was also very slow. In the opening of the newsreel (after the lines about Xanadu), both the internal and external rhythms of the sequence are rapid. This increased pace, coupled with the jarring narration on the soundtrack, shakes us out of the dreamlike state of the prologue.

Clearly, one of Welles's strategies in the early parts of *Citizen Kane* is to keep the viewer off balance. We settle comfortably into the newsreel because it resembles something with which we are familiar, but it concludes abruptly, and we find ourselves in a viewing room, with the arc light of the projector providing the only illumination. Again, light is used metaphorically: The reporters are in the dark, both literally and figuratively. They (and we, the viewers) cannot quite make sense of what has been shown. The newsreel, meant to be definitive, has failed to tell us who this man really was. What follows is—to use the term employed by Thompson at the end of the film—a jigsaw puzzle, in which we finally accumulate more pieces than any of the characters in the film.

Before continuing our examination of these pieces, let us briefly consider the structure of the film. The prologue shows Xanadu in a state of decay and then reveals Kane's subjective perception of the world at the moment of his death, a world he summarizes with the single word, "Rosebud." As yet, we do not understand this word, and the sign with which the film began—*No Trespassing*—indicates that perhaps we never will. Moreover, we are disoriented by the extravagance of the setting and the subsequent dreamlike nature of the shots within the bedroom. The newsreel at least identifies this man and summarizes the external events of his life. We have received no better understanding of the moment of his death; however, a clue to the meaning of "Rosebud" has been given us (in Walter Parks Thatcher's testimony before a Congressional committee), although it is doubtful if at this point in the film we can understand it. Now, by interviewing those closest to Kane (his second wife, Susan Alexander Kane; his former business manager, Bernstein; his friend from school days, Jedediah Leland; and Raymond, his butler at Xanadu), and by examining the diary of his deceased guardian, Walter Parks Thatcher, we begin to piece together the events in Kane's life, from youth to death. This technique permits Welles to show the same event from more than one perspective since the flashbacks overlap each other. Naturally, each character has a distinctive point of view, and the types of material conveyed within each flashback differ. Thatcher's flashback is the most impersonal and factual, presenting only what he could have witnessed firsthand, whereas Leland's and Susan's flashbacks present more personal material. In Leland's flashback, much of the material is related secondhand since he was not a participant in some of the scenes he presents. This mode is not unrealistic; rather, it indicates how close he had once been to Kane, whereas Kane's relationship with Thatcher had always been very formal. What results from these multiple points of view is a complex and at times contradictory portrait. Not one of the characters near Kane can solve the riddle of Rosebud, although many clues are provided. That information is finally accessible only to us, via the eye of the camera.

Through the elaborate use of flashbacks, different time periods are made to overlap, and several distinct types of time are also employed. In terms of narrative time, *Citizen Kane* is complicated by the fact that the film has two interlocking stories: the quest of Thompson and the other newspaper reporters for the meaning of "Rosebud," and the history of Kane's life, which their search encompasses. The first of these covers a period of several weeks and is presented chronologically, beginning in a viewing room and ending at Xanadu, where the newsmen abandon their search while the camera continues to probe among the ruins. The story of Kane's life begins with him as a young boy in Colorado in 1871 and concludes with his death in 1940, although Welles does not observe this chronology in his narration. Instead he begins with Kane's death, narrates the story of his life through flashbacks, and ends several weeks after Kane's death with the closing up of Xanadu. Contrasted with the narrative time (or here, two narrative times) is the screen time (for *Citizen Kane*, one hour, 59 minutes, 16 seconds). Welles also manipulates psychological time, and by doing so he causes us to feel such sensations as happiness, anxiety, or boredom, as time appears to move quickly or slowly.

Let us now isolate several more pieces of this vast puzzle and examine the cinematic means Welles employs to tell his story. The first person Thompson interviews is Susan Alexander, who is supporting herself by singing in a nightclub in Atlantic City. Welles cuts directly from the newsroom to the neon lights on the roof of the nightclub announcing her performance. Rain is falling steadily, and as the camera appears to crane up and over the top of the building, flashes of lightning provide illumination. Then the camera drops down and seems to pass through the sign and the skylight, penetrating the building without a single cut. Here Welles conceals his art. Actually, the shot is done with a miniature set, and the appearance of continuity is created by a dissolve occurring at the moment of the lightning flash. Since the dissolve matches the misting of the skylight, the viewer is unaware of it. By coming through the ceiling, our first view of Susan is from above. She sits at a table in an alcoholic stupor, and the high angle shot emphasizes her defenselessness and vulnerability. We have entered the nightclub without invitation (as we did with Kane's bedroom; again we remember the *No Trespassing* sign), and our reception is not friendly. It is no wonder that Thompson learns nothing.

The first informative flashback is not, like the others, narrated by a living participant but rather is gleaned from the diary of Kane's deceased guardian. Thompson, the indefatigable reporter, is visiting the Walter Parks Thatcher Memorial Library in Philadelphia, where, under the most carefully controlled conditions, he is permitted to read a portion of Thatcher's diary. As Thompson examines the precisely written entry, "I first encountered Mr. Kane in 1871. . . ," there is a slow pan to the right followed by a dissolve; snowflakes seem to cover the white page, which give way to a bucolic winter scene of young Kane playing in the snow and crying out "The Union forever," a phrase he repeats just before his parents break the news to him of his separation from them. Bernard Herrmann's soundtrack supports this change, as the somber melody of the Thatcher Library becomes a light, youthful play on strings and woodwinds. Herrmann has written of the importance of sound in preparing for visual transitions:

> . . . I used a great deal of what might be termed 'radio scoring.' The movies [in 1940] frequently overlook opportunities for musical clues which last only a few seconds—that is, from five to fifteen seconds at the most—the reason being that the eye usually covers the transition. On the other hand, in radio drama, every scene must be bridged by some sort of sound device, so that even five seconds of music becomes a vital instrument in telling the ear that the scene is shifting. I felt that in this film where the photographic contrasts were often so sharp and sudden, a brief cut—even two or three chords—might heighten the effect immeasurably.[6]

Herrmann had worked with Welles on radio, and they both drew on this experience successfully when turning to film.

The scene that follows provides a good example of the deep focus camera work of Gregg Toland. We begin with a shot of young Kane through the window, and then the camera tracks away from the window through the boarding house to reveal three planes of action: in the foreground sit Mrs.

[6]Herrmann, *Focus*, pp. 70–71.

Kane and Walter Parks Thatcher, discussing the papers that will determine the boy's future; in the middleground, and to the left, stands the boy's father, who is in disagreement with the other two; between them, in the extreme background visible through the window, is the boy, playing innocently outside. Here again the principle of contrast calls our attention to the young Kane: He is dark, against a white background, and his movement contrasts with the stasis of the others. Two distinct actions are occurring simultaneously; by keeping both scenes in focus, Welles indicates the relationship between them in the simplest possible manner (that is, without cutting from one to another). He has even choreographed the movement of the boy outside to underscore this relationship. At the moment of greatest tension, as Mr. Kane enters the room where his wife and Thatcher are signing the document and pleads, "Mary, I'm askin' you for the last time . . . ," the boy disappears from sight, although the window remains in view. When Thatcher mentions money to pacify the father, the boy again appears through the window. Deep focus work had been used in films before, but rarely to indicate complex relationships between apparently unrelated actions. The extreme difficulty of coordinating activity in the three planes has been described by Toland:

> It was a complex mixture of art and mechanics. A table and chair on rollers were to behave with clock-like precision as a three-ton camera boom moved over them. In proper timing lay the difficulty. When the props behaved on schedule, a child actor Buddy Swann would blow his lines. When those two items coordinated, the operation of the camera crane by nine men would be slightly out of synchronization. To bring all this action, dialogue, and mechanics into perfect time was the problem. But it was eventually solved.[7]

The sequence in Colorado ends with a long shot of Rosebud being obscured by the falling snow, as a train whistle blows in the distance. Kane's sudden inheritance has robbed him of this sled and everything it represents, although at this point in the film we do not understand its significance. The sled's meaning is partly clarified by a montage that follows, in which a conversation is continued through scenes separated in time and space. Here Welles uses a montage primarily to condense time, but it serves another function as well. We have just seen young Kane push Mr. Thatcher defiantly with Rosebud and then leave Rosebud behind in the snow. Now it is Christmas, and Thatcher is giving him a new sled to replace the old one. Welles is confronted with a simple problem here: How to cover the years from Kane's childhood to his maturity (when he can inherit the trust and become a more interesting character to us as viewers). He juxtaposes two holidays: young Kane's first Christmas with Thatcher, when he receives a sled as a present, and the New Year's Day many years later when he comes into his inherit-

---

[7]Charles Higham, *The Films of Orson Welles*, (Berkeley, Los Angeles, London: University of California Press, 1971), p. 12.

ance. These are linked by the conversation Thatcher begins in one time period and concludes in a later. More important, however, is the relationship
between Kane's loss of innocence and his inheritance, suggested by these
juxtapositions. The significance of this connection becomes fully clear to us
only later.

We have commented on Welles's metaphoric use of lighting in the
opening sequence; light and dark are played off against each other throughout the film, and most strikingly during the scene in the office of the *Inquirer*
when Kane reads his "Declaration of Principles." It is very late in the evening
when Kane tells Leland and Bernstein that he must "make the *New York Inquirer* as important to New York as the gas in that light." He reaches up and
extinguishes one of the gas lamps on the wall, thus providing a realistic basis
for what follows. Kane stands in full light, as are the seated figures of Leland
and Bernstein. The extinguished wall lamp is behind him. Then, as Kane begins to read his "Declaration of Principles," he steps forward and leans into
a shadow, which covers his countenance. The effect is a very subtle one, for
his words are undercut by the darkness that falls across his face. Like the reporters earlier, Kane is in the dark, both literally and figuratively, and it
comes as no surprise to us when he later betrays these lofty aims. By a careful manipulation of light, Welles has foreshadowed his betrayal.

Economy is a goal Welles pursues throughout his film, and nowhere is
this seen more clearly than in his depiction of Kane's first marriage. Welles
chronicles the marriage in a brief series of parallel scenes occurring at that
most domestic of moments: breakfast time. This sequence is part of Leland's
recollections. Although incarcerated in a hospital, Leland remains as sharp as
ever. Seated against a motionless background (actually a photograph), he declares, "It was a marriage just like any other marriage. . . ," and the picture
dissolves very slowly to the Kanes' breakfast room. For a moment both images are superimposed: Leland on the left, sitting erectly in his chair, and the
breakfast room on his right. Toland has described how this effect was
achieved:

> Most of the transitions in *Citizen Kane* are lap dissolves in which the
> background dissolves from one scene to the next shortly before the players
> in the foreground are dissolved. This was accomplished rather simply with
> two light-dimming outfits, one for the actors and one for the set.
>
> The dissolve is begun by dimming the lights on the background,
> eventually fading it out entirely. Then the lights on the people are
> dimmed to produce a fade-out on them. The fade-in is made the same
> way, fading in the set lights first, then the lights for the people.[8]

The slow dissolve beautifully captures Leland's struggle to recollect and re-
construct the past. In each of the six scenes, the positions of Kane and his
wife are the same, but the makeup, costumes, and setting are altered to dem-

[8]Toland, *Focus*, p. 76.

onstrate their aging and their shifting attitudes toward each other. The scenes are separated by swish pans, which suggest here the passage of time. From the flattering and ebullient conversations of the first shots to the silence of the last, with Mrs. Kane hiding behind the competitor's newspaper, the relationship is incisively developed. For the soundtrack, Herrmann created "the old classic form of the theme and variations":

> A waltz in the style of Waldteufel is the theme. It is heard during the first scene. Then, as discord crops up, the variations begin. Each scene is a separate variation. Finally, the waltz theme is heard bleakly played in the high registers of the violins.[9]

When the picture dissolves back to Leland, the afternoon sun has begun to set. In slightly more than two minutes of screen time, Welles has condensed the hour or so of narrative time it has taken Leland to relate his story, which in itself condensed the eight years of the Kanes' marriage. Moreover, psychological time is manipulated within the flashback. The shot that takes the long-

Citizen Kane. The past is slowly recollected: A superimposition of Leland and Mrs. Kane.

[9]Herrmann, *Focus,* p. 70.

Citizen Kane. Mrs. Kane barely conceals her disdain behind the competitor's newspaper.

est screen time (50 seconds) is the first, yet it seems to pass quickly because of the brisk internal rhythm; the final shot (20 seconds) of the couple seated in a frozen prose of hostility appears to drag on endlessly.

As we noted, the first sound montage in *Citizen Kane* is fairly simple, and although the viewer probably will not sense immediately the complexity of the connections between Kane's youth (the sled) and his inheritance, he or she can bridge the temporal and spatial gaps without difficulty. A much more complex sound montage occurs shortly after Kane encounters Susan Alexander for the first time. This montage is understandable, however, because the simpler sound montage has preceded it. Thus, Welles instructs his viewers in the course of the film.

Kane meets Susan Alexander on the way to a warehouse where the objects of his childhood (including, no doubt, Rosebud) have been stored. Susan is suffering from a toothache and leads him to her rented rooms, rooms that include among the bric-a-brac on her dressing table, the glass ball with a winter scene inside it that Kane clutches after she leaves him and again at the end of his life. In his nostalgic search for his youth, Kane has found Susan Alexander, whom he treats like a child and with whom he plays like a child. His parlor tricks cure her of her toothache, and at his request she sits at the piano and sings for him. Then begins an extraordinary series of shots, united

Citizen Kane. Through a sudden dissolve, Susan Alexander becomes a kept woman.

by the continuity of the soundtrack. As Susan sings, the picture dissolves to an identical composition with her continuing to perform on the left, and Kane seated on the right, but in far more lavish quarters. The juxtaposition of the two shots beautifully summarizes the development of their relationship. She concludes her song, and Kane begins to applaud. There is another dissolve, and as the applause continues (now magnified in intensity), Jedediah Leland is seen campaigning for Kane from an open car while a crowd claps. Leland speaks with great passion of "Charles Foster Kane, the fighting liberal, the friend of the working man, the next governor of this state, who entered upon this campaign . . ." Before he can complete the sentence, there is a dissolve to an enormous poster of Kane within a large conventional hall. The camera tilts down to reveal Kane, who finishes the sentence: ". . . with one purpose only . . . to point out and make public the dishonesty, the downright villainy of Boss Jim Gettys's political machine. . . ." The rally continues, concluding with a shot of Boss Jim Gettys, high in the balcony, putting on his hat and leaving the hall.

In this montage Welles condenses time to show the development of Kane's relationship with Susan Alexander and Kane's rise to political power. The juxtaposition of these actions is not gratuitous: The seeds of Kane's political downfall are sown in Susan's drawing room. Welles could hardly be more economical.

Welles's desire for simplicity is also evident in the presentation of Susan Alexander's suicide attempt. Preceding this is a brief montage of her unsuccessful opera career, in which her failure is frantically recapitulated. Newspaper headlines are superimposed on her stage appearances, juxtaposed with the flashing light announcing the beginning of the performance, the harried faces of her teacher and conductor, and so forth. The rhythm becomes increasingly rapid, and as Herrmann has pointed out, "sound-tracks of [Susan's] voice [are] blended with a rhythmical musical motif to produce an effect of mounting hysteria."[10] The montage concludes with Susan's voice running down like a broken record as a light flickers and it becomes dark. The metaphoric use of light here resembles that in the opening sequence. While the screen is dark, we hear heavy breathing, and gradually the picture fades in. Following the rapid rhythms (internal and external) of the previous sequence, we have a moment of stasis, and the contrast increases its effectiveness. Here too Welles and Toland employ deep focus photography: In the foreground is a close-up of a glass and a bottle of poison; behind, Susan lies on the bed, breathing laboriously; in the background is the door, behind which Kane knocks insistently before breaking into the room. Like the scene in the boarding house, there is a direct relationship between the three planes

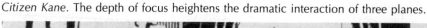

Citizen Kane. The depth of focus heightens the dramatic interaction of three planes.

[10]Herrmann, *Focus*, p. 71.

of action, and the deep focus photography permits this relationship to be shown simply and forcefully.

In Susan's recollections of life at Xanadu, where she and Kane reside after the failure of her opera career, Welles manipulates psychological time to convey her sense of tedium and purposelessness. Time appears to pass slowly, as Susan sprawls on the floor working jigsaw puzzles while Kane shuffles aimlessly about the cavernous rooms. At one point, Welles creates a montage of Susan's jigsaw puzzles. One dissolves into the next, each presenting a different season of the year. A rhythmical ticking on the soundtrack complements the visuals, and the combination deftly communicates the inexorable passage of time.

Welles uses a wide-angle lens in many of the scenes within Xanadu in order to distort space and make the distances within the frame appear greater. When Kane and Susan sit at opposite sides of the frame, the wide-angle lens emphasizes the physical distance between them and very aptly underlines their emotional separation. Of course, the settings are large and appear to dwarf the characters. (The fireplace, for example, is 10' by 18' by 27'.) This vastness can be contrasted with the earlier scenes in the newspaper offices, where the cramped space could hardly contain Kane. The energy of those earlier scenes is now gone; the slow rhythm (internal and external) of the sequence within Xanadu communicates the boredom and aimlessness of the couple, as Susan remembers it.

Thompson's final interview is with Kane's butler, Raymond, who has spent the last eleven years with Kane. In the previous flashback Susan had related her version of walking out on Kane; Raymond recounts Kane's reaction to this news after Susan has left. Kane flies into a rage, destroying the objects in Susan's bedroom, until he comes across the glass globe containing the winter scene; suddenly, all becomes quiet. He clutches the globe as he stumbles out of the room. This is our last view of Kane. He is identified with this globe, as he was in our first view of him in the film. Welles dissolves back to Thompson, who is unable to comprehend the significance of this object, and who ends his quest in defeat: ". . . I guess Rosebud is just a piece in a jigsaw puzzle, a missing piece." But the puzzle makes little sense without the selectivity of the camera eye. The camera cranes over the sea of objects, and, through a series of dissolves, brings us to the furnace where trash is being burned. Raymond has the last word in the film: "Throw that junk in, too," he commands, pointing to the sled; it is tossed into the flames, and as the camera dissolves closer, we are able to read the words clearly as the paint is burned off: Rosebud. The soundtrack also directs our attention to the importance of this discovery. In a film with very few close-ups, the opening and closing sequences are structured around two extreme close-ups: of Kane's lips, mouthing "Rosebud" at the beginning, and of the burning word "Rosebud" at the end. To the workmen, this sled is only a piece of junk; to Kane, it symbolizes all that he has lost in his rise to power.

Just as we are grasping this fact, the picture dissolves to a long shot of the castle as seen in the prologue of the film. This time, however, the window is dark, and smoke is billowing up from the chimney as Rosebud is consumed in flames. We return to the massive gate and the sign *No Trespassing*. In fact, within the world of the film, Thompson and the other reporters have not been able to trespass on Kane's life. But the filmmaker, who has at his disposal the means we have been discussing, achieves a measure of success where the others have failed. However, questions about Kane remain in the minds of most viewers, and the presence of these questions suggests some of the limitations of film itself as a medium. In the studies of individual films that follows, we shall explore the relative limitations and strengths of both film and literature.

In his first film Orson Welles has created a work in part about the power of narrative film. The work is also one that exploits the resources of film to the utmost. Like Orson Welles at the beginning of his career as a director, we can learn a great deal about the craft of film by viewing a single work repeatedly, and few films are as rewarding for that purpose as his own *Citizen Kane*.

Citizen Kane

Production Credits

Director	Orson Welles
Producer	Orson Welles
Screenplay by	Herman J. Mankiewicz, Orson Welles (with the assistance of Joseph Cotten and John Houseman)
Director of Photography	Gregg Toland
Art Directors	Van Nest Polglase, Perry Ferguson
Film Editors	Robert Wise (and Mark Robson)
Sets by	Darrell Silvera
Music by	Bernard Herrmann

USA. 1941. 119 minutes. Black & white.

Cast

Charles Foster Kane	Orson Welles
Jedediah Leland	Joseph Cotten
Susan Alexander Kane	Dorothy Comingore
Kane's mother	Agnes Moorehead
Emily Norton Kane	Ruth Warrick
James W. Gettys	Ray Collins

Mr. Carter	Erskine Sanford
Mr. Bernstein	Everett Sloane
Thompson, the reporter (and	
Newsreel, Narrator)	William Alland
Raymond, the butler	Paul Stewart
Walter Parks Thatcher	George Coulouris
Signor Matisti	Fortunio Bonanova
Headwaiter	Gus Schilling
Rawlston	Philip Van Zandt
Kane, Sr.	Harry Shannon
Kane's son	Sonny Bupp
Kane at age of eight	Buddy Swan

Further Reading

Bazin, André. *Orson Welles: A Critical View.* tr. Jonathan Rosenbaum. New York: Harper & Row, 1978.

Carringer, Robert. "*Citizen Kane, The Great Gatsby,* and Some Conventions of American Narrative." *Critical Inquiry,* 2, No. 2 (Winter 1975), 307–325.

———. "Rosebud, Dead or Alive." *PMLA,* 91, No. 2 (March 1976), 185–193.

Chatman, Seymour. *Story and Discourse: Narrative Structure in Fiction and Film.* Ithaca, New York: Cornell University Press, 1978.

Cook, David A. *A History of Narrative Film.* New York: W. W. Norton and Company, 1981.

Cowie, Peter. *A Ribbon of Dreams: The Cinema of Orson Welles.* New York: A. S. Barnes, 1973.

Gottesman, Ronald. *Focus on Citizen Kane.* Englewood Cliffs, N. J.: Prentice-Hall, 1971.

Higham, Charles. *The Films of Orson Welles.* Berkeley: University of California Press, 1970.

Kael, Pauline, Herman J. Mankiewicz, and Orson Welles. *The Citizen Kane Book.* Boston: Little, Brown and Co., 1971.

Kawin, Bruce F. *Mindscreen: Bergman, Godard, and First-Person Film.* Princeton, N. J.: Princeton University Press, 1978.

McBride, Joseph. *Orson Welles, Actor and Director.* New York: Viking Press, 1972.

Meryman, Richard. *Mank: The Wit, World, and Life of Herman Mankiewicz.* New York: William Morrow and Co., 1978.

Naremore, James. *The Magic World of Orson Welles.* New York: Oxford University Press, 1978.

Schatz, Thomas. *Hollywood Genres: Formulas, Filmmaking, and the Studio System.* Philadelphia: Temple University Press, 1981.

Solomon, Stanley J. ed. *The Classic Cinema: Essays in Criticism.* New York: Harcourt Brace Jovanovich, 1973.

PART TWO

Comparative Approaches: Literature and Film

3

Plot and Structure

Introduction

Every narrative work has a plot as well as a story, and we might begin by distinguishing between them. When someone asks you "what happened" in a fictional work, your answer is likely to be a summary of the events, usually in chronological order. In *The Stranger*, a man commits a murder, is sentenced, imprisoned, and finally executed. That is the story. The plot is the organization of these events and actions as presented by the narrator. This organization may follow a temporal pattern (chronological or associative), but it need not. For the plot, an author selects the most significant events and actions from an infinite number of possibilities and arranges them in the order that produces the maximum desired emotional and artistic effect.

As Aristotle noted long ago in the *Poetics*, such actions must have a beginning, a middle, and an end, or to use other terms, an introduction, a development, and a natural conclusion. However, as we noted above, these can be presented in any order. Welles begins Citizen Kane with the end of Kane's life and then returns to the point when his inheritance permitted his parents to send him away from his home. From there onward Welles presents the events of Kane's life more or less in chronological order, as related by those who knew him. A reordering of events may not affect the story, but it does change the plot. The implications of such changes will be examined in the essays on *The Turn of the Screw (The Innocents)*, *The Stranger*, and *The Grapes of Wrath*.

Plots are often identified by their tone and outcome. Thus, we can speak of a tragic plot, which usually ends with the isolation and death of the hero; a comic plot, which often concludes with a reunion or marriage, a satiric plot, and so on. A considerable variety of plot forms is possible.

In addition, many works include subplots or secondary plots, which are self-enclosed, but which illuminate the concerns of the main plot.

At the heart of most plots is conflict, which propels the action. Here, too, the possibilities are limitless. *The Collector* is primarily about the conflict between two characters, but one of these characters, Freddy, is also in conflict with his background. In *The Treasure of the Sierra Madre,* Howard, Curtin, and Dobbs are engaged in a struggle with the natural forces of their environment. But equally important are the conflicts among them, and within each one. *A Doll's House* chronicles the gradual awakening of a woman whose conflict is initially with her husband but more generally with the values of her society and the role that society has thrust upon her.

There are complications to every conflict, and an author, dramatist, or filmmaker can manipulate these to maintain the attention of readers or spectators. We wonder how things will turn out. Our unresolved expectations insure our continued interest. The techniques of surprise, mystery, and suspense are three ways of engaging and sustaining the interest of viewers or readers. Surprises are unexpected turns of events in the plot. These may occur throughout a work and even at the conclusion. However, surprises should appear plausible, and especially at the conclusion of a work, the natural outcome of the action. Suspense develops from our concern over the fate of a character and is accompanied by emotions of curiosity and fear. Suspense is strongest, of course, when we identify with the protagonist. Suspense plays upon our emotions, whereas mystery creates more of an intellectual puzzle. In a mystery we speculate about what is going to happen and why. On the basis of the information that the narrator gives us, we try to foresee the outcome. When a mystery is dramatized, our attention is usually focused on the attempts of the protagonist to solve a problem rather than on the problem itself.

Structure is a metaphoric term, transferred from architecture, which emphasizes the relationship of the parts to the whole. Many dramas employ divisions of acts, whereas novels sometimes have chapters, or structures determined by having been published serially. However, these activities vary from work to work. The scene, a formal unit in the drama defined by its spatial and temporal restrictions, also occurs in short stories and novels, although without being specified as such.

Each of these smaller units (act or chapter) has a structure of its own with a distinctive beginning and end, which is usually a climax to provoke the viewer or reader's interest and insure that he or she returns to the play or story. Henry James published *The Turn of the Screw* in *Collier's Weekly* (1898) in twelve installments. Each chapter reaches a small climax of its own; but the group of chapters published each week achieves a more momentous turn at the conclusion, so that the reader will be sure to purchase the next issue of the magazine. Similarly, with serialized novels on television, the script is written to achieve a small climax before each commercial, and a larger one at the end of the evening. The principal climax occurs on the final evening.

A nineteenth-century German critic, Gustav Freytag, developed a model of dramatic structure based on the pyramid. His terms are often employed and continue to be useful when considered descriptive rather than prescriptive. For Freytag a drama could be divided into five parts, which might or might not correspond to the division of acts. The five parts are: exposition; development or "rising action"; climax or turning point; "falling action"; conclusion or catastrophe. Some of these elements are present in any story, play, or novel. We can understand the usefulness of these terms by applying them to *Macbeth*.

The exposition or introduction establishes the time and place of the drama, introduces the characters (either directly, or through discussion by others), supplies information necessary to the understanding of the play, such as events that have taken place beforehand, and establishes the tone of the work. *In Macbeth* the ominous appearance of the witches establishes a supernatural atmosphere in which moral values appear to be turned upside down:

> Fair is foul, and foul is fair.
> Hover through the fog and filthy air.

The scene that follows introduces Macbeth through narration (the speech of the captain). The captain testifies to Macbeth's valor and speaks of events that have already occurred. Neither of these scenes contributes anything crucial to the story, but they are essential to the plot.

The development or rising action of the play occurs as new events complicate the original situation and produce conflicts. Sometimes a single action, called the exciting force, propels the action. In *Macbeth* the prophecy of the witches sets the conflict in motion, and the conflict continues through successive stages until Macbeth becomes King. By the beginning of Act III, Macbeth has fulfilled his aspirations. As Banquo notes:

> Thous hast it now—King, Cawdor, Glamis, all
> As the weird women promised; and I fear
> Thou playd'st most foully for 't.

The turning point occurs at the banquet. This scene, which should be a moment of communion and solidarity, is instead the point at which Macbeth's isolation begins. The gathering is disrupted by his visions of Banquo's ghost. From this moment onward, Macbeth's fortunes begin to fall.

Freytag envisaged the turning point as the apex of the pyramid. The falling action, usually shorter in time than the rising action, shows Macbeth losing control of events as his antagonists grow in strength. His isolation increases. The falling action is often precipitated by an action called the tragic force, which bears the same relation to falling action as exciting force does to rising action. In *Macbeth* the escape of Fleance is such an action.

The catastrophe involves a reversal of fortunes for the protagonist and usually culminates with his death. Macbeth is killed, and he dies alone, without the support of others. His death is followed by a restoration of order. Other types of plot, such as the comic, end with a denouement, taken from the French word for "unknotting." This term comes from the classical metaphor that compares a drama to a rope being knotted (the rising action) and unknotted (the falling action and conclusion).

In very general ways, the above pattern is applicable to the novel, short story, and film. Most narratives embody conflict of one sort or another, and the development of this conflict resembles the pattern just described.

It should be pointed out, however, that this form assumes a logical world of causality. Another plot form of long standing is the picaresque, where the events seem to be united only by the presence of the same character or group of characters in them all, as in *The Satyricon* of Petronius. There are also those writers who believe that the world is absurd or mysterious and who base their plots on factors other than causality. *The Stranger* would be a good example. In short, plot is not only the author's organization of the work but also an implicit indication of his or her view of the universe.

Additional Recommended Films

The Trial (1962), directed by Orson Welles, based on the novel by Franz Kafka. Both the novel and the filmscript are available in paperback.

The Ox-bow Incident (1943), directed by William Wellman, based on the novel by Walter Van Tilburg Clark. The novel is available in paperback, and the screenplay is available (although out of print) in hardback.

Tom Jones (1963), directed by Tony Richardson, based on the novel by Henry Fielding. The novel is available in paperback, and the script is out of print.

See Also:

A Doll's House (Chapter 3)
Jules and Jim (Chapter 4)
The Innocents (Chapter 5)
The Stranger (Chapter 6)
The Loneliness of the Long-Distance Runner (Chapter 6)
An Occurrence at Owl Creek Bridge (Chapter 9)
All the King's Men
The French Lieutenant's Woman
Great Expectations

The Grapes of Wrath

When John Steinbeck's novel *The Grapes of Wrath* appeared in 1939, it provoked an immediate outcry. Congressman Lyle Boren of Oklahoma denounced the work on the floor of the House as "a lie, a black infernal creation of a twisted distorted mind."[1] Other reactions (the California Chamber of Commerce, various farmers' organizations) were equally fervent, although perhaps less eloquent. One reviewer in a small town California newspaper began by confessing: "I have just read a few chapters of a book that is, in my opinion, the filthiest book I ever read . . . It requires no great skill to write a book such as *The Grapes of Wrath*. Anyone who can remember a filthy story and is willing to spend his time with morons, and then write everything he hears and sees, just as he hears and sees it, could do it."[2] The controversy resulting from the politically and socially volatile nature of the book's themes, as well as the strong language (for 1939), no doubt contributed to the popularity of the work, which rapidly climbed the best-seller list, where it remained for over a year. Hollywood has never shied away from best-sellers, but it might have in this case since the novel attacks many of the film studio's sources of financial support. Not the least of the problems, then, for John Ford, the director, and Darryl Zanuck, the producer, was the provocative nature of the subject.

But *The Grapes of Wrath* presents other problems to the filmmaker, more intrinsic to its medium. Among these is the length of the novel. At first glance, *The Grapes of Wrath* would seem impossible to condense. However, Steinbeck uses a great deal of physical description, both for character delineation and for establishing the setting. As George Bluestone has noted, ". . . the novel's prose relies wholly on dialogue and physical action to reveal character . . . Even at moments of highest tension, Steinbeck scrupulously avoids getting inside the minds of his people."[3] Bluestone argues that this makes Steinbeck's work extremely easy to film, and he quote's Ma's reaction to Tom's final departure to illustrate his point:

> "Good-bye," she said, and she walked quickly away. Her eyes were wet and burning, but she did not cry. Her footsteps were loud and careless on the leaves as she went through the bush. And as she went, out of the dim

[1] Quoted in Warren French, *Filmguide to The Grapes of Wrath* (Bloomington: Indiana University Press, 1973), p. 18.

[2] Carl Barkow, in a review from a Banning, California, newspaper, glued into the cover of an early copy of *The Grapes of Wrath* (fourth printing, April 1939), in my possession.

[3] George Bluestone, *Novels into Film*, (Berkeley and Los Angeles: University of California Press, 1968), p. 163.

sky the rain began to fall, big drops and few, splashing on the dry leaves heavily. Ma stopped and stood still in the dripping thicket. She turned about—took three steps back toward the mound of vines; and then she turned quickly and went back toward the boxcar camp.

Certainly nothing in this scene poses problems for the filmmaker; in fact, a visualization of this scene would be briefer than the literary version. So here the means of condensation are in part provided by the author, who has chosen an external approach to character.

There are thirty chapters in *The Grapes of Wrath,* but of these only fourteen deal directly with the story of the Joad family's migration from Oklahoma to California. The other sixteen are short "interchapters," which differ in style as well as subject from the main chapters. These interchapters both generalize the plight of the Joads and suggest the political and social consequences of their situation. The progression of interchapters parallels the Joads' circumstances. Some of these chapters deal with the anonymous individuals who share the adversity of the Joads, and others reflect the perspectives of those who have dealings with the migrants, such as the used-car dealer, the tractor driver ("Joe Davis's boy"), or the lunchroom attendants. The first interchapter (Chapter 1) gives a quasi-objective overview of the situation, but the tone of this chapter yields to the more polemical attitude of Chapters 14, 19, 21, and 25, as the condition of the Joads worsens. Chapter 21, in which Steinbeck discusses the likelihood of a revolution, concludes with an allusion to the novel's title: "On the highways the people moved like ants and searched for work, for food. And the anger began to ferment." This image is developed further at the end of Chapter 25, which shows the misuse of crops in California: ". . . in the eyes of the hungry there is a growing wrath. In the souls of the people the grapes of wrath are filling and growing heavy, growing heavy for the vintage."

Ford and his scriptwriter, Nunnally Johnson, have dropped the most speculative and abstract of the interchapters, but they have successfully adapted material from the others. They have done so by taking general situations from the interchapters and applying them directly to the Joads and other characters. Much of Chapter 5, for example, which concerns the takeover of the tenant farmers' land by the impersonal corporations, is incorporated into the first conversation between Tom Joad, Preacher Casy, and Muley Graves. Tom arrives at his home and is astonished to find it deserted. When he and Casy discover a former neighbor, Muley, one of Tom's first questions is, "Who done it?" In his only use of flashbacks, Ford has Muley relate how it happened, first showing the company agent in his shiny car dispatching the news to Muley and his family, and later the arrival of "Joe Davis's boy" on his tractor to drive them off. Muley and his family stand by helplessly as the diesel tractor moves closer and closer to their cabin, finally demolishing it. Ford and his photographer, Gregg Toland, forcefully capture the pathos of the scene.

The Grapes of Wrath. From general to specific: Ford portrays the destruction of the Muley family home.

Another example of a general scene made specific occurs just before the Joads leave Uncle John's cabin. The makeshift truck is fully packed when Tom arrives with Casy. Ford then includes some material from Chapter 9, in which Steinbeck chronicled the difficulties of departure for the migrants, and especially the pain of leaving behind possessions with sentimental value. An anonymous woman sorts through her goods:

> The woman sat among the doomed things, turning them over and looking past them and back. This book. My father had it . . . And his pipe— still smells rank. And this picture—an angel . . . Think we could get this china dog in? Aunt Sadie brought it from the St. Louis Fair. See? Wrote right on it. No, I guess not. Here's a letter my brother wrote the day before he died. Here's an old-time hat. These feathers—never got to use them. No, there isn't room.

In a simple scene Ford frames Ma Joad alone in the cabin, going over her keepsakes. Seated before a cracked mirror, she holds an odd pair of earrings up to her ears and then decides to take them with her. The scene is without dialogue; only the hushed tones of a concertina playing "Red River Valley," a mournful song of departure, provide accompaniment. The moment is very powerful.

Two of the interchapters (Chapters 12 and 15) deal with the westward movement of the migrants. Ford incorporates material from both into montage sequences of travel, in which the Joad vehicle is one of many. He also

The Grapes of Wrath. "The poignance of silence": Ma Joad sorts through her belongings.

personalizes the incident in the lunchroom from Chapter 15 by giving Pa Joad and the two youngest Joad children anonymous parts in the book.

In this way the generalizing intent of the interchapters is retained—with the exception of those chapters that are political or social (and essentially propagandistic)—and the focus remains on the Joads as part of a larger process: This, too, is a means of condensing the novel.

By assimilating these interchapters into the narrative of the Joad family, however, Ford has drastically altered the structure of Steinbeck's work. The plot of the novel includes not only the story of the Joads but also the interchapters that balance and extend that narrative. The film lacks the novel's alternating rhythms that are created by the juxtaposition of regular chapters and interchapters. On the basis of the example this film provides, it would seem that it is not possible for a narrative film to produce the contrasting rhythms that Steinbeck achieves in his novel.

Apart from the interchapters, the plot presents few problems for the filmmakers. Nonetheless, they have significantly altered the part of the plot that deals exclusively with the Joads.

In the novel, the fortunes of the Joad family reach a high point when they stay in the government camp. If one imagines Freytag's pyramid, this would be the turning point. The family has faced separation and loss, but, thanks to Ma Joad, it has endured and in some ways has become a stronger unit. Once they leave the government camp, however, their situation rapidly and steadily worsens. The fate of Rose of Sharon's stillborn child represents the inevitable decline of the Joad family. There is absolutely no reason, in terms of the properties of the medium of film, why this aspect of the plot could not have been preserved. However, the filmmakers' changes, resulting from political and social pressures, provide us with an apt illustration of the difference between story and plot.

When *The Grapes of Wrath* was published, the critical response to the ending was generally negative. In any event, the scene of Rose of Sharon nursing the dying old man would have been extremely difficult to film. The filmmakers solved this problem by dropping the incident entirely and rearranging the remaining material. The film culminates with the Joad family on the road, following the episode at the government camp and Tom's departure. The events are the same, but the rearrangement gives them an altered importance. By shifting the "falling action" before the climax or turning point, the plot becomes a line that moves continually upward. In spite of setbacks and hard times, the prospects of the Joad family steadily improve. Ma's final speech, taken from much earlier in the novel, leaves the viewer optimistic and encouraged: "We'll go on forever, Pa. We're the people."

In many ways the filmmakers have toned down the more radical implications of the novel, but in no way more fundamental than this reordering of its structure. By altering the plot, the story becomes vastly different from that of the novel.

In spite of the upbeat ending, however, the film contains shots and sequences of such undeniable force that their total effect undercuts Ma's optimistic words. The shots of Muley kneeling in the dusty soil, of Ma going over her possessions, of the hopeless faces and desperate surroundings of the Hooverville camp, of Casy being clubbed, of Tom's departure, and the last shot of the film—the sign *No Help Wanted,* viewed through the windshield of the truck—these and others have a cumulative power of despair and desolation that remains long after we have forgotten the surging music following Ma's final words. The shots are a testimony to the extraordinary impact of Gregg Toland's visuals and John Ford's direction in overcoming a flawed script.

The Grapes of Wrath

Production Credits

Director	John Ford
Producer	Darryl F. Zanuck
Screenplay by	Nunnally Johnson
Based on the novel by	John Steinbeck
Director of Photography	Gregg Toland
Art Directors	Richard Day, Mark Lee Kirk

Film Editor	Robert Simpson
Assistant Director	Edward O'Fearna
Sets by	Thomas Little
Music by	Alfred Newman

USA. 1940. 128 minutes. Black & white.

Cast

Tom	Henry Fonda
Ma	Jane Darwell
Pa	Russell Simpson
Grampa	Charley Grapewin
Granma	Zeffie Tilbury
Uncle John	Frank Darien
Noah	Frank Sully
Al	O.Z. Whitehead
Rosasharn	Dorris Bowdon
Connie Rivers	Eddie Quillan
Ruthie	Shirley Mills
Winfield	Darryl Hickman
Casy	John Carradine
Muley Graves	John Qualen
Caretaker at Wheat Patch	Grant Mitchell
Policeman	Ward Bond
Floyd	Paul Guilfoyle
Wilkie	Charles D. Brown
Deputy at the Keene Ranch	Joseph Sawyer

Further Reading

Baxter, John. *The Cinema of John Ford.* New York: A. S. Barnes, 1971.

Bluestone, George. *Novels Into Film.* Berkeley: University of California Press, 1971.

Bogdanovich, Peter. *John Ford.* Berkeley: University of California Press, 1968.

Campbell, Russell, "Trampling Out the Vintage: Sour Grapes." In *The Modern American Novel and the Movies,* Gerald Peary and Roger Shatzkin, eds. New York: Frederick Ungar, 1978.

Ford, Dan. *Pappy: The Life of John Ford.* Englewood Cliffs, N. J.: Prentice-Hall, 1979.

French, Warren. *Filmguide to The Grapes of Wrath.* Bloomington: Indiana University Press, 1973.

Gassner, John, and Dudley Nichols, eds. *Twenty Best Film Plays,* Vol. I. New York and London: Garland Publishing, Inc., 1977.

Johnson, Nora. *Flashback: Nora Johnson on Nunnally Johnson.* Garden City, New York: Doubleday, 1979.

Locke, Edwin. "Adaptation of Reality in *The Grapes of Wrath,*" *Films,* 1, No. 2 (1940), pp. 49–55.

McBride, Joseph, and Michael Wilmington. *John Ford.* London: Secker and Warburg, 1979.

Place, Janey. "The Grapes of Wrath: A Visual Analysis," *Film Comment,* 12, No. 5 (September–October 1976), 46–51.

_____. *The Non-Western Films of John Ford.* Secaucus, N. J.: Citadel Press: 1979.

Sarris, Andrew. *The John Ford Movie Mystery.* Bloomington: Indiana University Press, 1975.

Sinclair, Andrew. *John Ford.* New York: The Dial Press, 1979.

Stempel, Tom. Screenwriter: *The Life and Times of Nunnally Johnson.* San Diego: A. S. Barnes, 1980.

The Thirty-Nine Steps

The Thirty-Nine Steps (1935) is the quintessential Hitchcock, a blend of mirth, sexuality, and suspense. When one examines John Buchan's novel, where none of these qualities can be found, one realizes how markedly Hitchcock has changed his source. He has transformed Buchan's mystery into a quickly paced work of suspense, greatly simplified the plot, altered the structure, used the settings functionally, and made the work an exploration of the nature of male-female relationships. Hitchcock's film resembles its source but presents the viewer with a different vision of life, perceived in a radically different form.

As Hitchcock worked on the script of the film, he began to feel that Buchan's novel was far too complicated for his own needs. Thus, he decided to eliminate the political assassination, simplify the conspiracy, and shift the focus from the spies to the "innocent" protagonist, thereby removing the problem of detecting the spies as well as the spies' attempt to escape the country by boat. The "thirty-nine steps" no longer identified a geographical location but merely became the means of exposing the villain, who is easily recognizable in the film by the partial amputation of his little finger.

Accompanying the simplification of the story is a reconstruction of the book into a series of discrete sequences: "I saw it as a film of episodes," Hitchcock has noted. "As soon as we were through with one episode, I remember saying, 'Here we need a good short story.' "[4] Each of these sequences revolves around an elemental fear, and virtually all of them also deal with relations between the sexes. Neither of these subjects, however, plays any significant role in Buchan's novel.

The opening sequence or exposition of the film combines these two themes in such a structure. The sequence is based on two brief incidents in the novel that Hitchcock has expanded considerably: the murder of the American in Hannay's flat and the portion of an evening Hannay spends in

[4]François Truffaut, *Hitchcock* (New York: Simon & Schuster, 1967), p. 66.

a music hall. The film begins with the flashing letters M-U-S-I-C H-A-L-L moving from right to left across the screen. The hands of an unidentified spectator are seen buying a ticket, and the camera follows his legs and torso as he enters the theater and takes his seat. As he sits down, the "Mr. Memory" themes begins playing. This music will ultimately provide the connection between Mr. Memory and the "thirty-nine steps"; as is often the case with Hitchcock, this clue is presented to us in the first scene of the film. By beginning the film in this manner, Hitchcock has duplicated the actions of his viewers: We too are innocent spectators who have purchased tickets and entered a theater to be entertained passively. Like Hannay, we have all the evidence we need, but we do not know what to do with it.

The interrogation of Mr. Memory begins, and the opening question introduces the sexual motif that will permeate the other sequences: "Where's my old man been since last Saturday?" This question is the first of many references to unsuccessful male-female relationships. Other questions follow rapidly after that, and finally Hannay asks: "How far is Winnipeg from Montreal?" He is forced to repeat his question three times at intervals, before Mr. Memory responds to him: "Ah, a gentleman from Canada," he remarks, and this observation is followed by the applause of the audience. Hitchcock, with his usual economy, has characterized his protagonist by placing him in a dramatic situation. The question identifies him to us as a Canadian tourist (and this remains virtually all we ever know of his "real" background) as well as indicating to Annabelle that he is a foreigner, and hence the one person in the crowd she can trust with her secret.

By introducing Annabelle, Hitchcock has given the political intrigue a sexual dimension lacking in Buchan's novel. Annabelle demonstrates her aggressive sexuality the first time we see her, in her encounter with Hannay outside the theater,: "Well," she purrs, "I'd like to come home with you." "It's your funeral," Hannay glibly (and prophetically) replies, as he helps her board a bus. She is the archetypal femme fatale: dark, beautiful, mysterious, and foreign. Like us, Hannay is very skeptical. At his flat she wants the lights kept off, the mirror turned to the wall, and the telephone not answered. All these actions have sexual as well as political connotations. Yet Hannay remains strangely passive. His apartment characterizes him perfectly: The furniture (and even the telephone) is covered with sheets, suggesting both his transience and his cold, withdrawn passivity. He remains wrapped in his overcoat, as Annabelle explains that it was she who fired the shots at the Music Hall, and that, as she has been followed there, he is now equally involved. "A beautiful mysterious woman pursued by gunmen . . . It sounds like a spy story," he replies with a note of mockery. When he suggests that she simply call the police, she notes that: "They wouldn't believe me any more than you do," an insight confirmed by the rest of the film. But Hannay remains flippant: "Have you ever heard of a thing called persecution mania?" he asks. At her request he looks out of the window and observes two men in trench coats standing by a telephone booth. Hannay continues to be disbelieving, as Annabelle briefly tells him of a plot to take military secrets out of the country and then indicates her next destination on a map of Scotland. She retires to the other room, and he prepares for bed. Later, Hannay's sleep is interrupted as the door is suddenly thrust open and Annabelle staggers into the room and utters a warning. This action—the exciting force—signals Hannay's involvement in the political intrigue. Hannay is awakened to find himself living in a nightmare world. Hitchcock cuts from the recumbent body of Annabelle stretched across Hannay's bed with a knife in her back to an extreme close-up of Hannay's ringing telephone: As the camera slowly dollies away from it, Hannay backs into the frame to pick it up. The phone has become a menacing object, and Hannay's inability to answer it underlines his acceptance of Annabelle's story and his complicity in the action. Unlike Buchan, Hitchcock has us witness the event, thus forcing us to share Hannay's involvement.

An ironic reversal has taken place as a result of this sequence: not only has the passive, uninvolved spectator suddenly become a participant in the action, but he now also finds himself confronted with the same disbelief with which he had greeted Annabelle's story. Throughout the film Hannay attempts to tell people the truth, yet the only person who believes him at once is the villainous Professor. This becomes immediately apparent in the sequence that follows the murder of Annabelle. In the novel Hannay exchanges his clothes with a milkman quite easily, by offering him money. But in the film the milkman looks on with astonishment as Hannay attempts to relate the truth. Sensing defeat, Hannay changes the subject: "Are you married?" he asks. "Yes, but don't rub it in," replies the milkman. Hannay then fabricates a tale of sexual infidelity that the milkman immediately understands, and he gleefully agrees to exchange places, remarking that Hannay can return the favor some day. Again, the sexual humor has a cutting edge. As Hannay's own credibility begins to be questioned, he develops a "persecution mania" of his own. Hitchcock uses a subjective camera to show each passerby as a potential threat to Hannay, and we share his fears because we view them through his eyes.

Hannay's continuing attempts to explain his innocence are in vain: Pamela betrays him on the train and again at the Assembly Hall; the Scottish Inspector tries to lock him up, after remarking ironically that "I have no doubt you'll be able to convince Scotland Yard as easily as you've convinced me"; and, true to the Inspector's prediction, Scotland Yard follows Pamela and tries to arrest Hannay. Obviously, Hannay is no safer with the police than with the spies. Here too we are far from Buchan's novel, where Hannay is accorded a warm reception virtually everywhere he goes. The only cordial welcome he receives in the film is from the Professor, the genial family man who tells Hannay that it would be crude to lock him up, and then attempts to shoot him. The reception given Hannay by the jealous, penurious farmer typifies what one can expect in Hitchcock's world: suspicion and betrayal. The farmer's wife, longing for excitement, helps Hannay, but she pays for it with a beating. Whereas Buchan's protagonist is declared innocent long before the novel is over, Hitchcock's Hannay must prove his innocence, which he is unable to do until the final moments of the film. He remains a hunted fugitive throughout, and we are constantly reminded of this by his dangling handcuff.

For Buchan the topography functions primarily as a backdrop, but Hitchcock makes it an integral part of the story. In speaking of the early version of *The Man Who Knew Too Much*, Hitchcock noted that "the contrast between the snowy Alps and the congested streets of London was a decisive factor. That visual concept had to be embodied in the film."[5] In this film a similar contrast exists between the frenetic activity of the London streets and music halls and the desolate solitude of the Scottish countryside. Hitchcock exploits the visual properties of the Scottish moors, where the low scraggly shrubbery offers no place to hide, and Hannay is an easy prey for his pursuers. When Hannay has the protection of a crowd, as at the Music Hall or at the Assembly Hall, Hitchcock emphasizes the moblike nature of the group that pushes Hannay in one instance into Annabelle, in the other into the arms of the enemy agents. The only mob that works in his favor is the flock of sheep that, ironically, separates him and Pamela from the agents.

Hitchcock's theatrical settings also function dramatically, allowing him to manipulate the distinctions between spectator and actor. Hannay's first question not only characterizes him (to us and Annabelle), but it also involves him in the action by making him a participant in the theatrical spectacle. He continues to "perform" each time he uses a pseudonym or invents a past, notably at the Assembly Hall and at the Inn with Pamela. At the conclusion of the film, he returns to a theater where a "crazy month" is in progress. Just as Hannay identifies the tune that has been haunting him and makes the connection between Mr. Memory and the Professor, a Scotland Yard Inspector orders him to leave with a remark that reminds us of our role as spectators ("You don't want any trouble. . . . These people are here for entertainment"). Hannay pauses, and then asks Mr. Memory the question that frees them both and the denouement follows. The content of the question is no longer important; it is the mere fact of asking it and the response this elicits that are significant. The drama has come full cycle: The film ends where it began, at a spectacle, as Mr. Memory utters his dying confession while the show goes on.

Hitchcock's interest in the battle of the sexes finds its fullest expression in Hannay's relationships with Annabelle and Pamela. While Annabelle slowly disrobes in Hannay's apartment, he remains distant and cold, preferring the safety of innuendoes and fantasy to action. His sudden awakening, as she staggers into his room with a knife firmly planted between her shoulder blades, arouses something in him. The stabbing has clear sexual overtones and promotes feelings of guilt in Hannay for not having offered adequate protection and regret, for what might have been. The series of

<hr>

[5]Ibid., p. 61.

The Thirty-Nine Steps. The Professor plays his final "role" on the stage of the theater.

relationships that passes before him during the rest of the film provides negative examples that ultimately help him define his relationship with Pamela. We have already examined the references to failed marriages in the opening sequences of the film. The train trip to Scotland provides further examples, first in the conversation of the traveling salesman, and later in Hannay's abortive encounter with Pamela. The farm couple Hannay meets next are a barren, unhappy pair. The husband is driven by jealousy and a strict Calvinism; the wife is lonely and bored. However, her simple kindness to Hannay affects him at once and is ultimately responsible for saving his life.

The most blissful domestic situation is ironically that of the master criminal, whose wife and daughter are the picture of warmth, affection, and duty. In fact, he is the only person in the film who has a family: All other couples are childless. Hitchcock has a penchant for the attractive villain, and here he characterizes him by that idea that is still out of reach for Hannay.

Pamela presents a different sort of challenge to Hannay. From the moment of her kidnapping by the agents, she is bound to him emotionally by hatred and distrust and physically by handcuffs. On one level, the handcuffs represent the convergence of both forces that are pursuing him: the police (who have attached them to his wrists) and the spies (who have attached them to hers). But the handcuffs also represent what Hitchcock referred to as "sexual aberrations through restraint."[6] Hannay's excessive reliance on

[6]Ibid., p. 34.

clothing for protection has already been noted: He wears his overcoat in the theater and keeps it on when Pamela is in his flat. His "aberrations" with Pamela at the Inn are a source of comedy as she is forced to remove her stockings (encouraged by the innkeeper) while Hannay's hand lightly caresses her leg. As they lie together on the bed, Hannay displays a restraint that can be explained only in part by his fatigue. While he sleeps, Pamela slips the handcuff off and finds that his "gun" is only a pipe. Once the physical bond is broken, Pamela is free to discover the truth about Hannay. This is the turning point of the drama. She now helps him, and the principal threat to them is Scotland Yard. With the confession of Mr. Memory at the Palladium, Hannay becomes legally free, and in the final scene we see him acknowledge a different sort of bondage as he reaches across to take Pamela's hand, with the cuff still hanging from his wrist. Working with Pamela, Hannay has freed himself from external threats and from his own passive, restrained sexuality. Perhaps escape from this nightmare world is possible only through a union with someone of the opposite sex.

By having his protagonist remain a fugitive throughout the film, Hitchcock has completely changed the nature of Buchan's problem. It is no longer an intellectual puzzle ("Can Hannay identify the spies?") but rather an emotionally fraught situation ("Can Hannay solve the problem in order to free

The Thirty-Nine Steps. "Sexual aberrations through restraint": Hitchcock's hero and heroine bed down.

himself?''). This change is very much in keeping with Hitchcock's preference of suspense to mystery, and he refuses to provide an answer until the closing moments of the film.

Hitchcock's principal concerns—the exploration of man's elemental fears, the study of the relationships between men and women—are clearly not those of Buchan, and so he has transformed the story in accordance with his own interests. To do this he has changed the focus from mystery to suspense and restructured the story into a series of sequences. The movement of each is from precarious security to uncertainty: This is also the pattern of the film as a whole, with the suspense remaining unresolved until the final moments, when order is temporarily restored.

The Thirty-Nine Steps

Production Credits

Director	Alfred Hitchcock
Producers	Michael Balcon, Ivor Montagu
Screenplay by	Charles Bennett, Ian Hay, Alma Reville
Based on the novel by	John Buchan
Director of Photography	Bernard Knowles
Film Editor	Derek Twist
Sets by	Otto Werndorff, Albert Jullion
Music by	Louis Levy

Great Britain. 1935. 81 minutes. Black and White.

Cast

Richard Hannay	Robert Donat
Pamela	Madeleine Carroll
Annabelle Smith	Lucie Mannheim
Professor Jordan	Godfrey Tearle
Crofter's wife	Peggy Ashcroft
Crofter	John Laurie
Mrs. Jordan	Helen Haye
Sheriff	Frank Cellier
Mr. Memory	Wylie Watson

Further Reading

Camp, J. "John Buchan and Alfred Hitchcock." *Literature/Film Quarterly*, 6, No. 3 (Summer 1978), 230–40.

Durgnat, Raymond. *The Strange Case of Alfred Hitchcock.* Cambridge, Mass.: The M.I.T. Press, 1974.

Goldstein, R. M. "The 39 Steps." *Film News*, 36 (January /February 1979), 26.

Rothman, William. *Hitchcock—The Murderous Gaze.* Cambridge, Mass.: Harvard University Press, 1982.

Spoto, Donald. *The Art of Alfred Hitchcock: Fifty Years of his Motion Pictures*. New York: Hopkinson and Blake, 1976.

Truffaut, Francois with Helen G. Scott. *Hitchcock*. New York: Simon & Schuster, 1967.

Tyler, Parker. *Classics of the Foreign Film: A Pictorial Treasury*. New York: The Citadel Press, 1962.

 # The Member of the Wedding

Among the works in this volume, *A Member of the Wedding* has an unusual history. In 1945 Carson McCullers published her much acclaimed short novel. Several years later, with the help and encouragement of Tennessee Williams, she transformed it into a play that had a successful Broadway run of 501 performances. In 1952 Fred Zinnemann and scriptwriters Edna and Edward Anhalt produced a film version based on both the novel and the play, starring Julie Harris, Ethel Waters, and Brandon de Wilde, the same actors who had played the lead roles in the Broadway production. Although each version explores the universal search for identity and the loneliness and isolation that often accompany that search, they vary in significant ways. A comparison of the three provides a rare opportunity to examine how the medium shapes the message. As the director of the Broadway production, Harold Clurman, noted about McCullers's dramatization of her novel: "A play's form cannot be imposed by technical rules. A play's form rises out of its own organic nature."[7] The same applies to the forms of the novel and the film.

McCullers's novel is divided into three parts, each corresponding to one day in a weekend filled with significance for Frankie Addams. The first page of the novel acts as a prologue, describing the long summer that has preceded this weekend in August, and the last pages of Part Three serve as an epilogue, succinctly presenting the fates of the major characters through a conversation that takes place several months later between Frankie and Berenice the cook and the housekeeper. Within this three-part structure, the passage of time is carefully delineated. Except for a short flashback in Part One, in which we hear of the visit of Frankie's brother Jarvis and future sister-in-law Janice, the presentation is chronological. All other allusions to the past are conveyed through conversations between the characters. The single locale for Part One is the kitchen, where Frankie, John Henry (her seven-year-old cousin), and Berenice have spent the summer, playing cards, dallying over meals, and talking until their conversations have assumed an almost ritualistic tone.

---

[7] Harold Clurman, *On Directing* (New York: The Macmillan Company, 1972), p. 49.

Frankie is caught between childhood and adolescence, too old to treat John Henry as an equal and too young to be accepted by the girls whose club-house is within earshot of her yard. The visit of her brother and his fiancée has excited her, and she struggles to understand its meaning in her life. Suddenly, at the end of Part One, she has a revelation of its significance:

> Frankie stood looking into the sky. For when the old question came to her—the who she was and what she would be in the world, and why she was standing there that minute—when the old question came to her, she did not feel hurt and unanswered. At last she knew just who she was and understood where she was going. She loved her brother and the bride and she was a member of the wedding. The three of them would go into the world and they would always be together. And finally, after the scared spring and the crazy summer, she was no more afraid.

This revelation gives her the confidence to step beyond the confines of the kitchen and enter the world. She assumes a new identity to match this insight: Instead of being Frankie, she becomes F. Jasmine, the first syllable of her new name echoing the first syllables of Jarvis and Janice. Part Two begins:

> The day before the wedding was not like any day that F. Jasmine had ever known. It was the Saturday she went into town, and suddenly, after the closed blank summer, the town opened before her and in a new way she belonged.

Part Two (Saturday) is divided into three chapters, corresponding respectively to morning, afternoon, and evening, with the action alternating between her familiar home and the newly discovered town.

Part Three chronicles her eagerly anticipated bus trip to the wedding in the company of her father, John Henry, and Berenice, and her disappointing trip home. McCullers does not show us the ceremony itself; instead she concentrates on the reactions of those concerned, especially the dejected Frankie, who struggles to understand what has gone wrong and to cope with her sense of defeat.

The epilogue shows us the self-centered adolescent Frankie has become as a result of these experiences. The world of the kitchen (which included John Henry, Berenice and Honey Camden) is forever behind her. Adulthood lies ahead.

At one point in Part Two, as Frankie repeats her story of the wedding, the narrator comments, "the telling of the wedding had an end and a beginning, a shape like a song." The same could certainly be said about Carson McCullers's novel. The temporal pattern provides a structure, and the conflicts, adumbrated in the opening pages, are resolved in the epilogue.

In some ways, this work easily allows a theatrical adaptation. The three-part structure is based on a restricted time period, which can easily be duplicated on the stage. The work concerns a limited number of characters in a limited number of settings. Also, as we have noted, the most significant actions (the visit of Jarvis and Janice and the wedding ceremony) are not described; instead, these events are reflected through the reactions and dialogue of the other characters.

But there are also some obvious difficulties. The prologue, which establishes an emotional and temporal context for the weekend, cannot easily be dramatized. In addition, the work concerns internal conflicts, many of which are reflected through Frankie's consciousness and depicted in internal monologues. And although the kitchen is the principal location of the novel, there are several important journeys beyond this location: Frankie's exploration of the town on the morning of the wedding (Part Two, Chapter 1); Frankie's return to the more tawdry part of town the evening before the wedding (Part Two, Chapter 3); the long bus trip to Winter Hill, the site of the wedding, and the trip home (Part Three); and her flight through town after returning from the wedding (Part Three). Dramatizing these passages would require many changes of scene.

McCullers has created a three-act structure for her play, with each act corresponding to a day. The first act follows Part One of the novel very closely, except that the visit of Jarvis and Janice is now dramatized. Act Two focuses only upon the afternoon in the kitchen, eliminating Frankie's morning exploration of the town and her return to the town in the evening. In early versions of the play McCullers retained a scene between Frankie and the soldier, but it was dropped during try-outs, partly because it made the play too long (four hours), and partly because, in Harold Clurman's words, it "destroyed the play's unity on the stage."[8] Act Three corresponds to the third part of the novel, although the wedding is shifted to the groom's home, thereby eliminating the need for a trip. The wedding was originally shown in the play, but this scene was also dropped. Instead, the wedding takes place offstage, and we see the reactions of the characters in the kitchen. Similarly, when Frankie flees, our attention shifts to the plight of John Henry and the difficulties of Honey, which are depicted on the stage.

A significantly greater burden is placed on dialogue in the play since conversations now must convey not only the actions and activities occurring outside the kitchen, but the thoughts of the characters as well. As McCullers noted in an interview with Harvey Breit, the play "all had to spring from another medium. It was fascinating. The play has to be direct. The inner monologue has become the spoken word. It has to be more naked emotionally, too."[9] Emotions are more fully exposed in the play partly because physical movement becomes an important mode of expression. But thoughts and emotions are also conveyed verbally. For example, in the novel the narrator states: " . . . a thought and explanation suddenly came to her, so that she

[8]Ibid

[9]Harvey Breit, "Behind the Wedding: Carson McCullers Discusses the Novel She Converted Into a Stage Play," *The New York Times*, January 1, 1950, Section 2, page 3.

knew and almost said aloud: *They are the we of me."* In the play Frankie does say this aloud and, given her propensity for flowery language, the statement does not seem out of character. Similarly, descriptive passages are transformed into dialogue. During the card game the trio plays, the narrator in the novel comments: "They had played cards after dinner every single afternoon; if you would eat those old cards, they would taste like a combination of all the dinners of that August, together with a sweaty-handed nasty taste," a statement Frankie utters in desperation in the play when cards appear to be missing. Again, this type of transformation is believable because of Frankie's love of language.

In another significant shift of emphasis from novel to play, Berenice becomes the dominant character, and the theme of race becomes more prominent. This is partly a result of the physical limitations of the stage: The kitchen is now the principal locale, which makes the role of Berenice proportionately greater than in the novel. This shift also resulted from the casting of Ethel Waters as Berenice in the original Broadway production. Waters dominated the play, both through her presence as an actress and through minor changes in the script McCullers made to emphasize Berenice's more central role. For example, instead of concluding the play with the focus on Frankie, whose final conversation is interrupted by the ringing of the bell, McCullers ends with Berenice alone, mournfully humming "His Eye is on the Sparrow." Her sense of loss nearly overshadows Frankie's gain.

Fred Zinnemann draws upon both the novel and the play for his film, but he recasts his material to take advantage of his own medium. He respects the sense of enclosure represented by the world of the kitchen, but he follows Frankie beyond the confines of that world (as McCullers had in the novel) and effectively contrasts the two locations.

Zinnemann's film begins with an exterior shot of the three principals fishing in a river, as the credits unroll. On the soundtrack the humming we will later associate with Berenice blends with the jazz horn we will come to identify with Honey. Then, as Zinnemann cuts to a long shot of Frankie approaching on the sidewalk, a voice-over narration presents in condensed form the opening page of the novel, which acts as a prologue:

> It happened that green and crazy summer when Frankie was twelve years old. This was the summer when for a long time she had not been a member. She belonged to no club and was a member of nothing in the world. Frankie had become an unjoined person, and she was afraid. And then, on the last Friday of August, all this was changed: it was so sudden that Frankie puzzled the whole blank afternoon, and still she did not understand.

The lines are spoken by Julie Harris, as the humming of Berenice continues. Zinnemann then cuts directly to the visit of Jarvis and Janice and, except for minor changes in the dialogue, follows Act I of the play rather closely. After the departure of Janice and Jarvis, Zinnemann focuses exclusively upon the

The Member of the Wedding. Zinnemann heightens the claustrophobic confinement of the kitchen through his tight framing of the three protagonists.

trio in the kitchen. He uses his camera effectively both to isolate Frankie from the others through close-ups and, through depth of focus shots, to suggest the tensions between characters within a shot. The film follows the time scheme of both the novel and the play, and this first day ends with a scene in Frankie's bedroom. John Henry says his prayers, and he and Frankie are about to fall asleep when they hear the music of Honey's horn. Suddenly it stops. Frankie utters a wish that it be completed, but it never is. She looks out the window longingly, watching the moths fluttering at the screen. Zinnemann places his camera outside the window and holds a close-up of her as she repeats words from the novel:

> To me it is the irony of fate, the way they come here. Those moths could fly anywhere. Yet they keep hanging around the windows of this house.

Zinnemann's visualization of the scene beautifully complements Mc-Cullers's language. Frankie then realizes that she belongs to the wedding: "I love the two of them so much: they are the 'we' of me." This is the culminating moment of Part One of the novel and Act I of the play. Zinnemann, too, emphasizes this moment, by holding the close-up of Frankie within the bedroom, as she sits on the bed. She reaches up to her left and extinguishes the light. This action is followed by a fade-out and a fade-in on the next scene. The importance of Frankie's realization is heightened by these fades and by the contrasts that follow: The time changes to the next morning, and the scene shifts to the streets of the town. In addition, the music, used throughout the film to emphasize dramatic points and prepare us for transitions, modulates from something slow and melancholy to an upbeat, gay tune. In these ways Zinnemann suggests a definitive ending and a new beginning.

The scenes that follow, showing Frankie's trips to town, are drawn entirely from the novel. Although Zinnemann condenses this material (which, as we have seen, is entirely deleted from the play), he effectively conveys her new sense of belonging, as she bicycles from her middle-class neighborhood to the downtown area of her father's watch shop.

After Frankie's return home, Zinnemann follows Act II of the play. The scene in the kitchen builds toward the moment when Frankie and John Henry cluster around Berenice and John Henry initiates the singing of "His Eye Is on the Sparrow." In the novel this section concludes with the three of them crying together, "in the way that often on these summer evenings they would suddenly start a song." Here, too, we see how both play and film have been shaped to fit the casting of Ethel Waters as Berenice. "His Eye Is on the Sparrow" was one of her favorite spirituals (and the title she gave to her autobiography), and it beautifully draws together many of the themes of the film. The singing represents an extraordinary moment of unity, and Zinnemann deftly captures it with the most understated camera work before slowly fading out. His choice of the fade-out/fade-in (for the second time in the film) heightens the importance of this scene by bringing the drama to a halt. This is the cinematic technique closest to the dropping of the curtain in drama, and once again indicates a moment of climax.

Zinnemann fades in on the wedding ceremony, and the soundtrack (with the change from the spiritual to the wedding march) signals a transition. Unlike the play, he shows us the ceremony, and with good reason: He has made Frankie a member of the wedding by framing her in a long shot between Jarvis and Janice. Although the shot is presented objectively, it is a visual metaphor of her sense of the situation. Zinnemann expands upon the play again by taking us outside (as in the novel) and showing us Frankie's futile attempt to leave with Janice and Jarvis, and later by cutting from the kitchen to the seamy side of town, where Frankie is wandering fearfully, having run away from home. The unfamiliar, adult sounds of loneliness, sex, and violence combined with high contrast lighting create a menacing urban landscape quite unlike the one explored by Frankie earlier in the day. Zinnemann has combined Frankie's two encounters with the soldier into one, and this scene forms the climax of the sequence. The soldier's advances are met with Frankie's violence, after which she runs home, in fear and confusion, through the back streets of town. She finds no one home and calls out from her backyard. From John Henry's upstairs window her father and Berenice inform her that John Henry is ill. "Why is he sick, Berenice?" she asks, but no answer is forthcoming. The camera cranes up to the window, the light is extinguished, and there is a slow fade-out. As with the earlier fade-outs, this transition marks a definite ending. Zinnemann fades in on the same window and then pulls the camera back to reveal Frankie, no longer dressed like a tomboy but rather like a young woman.

Zinnemann follows the concluding scene of the play quite closely. With the most unobtrusive cinematic art, he emphasizes the growing estrangement between Frankie and Berenice. Berenice's stoical acceptance of grief beautifully modifies the youthful optimism of Frankie, for whom the events of the recent past have already receded. Nothing could underline Berenice's solitude more poignantly than the close-up of her as she hums "His Eye Is on the Sparrow," and struggles to hold back the tears.

Each of the three versions of *The Member of the Wedding* stands successfully on its own, and each has its own strengths. The similarities are evident: The story remains essentially the same in each, although the roles of Berenice and Honey Camden shift in emphasis from version to version. The play follows the temporal structure established in the novel, and Zinnemann adapts this structure to his film through a subtle use of the fade-out/fade in.

But, like a single tune played on three different instruments, the story is modified by changes required by the differences among the three forms. In the novel McCullers employs interior monologues and descriptive passages to convey the thoughts and feelings of the characters. The play exposes these emotions and ideas through verbal expression and physical movement. The economy of setting and time demanded by a play necessitates the cutting of scenes from the novel and the establishment of a more limited locale (for example, moving the wedding to the groom's home).

The film, like the novel, can transport the viewer virtually anywhere. Moreover, it can create meaning through editing, framing, and camera angle and use sound effectively for transition, emphasis, and mood. Zinnemann employs these resources with unobtrusive skill. Although the themes of identity, isolation, and the fragility of human existence run through all three versions, in each they are presented in a strikingly different variation.

The Member of the Wedding

Production Credits

Director	Fred Zinnemann
Producer	Stanley Kramer
Screenplay by	Edna and Edward Anhalt
Based on the novel and play by	Carson McCullers
Director of Photography	Hal Mohr, ASC
Production Design	Rudolph Sternad
Film Editor	William A. Lyon, ACE
Music by	Alex North

USA. 1952. 91 minutes
  Black & white.

Cast

Berenice Sadie Brown	Ethel Waters
Frankie Addams	Julie Harris
John Henry	Brandon de Wilde
Jarvis	Arthur Franz
Janice	Nancy Gates
Mr. Addams	William Hansen
Honey Camden Brown	James Edwards
T. T. Williams	Harry Bolden
Soldier	Dick Moore
Barney MacKean	Danny Mummert
Helen	June Hedin
Doris	Ann Carter

Further Reading

Giannetti, Louis D. "The Member of the Wedding." *Literature/Film Quarterly*, 4, No. 1 (Winter 1976), 28–38.

Goldstein, R. M. "*The Member of the Wedding.*" *Film News*, 36 (January /February 1979), 28.

Phillips, Gene D. "Fred Zinnemann: An Interview." *Journal of Popular Film and Television*, 7 (1978), 56–66.

Roud, Richard. "The Empty Streets." *Sight and Sound*, 26, No. 4 (Spring 1957), 191–95.

Waters, Ethel with Charles Samuels. *His Eye Is on the Sparrow*. Garden City, New York: Doubleday, 1951.

A Doll's House

Although written in 1879, Henrik Ibsen's *A Doll's House* seems remarkably contemporary. Ibsen focuses on the turning point in a woman's life as she decides to break away from the claustrophobic domesticity of her family life and seek fulfillment as an individual. Ibsen successfully employs the physical limitations of the stage to convey his heroine's sense of her oppressively confining surroundings and manipulates the temporal restrictions of drama to create a heightened sense of time, as each act hastens decisively toward the climax.

Joseph Losey clearly understands Ibsen's consummate use of the theatrical medium. In his own adaptation of *A Doll's House*, he attempts to reshape the structure of Ibsen's play and to expand the setting and narrative time without any loss of dramatic force. He extends the setting of the play by moving beyond the confines of the Helmer household, while maintaining that site as the center of his drama. The action takes place throughout the village of Røros, Norway, where the play was filmed. Losey makes extensive use of his settings to develop the themes of the play and to delineate characters.

Losey expands the narrative time of Ibsen's play from three days to nearly nine years. References within the play to past actions are dramatized, so that in the opening sequences of the film we are shown the characters creating their future. In addition, Losey makes frequent use of simultaneous time, both to compress the action and to enhance characterization.

The film contains eight scenes, set before the opening of Ibsen's play, that expand Ibsen's exposition in space and time. The movie begins with an establishing shot of a skating pond on a winter's afternoon. Beyond the pond lies a small, rustic restaurant. The scene is idyllic, and the camera slowly zooms across the pond as two young women end their skating and prepare to enter the restaurant. To the left of the restaurant against the white background stands a darkly clad figure. Our first view of Krogstad shows him spying on the actions of others, hardly a positive characteristic. Nora and Christine enter the coffee shop, take some pastries, and sit down at a table. As they converse, the camera slowly dollies around behind Christine to reveal Krogstad watching them through the window. Losey continually demonstrates how exposed these people's lives are. Characters are constantly observing others through windows, or unknowingly being observed themselves.

The apparently idle banter of this scene conveys important information to the viewer. Neither woman is married, and each is about to enter an alliance: Nora for love, and Christine for financial security. Nora promises to introduce Christine to her fiancé, Torvald, and later, as they are about to part, Nora insists that they correspond every week. These will be the first of Nora's broken promises. After Nora leaves, Krogstad enters, and the juxtaposition suggests a relationship between Nora and Krogstad that Losey will develop. Here we see Krogstad before his fall; he is an impecunious lawyer, who wants to marry for love but cannot do so. By adding this scene Losey implies that things might have turned out differently for Krogstad if Christine had accepted his offer of marriage. Although Krogstad already displays unpleasant characteristics, Christine is made to share responsibility for his actions.

The next two scenes dramatize the circumstances in which Nora is forced to borrow money from Krogstad. In the first of these, Nora and Dr. Rank are at the bedside of her dying father. She is pregnant and faced with the knowledge that her husband's health is also extremely bad. Dr. Rank assures her that her husband can be cured, but only by spending a year in warmer climates, and he expresses his happiness in the knowledge that they can afford to travel. Only later do we learn that this was not the case, and we begin to understand the pressures that have been upon Nora. In the scene that follows, Nora and Torvald depart for Italy. Torvald's illness is being kept a secret from him, and he is unhappy and reluctant to leave Norway. Torvald watches his wife and Dr. Rank talking in the street beneath his window and subsequently accuses them of being conspiratorial. Indeed they are, although we do not yet understand the extent of Nora's duplicity. When she has reentered the house, Nora tries to overhear her husband's conversation with Dr. Rank. Already secrets are being kept, secrets that will not be unraveled until years later. Finally, Nora and Torvald depart in the sleigh. Losey poignantly communicates Rank's isolation and grief through a high-angle long shot of him standing alone in the empty street.

Losey fades out to indicate the passage of time and then cuts directly from the darkened screen to a black and white photograph of the Helmer family in Italy, with the date, March 1885, in the lower right-hand corner. The camera dollies back to reveal Nora seated on the sofa reading a nursery story to her three children. Although Ibsen's play has not yet begun, we are now in the present. Significantly, Nora's roles as wife and mother precisely establish the time of each of the three preceding scenes: In the first scene, with Christine, Nora is engaged to be married; at her father's deathbed she is pregnant for the first time; and when she and Torvald leave for Italy, they take their first child, who is a baby. Now, in the fourth scene, surrounded by her three children, she is the picture of a loving and dutiful mother. Losey emphasizes the enormity of Nora's ultimate rejection of these roles by stressing them in his opening exposition.

Then, for the first time, Losey shifts from Nora to Torvald, whom we see entering his place of business, the bank. Even within this venerable structure there is no privacy, for the walls of the offices are glass. Losey cuts to the interior, where we expect to follow Torvald but discover instead Krogstad. Through Krogstad's conversation with his colleague, Olssen, we learn that Torvald may soon become bank manager, and we also get a lengthy and bitter tirade from Krogstad on the menial position he holds in the bank after many years of service. Losey creates sympathy for Krogstad by lengthening the period he has spent in the bank, thereby suggesting that he has more than paid for his crime. Torvald's later dismissal of him thus appears even more arbitrary than in the play.

Losey cuts back to Nora in a setting that evokes the opening scene of the film. Nora is alone in a coffee shop eating sweets; we observe her through the window, just as Krogstad had done earlier. When she leaves the coffee shop, Losey cuts to the interior, so that we see her departure through a window as well. The fact that her actions are so apparent to the townspeople as a whole makes her husband's blindness more striking.

As Nora heads homeward with her macaroons, Torvald completes his physical exam at Dr. Rank's apartment and is declared fit. But now Dr. Rank permits Torvald to see the possible evidence of his own illness through his microscope. Losey contrasts the fully recovered Torvald, about to be established as manager of the bank, with the formerly healthy Dr. Rank, whose rapid decay has begun.

Losey cuts from this scene to the inside of a train compartment, as the vehicle, bearing Christine, pulls into the station. The train is an intrusion into this bucolic landscape, through which, until this moment, everyone has traveled on sleigh (in the play Christine arrives by boat). This now liberated woman is similarly about to disturb the Helmer household. She will be joined by the forces of death (Dr. Rank) and corruption (Krogstad), with which Nora and Torvald must cope.

Losey, then, has created a new opening for his version by dramatizing material presented through conversations in Ibsen's play and by adding new material of his own. His opening is very slowly paced. Most shots are of long duration and employ a stationary camera. This leisurely presentation conveys an attitude toward life, an attitude established in the opening shots of the skating pond. Losey's spatial expansions also function thematically, far beyond the sense of realistic place that they contribute to the story. In the play Ibsen employs the limited setting of the Helmer home to underline Nora's entrapment: When at the conclusion of the drama, she is seen leaving that setting, the sense of liberation is enormous. Losey has risked losing this feeling of confinement by opening up his drama spatially. However, he has shown how restrictive life can be in such a town, where one's movements are constantly on display (everyone can see Nora purchasing macaroons in the coffee shop), and where rumors circulate freely ("Rumors are for pigs," Krogstad declares the first time we see him in the bank).

After the eight introductory scenes we have just discussed, Losey closely follows the development of Ibsen's play, and complications ensue rapidly. The film, like the play, reaches a climax with Torvald's discovery of Nora's secret, followed by the rapid falling action leading to the conclusion, which is Nora's departure. Although Losey adheres to Ibsen's plot for the rest of his film, he continues to expand the setting and to alter the dramatic structure by editing.

Losey moves Ibsen's scenes out of the Helmer house and edits them to suggest new relationships between actions and characters. For example, he cuts from the first scene of Nora disturbing Torvald in his study to a scene of Dr. Rank working at his desk in his study. The parallel created by the editing is reinforced by the similar action that follows. Dr. Rank is interrupted by his maid, who delivers a telegram, the contents of which are known to us and to him before he opens it. This, of course, prefigures Torvald's later receipt of Krogstad's letter, which will bring bad news of a different sort. The two men in Nora's life are very similar: the husband who acts like a father, and the father figure who she later discovers fantasizes about being her husband.

The relationship between Nora and Krogstad, already suggested in the opening sequence of the film, is also developed cinematically. We see Krogstad and Nora together for the first time in Nora's house on Christmas eve. Torvald, Christine, and Dr. Rank have left, and Nora is hiding from her children under the dining room table. She peeks out and whom does she discover at the end of the long corridor (in one of Losey's frequent deep focus shots) but Nils Krogstad. In the play the first of their conversations takes place entirely in the Helmer home, but Losey has divided this scene into two: one within the home and the other on a deserted bridge outside town. Nora and Krogstad are seen on the bridge in a long shot through the girders of a bridge in the foreground, making them resemble flies caught in a web. Losey cuts to a two shot as they confront each other in profile. The scene is rather static, with the lines of the bridge defining the space within which each operates. Nora and Krogstad are suspended between opposing possibilities, literally and figuratively. Except for their conversation and the rushing water below, the scene is silent, with little movement of characters or camera. Both are dressed in dark colors, which contrast starkly with the blue tint of the snow. The shots are of long duration, creating a very slowly paced scene. Nora still seems to have a measure of control here.

A Doll's House. Losey "opens up" the play spatially to heighten the dramatic tension as Krogstad faces Nora.

Losey has shifted the setting for Nora's second conversation with Krogstad from the Helmer house to a crowded toboggan slope, where Krogstad is spending the afternoon with his children. Losey cuts to this setting immediately after the scene in which Torvald sends the letter of dismissal to Krogstad. Krogstad's obvious enjoyment of his children and his devotion to them allies him with Nora and contrasts him with Torvald, who is never shown even touching his own children.

Nora joins her children at the toboggan slope after visiting Dr. Rank. She is more desperate now because she knows that Dr. Rank loves her, and as a result she feels that she cannot ask him for help. Slowly, she walks past the church to the top of the slope. Krogstad, at the bottom of the hill, observes her darkened figure against the sky, and the camera zooms in on her from his perspective. Nora too is an observer; not of Krogstad, however, but of her children, who are about to be taken home by their nannie. Her reverie is interrupted by Krogstad's calls, as he mounts the slope to join her.

This scene of confrontation is in marked contrast to the earlier scene on the bridge. Now Krogstad pursues Nora relentlessly, a pursuit emphasized by the moving camera. Gone, too, is any possibility of privacy; Nora and Krogstad stride along the crest of the hill in view of the entire town. Their encounters are becoming increasingly public as their secret begins to surface, and the accelerating internal rhythm of the shots pushes us toward the discovery scene. As Nora descends the slope by the church, Losey cuts to the interior of the empty church, which resonates with Krogstad's threats. The unforgiving patriarchal church, dominating the landscape in the opening and closing shots of the film, is yet another force Nora must confront and, like the other aspects of this patriarchal society, ultimately reject. The juxtaposition here with Krogstad's remarks is forceful.

The parallels between Nora and Krogstad are most striking in Losey's editing of the party sequence. Already, Krogstad has been shown as a family man, both in the scene on the slopes and in his comment to Nora (not in Ibsen's play) that his feeling for his family had prevented him from committing suicide. In Ibsen's play, Krogstad is a widower; in Losey's film, his wife has left him, just as Nora will leave Torvald. During the party sequence, Losey cuts from the jollity, color, and movement of the party to Krogstad's somber quarters. Krogstad's son awakens and cries out as Krogstad and Christine are talking, and Krogstad leaves the room to comfort him. Losey takes us back to the party, where Nora is about to perform the tarantella. But she must go in search of her tambourine, which gives her an opportunity to attempt to force the lock on the mailbox (thereby dramatizing an event that is only mentioned by Torvald in the play) and then to look in on her children for the last time. She bids the sleeping children farewell, and Losey cuts to Krogstad, coming out of his son's room. The parallel action builds sympathy for both of them, as each proceeds to take steps that will change their lives and the lives of their families. Losey returns us for the final time to the Helmer household, where the drama reaches its inevitable conclusion.

A Doll's House. Nora's final "performance" for her husband.

Losey's skill as a filmmaker and his understanding of the differences between drama and film are fully evident in this adaptation. He expands Ibsen's text spatially and temporally without losing any of the dramatic impact of the play, and alters the structure of the original drama in significant ways by reorganizing the scenes, adding new material, and creating new relationships between scenes through editing. Without betraying Ibsen's text, Losey succeeds in using the strengths of film as a medium to transform a play into a movie rather than merely transcribing its action onto film.

A Doll's House

Production Credits

Director	Joseph Losey
Producer	Joseph Losey
Screenplay by	David Mercer
Based on the play by	Henrik Ibsen
English translation by	Michael Meyer
Director of Photography	Gerry Fisher
Art Director	Eileen Diss

Film Editor	Reginald Beck
Music by	Michel Legrand

Great Britain. 1973. 109 minutes.
Color

Cast

Torvald Helmer	David Warner
Nora	Jane Fonda
Dr. Rank	Trevor Howard
Mrs. Linde	Delphine Seyrig
Nils Krogstad	Edward Fox
Ann Marie	Anna Wing
Olssen	Pierre Oudry

Further Reading

Dawson, Ian. "*A Doll's House.*" *Sight and Sound,* 42, No. 4 (Autumn 1973), 235–36.

Hirsch, Foster. *Joseph Losey.* Boston: Twayne Publishers, 1980.

Walker, Alexander. *Double Takes.* North Pomfred, Vermont: Hamish Hamilton, 1977.

A Doll's House
Henrik Ibsen

Translated from the Norwegian by William Archer

Characters

TORVALD HELMER
NORA, his wife
DOCTOR RANK
MRS. LINDEN*
NILS KROGSTAD
THE HELMERS' THREE CHILDREN
ANNA,† their nurse
A MAID-SERVANT (ELLEN)
A PORTER

The action passes in Helmer's house (a flat) in Christiania.

Act First

A room, comfortably and tastefully, but not expensively, furnished. In the back, on the right, a door leads to the hall; on the left another door leads to HELMER'S *study. Between the two doors a pianoforte. In the middle of the left wall a door, and nearer the front a window. Near the window a round table with armchairs and a small sofa. In the right wall, somewhat to the back, a door, and against the same wall, further forward, a porcelain stove; in front of it a couple of arm-chairs and a rocking-chair. Between the stove and the side-door a small table. Engravings on the walls. A what-not with china and bric-à-brac. A small bookcase filled with handsomely bound books. Carpet. A fire in the stove. It is a winter day.*

A bell rings in the hall outside. Presently the outer door of the flat is heard to open. Then NORA *enters, humming gaily. She is in outdoor dress, and carries several parcels, which she lays on the right-hand table. She leaves the door into the hall open, and a* PORTER *is seen outside, carrying a Christmas-tree and a basket, which he gives to the* MAID-SERVANT *who has opened the door.*

NORA. Hide the Christmas-tree carefully, Ellen; the children must on no account see it before this evening, when it's lighted up. *(To the* PORTER, *taking out her purse.)* How much?
PORTER. Fifty öre.
NORA. There is a crown. No, keep the change. *(The* PORTER *thanks her and goes.* NORA *shuts the door. She continues smiling in quiet glee as she takes off her outdoor things. Taking from her pocket a bag of macaroons, she eats one or two. Then she goes on tip-toe to her husband's door and listens.)*

*In the original "Fru Linde."
†In the original "Anne-Marie."

NORA. Yes; he is at home. *(She begins humming again, crossing to the table on the right.)*

HELMER. *(In his room.)* Is that my lark twittering there?

NORA. *(Busy opening some of her parcels.)* Yes, it is.

HELMER. Is it the squirrel frisking around?

NORA. Yes!

HELMER. When did the squirrel get home?

NORA. Just this minute. *(Hides the bag of macaroons in her pocket and wipes her mouth.)* Come here, Torvald, and see what I've been buying.

HELMER. Don't interrupt me. *(A little later he opens the door and looks in, pen in hand.)* Buying, did you say? What! All that? Has my little spendthrift been making the money fly again?

NORA. Why, Torvald, surely we can afford to launch out a little now. It's the first Christmas we haven't had to pinch.

HELMER. Come come; we can't afford to squander money.

NORA. Oh yes, Torvald, do let us squander a little, now—just the least little bit! You know you'll soon be earning heaps of money.

HELMER. Yes, from New Year's Day. But there's a whole quarter before my first salary is due.

NORA. Never mind; we can borrow in the meantime.

HELMER. Nora! *(He goes up to her and takes her playfully by the ear.)* Still my little featherbrain! Supposing I borrowed a thousand crowns to-day, and you made ducks and drakes of them during Christmas week, and then on New Year's Eve a tile blew off the roof and knocked my brains out——

NORA. *(Laying her hand on his mouth.)* Hush! How can you talk so horridly?

HELMER. But supposing it were to happen—what then?

NORA. If anything so dreadful happened, it would be all the same to me whether I was in debt or not.

HELMER. But what about the creditors?

NORA. They! Who cares for them? They're only strangers.

HELMER. Nora, Nora! What a woman you are! But seriously, Nora, you know my principles on these points. No debts! No borrowing! Home life ceases to be free and beautiful as soon as it is founded on borrowing and debt. We two have held out bravely till now, and we are not going to give in at the last.

NORA. *(Going to the fireplace.)* Very well—as you please, Torvald.

HELMER. *(Following her.)* Come come; my little lark mustn't droop her wings like that. What? Is my squirrel in the sulks? *(Takes out his purse.)* Nora, what do you think I have here?

NORA. *(Turning round quickly.)* Money!

HELMER. There! *(Gives her some notes.)* Of course I know all sorts of things are wanted at Christmas.

NORA. *(Counting.)* Ten, twenty, thirty, forty. Oh, thank you, thank you, Torvald! This will go a long way.

HELMER. I should hope so.

NORA. Yes, indeed; a long way! But come here, and let me show you all I've been buying. And so cheap! Look, here's a new suit for Ivar, and a little sword. Here are a horse and a trumpet for Bob. And here a doll and a cradle for Emmy. They're only common; but they're good enough for her to pull to pieces. And dress-stuffs and kerchiefs for the servants. I ought to have got something better for old Anna.

HELMER. And what's in that other parcel?

NORA. *(Crying out.)* No, Torvald, you're not to see that until this evening.

HELMER. Oh! Ah! But now tell me, you little spendthrift, have you thought of anything for yourself?

NORA. For myself! Oh, I don't want anything.

HELMER. Nonsense! Just tell me something sensible you would like to have.

NORA. No, really I don't know of anything—— Well, listen, Torvald——

HELMER. Well?

NORA. *(Playing with his coat-buttons, without looking him in the face.)* If you really want to give me something, you might, you know—you might——

HELMER. Well? Out with it!

NORA. *(Quickly.)* You might give me money, Torvald. Only just what you think you can spare; then I can buy something with it later on.

HELMER. But, Nora——

NORA. Oh, please do, dear Torvald, please do! I should hang the money in lovely gilt paper on the Christmas-tree. Wouldn't that be fun?

HELMER. What do they call the birds that are always making the money fly?

NORA. Yes, I know—spendthrifts,* of course. But please do as I ask you, Torvald. Then I shall have time to think what I want most. Isn't that very sensible, now?

HELMER. *(Smiling.)* Certainly; that is to say, if you really kept the money I gave you, and really spent it on something for yourself. But it all goes in housekeeping, and for all manner of useless things, and then I have to pay up again.

NORA. But, Torvald——

HELMER. Can you deny it, Nora dear? *(He puts his arm round her.)* It's a sweet little lark, but it gets through a lot of money. No one would believe how much it costs a man to keep such a little bird as you.

NORA. For shame! How can you say so? Why, I save as much as ever I can.

HELMER. *(Laughing.)* Very true—as much as you can—but that's precisely nothing.

NORA. *(Hums and smiles with convert glee.)* H'm! If you only knew, Torvald, what expenses we larks and squirrels have.

HELMER. You're a strange little being! Just like your father—always on the look-out for all the money you can lay your hands on; but the moment you have it, it seems to slip through your fingers; you never know what

---

*"Spillefugl," literally "playbird," means a gambler.

becomes of it. Well, one must take you as you are. It's in the blood. Yes, Nora, that sort of thing is hereditary.

NORA. I wish I had inherited many of papa's qualities.

HELMER. And I don't wish you anything but just what you are—my own, sweet little song-bird. But I say—it strikes me you look so—so—what shall I call it?—so suspicious to-day——

NORA. Do I?

HELMER. You do, indeed. Look me full in the face.

NORA. *(Looking at him.)* Well?

HELMER. *(Threatening with his finger.)* Hasn't the little sweet-tooth been play-ing pranks to-day?

NORA. No; how can you think such a thing!

HELMER. Didn't she just look in at the confectioner's?

NORA. No, Torvald; really——

HELMER. Not to sip a little jelly?

NORA. No; certainly not.

HELMER. Hasn't she even nibbled a macaroon or two?

NORA. No, Torvald, indeed, indeed!

HELMER. Well, well, well; of course I'm only joking.

NORA. *(Goes to the table on the right.)* I shouldn't think of doing what you dis-approve of.

HELMER. No, I'm sure of that; and, besides, you've given me your word—— *(Going towards her.)* Well, keep your little Christmas secrets to yourself, Nora darling. The Christmas-tree will bring them all to light, I daresay.

NORA. Have you remembered to invite Doctor Rank?

HELMER. No. But it's not necessary; he'll come as a matter of course. Besides, I shall ask him when he looks in to-day. I've ordered some capital wine. Nora, you can't think how I look forward to this evening.

NORA. And I too. How the children will enjoy themselves, Torvald!

HELMER. Ah, it's glorious to feel that one has an assured position and ample means. Isn't it delightful to think of?

NORA. Oh, it's wonderful!

HELMER. Do you remember last Christmas? For three whole weeks before-hand you shut yourself up every evening till long past midnight to make flowers for the Christmas-tree, and all sorts of other marvels that were to have astonished us. I was never so bored in my life.

NORA. I didn't bore myself at all.

HELMER. *(Smiling.)* But it came to little enough in the end, Nora.

NORA. Oh, are you going to tease me about that again? How could I help the cat getting in and pulling it all to pieces?

HELMER. To be sure you couldn't, my poor little Nora. You did your best to give us all pleasure, and that's the main point. But, all the same, it's a good thing the hard times are over.

NORA. Oh, isn't it wonderful?

HELMER. Now I needn't sit here boring myself all alone; and you needn't tire your blessed eyes and your delicate little fingers——

NORA. *(Clapping her hands.)* No, I needn't, need I, Torvald? Oh, how wonderful it is to think of? *(Takes his arm.)* And now I'll tell you how I think we ought to manage, Torvald. As soon as Christmas is over—— *(The hall-door bell rings.)* Oh, there's a ring! *(Arranging the room.)* That's somebody come to call. How tiresome!

HELMER. I'm "not at home" to callers; remember that.

ELLEN. *(In the doorway.)* A lady to see you, ma'am.

NORA. Show her in.

ELLEN. *(To HELMER.)* And the doctor has just come, sir.

HELMER. Has he gone into my study?

ELLEN. Yes, sir. *(HELMER goes into his study.* ELLEN *ushers in* MRS. LINDEN, *in travelling costume, and goes out, closing the door.)*

MRS. LINDEN. *(Embarrassed and hesitating.)* How do you do, Nora?

NORA. *(Doubtfully.)* How do you do?

MRS. LINDEN. I see you don't recognise me!

NORA. No, I don't think—oh yes!—I believe—— *(Suddenly brightening.)* What, Christina! Is is really you?

MRS. LINDEN. Yes; really I!

NORA. Christina! And to think I didn't know you! But how could I—— *(More softly.)* How changed you are, Christina!

MRS. LINDEN. Yes, no doubt. In nine or ten years——

NORA. Is it really so long since we met? Yes, so it is. Oh, the last eight years have been a happy time, I can tell you. And now you have come to town? All that long journey in mid-winter! How brave of you!

MRS. LINDEN. I arrived by this morning's steamer.

NORA. To have a merry Christmas, of course. Oh, how delightful! Yes, we will have a merry Christmas. Do take your things off. Aren't you frozen? *(Helping her.)* There; now we'll sit cosily by the fire. No, you take the arm-chair; I shall sit in this rocking-chair. *(Seizes her hands.)* Yes, now I can see the dear old face again. It was only at the first glance—— But you're a little paler, Christina—and perhaps a little thinner.

MRS. LINDEN. And much, much older, Nora.

NORA. Yes, perhaps a little older—not much—ever so little. *(She suddenly checks herself; seriously.)* Oh, what a thoughtless wretch I am! Here I sit chattering on, and—— Dear, dear Christina, can you forgive me!

MRS. LINDEN. What do you mean, Nora?

NORA. *(Softly.)* Poor Christina! I forgot: you are a widow.

MRS. LINDEN. Yes; my husband died three years ago.

NORA. I know, I know; I saw it in the papers. Oh, believe me, Christina, I did mean to write to you; but I kept putting it off, and something always came in the way.

MRS. LINDEN. I can quite understand that, Nora dear.

NORA. No, Christina; it was horrid of me. Oh, you poor darling! how much you must have gone through!—And he left you nothing?

MRS. LINDEN. Nothing.

NORA. And no children?

MRS. LINDEN. None.

NORA. Nothing, nothing at all?

MRS. LINDEN. Not even a sorrow or a longing to dwell upon.

NORA. *(Looking at her incredulously.)* My dear Christina, how is that possible?

MRS. LINDEN. *(Smiling sadly and stroking her hair.)* Oh, it happens so sometimes, Nora.

NORA. So utterly alone! How dreadful that must be! I have three of the loveliest children. I can't show them to you just now; they're out with their nurse. But now you must tell me everything.

MRS. LINDEN. No, no; I want you to tell me——

NORA. No, you must begin; I won't be egotistical to-day. To-day I'll think only of you. Oh! but I must tell you one thing—perhaps you've heard of our great stroke of fortune?

MRS. LINDEN. No. What is it?

NORA. Only think! my husband has been made manager of the Joint Stock Bank.

MRS. LINDEN. Your husband! Oh, how fortunate!

NORA. Yes; isn't it? A lawyer's position is so uncertain, you see, especially when he won't touch any business that's the least bit—shady, as of course Torvald never would; and there I quite agree with him. Oh! you can imagine how glad we are. He is to enter on his new position at the New Year, and then he'll have a large salary, and percentages. In future we shall be able to live quite differently—just as we please, in fact. Oh, Christina, I feel so lighthearted and happy! It's delightful to have lots of money, and no need to worry about things, isn't it?

MRS. LINDEN. Yes; at any rate it must be delightful to have what you need.

NORA. No, not only what you need, but heaps of money—heaps!

MRS. LINDEN. *(Smiling.)* Nora, Nora, haven't you learnt reason yet? In our schooldays you were a shocking little spendthrift.

NORA. *(Quietly smiling.)* Yes; that's what Torvald says I am still. *(Holding up her forefinger.)* But "Nora, Nora" is not so silly as you all think. Oh! I haven't had the chance to be much of a spendthrift. We have both had to work.

MRS. LINDEN. You too?

NORA. Yes, light fancy work: crochet, and embroidery, and things of that sort; *(Carelessly)* and other work too. You know, of course, that Torvald left the Government service when we were married. He had little chance of promotion, and of course he required to make more money. But in the first year after our marriage he overworked himself terribly. He had to undertake all sorts of extra work, you know, and to slave early and late. He couldn't stand it, and fell dangerously ill. Then the doctors declared he must go to the South.

MRS. LINDEN. You spent a whole year in Italy, didn't you?

NORA. Yes, we did. It wasn't easy to manage, I can tell you. It was just after Ivar's birth. But of course we had to go. Oh, it was a wonderful, delicious journey! And it saved Torvald's life. But it cost a frightful lot of money, Christina.

MRS. LINDEN. So I should think.

NORA. Twelve hundred dollars! Four thousand eight hundred crowns!* Isn't that a lot of money?

MRS. LINDEN. How lucky you had the money to spend!

NORA. We got it from father, you must know.

MRS. LINDEN. Ah, I see. He died just about that time, didn't he?

NORA. Yes, Christina, just then. And only think! I couldn't go and nurse him! I was expecting little Ivar's birth daily; and then I had my poor sick Torvald to attend to. Dear, kind old father! I never saw him again, Christina. Oh! that's the hardest thing I have had to bear since my marriage.

MRS. LINDEN. I know how fond you were of him. But then you went to Italy?

NORA. Yes; you see, we had the money, and the doctors said we must lose no time. We started a month later.

MRS. LINDEN. And your husband came back completely cured.

NORA. Sound as a bell.

MRS. LINDEN. But—the doctor?

NORA. What do you mean?

MRS. LINDEN. I thought as I came in your servant announced the doctor——

NORA. Oh, yes; Doctor Rank. But he doesn't come professionally. He is our best friend, and never lets a day pass without looking in. No, Torvald hasn't had an hour's illness since that time. And the children are so healthy and well, and so am I. *(Jumps up and claps her hands.)* Oh, Christina, Christina, what a wonderful thing it is to live and to be happy!— Oh, but it's really too horrid of me! Here am I talking about nothing but my own concerns. *(Seats herself upon a footstool close to* CHRISTINA, *and lays her arms on her friend's lap.)* Oh, don't be angry with me! Now tell me, is it really true that you didn't love your husband? What made you marry him, then?

MRS. LINDEN. My mother was still alive, you see, bedridden and helpless; and then I had my two younger brothers to think of. I didn't think it would be right for me to refuse him.

NORA. Perhaps it wouldn't have been. I suppose he was rich then?

MRS. LINDEN. Very well off, I believe. But his business was uncertain. It fell to pieces at his death, and there was nothing left.

NORA. And then——?

MRS. LINDEN. Then I had to fight my way to keeping a shop, a little school, anything I could turn my hand to. The last three years have been one long struggle for me. But now it is over, Nora. My poor mother no longer needs me; she is at rest. And the boys are in business, and can look after themselves.

*The dollar (4s. 6d.) was the old unit of currency in Norway. The crown was substituted for it shortly before the date of this play.

NORA. How free your life must feel!

MRS. LINDEN. No, Nora; only inexpressibly empty. No one to live for! *(Stands up restlessly.)* That's why I could not bear to stay any longer in that out-of-the-way corner. Here it must be easier to find something to take one up—to occupy one's thoughts. If I could only get some settled employment—some office work.

NORA. But, Christina, that's such drudgery, and you look worn out already. It would be ever so much better for you to go to some watering-place and rest.

MRS. LINDEN. *(Going to the window.)* I have no father to give me the money, Nora.

NORA. *(Rising.)* Oh, don't be vexed with me.

MRS. LINDEN. *(Going to her.)* My dear Nora, don't you be vexed with me. The worst of a position like mine is that it makes one so bitter. You have no one to work for, yet you have to be always on the strain. You must live; and so you become selfish. When I heard of the happy change in your fortunes—can you believe it?—I was glad for my own sake more than for yours.

NORA. How do you mean? Ah, I see! You think Torvald can perhaps do something for you.

MRS. LINDEN. Yes; I thought so.

NORA. And so he shall, Christina. Just you leave it all to me. I shall lead up to it beautifully!—I shall think of some delightful plan to put him in a good humour! Oh, I should so love to help you.

MRS. LINDEN. How good of you, Nora, to stand by me so warmly! Doubly good in you, who knows so little of the troubles and burdens of life.

NORA. I? I know so little of——?

MRS. LINDEN. *(Smiling.)* Oh, well—a little fancy-work, and so forth.—You're a child, Nora.

NORA. *(Tosses her head and paces the room.)* Oh, come, you mustn't be so patronising!

MRS. LINDEN. No?

NORA. You're like the rest. You all think I'm fit for nothing really serious——

MRS. LINDEN. Well, well——

NORA. You think I've had no troubles in this weary world.

MRS. LINDEN. My dear Nora, you've just told me all your troubles.

NORA. Pooh—those trifles! *(Softly.)* I haven't told you the great thing.

MRS. LINDEN. The great thing? What do you mean?

NORA. I know you look down upon me, Christina; but you have no right to. You are proud of having worked so hard and so long for your mother.

MRS. LINDEN. I am sure I don't look down upon any one; but it's true I am both proud and glad when I remember that I was able to keep my mother's last days free from care.

NORA. And you're proud to think of what you have done for your brothers, too.

MRS. LINDEN. Have I not the right to be?

NORA. Yes indeed. But now let me tell you, Christina—I, too, have something to be proud and glad of.

MRS. LINDEN. I don't doubt it. But what do you mean?

NORA. Hush! Not so loud. Only think, if Torvald were to hear! He mustn't—not for worlds! No one must know about it, Christina—no one but you.

MRS. LINDEN. Why, what can it be?

NORA. Come over here. (*Draws her down beside her on the sofa.*) Yes, Christina—I, too, have something to be proud and glad of. I saved Torvald's life.

MRS. LINDEN. Saved his life? How?

NORA. I told you about our going to Italy. Torvald would have died but for that.

MRS. LINDEN. Well—and your father gave you the money.

NORA. (*Smiling.*) Yes, so Torvald and every one believes; but——

MRS. LINDEN. But——?

NORA. Papa didn't give us one penny. It was *I* that found the money.

MRS. LINDEN. You? All that money?

NORA. Twelve hundred dollars. Four thousand eight hundred crowns. What do you say to that?

MRS. LINDEN. My dear Nora, how did you manage it? Did you win it in the lottery?

NORA. (*Contemptuously.*) In the lottery? Pooh! Any one could have done that!

MRS. LINDEN. Then wherever did you get it from?

NORA. (*Hums and smiles mysteriously.*) H'm; tra-la-la-la!

MRS. LINDEN. Of course you couldn't borrow it.

NORA. No? Why not?

MRS. LINDEN. Why, a wife can't borrow without her husband's consent.

NORA. (*Tossing her head.*) Oh! when the wife has some idea of business, and knows how to set about things——

MRS. LINDEN. But, Nora, I don't understand——

NORA. Well, you needn't. I never said I borrowed the money. There are many ways I may have got it. (*Throws herself back on the sofa.*) I may have got it from some admirer. When one is so—attractive as I am——

MRS. LINDEN. You're too silly, Nora.

NORA. Now I'm sure you're dying of curiosity, Christina——

MRS. LINDEN. Listen to me, Nora dear: haven't you been a little rash?

NORA. (*Sitting upright again.*) Is it rash to save one's husband's life?

MRS. LINDEN. I think it was rash of you, without his knowledge——

NORA. But it would have been fatal for him to know! Can't you understand that? He wasn't even to suspect how ill he was. The doctors came to me privately and told me his life was in danger—that nothing could save him but a winter in the South. Do you think I didn't try diplomacy first? I told him how I longed to have a trip abroad, like other young wives; I wept and prayed; I said he ought to think of my condition, and not to thwart me; and then I hinted that he could borrow the money. But then,

Christina, he got almost angry. He said I was frivolous, and that it was his duty as a husband not to yield to my whims and fancies—so he called them. Very well, thought I, but saved you must be; and then I found the way to do it.

MRS. LINDEN. And did your husband never learn from your father that the money was not from him?

NORA. No; never. Papa died at that very time. I meant to have told him all about it, and begged him to say nothing. But he was so ill—unhappily, it wasn't necessary.

MRS. LINDEN. And you have never confessed to your husband?

NORA. Good heavens! What can you be thinking of? Tell him, when he has such a loathing of debt? And besides—how painful and humiliating it would be for Torvald, with his manly self-respect, to know that he owed anything to me! It would utterly upset the relation between us; our beautiful, happy home would never again be what it is.

MRS. LINDEN. Will you never tell him?

NORA. (*Thoughtfully, half-smiling.*) Yes, some time perhaps–many, many years hence, when I'm—not so pretty. You mustn't laugh at me! Of course I mean when Torvald is not so much in love with me as he is now; when it doesn't amuse him any longer to see me dancing about, and dressing up and acting. Then it might be well to have something in reserve. (*Breaking off.*) Nonsense! nonsense! That time will never come. Now, what do you say to my grand secret, Christina? Am I fit for nothing now? You may believe it has cost me a lot of anxiety. It has been no joke to meet my engagements punctually. You must know, Christina, that in business there are things called instalments, and quarterly interest, that are terribly hard to provide for. So I've had to pinch a little here and there, wherever I could. I couldn't save much out of the housekeeping, for of course Torvald had to live well. And I couldn't let the children go about badly dressed; all I got for them, I spent on them, the blessed darlings!

MRS. LINDEN. Poor Nora! So it had to come out of your own pocketmoney.

NORA. Yes, of course. After all, the whole thing was my doing. When Torvald gave me money for clothes, and so on, I never spent more than half of it; I always bought the simplest and cheapest things. It's a mercy that everything suits me so well—Torvald never had any suspicions. But it was often very hard, Christina dear. For it's nice to be beautifully dressed—now, isn't it?

MRS. LINDEN. Indeed it is.

NORA. Well, and besides that, I made money in other ways. Last winter I was so lucky—I got a heap of copying to do. I shut myself up every evening and wrote far into the night. Oh, sometimes I was so tired, so tired. And yet it was splendid to work in that way and earn money. I almost felt as if I was a man.

MRS. LINDEN. Then how much have you been able to pay off?

NORA. Well, I can't precisely say. It's difficult to keep that sort of business clear. I only know that I've paid everything I could scrape together. Sometimes I really didn't know where to turn. *(Smiles.)* Then I used to sit here and pretend that a rich old gentleman was in love with me——

MRS. LINDEN. What! What gentleman?

NORA. Oh, nobody!—that he was dead now, and that when his will was opened, there stood in large letters: "Pay over at once everything of which I die possessed to that charming person, Mrs. Nora Helmer."

MRS. LINDEN. But, my dear Nora—what gentleman do you mean?

NORA. Oh dear, can't you understand? There wasn't any old gentleman: it was only what I used to dream and dream when I was at my wits' end for money. But it doesn't matter now—the tiresome old creature may stay where he is for me. I care nothing for him or his will; for now my troubles are over. *(Springing up.)* Oh, Christina, how glorious it is to think of! Free from all anxiety! Free, quite free. To be able to play and romp about with the children; to have things tasteful and pretty in the house, exactly as Torvald likes it! And then the spring will soon be here, with the great blue sky. Perhaps then we shall have a little holiday. Perhaps I shall see the sea again. Oh, what a wonderful thing it is to live and to be happy! *(The hall-door bell rings.)*

MRS. LINDEN. *(Rising.)* There's a ring. Perhaps I had better go.

NORA. No; do stay. No one will come here. It's sure to be someone for Torvald.

ELLEN. *(In the doorway.)* If you please, ma'am, there's a gentleman to speak to Mr. Helmer.

NORA. Who is the gentleman?

KROGSTAD. *(In the doorway.)* It is I, Mrs. Helmer. (MRS. LINDEN *starts and turns away to the window.)*

NORA. *(Goes a step towards him, anxiously, speaking low.)* You? What is it? What do you want with my husband?

KROGSTAD. Bank business—in a way. I hold a small post in the Joint Stock Bank, and your husband is to be our new chief, I hear.

NORA. Then it is——?

KROGSTAD. Only tiresome business, Mrs. Helmer; nothing more.

NORA. Then will you please go to his study. (KROGSTAD *goes. She bows indifferently while she closes the door into the hall. Then she goes to the stove and looks to the fire.)*

MRS. LINDEN. Nora—who was that man?

NORA. A Mr. Krogstad—a lawyer.

MRS. LINDEN. Then it was really he?

NORA. Do you know him?

MRS. LINDEN. I used to know him—many years ago. He was in a lawyer's office in our town.

NORA. Yes, so he was.

MRS. LINDEN. How he has changed!

NORA. I believe his marriage was unhappy.

MRS. LINDEN. And he is a widower now?

NORA. With a lot of children. There! Now it will burn up. *(She closes the stove, and pushes the rocking-chair a little aside.)*

MRS. LINDEN. His business is not of the most creditable, they say?

NORA. Isn't it? I daresay not. I don't know. But don't let us think of business—it's so tiresome.

DR. RANK *comes out of* HELMER'S *room.*

RANK. *(Still in the doorway.)* No, no; I'm in your way. I shall go and have a chat with your wife. *(Shuts the door and sees* MRS. LINDEN.*)* Oh, I beg your pardon. I'm in the way here too.

NORA. No, not in the least. *(Introduces them.)* Doctor Rank—Mrs. Linden.

RANK. Oh, indeed; I've often heard Mrs. Linden's name; I think I passed you on the stairs as I came up.

MRS. LINDEN. Yes; I go so very slowly. Stairs try me so much.

RANK. Ah—you are not very strong?

MRS. LINDEN. Only overworked.

RANK. Nothing more? Then no doubt you've come to town to find rest in a round of dissipation?

MRS. LINDEN. I have come to look for employment.

RANK. Is that an approved remedy for overwork?

MRS. LINDEN. One must live, Doctor Rank.

RANK. Yes, that seems to be the general opinion.

NORA. Come, Doctor Rank—you want to live yourself.

RANK. To be sure I do. However wretched I may be, I want to drag on as long as possible. All my patients, too, have the same mania. And it's the same with people whose complaint is moral. At this very moment Helmer is talking to just such a moral incurable——

MRS. LINDEN. *(Softly.)* Ah!

NORA. Whom do you mean?

RANK. Oh, a fellow named Krogstad, a man you know nothing about—corrupt to the very core of his character. But even he began by announcing, as a matter of vast importance, that he must live.

NORA. Indeed? And what did he want with Torvald?

RANK. I haven't an idea; I only gathered that it was some bank business.

NORA. I didn't know that Krog—that this Mr. Krogstad had anything to do with the Bank?

RANK. Yes. He has got some sort of place there. *(To* MRS. LINDEN.*)* I don't know whether in your part of the country, you have people who go grubbing and sniffing around in search of moral rottenness—and then, when they have found a "case," don't rest till they have got their man into some good position, where they can keep a watch upon him. Men with a clean bill of health they leave out in the cold.

MRS. LINDEN. Well, I suppose the—delicate characters require most care.

RANK. *(Shrugs his shoulders.)* There we have it! It's that notion that makes society a hospital.

(NORA, *deep in her own thoughts, breaks into half-stifled laughter and claps her hands.*)

RANK. Why do you laugh at that? Have you any idea what "society" is?

NORA. What do I care for your tiresome society? I was laughing at something else—something excessively amusing. Tell me, Doctor Rank, are all the employees at the Bank dependent on Torvald now?

RANK. Is that what strikes you as excessively amusing?

NORA. (*Smiles and hums.*) Never mind, never mind! (*Walks about the room*) Yes, it is funny to think that we—that Torvald has such power over so many people. (*Takes the bag from her pocket*) Doctor Rank, will you have a macaroon?

RANK. What!—macaroons! I thought they were contraband here.

NORA. Yes; but Christina brought me these.

MRS. LINDEN. What! I——?

NORA. Oh, well! Don't be frightened. You couldn't possibly know that Torvald had forbidden them. The fact is, he's afraid of me spoiling my teeth. But, oh bother, just for once!—That's for you, Doctor Rank! (*Puts a macaroon into his mouth.*) And you too, Christina. And I'll have one while we're about it—only a tiny one, or at most two. (*Walks about again.*) Oh dear, I am happy! There's only one thing in the world I really want.

RANK. Well; what's that?

NORA. There's something I should so like to say—in Torvald's hearing.

RANK. Then why don't you say it?

NORA. Because I daren't, it's so ugly.

MRS. LINDEN. Ugly!

RANK. In that case you'd better not. But to us you might—— What is it you would so like to say in Helmer's hearing?

NORA. I should so love to say "Damn it all!"*

RANK. Are you out of your mind?

MRS. LINDEN. Good gracious, Nora——!

RANK. Say it—there he is!

NORA. (*Hides the macaroons,*) Hush—sh—sh!

HELMER *comes out of his room, hat in hand, with his overcoat on his arm.*

NORA. (*Going to him.*) Well, Torvald dear, have you got rid of him?

HELMER. Yes; he has just gone.

NORA. Let me introduce you—this is Christina, who has come to town——

HELMER. Christina? Pardon me, I don't know——

NORA. Mrs. Linden, Torvald dear—Christina Linden.

HELMER. (*To* MRS. LINDEN.) Indeed! A school-friend of my wife's, no doubt?

MRS. LINDEN. Yes; we knew each other as girls.

NORA. And only think! she has taken this long journey on purpose to speak to you.

---

*"Död og pine," literally "death and torture"; but by usage a comparatively midl oath.

HELMER. To speak to me!

MRS. LINDEN. Well, not quite——

NORA. You see, Christina is tremendously clever at officework, and she's so anxious to work under a first-rate man of business in order to learn still more——

HELMER. *(To* MRS. LINDEN.*)* Very sensible indeed.

NORA. And when she heard you were appointed manager—it was telegraphed, you know—she started off at once and—— Torvald, dear, for my sake, you must do something for Christina. Now can't you?

HELMER. It's not impossible. I presume Mrs. Linden is a widow?

MRS. LINDEN. Yes.

HELMER. And you have already had some experience of business?

MRS. LINDEN. A good deal.

HELMER. Well, then, it's very likely I may be able to find a place for you.

NORA. *(Clapping her hands).* There now! There now!

HELMER. You have come at a fortunate moment, Mrs. Linden.

MRS. LINDEN. Oh, how can I thank you——?

HELMER. *(Smiling).* There is no occasion. *(Puts on his overcoat.)* But for the present you must excuse me——

RANK. Wait; I am going with you. *(Fetches his fur coat from the hall and warms it at the fire.)*

NORA. Don't be long, Torvald dear.

HELMER. Only an hour; not more.

NORA. Are you going too, Christina?

MRS. LINDEN. *(Putting on her walking things.)* Yes; I must set about looking for lodgings.

HELMER. Then perhaps we can go together?

NORA. *(Helping her.)* What a pity we haven't a spare room for you; but it's impossible——

MRS. LINDEN. I shouldn't think of troubling you. Good-bye, dear Nora, and thank you for all your kindness.

NORA. Good-bye for the present. Of course you'll come back this evening. And you, too, Doctor Rank. What! If you're well enough? Of course you'll be well enough. Only wrap up warmly. *(They go out, talking, into the hall. Outside on the stairs are heard children's voices.)* There they are! There they are! *(She runs to the outer door and opens it. The nurse, ANNA, enters the hall with the children.)* Come in! Come in! *(Stoops down and kisses the children.)* Oh, my sweet darlings! Do you see them, Christina? Aren't they lovely?

RANK. Don't let us stand here chattering in the draught.

HELMER. Come, Mrs. Linden; only mothers can stand such a temperature.

DR. RANK, HELMER, *and* MRS. LINDEN *go down the stairs,* ANNA *enters the room with the children;* NORA *also, shutting the door.)*

NORA. How fresh and bright you look! And what red cheeks you've got! Like apples and roses. *(The children chatter to her during what follows.)* Have you had great fun? That's splendid! Oh, really! You've been giving Emmy and Bob a ride on your sledge!—both at once, only think! Why, you're quite a man, Ivar. Oh, give her to me a little, Anna. My sweet little dolly! *(Takes the smallest from the nurse and dances with her.)* Yes, yes; mother will dance with Bob too. What! Did you have a game of snowballs? Oh, I wish I'd been there. No; leave them, Anna; I'll take their things off. Oh, yes, let me do it; it's such fun. Go to the nursery; you look frozen. You'll find some hot coffee on the stove.

(The NURSE *goes into the room on the left.* NORA *takes off the children's things and throws them down anywhere, while the children talk all together.*

Really! A big dog ran after you? But he didn't bite you? No; dogs don't bite dear little dolly children. Don't peep into those parcels, Ivar. What is it? Wouldn't you like to know? Take care—it'll bite! What? Shall we have a game? What shall we play at? Hide-and-seek? Yes, let's play hide-and-seek. Bob shall hide first. Am I to? Yes, let me hide first.

(She and the children play, with laughter and shouting, in the room and the adjacent one to the right.) At last NORA *hides under the table; the children come rushing in, look for her, but cannot find her, hear her half-choked laughter, rush to the table, lift up the cover and see her. Loud shouts. She creeps out, as though to frighten them. Fresh shouts. Meanwhile there has been a knock at the door leading into the hall. No one has heard it. Now, the door is half opened and* KROGSTAD *appears. He waits a little; the game is renewed.)*

KROGSTAD. I beg your pardon, Mrs. Helmer——
NORA. *(With a suppressed cry, turns round and half jumps up.)* Ah! What do you want?
KROGSTAD. Excuse me; the outer door was ajar—somebody must have forgotten to shut it——
NORA. *(Standing up.)* My husband is not at home, Mr. Krogstad.
KROGSTAD. I know it.
NORA. Then what do you want here?
KROGSTAD. To say a few words to you.
NORA. To me? *(To the children, softly.)* Go in to Anna. What? No, the strange man won't hurt mamma. When he's gone we'll go on playing. *(She leads the children into the left-hand room, and shuts the door behind them. Uneasy, in suspense.)* It is to me you wish to speak?
KROGSTAD. Yes, to you.
NORA. To-day? But it's not the first yet——
KROGSTAD. No, to-day is Christmas Eve. It will depend upon yourself whether you have a merry Christmas.
NORA. What do you want? I'm not ready to-day——
KROGSTAD. Never mind that just now. I have come about another matter. You have a minute to spare?
NORA. Oh, yes, I suppose so; although——

KROGSTAD. Good. I was sitting in the restaurant opposite, and I saw your husband go down the street——

NORA. Well?

KROGSTAD. ——with a lady.

NORA. What then?

KROGSTAD. May I ask if the lady was a Mrs. Linden?

NORA. Yes.

KROGSTAD. Who has just come to town?

NORA. Yes. To-day.

KROGSTAD. I believe she is an intimate friend of yours.

NORA. Certainly. But I don't understand——

KROGSTAD. I used to know her too.

NORA. I know you did.

KROGSTAD. Ah! You know all about it. I thought as much. Now, frankly, is Mrs. Linden to have a place in the Bank?

NORA. How dare you catechise me in this way, Mr. Krogstad—you, a subordinate of my husband's? But since you ask, you shall know. Yes, Mrs. Linden is to be employed. And it is I who recommended her, Mr. Krogstad. Now you know.

KROGSTAD. Then my guess was right.

NORA. *(Walking up and down.)* You see one has a wee bit of influence, after all. It doesn't follow because one's only a woman—— When people are in a subordinate position, Mr. Krogstad, they ought really to be careful how they offend anybody who—h'm——

KROGSTAD. ——who has influence?

NORA. Exactly.

KROGSTAD. *(Taking another tone.)* Mrs. Helmer, will you have the kindness to employ your influence on my behalf?

NORA. What? How do you mean?

KROGSTAD. Will you be so good as to see that I retain my subordinate position in the Bank?

NORA. What do you mean? Who wants to take it from you?

KROGSTAD. Oh, you needn't pretend ignorance. I can very well understand that it cannot be pleasant for your friend to meet me; and I can also understand now for whose sake I am to be hounded out.

NORA. But I assure you——

KROGSTAD. Come come now, once for all: there is time yet, and I advise you to use your influence to prevent it.

NORA. But Mr. Krogstad, I have no influence—absolutely none.

KROGSTAD. None? I thought you said a moment ago——

NORA. Of course not in that sense. I! How can you imagine that I should have any such influence over my husband?

KROGSTAD. Oh, I know your husband from our college days. I don't think he is any more inflexible than other husbands.

NORA. If you talk disrespectfully of my husband, I must request you to leave the house.

KROGSTAD. You are bold, madam.

NORA. I am afraid of you no longer. When New Year's Day is over, I shall soon be out of the whole business.

KROGSTAD. *(Controlling himself.)* Listen to me, Mrs. Helmer. If need be, I shall fight as though for my life to keep my little place in the Bank.

NORA. Yes, so it seems.

KROGSTAD. It's not only for the salary: that is what I care least about. It's something else—— Well, I had better make a clean breast of it. Of course you know, like every one else, that some years ago I—got into trouble.

NORA. I think I've heard something of the sort.

KROGSTAD. The matter never came into court; but from that moment all paths were barred to me. Then I took up the business you know about. I had to turn my hand to something; and I don't think I've been one of the worst. But now I must get clear of it all. My sons are growing up; for their sake I must try to recover my character as well as I can. This place in the Bank was the first step; and now your husband wants to kick me off the ladder, back into the mire.

NORA. But I assure you, Mr. Krogstad, I haven't the least power to help you.

KROGSTAD. That is because you have not the will; but I can compel you.

NORA. You won't tell my husband that I owe you money?

KROGSTAD. H'm; suppose I were to?

NORA. It would be shameful of you. *(With tears in her voice.)* The secret that is my joy and my pride—that he should learn it in such an ugly, coarse way—and from you. It would involve me in all sorts of unpleasantness—

KROGSTAD. Only unpleasantness?

NORA. *(Hotly.)* But just do it. It's you that will come off worst, for then my husband will see what a bad man you are, and then you certainly won't keep your place.

KROGSTAD. I asked whether it was only domestic unpleasantness you feared?

NORA. If my husband gets to know about it, he will of course pay you off at once, and then we shall have nothing more to do with you.

KROGSTAD. *(Coming a pace nearer.)* Listen, Mrs. Helmer: either your memory is defective, or you don't know much about business. I must make the position a little clearer to you.

NORA. How so?

KROGSTAD. When your husband was ill, you came to me to borrow twelve hundred dollars.

NORA. I knew of nobody else.

KROGSTAD. I promised to find you the money—

NORA. And you did find it.

KROGSTAD. I promised to find you the money, on certain conditions. You were so much taken up at the time about your husband's illness, and so eager to have the wherewithal for your journey, that you probably did not give much thought to the details. Allow me to remind you of them. I promised to find you the amount in exchange for a note of hand, which I drew up.

NORA. Yes, and I signed it.

KROGSTAD. Quite right. But then I added a few lines, making your father security for the debt. Your father was to sign this.

NORA. Was to——? He did sign it!

KROGSTAD. I had left the date blank. That is to say, your father was himself to date his signature. Do you recollect that?

NORA. Yes, I believe——

KROGSTAD. Then I gave you the paper to send to your father, by post. Is not that so?

NORA. Yes.

KROGSTAD. And of course you did so at once; for within five or six days you brought me back the document with your father's signature; and I handed you the money.

NORA. Well? Have I not made my payments punctually?

KROGSTAD. Fairly—yes. But to return to the point: You were in great trouble at the time, Mrs. Helmer.

NORA. I was indeed!

KROGSTAD. Your father was very ill, I believe?

NORA. He was on his death-bed.

KROGSTAD. And died soon after?

NORA. Yes.

KROGSTAD. Tell me, Mrs. Helmer: do you happen to recollect the day of his death? The day of the month, I mean?

NORA. Father died on the 29th of September.

KROGSTAD. Quite correct. I have made inquiries. And here comes in the remarkable point—*(Produces a paper.)* which I cannot explain.

NORA. What remarkable point? I don't know——

KROGSTAD. The remarkable point, madam, that your father signed this paper three days after his death!

NORA. What! I don't understand——

KROGSTAD. Your father died on the 29th of September. But look here: he has dated his signature October 2nd! Is not that remarkable, Mrs. Helmer? *(NORA is silent.)* Can you explain it? *(NORA continues silent.)* It is noteworthy, too, that the words "October 2nd" and the year are not in your father's handwriting, but in one which I believe I know. Well, this may be explained; your father may have forgotten to date his signature, and somebody may have added the date at random, before the fact of your father's death was known. There is nothing wrong in that. Everything depends on the signature. Of course it is genuine, Mrs. Helmer? It was really your father himself who wrote his name here?

NORA. *(After a short silence, throws her head back and looks defiantly at him.)* No, it was not. *I* wrote father's name.

KROGSTAD. Ah—Are you aware, madam, that that is a dangerous admission?

NORA. How so? You will soon get your money.

KROGSTAD. May I ask you one more question? Why did you not send the paper to your father?

NORA. It was impossible. Father was ill. If I had asked him for his signature, I should have had to tell him why I wanted the money; but he was so ill I really could not tell him that my husband's life was in danger. It was impossible.

KROGSTAD. Then it would have been better to have given up your tour.

NORA. No, I couldn't do that; my husband's life depended on that journey. I couldn't give it up.

KROGSTAD. And did it never occur to you that you were playing me false?

NORA. That was nothing to me. I didn't care in the least about you. I couldn't endure you for all the cruel difficulties you made, although you knew how ill my husband was.

KROGSTAD. Mrs. Helmer, you evidently do not realise what you have been guilty of. But I can assure you it was nothing more and nothing worse that made me an outcast from society.

NORA. You! You want me to believe that you did a brave thing to save your wife's life?

KROGSTAD. The law takes no account of motives.

NORA. Then it must be a very bad law.

KROGSTAD. Bad or not, if I produce this document in court, you will be condemned according to law.

NORA. I don't believe that. Do you mean to tell me that a daughter has no right to spare her dying father trouble and anxiety?—that a wife has no right to save her husband's life? I don't know much about the law, but I'm sure you'll find, somewhere or another, that that is allowed. And you don't know that—you, a lawyer! You must be a bad one, Mr. Krogstad.

KROGSTAD. Possibly. But business—such business as ours—I do understand. You believe that? Very well; now do as you please. But this I may tell you, that if I am flung into the gutter a second time, you shall keep me company. *(Bows and goes out through hall.)*

NORA. *(Stands a while thinking, then tosses her head.)* Oh nonsense! He wants to frighten me. I'm not so foolish as that. *(Begins folding the children's clothes. Pauses.)* But——? No, it's impossible! Why, I did it for love!

CHILDREN. *(At the door, left.)* Mamma, the strange man has gone now.

NORA. Yes, yes, I know. But don't tell any one about the strange man. Do you hear? Not even papa!

CHILDREN. No, mamma; and now will you play with us again?

NORA. No, no; not now.

CHILDREN. Oh, do, mamma; you know you promised.

NORA. Yes, but I can't just now. Run to the nursery; I have so much to do. Run along, run along, and be good, my darlings! *(She pushes them gently into the inner room, and closes the door behind them. Sits on the sofa, embroiders a few stitches, but soon pauses.)* No! *(Throws down the work, rises, goes to the hall door and calls out.)* Ellen, bring in the Christmas-tree! *(Goes to table, left, and opens the drawer; again pauses.)* No, it's quite impossible!

ELLEN. *(With Christmas-tree.)* Where shall I stand it, ma'am?

NORA. There, in the middle of the room.

ELLEN. Shall I bring in anything else?

NORA. No, thank you, I have all I want. (ELLEN, *having put down the tree, goes out.*)

NORA. (*Busy dressing the tree.*) There must be a candle here—and flowers there.—That horrible man! Nonsense, nonsense! there's nothing to be afraid of. The Christmas-tree shall be beautiful. I'll do everything to please you, Torvald; I'll sing and dance, and——

Enter HELMER *by the hall door, with a bundle of documents.*

NORA. Oh! You're back already!

HELMER. Yes. Has anybody been here?

NORA. Here? No.

HELMER. That's odd. I saw Krogstad come out of the house.

NORA. Did you? Oh, yes, by-the-bye, he was here for a minute.

HELMER. Nora, I can see by your manner that he has been begging you to put in a good word for him.

NORA. Yes.

HELMER. And you were to do it as if of your own accord? You were to say nothing to me of his having been here. Didn't he suggest that too?

NORA. Yes, Torvald; but——

HELMER. Nora, Nora! And you could condescend to that! To speak to such a man, to make him a promise! And then to tell me an untruth about it!

NORA. An untruth!

HELMER. Didn't you say that nobody had been here? (*Threatens with his finger.*) My little bird must never do that again! "A song-bird must sing clear and true"; no false notes. (*Puts his arm round her.*) That's so, isn't it? Yes, I was sure of it. (*Lets her go.*) And now we'll say no more about it. (*Sits down before the fire.*) Oh, how cosy and quiet it is here! (*Glances into his documents.*)

NORA. *Busy with the tree, after a short silence.*) Torvald!

HELMER. Yes.

NORA. I'm looking forward so much to the Stenborgs' fancy ball the day after to-morrow.

HELMER. And I'm on tenterhooks to see what surprise you have in store for me.

NORA. Oh, it's too tiresome!

HELMER. What is?

NORA. I can't think of anything good. Everything seems so foolish and meaningless.

HELMER. Has little Nora made that discovery?

NORA. (*Behind his chair, with her arms on the back.*) Are you very busy, Torvald?

HELMER. Well——

NORA. What papers are those?

HELMER. Bank business.

NORA. Already!

HELMER. I have got the retiring manager to let me make some necessary changes in the staff and the organization. I can do this during Christmas week. I want to have everything straight by the New Year.

NORA. Then that's why that poor Krogstad——

HELMER. H'm.

NORA. *(Still leaning over the chair-back and slowly stroking his hair.)* If you hadn't been so very busy, I should have asked you a great, great favour, Torvald.

HELMER. What can it be? Out with it.

NORA. Nobody has such perfect taste as you; and I should so love to look well at the fancy ball. Torvald, dear, couldn't you take me in hand, and settle what I'm to be, and arrange my costume for me?

HELMER. Aha! So my wilful little woman is at a loss, and making signals of distress.

NORA. Yes, please, Torvald. I can't get on without your help.

HELMER. Well, well, I'll think it over, and we'll soon hit upon something.

NORA. Oh, how good that is of you! *(Goes to the tree again; pause.)* How well the red flowers show.—Tell me, was it anything so very dreadful this Krogstad got into trouble about?

HELMER. Forgery, that's all. Don't you know what that means?

NORA. Mayn't he have been driven to it by need?

HELMER. Yes; or, like so many others, he may have done it in pure heedlessness. I am not so hard-hearted as to condemn a man absolutely for a single fault.

NORA. No, surely not, Torvald!

HELMER. Many a man can retrieve his character, if he owns his crime and takes the punishment.

NORA. Punishment——?

HELMER. But Krogstad didn't do that. He evaded the law by means of tricks and subterfuges; and that is what has morally ruined him.

NORA. Do you think that——?

HELMER. Just think how a man with a thing of that sort on his conscience must be always lying and canting and shamming. Think of the mask he must wear even towards those who stand nearest him—towards his own wife and children. The effect on the children—that's the most terrible part of it, Nora.

NORA. Why?

HELMER. Because in such an atmosphere of lies home life is poisoned and contaminated in every fibre. Every breath the children draw contains some germ of evil.

NORA. *(Closer behind him.)* Are you sure of that?

HELMER. As a lawyer, my dear, I have seen it often enough. Nearly all cases of early corruption may be traced to lying mothers.

NORA. Why—mothers?

HELMER. It generally comes from the mother's side; but of course the father's influence may act in the same way. Every lawyer knows it too well. And here has this Krogstad been poisoning his own children for years past by a life of lies and hypocrisy—that is why I call him morally ruined. *(Holds out both hands to her.)* So my sweet little Nora must promise not to plead his cause. Shake hands upon it. Come, come, what's this? Give me your hand. That's right. Then it's a bargain. I assure you it would have been impossible for me to work with him. It gives me a positive sense of physical discomfort to come in contact with such people.

(NORA draws her hand away, and moves to the other side of the Christmas-tree.)

NORA. How warm it is here. And I have so much to do.

HELMER. *(Rises and gathers up his papers.)* Yes, and I must try to get some of these papers looked through before dinner. And I shall think over your costume too. Perhaps I may even find something to hang in gilt paper on the Christmas-tree. *(Lays his hand on her head.)* My precious little song-bird! *(He goes into his room and shuts the door.)*

NORA. *(Softly, after a pause.)* It can't be. It's impossible. It must be impossible!

ANNA. *(At the door, left.)* The little ones are begging so prettily to come to mamma.

NORA. No, no, no; don't let them come to me! Keep them with you, Anna.

ANNA. Very well, ma'am. *(Shuts the door.)*

NORA. *(Pale with terror.)* Corrupt my children!—Poison my home! *(Short pause. She throws back her head.)* It's not true! It can never, never be true!

Act Second

The same room. In the corner, beside the piano, stands the Christmas-tree, stripped, and with the candles burnt out. NORA'S outdoor things lie on the sofa.

NORA, alone, is walking about restlessly. At last she stops by the sofa, and takes up her cloak.

NORA. *(Dropping the cloak.)* There's somebody coming! *(Goes to the hall door and listens.)* Nobody; of course nobody will come to-day, Christmas-day; nor to-morrow either. But perhaps——*(Opens the door and looks out.)*—No, nothing in the letter box; quite empty. *(Comes forward.)* Stuff and nonsense! Of course he won't really do anything. Such a thing couldn't happen. It's impossible! Why, I have three little children.

ANNA enters from the left, with a large cardboard box.

ANNA. I've found the box with the fancy dress at last.

NORA. Thanks; put it down on the table.

ANNA. *(Does so.)* But I'm afraid it's very much out of order.

NORA. Oh, I wish I could tear it into a hundred thousand pieces!

ANNA. Oh, no. It can easily be put to rights—just a little patience.

NORA. I shall go and get Mrs. Linden to help me.

ANNA. Going out again? In such weather as this! You'll catch cold, ma'am, and be ill.

NORA. Worse things might happen.—What are the children doing?

ANNA. They're playing with their Christmas presents, poor little dears; but——

NORA. Do they often ask for me?

ANNA. You see they've been so used to having their mamma with them.

NORA. Yes; but, Anna, I can't have them so much with me in future.

ANNA. Well, little children get used to anything.

NORA. Do you think they do? Do you believe they would forget their mother if she went quite away?

ANNA. Gracious me! Quite away?

NORA. Tell me, Anna—I've so often wondered about it—how could you bring yourself to give your child up to strangers?

ANNA. I had to when I came to nurse my little Miss Nora.

NORA. But how could you make up your mind to it?

ANNA. When I had the chance of such a good place? A poor girl who's been in trouble must take what comes. That wicked man did nothing for me.

NORA. But your daughter must have forgotten you.

ANNA. Oh, no, ma'am, that she hasn't. She wrote to me both when she was confirmed and when she was married.

NORA. *(Embracing her.)* Dear old Anna—you were a good mother to me when I was little.

ANNA. My poor little Nora had no mother but me.

NORA. And if my little ones had nobody else, I'm sure you would—— Nonsense, nonsense! *(Opens the box.)* Go in to the children. Now I must—— You'll see how lovely I shall be to-morrow.

ANNA. I'm sure there will be no one at the ball so lovely as my Miss Nora. *(She goes into the room on the left.)*

NORA. *(Takes the costume out of the box, but soon throws it down again.)* Oh, if I dared go out. If only nobody would come. If only nothing would happen here in the meantime. Rubbish; nobody is coming. Only not to think. What a delicious muff! Beautiful gloves, beautiful gloves! To forget—to forget! One, two, three, four, five, six—— *(With a scream.)* Ah, there they come. *(Goes toward the door, then stands irresolute.)*

MRS. LINDEN *enters from the hall where she has taken off her things.*

NORA. Oh, it's you Christina. There's nobody else there? I'm so glad you have come.

MRS. LINDEN. I hear you called at my lodgings.

NORA. Yes, I was just passing. There's something you must help me with. Let us sit here on the sofa—so. To-morrow evening there's to be a fancy ball at Consul Stenborg's overhead, and Torvald wants me to appear as a Neapolitan fisher-girl, and dance the tarantella; I learned it at Capri.

MRS. LINDEN. I see—quite a performance.

NORA. Yes, Torvald wishes it. Look, this is the costume; Torvald had it made for me in Italy. But now it's all so torn, I don't know——

MRS. LINDEN. Oh, we shall soon set that to rights. It's only the trimming that has come loose here and there. Have you a needle and thread? Ah, here's the very thing.

NORA. Oh, how kind of you.

MRS. LINDEN. *(Sewing.)* So you're to be in costume to-morrow, Nora? I'll tell you what—I shall come in for a moment to see you in all your glory. But I've quite forgotten to thank you for the pleasant evening yesterday.

NORA. *(Rises and walks across the room.)* Oh, yesterday, it didn't seem so pleasant as usual.—You should have come to town a little sooner, Christina.—Torvald has certainly the art of making home bright and beautiful.

MRS. LINDEN. You too, I should think, or you wouldn't be your father's daughter. But tell me—is Doctor Rank always so depressed as he was last evening?

NORA. No, yesterday it was particularly noticeable. You see, he suffers from a dreadful illness. He has spinal consumption, poor fellow. They say his father was a horrible man, who kept mistresses and all sorts of things—so the son has been sickly from his childhood, you understand.

MRS. LINDEN. *(Lets her sewing fall into her lap.)* Why, my darling Nora, how do you come to know such things?

NORA. *(Moving about the room.)* Oh, when one has three children, one sometimes has visits from women who are half—half doctors—and they talk of one thing and another.

MRS. LINDEN. *(Goes on sewing; a short pause.)* Does Doctor Rank come here every day?

NORA. Every day of his life. He has been Torvald's most intimate friend from boyhood, and he's a good friend of mine too. Doctor Rank is quite one of the family.

MRS. LINDEN. But tell me—is he quite sincere? I mean, isn't he rather given to flattering people?

NORA. No, quite the contrary. Why should you think so?

MRS. LINDEN. When you introduced us yesterday he said he had often heard my name; but I noticed afterwards that your husband had no notion who I was. How could Doctor Rank——?

NORA. He was quite right, Christina. You see, Torvald loves me so indescribably, he wants to have me all to himself, as he says. When we were first married he was almost jealous if I even mentioned any of my old friends at home; so naturally I gave up doing it. But I often talk of the old times to Doctor Rank, for he likes to hear about them.

MRS. LINDEN. Listen to me, Nora! You are still a child in many ways. I am older than you, and have had more experience. I'll tell you something? You ought to get clear of all this with Dr. Rank.

NORA. Get clear of what?

MRS. LINDEN. The whole affair, I should say. You were talking yesterday of a
    rich admirer who was to find you money——

NORA. Yes, one who never existed, worse luck. What then?

MRS. LINDEN. Has Doctor Rank money?

NORA. Yes, he has.

MRS. LINDEN. And nobody to provide for?

NORA. Nobody. But——?

MRS. LINDEN. And he comes here every day?

NORA. Yes, I told you so.

MRS. LINDEN. I should have thought he would have had better taste.

NORA. I don't understand you a bit.

MRS. LINDEN. Don't pretend, Nora. Do you suppose I can't guess who lent
    you the twelve hundred dollars?

NORA. Are you out of your senses? How can you think such a thing? A friend
    who comes here every day! Why, the position would be unbearable!

MRS. LINDEN. Then it really is not he?

NORA. No, I assure you. It never for a moment occurred to me—— Besides,
    at that time he had nothing to lend; he came into his property afterwards.

MRS. LINDEN. Well, I believe that was lucky for you, Nora dear.

NORA. No, really, it would never have struck me to ask Dr. Rank—— And
    yet, I'm certain that if I did——

MRS. LINDEN. But of course you never would.

NORA. Of course not. It's inconceivable that it should ever be necessary. But
    I'm quite sure that if I spoke to Doctor Rank——

MRS. LINDEN. Behind your husband's back?

NORA. I must get clear of the other thing; that's behind his back too. I must
    get clear of that.

MRS. LINDEN. Yes, yes, I told you so yesterday; but——

NORA. (*Walking up and down.*) A man can manage these things much better
    than a woman.

MRS. LINDEN. One's own husband, yes.

NORA. Nonsense. (*Stands still.*) When everything is paid, one gets back the
    paper.

MRS. LINDEN. Of course.

NORA. And can tear it into a hundred thousand pieces, and burn it up, the
    nasty, filthy thing!

MRS. LINDEN. (*Looks at her fixedly, lays down her work, and rises slowly.*) Nora,
    you are hiding something from me.

NORA. Can you see it in my face?

MRS. LINDEN. Something has happened since yesterday morning. Nora, what
    is it?

NORA. (*Going towards her.*) Christina——! (*Listens.*) Hush! There's Torvald
    coming home. Do you mind going into the nursery for the present? Tor-
    vald can't bear to see dressmaking going on. Get Anna to help you.

MRS. LINDEN. *(Gathers some of the things together.)* Very well; but I shan't go away until you have told me all about it. *(She goes out to the left, as* HELMER *enters from the hall.)*

NORA. *(Runs to meet him.)* Oh, how I've been longing for you to come, Torvald dear!

HELMER. Was that the dressmaker——?

NORA. No, Christina. She's helping me with my costume. You'll see how nice I shall look.

HELMER. Yes, wasn't that a happy thought of mine?

NORA. Splendid! But isn't it good of me, too, to have given in to you about the tarantella?

HELMER. *(Takes her under the chin.)* Good of you! To give in to your own husband? Well well, you little madcap, I know you don't mean it. But I won't disturb you. I daresay you want to be "trying on."

NORA. And you are going to work, I suppose?

HELMER. Yes. *(Shows her a bundle of papers.)* Look here. I've just come from the Bank—— *(Goes towards his room.)*

NORA. Torvald.

HELMER. *(Stopping.)* Yes?

NORA. If your little squirrel were to beg you for something so prettily—

HELMER. Well?

NORA. Would you do it?

HELMER. I must know first what it is.

NORA. The squirrel would skip and play all sorts of tricks if you would only be nice and kind.

HELMER. Come, then, out with it.

NORA. Your lark would twitter from morning till night——

HELMER. Oh, that she does in any case.

NORA. I'll be an elf and dance in the moonlight for you, Torvald.

HELMER. Nora—you can't mean what you were hinting at this morning?

NORA. *(Coming nearer.)* Yes, Torvald, I beg and implore you!

HELMER. Have you really the courage to begin that again?

NORA. Yes, yes; for my sake, you must let Krogstad keep his place in the Bank.

HELMER. My dear Nora, it's his place I intend for Mrs. Linden.

NORA. Yes, that's so good of you. But instead of Krogstad, you could dismiss some other clerk.

HELMER. Why, this is incredible obstinacy! Because you have thoughtlessly promised to put in a word for him, I am to——!

NORA. It's not that, Torvald. It's for your own sake. This man writes for the most scurrilous newspapers; you said so yourself. He can do you no end of harm. I'm so terribly afraid of him——

HELMER. Ah, I understand; it's old recollections that are frightening you.

NORA. What do you mean?

HELMER. Of course you're thinking of your father.

NORA. Yes—yes, of course. Only think of the shameful slanders wicked people used to write about father. I believe they would have got him dismissed if you hadn't been sent to look into the thing and been kind to him, and helped him.

HELMER. My little Nora, between your father and me there is all the difference in the world. Your father was not altogether unimpeachable. I am; and I hope to remain so.

NORA. Oh, no one knows what wicked men may hit upon. We could live so quietly and happily now, in our cosy, peaceful home, you and I and the children, Torvald! That's why I beg and implore you——

HELMER. And it is just by pleading his cause that you make it impossible for me to keep him. It's already known at the Bank that I intend to dismiss Krogstad. If it were now reported that the new manager let himself be turned round his wife's little finger——

NORA. What then?

HELMER. Oh, nothing, so long as a wilful woman can have her way——! I am to make myself a laughing-stock to the whole staff, and set people saying that I am open to all sorts of outside influence? Take my word for it, I should soon feel the consequences. And besides—there is one thing that makes Krogstad impossible for me to work with——

NORA. What thing?

HELMER. I could perhaps have overlooked his moral failings at a pinch——

NORA. Yes, couldn't you, Torvald?

HELMER. And I hear he is good at his work. But the fact is, he was a college chum of mine—there was one of those rash friendships between us that one so often repents of later. I may as well confess it at once—he calls me by my Christian name;* and he is tactless enough to do it even when others are present. He delights in putting on airs of familiarity—Torvald here, Torvald there! I assure you it's most painful to me. He would make my position at the bank perfectly unendurable.

NORA. Torvald, surely you're not serious?

HELMER. No? Why not?

NORA. That's such a petty reason.

HELMER. What! Petty! Do you consider me petty!

NORA. No, on the contrary, Torvald dear; and that's just why——

HELMER. Never mind; you call my motives petty; then I must be petty too. Petty! Very well!—Now we'll put an end to this, once for all. (*Goes to the door into the hall and calls.*) Ellen!

NORA. What do you want?

HELMER. (*Searching among his papers.*) To settle the thing. (ELLEN *enters.*) Here; take this letter; give it to a messenger. See that he takes it at once. The address is on it. Here's the money.

ELLEN. Very well, sir. (*Goes with the letter.*)

HELMER. (*Putting his papers together.*) There, Madam Obstinacy.

*In the original, "We say 'thou' to each other."

NORA. *(Breathless.)* Torvald—What was in the letter?

HELMER. Krogstad's dismissal.

NORA. Call it back again, Torvald! There's still time. Oh, Torvald, call it back again! For my sake, for your own, for the children's sake! Do you hear, Torvald? Do it! You don't know what that letter may bring upon us all.

HELMER. Too late.

NORA. Yes, too late.

HELMER. My dear Nora, I forgive your anxiety, though it's anything but flattering to me. Why should you suppose that *I* would be afraid of a wretched scribbler's spite? But I forgive you all the same, for it's a proof of your great love for me. *(Takes her in his arms.)* That's as it should be, my own dear Nora. Let what will happen—when it comes to the pinch, I shall have strength and courage enough. You shall see: my shoulders are broad enough to bear the whole burden.

NORA. *(Terror-struck.)* What do you mean by that?

HELMER. The whole burden, I say——

NORA. *(With decision.)* That you shall never, never do!

HELMER. Very well; then we'll share it, Nora, as man and wife. That is how it should be. *(Petting her.)* Are you satisfied now? Come, come, come, don't look like a scared dove. It's all nothing—foolish fancies.—Now you ought to play the tarantella through and practise with the tambourine. I shall sit in my inner room and shut both doors, so that I shall hear nothing. You can make as much noise as you please. *(Turns round in doorway.)* And when Rank comes, just tell him where I'm to be found. *(He nods to her, and goes with his papers into his room, closing the door.)*

NORA. *(Bewildered with terror, stands as though rooted to the ground, and whispers.)* He would do it. Yes, he would do it. He would do it, in spite of all the world.—No, never that, never, never! Anything rather than that! Oh, for some way of escape! What shall I do——! *(Hall bell rings.)* Doctor Rank——!—Anything, anything, rather than——!

(NORA draws her hands over her face, pulls herself together, goes to the door and opens it. RANK stands outside hanging up his fur coat. During what follows it begins to grow dark.)

NORA. Good afternoon, Doctor Rank, I knew you by your ring. But you mustn't go to Torvald now. I believe he's busy.

RANK. And you? *(Enters and closes the door.)*

NORA. Oh, you know very well, I have always time for you.

RANK. Thank you. I shall avail myself of your kindness as long as I can.

NORA. What do you mean? As long as you can?

RANK. Yes. Does that frighten you?

NORA. I think it's an odd expression. Do you expect anything to happen?

RANK. Something I have long been prepared for; but I didn't think it would come so soon.

NORA. *(Catching at his arm.)* What have you discovered? Doctor Rank, you must tell me!

RANK. (*Sitting down by the stove.*) I am running down hill. There's no help for it.

NORA. (*Draws a long breath of relief.*) It's you——?

RANK. Who else should it be?—Why lie to one's self? I am the most wretched of all my patients, Mrs. Helmer. In these last days I have been auditing my life-account—bankrupt! Perhaps before a month is over, I shall lie rotting in the church-yard.

NORA. Oh! What an ugly way to talk.

RANK. The thing itself is so confoundedly ugly, you see. But the worst of it is, so many other ugly things have to be gone through first. There is only one last investigation to be made, and when that is over I shall know pretty certainly when the break-up will begin. There's one thing I want to say to you: Helmer's delicate nature shrinks so from all that is horrible: I will not have him in my sick-room——

NORA. But, Doctor Rank——

RANK. I won't have him, I say—not on any account! I shall lock my door against him.—As soon as I am quite certain of the worst, I shall send you my visiting-card with a black cross on it; and then you will know that the final horror has begun.

NORA. Why, you're perfectly unreasonable to-day; and I did so want you to be in a really good humour.

RANK. With death staring me in the face?—And to suffer thus for another's sin! Where's the justice of it? And in one way or another you can trace in every family some such inexorable retribution——

NORA. (*Stopping her ears.*) Nonsense, nonsense! Now cheer up!

RANK. Well, after all, the whole thing's only worth laughing at. My poor innocent spine must do penance for my father's wild oats.

NORA. (*At table, left.*) I suppose he was too fond of asparagus and Strasbourg pâté, wasn't he?

RANK. Yes; and truffles.

NORA. Yes, truffles, to be sure. And oysters, I believe?

RANK. Yes, oysters; oysters, of course.

NORA. And then all the port and champagne! It's sad that all these good things should attack the spine.

RANK. Especially when the luckless spine attacked never had any good of them.

NORA. Ah, yes, that's the worst of it.

RANK. (*Looks at her searchingly.*) H'm——

NORA. (*A moment later.*) Why did you smile?

RANK. No; it was you that laughed.

NORA. No; it was you that smiled, Doctor Rank.

RANK. (*Standing up.*) I see you're deeper than I thought.

NORA. I'm in such a crazy mood to-day.

RANK. So it seems.

NORA. (*With her hands on his shoulders.*) Dear, dear, Doctor Rank, death shall not take you away from Torvald and me.

RANK. Oh, you'll easily get over the loss. The absent are soon forgotten.

NORA. *(Looks at him anxiously.)* Do you think so?

RANK. People make fresh ties, and then——

NORA. Who make fresh ties?

RANK. You and Helmer will, when I am gone. You yourself are taking time by the forelock, it seems to me. What was that Mrs. Linden doing here yesterday?

NORA. Oh!—you're surely not jealous of poor Christina?

RANK. Yes, I am. She will be my successor in this house. When I am out of the way, this woman will perhaps——

NORA. Hush! Not so loud! She's in there.

RANK. To-day as well? You see!

NORA. Only to put my costume in order—dear me, how unreasonable you are! *(Sits on sofa.)* Now do be good, Doctor Rank! To-morrow you shall see how beautifully I shall dance; and then you may fancy that I'm doing it all to please you—and of course Torvald as well. *(Takes various things out of box.)* Doctor Rank, sit down here, and I'll show you something.

RANK. *(Sitting.)* What is it?

NORA. Look here. Look!

RANK. Silk stockings.

NORA. Flesh-coloured. Aren't they lovely? It's so dark here now; but to-morrow—— No, no, no; you must only look at the feet. Oh, well, I suppose you may look at the rest too.

RANK. H'm——

NORA. What are you looking so critical about? Do you think they won't fit me?

RANK. I can't possibly give any competent opinion on that point.

NORA. *(Looking at him for a moment.)* For shame! *(Hits him lightly on the ear with the stockings.)* Take that. *(Rolls them up again.)*

RANK. And what other wonders am I to see?

NORA. You sha'n't see anything more; for you don't behave nicely. *(She hums a little and searches among the things.)*

RANK. *(After a short silence.)* When I sit here gossiping with you, I can't imagine—I simply cannot conceive—what would have become of me if I had never entered this house.

NORA. *(Smiling.)* Yes, I think you do feel at home with us.

RANK. *(More softly—looking straight before him.)* And now to have to leave it all——

NORA. Nonsense. You sha'n't leave us.

RANK. *(In the same tone.)* And not to be able to leave behind the slightest token of gratitude; scarcely even a passing regret—nothing but an empty place, that can be filled by the first comer.

NORA. And if I were to ask you for——? No——

RANK. For what?

NORA. For a great proof of your friendship.

RANK. Yes—yes?

NORA. I mean—for a very, very great service——

RANK. Would you really, for once, make me so happy?

NORA. Oh, you don't know what it is.

RANK. Then tell me.

NORA. No, I really can't, Doctor Rank. It's far, far too much—not only a service, but help and advice besides——

RANK. So much the better. I can't think of what you can mean. But go on. Don't you trust me?

NORA. As I trust no one else. I know you are my best and truest friend. So I will tell you. Well then, Doctor Rank, there is something you must help me to prevent. You know how deeply, how wonderfully Torvald loves me; he wouldn't hesitate a moment to give his very life for my sake.

RANK. (Bending towards her.) Nora—do you think he is the only one who——?

NORA. (With a slight start.) Who——?

RANK. Who would gladly give his life for you?

NORA. (Sadly.) Oh!

RANK. I have sworn that you shall know it before I—go. I shall never find a better opportunity.—Yes, Nora, now I have told you; and now you know that you can trust me as you can no one else.

NORA. (Standing up; simply and calmly.) Let me pass, please.

RANK. (Makes way for her, but remains sitting.) Nora——

NORA. (In the doorway.) Ellen, bring the lamp. (Crosses to the stove.) Oh dear, Doctor Rank, that was too bad of you.

RANK. (Rising.) That I have loved you as deeply as—any one else? Was that too bad of me?

NORA. No, but that you should have told me so. It was so unnecessary——

RANK. What do you mean? Did you know——? (ELLEN enters with the lamp; sets it on the table and goes out again.)

RANK. Nora—Mrs. Helmer—I ask you, did you know?

NORA. Oh, how can I tell what I knew or didn't know? I really can't say—— How could you be so clumsy, Doctor Rank? It was all so nice!

RANK. Well, at any rate, you know now that I am at your service, body and soul. And now, go on.

NORA. (Looking at him.) Go on—now?

RANK. I beg you to tell me what you want.

NORA. I can tell you nothing now.

RANK. Yes, yes! You mustn't punish me in that way. Let me do for you whatever a man can.

NORA. You can do nothing for me now.—Besides, I really want no help. You shall see it was only my fancy. Yes, it must be so. Of course! (Sits in the rocking-chair, looks at him and smiles.) You are a nice person, Doctor Rank! Aren't you ashamed of yourself, now that the lamp is on the table?

RANK. No; not exactly. But perhaps I ought to go—forever.

NORA. No, indeed you mustn't. Of course you must come and go as you've always done. You know very well that Torvald can't do without you.

RANK. Yes, but you?

NORA. Oh, you know I always like to have you here.

RANK. That is just what led me astray. You are a riddle to me. It has often seemed to me as if you liked being with me almost as much as being with Helmer.

NORA. Yes; don't you see? There are people one loves, and others one likes to talk to.

RANK. Yes—there's something in that.

NORA. When I was a girl, of course I loved papa best. But it always delighted me to steal into the servants' room. In the first place they never lectured me, and in the second it was such fun to hear them talk.

RANK. Ah, I see; that it's their place I have taken?

NORA. (*Jumps up and hurries toward him.*) Oh, my dear Doctor Rank, I don't mean that. But you understand, with Torvald it's the same as with papa——

ELLEN *enters from the hall.*

ELLEN. Please, ma'am—— (*Whispers to* NORA, *and gives her a card.*)

NORA. (*Glancing at card.*) Ah! (*Puts it in her pocket.*)

RANK. Anything wrong?

NORA. No, no, not in the least. It's only—it's my new costume——

RANK. Your costume! Why, it's there.

NORA. Oh, that one, yes. But this is another that—I have ordered it—Torvald mustn't know——

RANK. Aha! So that's the great secret.

NORA. Yes, of course. Please go to him; he's in the inner room. Do keep him while I——

RANK. Don't be alarmed; he sha'n't escape. (*Goes into* HELMER'S *room.*)

NORA. (*To* ELLEN.) Is he waiting in the kitchen?

ELLEN. Yes, he came up the back stair——

NORA. Didn't you tell him I was engaged?

ELLEN. Yes, but it was no use.

NORA. He won't go away?

ELLEN. No, ma'am, not until he has spoken to you.

NORA. Then let him come in; but quietly. And, Ellen—say nothing about it; it's a surprise for my husband.

ELLEN. Oh, yes, ma'am, I understand. (*She goes out.*)

NORA. It is coming! The dreadful thing is coming, after all. No, no, no, it can never be; it shall not!

(*She goes to* HELMER'S *door and slips the bolt.* ELLEN *opens the hall door for* KROGSTAD, *and shuts it after him. He wears a travelling-coat, high boots, and a fur cap.*)

NORA. (*Goes toward him.*) Speak softly; my husband is at home.

KROGSTAD. All right. That's nothing to me.

NORA. What do you want?

KROGSTAD. A little information.

NORA. Be quick, then. What is it?

KROGSTAD. You know I have got my dismissal.

NORA. I couldn't prevent it, Mr. Krogstad. I fought for you to the last, but it was of no use.

KROGSTAD. Does your husband care for you so little? He knows what I can bring upon you, and yet he dares——

NORA. How could you think I should tell him?

KROGSTAD. Well, as a matter of fact, I didn't think it. It wasn't like my friend Torvald Helmer to show so much courage——

NORA. Mr. Krogstad, be good enough to speak respectfully of my husband.

KROGSTAD. Certainly, with all due respect. But since you are so anxious to keep the matter secret, I suppose you are a little clearer than yesterday as to what you have done.

NORA. Clearer than you could ever make me.

KROGSTAD. Yes, such a bad lawyer as I——

NORA. What is it you want?

KROGSTAD. Only to see how you are getting on, Mrs. Helmer. I've been thinking about you all day. Even a mere money-lender, a gutter-journalist, a,—in short, a creature like me—has a little bit of what people call feeling.

NORA. Then show it; think of my little children.

KROGSTAD. Did you and your husband think of mine? But enough of that. I only wanted to tell you that you needn't take this matter too seriously. I shall not lodge any information, for the present.

NORA. No, surely not. I knew you wouldn't.

KROGSTAD. The whole thing can be settled quite amicably. Nobody need know. It can remain among us three.

NORA. My husband must never know.

KROGSTAD. How can you prevent it? Can you pay off the balance?

NORA. No, not at once.

KROGSTAD. Or have you any means of raising the money in the next few days?

NORA. None—that I will make use of.

KROGSTAD. And if you had, it would not help you now. If you offered me ever so much money down, you should not get back your I.O.U.

NORA. Tell me what you want to do with it.

KROGSTAD. I only want to keep it—to have it in my possession. No outsider shall hear anything of it. So, if you have any desperate scheme in your head——

NORA. What if I have?

KROGSTAD. If you should think of leaving your husband and children——

NORA. What if I do?

KROGSTAD. Or if you should think of—something worse——

NORA. How do you know that?

KROGSTAD. Put all that out of your head.

NORA. How did you know what I had in my mind?

KROGSTAD. Most of us think that at first. I thought of it, too; but I hadn't the courage——

NORA. *(Tonelessly.)* Nor I.

KROGSTAD. *(Relieved.)* No, one hasn't. You haven't the courage either, have you?

NORA. I haven't, I haven't.

KROGSTAD. Besides, it would be very foolish.—Just one domestic storm, and it's all over. I have a letter in my pocket for your husband——

NORA. Telling him everything?

KROGSTAD. Sparing you as much as possible.

NORA. *(Quickly.)* He must never read that letter. Tear it up. I will manage to get the money somehow——

KROGSTAD. Pardon me, Mrs. Helmer, but I believe I told you——

NORA. Oh, I'm not talking about the money I owe you. Tell me how much you demand from my husband—I will get it.

KROGSTAD. I demand no money from your husband.

NORA. What do you demand then?

KROGSTAD. I will tell you. I want to regain my footing in the world. I want to rise; and your husband shall help me to do it. For the last eighteen months my record has been spotless; I have been in bitter need all the time; but I was content to fight my way up, step by step. Now, I've been thrust down again, and I will not be satisfied with merely being reinstated as a matter of grace. I want to rise, I tell you. I must get into the Bank again, in a higher position than before. Your husband shall create a place on purpose for me——

NORA. He will never do that!

KROGSTAD. He will do it; I know him—he won't dare to show fight! And when he and I are together there, you shall soon see! Before a year is out I shall be the manager's right hand. It won't be Torvald Helmer, but Nils Krogstad, that manages the Joint Stock Bank.

NORA. That shall never be.

KROGSTAD. Perhaps you will——?

NORA. Now I have the courage for it.

KROGSTAD. Oh, you don't frighten me! A sensitive, petted creature like you——

NORA. You shall see, you shall see!

KROGSTAD. Under the ice, perhaps? Down into the cold, black water? And next spring to come up again, ugly, hairless, unrecognisable——

NORA. You can't terrify me.

KROGSTAD. Nor you me. People don't do that sort of thing, Mrs. Helmer. And, after all, what would be the use of it? I have your husband in my pocket, all the same.

NORA. Afterwards? When I am no longer——?

KROGSTAD. You forget, your reputation remains in my hands! *(NORA stands speechless and looks at him.)* Well, now you are prepared. Do nothing foolish. As soon as Helmer has received my letter, I shall expect to hear from him. And remember that it is your husband himself who has forced me back again into such paths. That I will never forgive him. Good-bye, Mrs. Helmer. *(Goes out through the hall. NORA hurries to the door, opens it a little, and listens.)*

NORA. He's going. He's not putting the letter into the box. No, no, it would be impossible! *(Opens the door further and further.)* What's that. He's standing still; not going down stairs. Has he changed his mind? Is he——? *(A letter falls into the box.* KROGSTAD's *footsteps are heard gradually receding down the stair.* NORA *utters a suppressed shriek, and rushes forward towards the sofa-table; pause.)* In the letter-box! *(Slips shrinkingly up to the hall door.)* There it lies.—Torvald, Torvald—now we are lost!

MRS. LINDEN *enters from the left with the costume.*

MRS. LINDEN. There, I think it's all right now. Shall we just try in on?
NORA. *(Hoarsely and softly.)* Christina, come here.
MRS. LINDEN. *(Throws down the dress on the sofa.)* What's the matter? You look quite distracted.
NORA. Come here. Do you see that letter? There, see—through the glass of the letter-box.
MRS. LINDEN. Yes, yes, I see it.
NORA. That letter is from Krogstad——
MRS. LINDEN. Nora—it was Krogstad who lent you the money?
NORA. Yes; and now Torvald will know everything.
MRS. LINDEN. Believe me, Nora, it's the best thing for both of you.
NORA. You don't know all yet. I have forged a name——
MRS. LINDEN. Good heavens!
NORA. Now, listen to me, Christina; you shall bear me witness——
MRS. LINDEN. How "witness"? What am I to——?
NORA. If I should go out of my mind—it might easily happen——
MRS. LINDEN. Nora!
NORA. Or if anything else should happen to me—so that I couldn't be here——!
MRS. LINDEN. Nora, Nora, you're quite beside yourself!
NORA. In case any one wanted to take it all upon himself—the whole blame— you understand——
MRS. LINDEN. Yes, yes; but how can you think——?
NORA. You shall bear witness that it's not true, Christina. I'm not out of my mind at all; I know quite well what I'm saying; and I tell you nobody else knew anything about it; I did the whole thing, I myself. Remember that.
MRS. LINDEN. I shall remember. But I don't understand what you mean——
NORA. Oh, how should you? It's the miracle coming to pass.
MRS. LINDEN. The miracle?
NORA. Yes, the miracle. But it's so terrible, Christina; it mustn't happen for all the world.
MRS. LINDEN. I shall go straight to Krogstad and talk to him.
NORA. Don't; he'll do you some harm.
MRS. LINDEN. Once he would have done anything for me.
NORA. He?
MRS. LINDEN. Where does he live?

NORA. Oh, how can I tell—? Yes— *(Feels in her pocket.)* Here's his card. But the letter, the letter——!

HELMER. *(Knocking outside.)* Nora!

NORA. *(Shrieks in terror.)* Oh, what is it? What do you want?

HELMER. Well, well, don't be frightened. We're not coming in; you've bolted the door. Are you trying on your dress?

NORA. Yes, yes, I'm trying it on. It suits me so well, Torvald.

MRS. LINDEN. *(Who has read the card.)* Why, he lives close by here.

NORA. Yes, but it's no use now. We are lost. The letter is there in the box.

MRS. LINDEN. And your husband has the key?

NORA. Always.

MRS. LINDEN. Krogstad must demand his letter back, unread. He must find some pretext——

NORA. But this is the very time when Torvald generally——

MRS. LINDEN. Prevent him. Keep him occupied. I shall come back as quickly as I can. *(She goes out hastily by the hall door.)*

NORA. *(Opens HELMER's door and peeps in.)* Torvald!

HELMER. Well, may one come into one's own room again at last? Come, Rank, we'll have a look—— *(In the doorway.)* But how's this?

NORA. What, Torvald dear?

HELMER. Rank led me to expect a grand transformation.

RANK. *(In the doorway.)* So I understood. I suppose I was mistaken.

NORA. No, no one shall see me in my glory till to-morrow evening.

HELMER. Why, Nora dear, you look so tired. Have you been practising too hard?

NORA. No, I haven't practised at all yet.

HELMER. But you'll have to——

NORA. Oh yes, I must, I must! But, Torvald, I can't get on at all without your help. I've forgotten everything.

HELMER. Oh, we shall soon freshen it up again.

NORA. Yes, do help me, Torvald. You must promise me—— Oh, I'm so nervous about it. Before so many people—— This evening you must give yourself up entirely to me. You mustn't do a stroke of work; you mustn't even touch a pen. Do promise, Torvald dear!

HELMER. I promise. All this evening I shall be your slave. Little helpless thing——! But, by-the-bye, I must just—— *(Going to hall door.)*

NORA. What do you want there?

HELMER. Only to see if there are any letters.

NORA. No, no, don't do that, Torvald.

HELMER. Why not?

NORA. Torvald, I beg you not to. There are none there.

HELMER. Let me just see. *(Is going.)* (NORA, *at the piano, plays the first bars of the tarantella.*)

HELMER. *(At the door, stops.)* Aha!

NORA. I can't dance to-morrow if I don't rehearse with you first.

HELMER. *(Going to her.)* Are you really so nervous, dear Nora?

NORA. Yes, dreadfully! Let me rehearse at once. We have time before dinner. Oh, do sit down and play for me, Torvald dear; direct me and put me right, as you used to do.

HELMER. With all the pleasure in life, since you wish it. *(Sits at piano.)*

(NORA snatches the tambourine out of the box, and hurriedly drapes herself in a long parti-coloured shawl; then, with a bound, stands in the middle of the floor.)

NORA. Now play for me! Now I'll dance! *(HELMER plays and NORA dances.* RANK *stands at the piano behind* HELMER *and looks on.)*

HELMER. *(Playing.)* Slower! Slower!

NORA. Can't do it slower!

HELMER. Not so violently, Nora.

NORA. I must! I must!

HELMER. *(Stops.)* No, no, Nora—that will never do.

NORA. *(Laughs and swings her tambourine.)* Didn't I tell you so!

RANK. Let me play for her.

HELMER. *(Rising.)* Yes, do—then I can direct her better.

(RANK sits down to the piano and plays; NORA dances more and more wildly. HELMER stands by the stove and addresses frequent corrections to her; she seems not to hear. Her hair breaks loose, and falls over her shoulders. She does not notice it, but goes on dancing. MRS. LINDEN *enters and stands spellbound in the doorway.)*

MRS. LINDEN. Ah——!

NORA. *(Dancing.)* We're having such fun here, Christina!

HELMER. Why, Nora dear, you're dancing as if it were a matter of life and death.

NORA. So it is.

HELMER. Rank, stop! This is the merest madness. Stop, I say! *(RANK stops playing, and NORA comes to a sudden standstill.)*

HELMER. *(Going towards her.)* I couldn't have believed it. You're positively forgotten all I taught you.

NORA. *(Throws the tambourine away.)* You see for yourself.

HELMER. You really do want teaching.

NORA. Yes, you see how much I need it. You must practise with me up to the last moment. Will you promise me, Torvald?

HELMER. Certainly, certainly.

NORA. Neither to-day nor to-morrow must you think of anything but me. You mustn't open a single letter—mustn't look at the letter-box.

HELMER. Ah, you're still afraid of that man——

NORA. Oh yes, yes, I am.

HELMER. Nora, I can see it in your face—there's a letter from him in the box.

NORA. I don't know, I believe so. But you're not to read anything now; nothing ugly must come between us until all is over.

RANK. *(Softly, to HELMER.)* You mustn't contradict her.

HELMER. *(Putting his arm around her.)* The child shall have her own way. But to-morrow night, when the dance is over——

NORA. Then you shall be free. (ELLEN *appears in the doorway, right.*)

ELLEN. Dinner is on the table, ma'am.

NORA. We'll have some champagne, Ellen.

ELLEN. Yes, ma'am. *(Goes out.)*

HELMER. Dear me! Quite a banquet.

NORA. Yes, and we'll keep it up till morning. *(Calling out.)* And macaroons, Ellen—plenty—just this once.

HELMER. *(Seizing her hand.)* Come, come, don't let us have this wild excitement! Be my own little lark again.

NORA. Oh yes, I will. But now go into the dining-room; and you too, Doctor Rank. Christina, you must help me to do up my hair.

RANK. *(Softly, as they go.)* There's nothing in the wind? Nothing—I mean——?

HELMER. Oh no, nothing of the kind. It's merely this babyish anxiety I was telling you about. *(They go out to the right.)*

NORA. Well?

MRS. LINDEN. He's gone out of town.

NORA. I saw it in your face.

MRS. LINDEN. He comes back to-morrow evening. I left a note for him.

NORA. You shouldn't have done that. Things must take their course. After all, there's something glorious in waiting for the miracle.

MRS. LINDEN. What is it you're waiting for?

NORA. Oh, you can't understand. Go to them in the dining-room; I shall come in a moment. (MRS. LINDEN *goes into the dining-room.* NORA *stands for a moment as though collecting her thoughts; then looks at her watch.*)

NORA. Five. Seven hours till midnight. Then twenty-four hours till the next midnight. Then the tarantella will be over. Twenty-four and seven? Thirty-one hours to live.

HELMER *appears at the door, right.*

HELMER. What has become of my little lark?

NORA. *(Runs to him with open arms.)* Here she is!

Act Third

The same room. The table, with the chairs around it, in the middle. A lighted lamp on the table. The door to the hall stands open. Dance music is heard from the floor above.

　　MRS. LINDEN *sits by the table and absently turns the pages of a book. She tries to read, but seems unable to fix her attention; she frequently listens and looks anxiously towards the hall door.*

MRS. LINDEN. *(Looks at her watch.)* Not here yet; and the time is nearly up. If only he hasn't—— *(Listens again.)* Ah, there he is. *(She goes into the hall and cautiously opens the outer door; soft footsteps are heard on the stairs; she whispers.)* Come in; there is no one here.

KROGSTAD. *(In the doorway.)* I found a note from you at my house. What does it mean?

MRS. LINDEN. I must speak to you.

KROGSTAD. Indeed? And in this house?

MRS. LINDEN. I could not see you at my rooms. They have no separate entrance. Come in; we are quite alone. The servants are asleep, and the Helmers are at the ball upstairs.

KROGSTAD. *(Coming into the room.)* Ah! So the Helmers are dancing this evening? Really?

MRS. LINDEN. Yes. Why not?

KROGSTAD. Quite right. Why not?

MRS. LINDEN. And now let us talk a little.

KROGSTAD. Have we two anything to say to each other?

MRS. LINDEN. A great deal.

KROGSTAD. I should not have thought so.

MRS. LINDEN. Because you have never really understood me.

KROGSTAD. What was there to understand? The most natural thing in the world—a heartless woman throws a man over when a better match offers.

MRS. LINDEN. Do you really think me so heartless? Do you think I broke with you lightly?

KROGSTAD. Did you not?

MRS. LINDEN. Do you really think so?

KROGSTAD. If not, why did you write me that letter?

MRS. LINDEN. Was it not best? Since I had to break with you, was it not right that I should try to put an end to all that you felt for me?

KROGSTAD. *(Clenching his hands together.)* So that was it? And all this—for the sake of money!

MRS. LINDEN. You ought not to forget that I had a helpless mother and two little brothers. We could not wait for you, Nils, as your prospects then stood.

KROGSTAD. Perhaps not; but you had no right to cast me off for the sake of others, whoever the others might be.

MRS. LINDEN. I don't know. I have often asked myself whether I had the right.

KROGSTAD. *(More softly.)* When I had lost you, I seemed to have no firm ground left under my feet. Look at me now. I am a shipwrecked man clinging to a spar.

MRS. LINDEN. Rescue may be at hand.

KROGSTAD. It was at hand; but then you came and stood in the way.

MRS. LINDEN. Without my knowledge, Nils. I did not know till to-day that it was you I was to replace in the Bank.

KROGSTAD. Well, I take your word for it. But now that you do know, do you mean to give way?

MRS. LINDEN. No, for that would not help you in the least.

KROGSTAD. Oh, help, help——! I should do it whether or no.

MRS. LINDEN. I have learnt prudence. Life and bitter necessity have schooled me.

KROGSTAD. And life has taught me not to trust fine speeches.

MRS. LINDEN. Then life has taught you a very sensible thing. But deeds you will trust?

KROGSTAD. What do you mean?

MRS. LINDEN. You said you were a shipwrecked man, clinging to a spar.

KROGSTAD. I have good reason to say so.

MRS. LINDEN. I too am shipwrecked, and clinging to a spar. I have no one to mourn for, no one to care for.

KROGSTAD. You made your own choice.

MRS. LINDEN. No choice was left me.

KROGSTAD. Well, what then?

MRS. LINDEN. Nils, how if we two shipwrecked people could join hands?

KROGSTAD. What!

MRS. LINDEN. Two on a raft have a better chance than if each clings to a separate spar.

KROGSTAD. Christina!

MRS. LINDEN. What do you think brought me to town?

KROGSTAD. Had you any thought of me?

MRS. LINDEN. I must have work or I can't bear to live. All my life, as long as I can remember, I have worked; work has been my one great joy. Now I stand quite alone in the world, aimless and forlorn. There is no happiness in working for one's self. Nils, give me somebody and something to work for.

KROGSTAD. I cannot believe in all this. It is simply a woman's romantic craving for self-sacrifice.

MRS. LINDEN. Have you ever found me romantic?

KROGSTAD. Would you really——? Tell me: do you know all my past?

MRS. LINDEN. Yes.

KROGSTAD. And do you know what people say of me?

MRS. LINDEN. Did you not say just now that with me you could have been another man?

KROGSTAD. I am sure of it.

MRS. LINDEN. Is it too late?

KROGSTAD. Christina, do you know what you are doing? Yes, you do; I see it in your face. Have you the courage then——?

MRS. LINDEN. I need someone to be a mother to, and your children need a mother. You need me, and I—I need you. Nils, I believe in your better self. With you I fear nothing.

KROGSTAD. (*Seizing her hands.*) Thank you—thank you, Christina. Now I shall make others see me as you do—Ah, I forgot——

MRS. LINDEN. (*Listening.*) Hush! The tarantella! Go! go!

KROGSTAD. Why? What is it?

MRS. LINDEN. Don't you hear the dancing overhead? As soon as that is over they will be here.

KROGSTAD. Oh yes, I shall go. Nothing will come of this, after all. Of course, you don't know the step I have taken against the Helmers.

MRS. LINDEN. Yes, Nils, I do know.

KROGSTAD. And yet you have the courage to——?

MRS. LINDEN. I know to what lengths despair can drive a man.

KROGSTAD. Oh, if I could only undo it!

MRS. LINDEN. You could. Your letter is still in the box.

KROGSTAD. Are you sure?

MRS. LINDEN. Yes, but——

KROGSTAD. (*Looking to her searchingly.*) Is that what it all means? You want to save your friend at any price. Say it out—is that your idea?

MRS. LINDEN. Nils, a woman who has once sold herself for the sake of others, does not do so again.

KROGSTAD. I shall demand my letter back again.

MRS. LINDEN. No, no.

KROGSTAD. Yes, of course. I shall wait till Helmer comes; I shall tell him to give it back to me—that it's only about my dismissal—that I don't want it read——

MRS. LINDEN. No, Nils, you must not recall the letter.

KROGSTAD. But tell me, wasn't that just why you got me to come here?

MRS. LINDEN. Yes, in my first alarm. But a day has passed since then, and in that day I have seen incredible things in this house. Helmer must know everything; there must be an end to this unhappy secret. These two must come to a full understanding. They must have done with all these shifts and subterfuges.

KROGSTAD. Very well, if you like to risk it. But one thing I can do, and at once——

MRS. LINDEN. (*Listening.*) Make haste! Go, go! The dance is over; we're not safe another moment.

KROGSTAD. I shall wait for you in the street.

MRS. LINDEN. Yes, do; you must see me home.

KROGSTAD. I never was so happy in all my life! (KROGSTAD *goes out by the outer door. The door between the room and the hall remains open.*)

MRS. LINDEN. (*Arranging the room and getting her outdoor things together.*) What a change! What a change! To have someone to work for, to live for; a home to make happy! Well, it shall not be my fault if I fail—I wish they would come—(*Listens.*) Ah, here they are! I must get my things on. (*Takes bonnet and cloak.* HELMER'S *and* NORA'S *voices are heard outside, a key is turned in the lock, and* HELMER *drags* NORA *almost by force into the hall. She wears the Italian costume with a large black shawl over it. He is in evening dress and wears a black domino, open.*)

NORA. (*Struggling with him in the doorway.*) No, no, no! I won't go in! I want to go upstairs again; I don't want to leave so early!

HELMER. But, my dearest girl——!

NORA. Oh, please, please, Torvald, I beseech you—only one hour more!

HELMER. Not one minute more, Nora dear; you know what we agreed. Come, come in; you're catching cold here. (*He leads her gently into the room in spite of her resistance.*)

MRS. LINDEN. Good-evening.

NORA. Christina!

HELMER. What, Mrs. Linden! You here so late?

MRS. LINDEN. Yes, I ought to apologise. I did so want to see Nora in her costume.

NORA. Have you been sitting here waiting for me?

MRS. LINDEN. Yes; unfortunately I came too late. You had gone upstairs already, and I felt I couldn't go away without seeing you.

HELMER. (*Taking* NORA's *shawl off.*) Well then, just look at her! I assure you she's worth it. Isn't she lovely, Mrs. Linden?

MRS. LINDEN. Yes, I must say——

HELMER. Isn't she exquisite? Everyone said so. But she's dreadfully obstinate, dear little creature. What's to be done with her? Just think, I had almost to force her away.

NORA. Oh, Torvald, you'll be sorry some day that you didn't let me stay, if only for one half-hour more.

HELMER. There! You hear her, Mrs. Linden? She dances her tarantella with wild applause, and well she deserved it, I must say—though there was, perhaps, a little too much nature in her rendering of the idea—more than was, strictly speaking, artistic. But never mind—the point is, she made a great success, a tremendous success. Was I to let her remain after that— to weaken the impression? Not if I know it. I took my sweet little Capri girl—my capricious little Capri girl, I might say—under my arm; a rapid turn round the room, a curtsey to all sides, and—as they say in novels— the lovely apparition vanished! An exit should always be effective, Mrs. Linden; but I can't get Nora to see it. By Jove! it's warm here. (*Throws his domino on a chair and opens the door to his room.*) What! No light there? Oh, of course. Excuse me—— (*Goes in and lights candles.*)

NORA. (*Whispers breathlessly.*) Well?

MRS. LINDEN. (*Softly.*) I've spoken to him.

NORA. And——?

MRS. LINDEN. Nora—you must tell your husband everything——

NORA. (*Tonelessly.*) I knew it!

MRS. LINDEN. You have nothing to fear from Krogstad; but you must speak out.

NORA. I shall not speak!

MRS. LINDEN. Then the letter will.

NORA. Thank you, Christina. Now I know what I have to do. Hush——!

HELMER. (*Coming back.*) Well, Mrs. Linden, have you admired her?

MRS. LINDEN. Yes; and now I must say good-night.

HELMER. What, already? Does this knitting belong to you?

MRS. LINDEN. (*Takes it.*) Yes, thanks; I was nearly forgetting it.

HELMER. Then you do knit?

MRS. LINDEN. Yes.

HELMER. Do you know, you ought to embroider instead?

MRS. LINDEN. Indeed! Why?

HELMER. Because it's so much prettier. Look now! You hold the embroidery in the left hand, so, and then work the needle with the right hand, in a long, graceful curve—don't you?

MRS. LINDEN. Yes, I suppose so.

HELMER. But knitting is always ugly. Just look—your arms close to your sides, and the needles going up and down—there's something Chinese about it.—They really gave us splendid champagne to-night.

MRS. LINDEN. Well, good-night, Nora, and don't be obstinate any more.

HELMER. Well said, Mrs. Linden!

MRS. LINDEN. Good-night, Mr. Helmer.

HELMER. (*Accompanying her to the door.*) Good-night, good-night; I hope you'll get safely home. I should be glad to—but you have such a short way to go. Good-night, good-night. (*She goes;* HELMER *shuts the door after her and comes forward again.*) At last we've got rid of her: she's a terrible bore.

NORA. Aren't you very tired, Torvald?

HELMER. No, not in the least.

NORA. Nor sleepy?

HELMER. Not a bit. I feel particularly lively. But you? You do look tired and sleepy.

NORA. Yes, very tired. I shall soon sleep now.

HELMER. There, you see. I was right after all not to let you stay longer.

NORA. Oh, everything you do is right.

HELMER. (*Kissing her forehead.*) Now my lark is speaking like a reasonable being. Did you notice how jolly Rank was this evening?

NORA. Indeed? Was he? I had no chance of speaking to him.

HELMER. Nor I, much; but I haven't seen him in such good spirits for a long time. (*Looks at* NORA *a little, then comes nearer her.*) It's splendid to be back in our own home, to be quite alone together!—Oh, you enchanting creature!

NORA. Don't look at me in that way, Torvald.

HELMER. I am not to look at my dearest treasure?—at all the loveliness that is mine, mine only, wholly and entirely mine?

NORA. (*Goes to the other side of the table.*) You mustn't say these things to me this evening.

HELMER. (*Following.*) I see you have the tarantella still in your blood—and that makes you all the more enticing. Listen! the other people are going now. (*More softly.*) Nora—soon the whole house will be still.

NORA. Yes, I hope so.

HELMER. Yes, don't you, Nora darling? When we are among strangers, do you know why I speak so little to you, and keep so far away, and only steal a glance at you now and then—do you know why I do it? Because I am fancying that we love each other in secret, that I am secretly betrothed to you, and that no one dreams that there is anything between us.

NORA. Yes, yes, yes. I know all your thoughts are with me.

HELMER. And then, when the time comes to go, and I put the shawl about your smooth, soft shoulders, and this glorious neck of yours, I imagine you are my bride, that our marriage is just over, that I am bringing you for the first time to my home—that I am alone with you for the first time—quite alone with you, in your trembling loveliness! All this evening I have been longing for you, and you only. When I watched you swaying and whirling in the tarantella—my blood boiled—I could endure it no longer; and that's why I made you come home with me so early——

NORA. Go now, Torvald! Go away from me. I won't have all this.

HELMER. What do you mean? Ah, I see you're teasing me, little Nora! Won't—won't! Am I not your husband——? *(A knock at the outer door.)*

NORA. *(Starts.)* Did you hear——?

HELMER. *(Going towards the hall.)* Who's there?

RANK. *(Outside.)* It is I; may I come in for a moment?

HELMER. *(In a low tone, annoyed.)* Oh, what can he want just now? *(Aloud.)* Wait a moment. *(Opens door.)* Come, it's nice of you to look in.

RANK. I thought I heard your voice, and that put it into my head. *(Looks round.)* Ah, this dear old place! How cosy you two are here!

HELMER. You seemed to find it pleasant enough upstairs, too.

RANK. Exceedingly. Why not? Why shouldn't one take one's share of everything in this world? All one can, at least, and as long as one can. The wine was splendid——

HELMER. Especially the champagne.

RANK. Did you notice it? It's incredible the quantity I contrived to get down.

NORA. Torvald drank plenty of champagne, too.

RANK. Did he?

NORA. Yes, and it always puts him in such spirits.

RANK. Well, why shouldn't one have a jolly evening after a well-spent day?

HELMER. Well-spent! Well, I haven't much to boast of in that respect.

RANK. *(Slapping him on the shoulder.)* But I have, don't you see?

NORA. I suppose you have been engaged in a scientific investigation, Doctor Rank?

RANK. Quite right.

HELMER. Bless me! Little Nora talking about scientific investigations!

NORA. Am I to congratulate you on the result?

RANK. By all means.

NORA. It was good then?

RANK. The best possible, both for doctor and patient—certainty.

NORA. *(Quickly and searchingly.)* Certainty?

RANK. Absolute certainty. Wasn't I right to enjoy myself after that?

NORA. Yes, quite right, Doctor Rank.

HELMER. And so say I, provided you don't have to pay for it to-morrow.

RANK. Well, in this life nothing is to be had for nothing.

NORA. Doctor Rank—I'm sure you are very fond of masquerades?

RANK. Yes, when there are plenty of amusing disguises——

NORA. Tell me, what shall we two be at our next masquerade?

HELMER. Little featherbrain! Thinking of your next already!

RANK. We two? I'll tell you. You must go as a good fairy.

HELMER. Ah, but what costume would indicate that?

RANK. She has simply to wear her everyday dress.

HELMER. Capital! But don't you know what you will be yourself?

RANK. Yes, my dear friend, I am perfectly clear upon that point.

HELMER. Well?

RANK. At the next masquerade I shall be invisible.

HELMER. What a comical idea!

RANK. There's a big black hat—haven't you heard of the invisible hat? It comes down all over you, and then no one can see you.

HELMER. *(With a suppressed smile.)* No, you're right there.

RANK. But I'm quite forgetting what I came for. Helmer, give me a cigar—one of the dark Havanas.

HELMER. With the greatest pleasure. *(Hands cigar-case.)*

RANK. *(Takes one and cuts the end off.)* Thank you.

NORA. *(Striking a wax match.)* Let me give you a light.

RANK. A thousand thanks. *(She holds the match. He lights his cigar at it.)*

RANK. And now, good-bye!

HELMER. Good-bye, good-bye, my dear fellow.

NORA. Sleep well, Doctor Rank.

RANK. Thanks for the wish.

NORA. Wish me the same.

RANK. You? Very well, since you ask me—Sleep well. And thanks for the light. *(He nods to them both and goes out.)*

HELMER. *(In an undertone.)* He's been drinking a good deal.

NORA. *(Absently.)* I daresay. *(HELMER takes his bunch of keys from his pocket and goes into the hall.)* Torvald, what are you doing there?

HELMER. I must empty the letter-box; it's quite full; there will be no room for the newspapers to-morrow morning

NORA. Are you going to work to-night?

HELMER. You know very well I am not—Why, how is this? Someone has been at the lock.

NORA. The lock——?

HELMER. I'm sure of it. What does it mean? I can't think that the servants——? Here's a broken hair-pin. Nora, it's one of yours.

NORA. *(Quickly.)* It must have been the children——

HELMER. Then you must break them of such tricks.—There! At last I've got it open. (*Takes contents out and calls into the kitchen.*) Ellen!—Ellen, just put the hall door lamp out. (*He returns with letters in his hand, and shuts the inner door.*)

HELMER. Just see how they've accumulated. (*Turning them over.*) Why, what's this?

NORA. (*At the window.*) The letter! Oh no, no, Torvald!

HELMER. Two visiting-cards—from Rank.

NORA. From Doctor Rank?

HELMER. (*Looking at them.*) Doctor Rank. They were on the top. He must just have put them in.

NORA. Is there anything on them?

HELMER. There's a black cross over the name. Look at it. What an unpleasant idea! It looks just as if he were announcing his own death.

NORA. So he is.

HELMER. What! Do you know anything? Has he told you anything?

NORA. Yes. These cards mean that he has taken his last leave of us. He is going to shut himself up and die.

HELMER. Poor fellow! Of course I knew we couldn't hope to keep him long. But so soon——! And to go and creep into his lair like a wounded animal——

NORA. When we must go, it is best to go silently. Don't you think so, Torvald?

HELMER. (*Walking up and down.*) He had so grown into our lives, I can't realise that he is gone. He and his sufferings and his loneliness formed a sort of cloudy background to the sunshine of our happiness—Well, perhaps it's best as it is—at any rate for him. (*Stands still.*) And perhaps for us too, Nora. Now we two are thrown entirely upon each other. (*Takes her in his arms.*) My darling wife! I feel as if I could never hold you close enough. Do you know, Nora, I often wish some danger might threaten you, that I might risk body and soul, and everything, everything, for your dear sake.

NORA. (*Tears herself from him and says firmly.*) Now you shall read your letters, Torvald.

HELMER. No, no; not to-night. I want to be with you, my sweet wife.

NORA. With the thought of your dying friend——?

HELMER. You are right. This has shaken us both. Unloveliness has come between us—thoughts of death and decay. We must seek to cast them off. Till then—we will remain apart.

NORA. (*Her arms round his neck.*) Torvald! Good-night! good-night!

HELMER. (*Kissing her forehead.*) Good-night, my little songbird. Sleep well, Nora. Now I shall go and read my letters. (*He goes with the letters in his hand into his room and shuts the door.*)

NORA. (*With wild eyes, gropes about her, seizes* HELMER'S *domino, throws it round her, and whispers quickly, hoarsely, and brokenly.*) Never to see him again. Never, never, never. (*Throws her shawl over her head.*) Never to see the children again. Never, never,—Oh that black, icy water! Oh that bottom-less——! If it were only over! Now he has it; he's reading it. Oh, no, no, no, not yet. Torvald, good-bye——! Good-bye, my little ones——! *(She is rushing out by the hall; at the same moment* HELMER *flings his door open, and stands there with an open letter in his hand.)*

HELMER. Nora!

NORA. *(Shrieks.)* Ah——!

HELMER. What is this? Do you know what is in this letter?

NORA. Yes, I know. Let me go! Let me pass!

HELMER. *(Holds her back.)* Where do you want to go?

NORA. *(Tries to break away from him.)* You shall not save me, Torvald.

HELMER. *(Falling back.)* True! Is what he writes true? No, no, it is impossible that this can be true.

NORA. It is true. I have loved you beyond all else in the world.

HELMER. Pshaw—no silly evasions!

NORA. *(A step nearer him.)* Torvald——!

HELMER. Wretched woman—what have you done!

NORA. Let me go—you shall not save me! You shall not take my guilt upon yourself!

HELMER. I don't want any melodramatic airs. *(Locks the outer door.)* Here you shall stay and give an account of yourself. Do you understand what you have done? Answer! Do you understand it?

NORA. *(Looks at him fixedly, and says with a stiffening expression.)* Yes; now I begin fully to understand it.

HELMER. *(Walking up and down.)* Oh! what an awful awakening! During all these eight years—she who was my pride and my joy—a hypocrite, a liar—worse, worse—a criminal. Oh, the unfathomable hideousness of it all! Ugh! Ugh! *(NORA says nothing, and continues to look fixedly at him.)*

HELMER. I ought to have known how it would be. I ought to have foreseen it. All your father's want of principle—be silent—all your father's want of principle you have inherited—no religion, no morality, no sense of duty. How I am punished for screening him! I did it for your sake; and you reward me like this.

NORA. Yes—like this.

HELMER. You have destroyed my whole happiness. You have ruined my future. Oh, it's frightful to think of! I am in the power of a scoundrel; he can do whatever he pleases with me, demand whatever he chooses; he can domineer over me as much as he likes, and I must submit. And all this disaster and ruin is brought upon me by an unprincipled woman!

NORA. When I am out of the world, you will be free.

HELMER. Oh, no fine phrases. Your father, too, was always ready with them. What good would it do me, if you were "out of the world," as you say? No good whatever! He can publish the story all the same; I might even be suspected of collusion. People will think I was at the bottom of it all and egged you on. And for all this I have you to thank—you whom I

have done nothing but pet and spoil during our whole married life. Do
you understand now what you have done to me?

NORA. *(With cold calmness.)* Yes.

HELMER. The thing is so incredible, I can't grasp it. But we must come to an
understanding. Take that shawl off. Take it off, I say! I must try to pacify
him in one way or another—the matter must be hushed up, cost what it
may.—As for you and me, we must make no outward change in our way
of life—no outward change, you understand. Of course, you will continue
to live here. But the children cannot be left in your care. I dare not trust
them to you.—Oh, to have to say this to one I have loved so tenderly—
whom I still——! But that must be a thing of the past. Henceforward
there can be no question of happiness, but merely of saving the ruins, the
shreds, the show——*(A ring;* HELMER *starts.)* What's that? So late! Can
it be the worst? Can he——? Hide yourself, Nora; say you are ill. *(*NORA
stands motionless. HELMER *goes to the door and opens it.)*

ELLEN. *(Half dressed, in the hall.)* Here is a letter for you, ma'am.

HELMER. Give it to me. *(Seizes the letter and shuts the door.)* Yes, from him.
You shall not have it. I shall read it.

NORA. Read it!

HELMER. *(By the lamp.)* I have hardly the courage to. We may both be lost,
both you and I. Ah! I must know. *(Hastily tears the letter open; reads a few
lines, looks at an enclosure; with a cry of joy.)* Nora! *(*NORA *looks inquiringly
at him.)*

HELMER. Nora!—Oh! I must read it again.—Yes, yes, it is so. I am saved!
Nora, I am saved!

NORA. And I?

HELMER. You too, of course; we are both saved, both of us. Look here—he
sends you back your promissory note. He writes that he regrets and apol-
ogises, that a happy turn in his life——Oh, what matter what he writes.
We are saved, Nora! No one can harm you. Oh, Nora, Nora——; but
first to get rid of this hateful thing. I'll just see——*(Glances at the I.O.U.)*
No, I will not look at it; the whole thing shall be nothing but a dream to
me. *(Tears the I.O.U. and both letters in pieces. Throws them into the fire and
watches them burn.)* There! it's gone!—He said that ever since Christmas
Eve—— Oh, Nora, they must have been three terrible days for you!

NORA. I have fought a hard fight for the last three days.

HELMER. And in your agony you saw no other outlet but——No; we won't
think of that horror. We will only rejoice and repeat—it's over, all over!
Don't you hear, Nora? You don't seem able to grasp it. Yes, it's over.
What is this set look on your face? Oh, my poor Nora, I understand; you
cannot believe that I have forgiven you. But I have, Nora; I swear it. I
have forgiven everything. I know that what you did was all for love of
me.

NORA. That is true.

HELMER. You loved me as a wife should love her husband. It was only the means that, in your inexperience, you misjudged. But do you think I love you the less because you cannot do without guidance? No, no. Only lean on me; I will counsel you, and guide you. I should be no true man if this very womanly helplessness did not make you doubly dear in my eyes. You mustn't dwell upon the hard things I said in my first moment of terror, when the world seemed to be tumbling about my ears. I have forgiven you, Nora—I swear I have forgiven you.

NORA. I thank you for your forgiveness. *(Goes out, to the right.)*

HELMER. No, stay——! *(Looking through the doorway.)* What are you going to do?

NORA. *(Inside.)* To take off my masquerade dress.

HELMER. *(In the doorway.)* Yes, do, dear. Try to calm down, and recover your balance, my scared little song-bird. You may rest secure. I have broad wings to shield you. *(Walking up and down near the door.)* Oh, how lovely—how cosy our home is, Nora! Here you are safe; here I can shelter you like a hunted dove whom I have saved from the claws of the hawk. I shall soon bring your poor beating heart to rest; believe me, Nora, very soon. To-morrow all this will seem quite different—everything will be as before. I shall not need to tell you again that I forgive you; you will feel for yourself that it is true. How could you think I could find it in my heart to drive you away, or even so much as to reproach you? Oh, you don't know a true man's heart, Nora. There is something indescribably sweet and soothing to a man in having forgiven his wife—honestly forgiven her, from the bottom of his heart. She becomes his property in a double sense. She is as though born again; she has become, so to speak, at once his wife and his child. That is what you shall henceforth be to me, my bewildered, helpless darling. Don't be troubled about anything, Nora; only open your heart to me, and I will be both will and conscience to you. *(NORA enters in everyday dress.)* Why, what's this? Not gone to bed? You have changed your dress?

NORA. Yes, Torvald; now I have changed my dress.

HELMER. But why now, so late——?

NORA. I shall not sleep to-night.

HELMER. But, Nora dear——

NORA. *(Looking at her watch.)* It's not so late yet. Sit down, Torvald; you and I have much to say to each other. (She sits at one side of the table.)

HELMER. Nora—what does this mean? Your cold, set face——

NORA. Sit down. It will take some time. I have much to talk over with you. *(HELMER sits at the other side of the table.)*

HELMER. You alarm me, Nora. I don't understand you.

NORA. No, that is just it. You don't understand me; and I have never understood you—till to-night. No, don't interrupt. Only listen to what I say.—We must come to a final settlement, Torvald.

HELMER. How do you mean?

NORA. *(After a short silence.)* Does not one thing strike you as we sit here?

HELMER. What should strike me?

NORA. We have been married eight years. Does it not strike you that this is the first time we two, you and I, man and wife, have talked together seriously?

HELMER. Seriously! What do you call seriously?

NORA. During eight whole years, and more—ever since the day we first met—we have never exchanged one serious word about serious things.

HELMER. Was I always to trouble you with the cares you could not help me to bear?

NORA. I am not talking of cares. I say that we have never yet set ourselves seriously to get to the bottom of anything.

HELMER. Why, my dearest Nora, what have you to do with serious things?

NORA. There we have it! You have never understood me—I have had great injustice done me, Torvald; first by father, and then by you.

HELMER. What! By your father and me?—By us, who have loved you more than all the world?

NORA. *(Shaking her head.)* You have never loved me. You only thought it amusing to be in love with me.

HELMER. Why, Nora, what a thing to say!

NORA. Yes, it is so, Torvald. While I was at home with father, he used to tell me all his opinions, and I held the same opinions. If I had others I said nothing about them, because he wouldn't have liked it. He used to call me his doll-child, and played with me as I played with my dolls. Then I came to live in your house——

HELMER. What an expression to use about our marriage!

NORA. *(Undisturbed.)* I mean I passed from father's hands into yours. You arranged everything according to your taste; and I got the same tastes as you; or I pretended to—I don't know which—both ways, perhaps; sometimes one and sometimes the other. When I look back on it now, I seem to have been living here like a beggar, from hand to mouth. I lived by performing tricks for you, Torvald. But you would have it so. You and father have done me a great wrong. It is your fault that my life has come to nothing.

HELMER. Why, Nora, how unreasonable and ungrateful you are! Have you not been happy here?

NORA. No, never. I thought I was; but I never was.

HELMER. Not—not happy!

NORA. No; only merry. And you have always been so kind to me. But our house has been nothing but a play-room. Here I have been your doll-wife, just as at home I used to be papa's doll-child. And the children, in their turn, have been my dolls. I thought it fun when you played with me, just as the children did when I played with them. That has been our marriage, Torvald.

HELMER. There is some truth in what you say, exaggerated and overstrained though it be. But henceforth it shall be different. Play-time is over; now comes the time for education.

NORA. Whose education? Mine, or the children's?

HELMER. Both, my dear Nora.

NORA. Oh, Torvald, you are not the man to teach me to be a fit wife for you.

HELMER. And you can say that?

NORA. And I—how have I prepared myself to educate the children?

HELMER. Nora!

NORA. Did you not say yourself, a few minutes ago, you dared not trust them to me?

HELMER. In the excitement of the moment! Why should you dwell upon that?

NORA. No—you were perfectly right. That problem is beyond me. There is another to be solved first—I must try to educate myself. You are not the man to help me in that. I must set about it alone. And that is why I am leaving you.

HELMER. *(Jumping up.)* What—do you mean to say——?

NORA. I must stand quite alone if I am ever to know myself and my surroundings; so I cannot stay with you.

HELMER. Nora! Nora!

NORA. I am going at once. I daresay Christina will take me in for to-night——

HELMER. You are mad! I shall not allow it! I forbid it!

NORA. It is of no use your forbidding me anything now. I shall take with me what belongs to me. From you I will accept nothing, either now or afterwards.

HELMER. What madness this is!

NORA. To-morrow I shall go home—I mean to what was my home. It will be easier for me to find some opening there.

HELMER. Oh, in your blind inexperience——

NORA. I must try to gain experience, Torvald.

HELMER. To forsake your home, your husband, and your children! And you don't consider what the world will say.

NORA. I can pay no heed to that. I only know that I must do it.

HELMER. This is monstrous! Can you forsake your holiest duties in this way?

NORA. What do you consider my holiest duties?

HELMER. Do I need to tell you that? Your duties to your husband and your children.

NORA. I have other duties equally sacred.

HELMER. Impossible! What duties do you mean?

NORA. My duties towards myself.

HELMER. Before all else you are a wife and a mother.

NORA. That I no longer believe. I believe that before all else I am a human being, just as much as you are—or at least that I should try to become one. I know that most people agree with you, Torvald, and that they say so in books. But henceforth I can't be satisfied with what most people say, and what is in books. I must think things out for myself, and try to get clear about them.

HELMER. Are you not clear about your place in your own home? Have you not an infallible guide in questions like these? Have you not religion?

NORA. Oh, Torvald, I don't really know what religion is.

HELMER. What do you mean?

NORA. I know nothing but what Pastor Hansen told me when I was confirmed. He explained that religion was this and that. When I get away from all this and stand alone, I will look into that matter too. I will see whether what he taught me is right, or, at any rate, whether it is right for me.

HELMER. Oh, this is unheard of! And from so young a woman! But if religion cannot keep you right, let me appeal to your conscience—for I suppose you have some moral feeling? Or, answer me: perhaps you have none?

NORA. Well, Torvald, it's not easy to say. I really don't know—I am all at sea about these things. I only know that I think quite differently from you about them. I hear, too, that the laws are different from what I thought; but I can't believe that they can be right. It appears that a woman has no right to spare her dying father, or to save her husband's life! I don't believe that.

HELMER. You talk like a child. You don't understand the society in which you live.

NORA. No, I do not. But now I shall try to learn. I must make up my mind which is right—society or I.

HELMER. Nora, you are ill; you are feverish; I almost think you are out of your senses.

NORA. I have never felt so much clearness and certainty as to-night.

HELMER. You are clear and certain enough to forsake husband and children?

NORA. Yes, I am.

HELMER. Then there is one explanation possible.

NORA. What is that?

HELMER. You no longer love me.

NORA. No; that is just it.

HELMER. Nora!—Can you say so!

NORA. Oh, I'm so sorry, Torvald; for you've always been so kind to me. But I can't help it. I do not love you any longer.

HELMER. (*Mastering himself with difficulty.*) Are you clear and certain on this point too?

NORA. Yes, quite. That is why I will not stay here any longer.

HELMER. And can you also make clear to me how I have forfeited your love?

NORA. Yes, I can. It was this evening, when the miracle did not happen; for then I saw you were not the man I had imagined.

HELMER. Explain yourself more clearly; I don't understand.

NORA. I have waited so patiently all these eight years; for of course I saw clearly enough that miracles don't happen every day. When this crushing blow threatened me, I said to myself so confidently, "Now comes the miracle!" When Krogstad's letter lay in the box, it never for a moment occurred to me that you would think of submitting to that man's conditions. I was convinced that you would say to him, "Make it known to all the world"; and that then——

HELMER. Well? When I had given my own wife's name up to disgrace and shame——?

NORA. Then I firmly believed that you would come forward, take everything upon yourself, and say, "I am the guilty one."

HELMER. Nora——!

NORA. You mean I would never have accepted such a sacrifice? No, certainly not. But what would my assertions have been worth in opposition to yours?—That was the miracle that I hoped for and dreaded. And it was to hinder that that I wanted to die.

HELMER. I would gladly work for you day and night, Nora—bear sorrow and want for your sake. But no man sacrifices his honour, even for one he loves.

NORA. Millions of women have done so.

HELMER. Oh, you think and talk like a silly child.

NORA. Very likely. But you neither think nor talk like the man I can share my life with. When your terror was over—not for what threatened me, but for yourself—when there was nothing more to fear—then it seemed to you as though nothing had happened. I was your lark again, your doll, just as before—whom you would take twice as much care of in future, because she was so weak and fragile. *(Stands up.)* Torvald—in that moment it burst upon me that I had been living here these eight years with a strange man, and had borne him three children.—Oh, I can't bear to think of it! I could tear myself to pieces!

HELMER. *(Sadly.)* I see it, I see it; an abyss has opened between us.—But, Nora, can it never be filled up?

NORA. As I now am, I am no wife for you.

HELMER. I have strength to become another man.

NORA. Perhaps—when your doll is taken away from you.

HELMER. To part—to part from you! No, Nora, no; I can't grasp the thought.

NORA. *(Going into room on the right.)* The more reason for the thing to happen.

(She comes back with out-door things and a small travelling-bag, which she places on a chair.)

HELMER. Nora, Nora, not now! Wait till to-morrow.

NORA. *(Putting on cloak.)* I can't spend the night in a strange man's house.

HELMER. But can we not live here, as brother and sister——?

NORA. *(Fastening her hat.)* You know very well that wouldn't last long. *(Puts on the shawl.)* Good-bye, Torvald. No, I won't go to the children. I know they are in better hands than mine. As I now am, I can be nothing to them.

HELMER. But some time, Nora—some time——?

NORA. How can I tell? I have no idea what will become of me.

HELMER. But you are my wife, now and always!

NORA. Listen, Torvald—when a wife leaves her husband's house, as I am doing, I have heard that in the eyes of the law he is free from all duties towards her. At any rate, I release you from all duties. You must not feel yourself bound, any more than I shall. There must be perfect freedom on both sides. There, I give you back your ring. Give me mine.

HELMER. That too?

NORA. That too.

HELMER. Here it is.

NORA. Very well. Now it is all over. I lay the keys here. The servants know about everything in the house—better than I do. To-morrow, when I have started, Christina will come to pack up the things I brought with me from home. I will have them sent after me.

HELMER. All over! all over! Nora, will you never think of me again?

NORA. Oh, I shall often think of you, and the children, and this house.

HELMER. May I write to you, Nora?

NORA. No—never. You must not.

HELMER. But I must send you——

NORA. Nothing, nothing.

HELMER. I must help you if you need it.

NORA. No, I say. I take nothing from strangers.

HELMER. Nora—can I never be more than a stranger to you?

NORA. *(Taking her travelling-bag.)* Oh, Torvald, then the miracle of miracles would have to happen——

HELMER. What is the miracle of miracles?

NORA. Both of us would have to change so that——Oh, Torvald, I no longer believe in miracles.

HELMER. But *I* will believe. Tell me! We must so change that——?

NORA. That communion between us shall be a marriage. Good-bye. *(She goes out by the hall door.)*

HELMER. *(Sinks into a chair by the door with his face in his hands.)* Nora! Nora! *(He looks round and rises.)* Empty. She is gone. *(A hope springs up in him.)* Ah! The miracle of miracles——?! *(From below is heard the reverberation of a heavy door closing.)*

4

Character

Introduction

Works of fiction are populated by people, or by animals, machines, or ideas that are generally given human characteristics. We expect these characters to be credible in their own fictive worlds, whether they develop during the course of the story, or whether they remain unchanged. Ma Joad, for example, is fully characterized the first time John Steinbeck introduces her in *The Grapes of Wrath* and, in spite of considerable alterations in her circumstances, she is essentially the same when the novel concludes. Macbeth, on the other hand, develops as a character throughout the duration of the play. We don't feel we know him until the play is over. Unlike Ma Joad, Macbeth changes rapidly in a very short span of time; his disintegration is fully credible because he retains an important degree of psychological consistency. Both these characters play major roles in their respective works, and we expect them to be more fully realized than minor characters would be. E. M. Forster has called the latter "flat characters," as opposed to the "round characters" (such as Ma Joad or Macbeth) who are the protagonists. Characters can also be abstractions, although these occur most often in works of allegorical fiction. But Graham Greene's "The Basement Room" includes someone called "Justice," which designates the way he is perceived by the young protagonist of the story. In film, however, minor characters and abstractions are necessarily physical beings and thus have a specificity their literary counterparts often lack.

Creating such characters is a major task for the novelist, playwright, or filmmaker, but each has many methods at his or her disposal. One of the most obvious of these is appearance. Our first direct impressions of people are based on their physical attributes and choice of clothing, since most people convey messages by what they wear and how they wear it, even though these messages may be misleading. On seeing the witches in Macbeth, Banquo's opening comment concerns their appearance:

> What are these,
> So withered and so wild in their attire
> That look not like th' inhabitants o' th' earth
> And yet are on 't?

Changes in appearance can often signal more fundamental changes. When Ross confronts Banquo and Macbeth shortly after the witches' prophecy and addresses Macbeth as Thane of Cawdor, Macbeth replies:

> The Thane of Cawdor lives. Why do you dress me
> In borrowed robes?

Images of clothing are used throughout the play to indicate Macbeth's situation. Later, Banquo notes:

> New honors come upon him
> Like our strange garments, cleave not to their mould
> But with the aid of use.

And in the last act, when Macbeth has lost his power, Angus comments upon his forlorn state:

> Those he commands move only in command,
> Nothing in love. Now does he feel his title
> Hang loose about him, like a giant's robe
> Upon a dwarfish thief.

Macbeth's physical changes are an index of his moral decline.

Early fiction frequently employed lengthy physical descriptions, and these often slowed down the pace of the narrative or stopped it entirely, which is sometimes true of Steinbeck's descriptions. When Ma Joad is presented for the first time, Steinbeck halts the action and devotes a page to her appearance and role in the family. With this description her character is complete and the action can resume. However, modern writers are more apt to seize on a few significant physical details and to fill in the character as the work unfolds. Here filmmakers have an advantage: Because of the nature of the medium, they can present a character's appearance while telling the story. Ma Joad's physical appearance is important in John Ford's film, but she is simultaneously shown in action, which advances the plot and develops her character just as much as her appearance does.

As we learn from the physical appearance of a character, so do we learn from the appearance of the world that surrounds him, and the ways he interacts with it. *Macbeth* opens with a scene on the heath, where thunder and lightning form a backdrop for the incantations of the three witches:

> Fair is foul, and foul is fair.
> Hover through the fog and filthy air.

The darkness and chaotic nature of this scene, enforced by the reversal of moral values in the language of the witches, establish an important mood for the dramatic action. The scenes following occur primarily at night, until the last act where the predominance of daylight suggests a restoration of order. The setting, in its most general form, evokes moral values that inform the themes of the play.

A character's personal environment also reflects him. The choice of decorations in a home, for example, can reveal a great deal about the inhabitants. When Miranda awakens in Wyler's film, *The Collector* and finds herself imprisoned in a basement room, her horror is increased as she discovers that this environment has been made for her alone. The room is decorated as her captor believes she would have decorated her own room, and thus, it reveals his understanding (however limited) of her character. Tony Richardson uses the bleak home environment in *The Loneliness of the Long-Distance Runner* to characterize his protagonist and his family. The exterior urban landscape functions in the same way. In one of the most tender moments of the film, the two couples are seated on a hill talking to each other for the first time when a train suddenly crosses the barren landscape, reminding them (and us) that they are in an industrial wasteland. When they embrace, Richardson emphasizes the barbed wire fence behind them. How differently we would respond to this scene if the setting were pastoral! In film, setting, like a character's appearance, can be presented while the action is occurring. In addition, settings assume an added significance in film because of their virtual omnipresence.

The importance of heredity, like environment, depends on the needs of the artist for each particular work. All human characters in a work of fiction theoretically have families and past histories that have helped form them. In *The Loneliness of the Long-Distance Runner*, the protagonist's family is shown to be an important determinant of his character. Miss Julie's struggle with the influence of her dead mother becomes the focus of Strindberg's drama. The protagonist of *The Collector* is driven in part by feelings of social inferiority resulting from his background. The extent to which heredity is emphasized depends on the purposes of the writer and filmmaker, but the possibilities are considerable.

Figurative language is also an important tool of characterization: It can be employed to illuminate the teller of the tale (for example, in a first-person narration), and/or the object to which it is applied. When, at the end of Part I of *The Stranger*, Meursault squeezes the trigger of his pistol and describes "each successive shot" as "another loud, fateful rap on the door of my undoing," he is revealing more about his perception of his own fate than about the sounds of a gun. With an omniscient narrator, we learn more about the object being described, as when the narrator of "The Basement Room" describes Mrs. Baines's voice as being "like the voice in a nightmare." As we shall see in our chapter on figurative language, these means can also be employed by the filmmaker. But all of the above methods are primarily descriptive and take us only so far. To understand characters more fully, we must observe them in action and also get a sense of their interior lives.

There have traditionally been two ways of presenting character, neither of them necessarily used exclusively: "showing," also called "the dramatic method," and "telling," where the narrator can intervene and explain actions and motivations. A novelist employing the dramatic method of characterization sets a character before us and lets us draw conclusions from what we observe, as we do at the performance of a play, or daily, with the people we meet. Thus, we watch characters speaking, both to others and at times to themselves, and we also notice their physical gestures and mannerisms. At the same time, we hear and see the speeches and actions of others, which confirm or deny what a character is saying. Of course, novelists determine how their character acts and what is said; however, with the dramatic method, novelists try to remove themselves as much as possible from their stories.

Whether in fiction, drama, or film, dialogue is used simultaneously for characterization and for plot development. The use of language (both the character's vocabulary and patterns of speech) is as important as what is said. Compare the first lines spoken by Mrs. Baines in "The Basement Room" with those of her husband:

Be off out of here, Master Philip. . . .

Come in, Phil, and make yourself at home. Wait a moment and I'll do the honours. . . .

The terseness of the first command and the formality of address contrast markedly with the genial informality of Baines's invitation. In fiction as in life, we can identify characters by their voices or range of voices. The language must be in character: Baines could never talk like Macbeth, or vice versa.

By showing characters speaking or thinking, authors can indicate how characters' attitudes about themselves conflict with the attitudes others have of them. Neither what characters say about themselves nor what others say about them is necessarily true: We can evaluate such statements in the context of the story or play and judge them accordingly. Authors can also show how characters' attitudes about themselves conflict with their real motivations. For example, characters may consider themselves altruistic and may even perform generous deeds when actually motivated by selfish desires. Here we are dealing more with modes of characterization that penetrate the interior of a character. The tension between illusion and reality can be a good source of characterization for the writer. One way of showing this tension in novels is the stream of consciousness technique, where we are given access to the character's thoughts in an apparently random sequence of associations. Another way is contrasting the attitudes of others toward the character, which would either confirm or undercut his or her self-image. Through the favorable testimony of the narrators of the prefatory chapter, Henry James creates a strong bias in his readers' minds toward the governess who narrates the principal story in *The Turn of the Screw*. In film the total visual context (including lighting, composition, camera position, choice of lens, etc.) shapes our attitude toward what we see and hear. When, for example, Kane reads his "Declaration of Principles" to Leland and Bernstein in *Citizen Kane*, the dark shadows on his face and the low camera angle undercut the lofty ideals he espouses.

Actions, like words, reveal a great deal about a character. In *The Treasure of the Sierra Madre*, Curtin and Dobbs have equal opportunities to betray each other for Howard's gold, but only Dobbs seizes the opportunity. Macbeth and Banquo both receive prophecies from the witches, but only Macbeth acts on them. As Henry James noted: "What is character but determination of incident? What is incident but the illustration of character?" The elements of plot and character may be separated for the purposes of discussion, but in a work of fiction these are intertwined.

Many of these methods are employed equally when "telling," but we remain more aware of the narrator's presence with that type of presentation. Clearly, in attempting to "show" their protagonists in action and to develop their characters more objectively, the modern novelist and short story writer have drawn heavily on the playwright's techniques. Filmmakers, in turn, embrace many of the methods of the playwright, novelist, and short story writer, and to these techniques they add those that are the property of their medium alone.

Additional Recommended Films

Greed (1924), directed by Eric Von Stroheim, based on the novel *McTeague* by Frank Norris. The novel and the script are available in paperback.

All the King's Men (1949), directed by Robert Rossen, based on the novel by Robert Penn Warren. The novel and the script are available in paperback.

The French Lieutenant's Woman (1982), directed by Karel Reisz, based on the novel by John Fowles. The novel is available in paperback and the script in hardback.

See Also:

The Grapes of Wrath (Chapter 3)
The Member of the Wedding (Chapter 3)
The Collector (Chapter 5)
The Innocents (Chapter 5)
Blow-up (Chapter 6)
Women in Love (Chapter 7)
The Rocking-Horse Winner (Chapter 8)

The Treasure of the Sierra Madre

The Treasure of the Sierra Madre (1948) was John Huston's first postwar film, and critics hailed it as the fulfillment of the promise shown in his early narrative films, such as *The Maltese Falcon* (1941), and his wartime documentaries. The subject was not one calculated to have great audience appeal, for Huston's movie is a study of greed, fear, and the breakdown of personality in the absence of those controls imposed by civilization. Moreover, there is no romantic interest, and the movie lacks the happy ending typical of Hollywood productions of that period. Yet *The Treasure of the Sierra Madre* was a popular success, and Huston received two Academy Awards for best script and for best direction. In addition, his father, Walter Huston, won an Academy Award for best supporting actor.

Huston's film is based on B. Traven's novel, *The Treasure of the Sierra Madre* (1935). Traven chronicles the white man's relentless and corrupting pursuit of wealth by focusing on three American drifters living in Mexico in the 1920s who decide to try their luck at prospecting in a remote, isolated mountain area. But Traven has greater ambitions than merely writing an adventure story. He contrasts the Indians' and the white men's cultures and examines the economic and social exploitation that has resulted from their confrontation. Traven depicts the Indians' struggle to preserve their values in the face of domination by Spanish conquerors and later by Americans. The prospecting of the three Americans exemplifies a historical process that has been occurring for several centuries. Huston eliminates the historical material and the social commentary that accompanies it, although he retains the contrast of the two cultures through Howard's contact with the Indians. As a film *The Treasure of the Sierra Madre* becomes primarily a drama of man in conflict with himself.

Huston clearly conceives of the three men as a unit, much like aspects of a single self. Howard has the strongest sense of personal identity. He provides moral leadership and practical knowledge and is the only person in touch with the environment and the uncorrupted forces represented by the Indians. It is he who suggests that the mountain be put back together after its riches have been plundered, and when, at the end of the film, he returns to live with the Indians, we feel that he has made an appropriate choice. In both the book and film Curtin is the least clearly delineated of the characters. He has a conscience and a boyish naiveté. Yet Curtin is unable to act without another's support. In the film he shares Howard's love of the land, and this finally provides him with a vocation. Fred C. Dobbs has the greatest potential for mercurial malevolence: When the last vestiges of civilized restraint are removed, his base instincts take over. Together, the three form a system of checks and balances, which Huston emphasizes by framing. In the early shot of Dobbs and Curtin shaking hands while Howard sits between them, Howard provides a strong center, literally balancing the shot, as he does time and again in the first parts of the film. Huston frequently stresses the importance of the unity of the three. Howard is not present when the mine collapses, and Curtin momentarily thinks of leaving Dobbs inside to die. On yet another occasion, believing him to be stealing his gold, Dobbs draws his gun on Curtin. When Howard joins them, order is restored. The final breakdown occurs when the Indians insist on taking Howard back to their village to repay him for saving the life of the Indian boy, thereby leaving Curtin and Dobbs alone together.

Fred C. Dobbs is the most important of the protagonists, and the ways Huston develops his character amply illustrate the means a director has at his command. The film begins with a dissolve to a close-up of a poster displaying winning lottery numbers. The time (February 14, 1925), the place (Mexico), and an important theme of the film (the lure of easy money) are established in the first shot. Then the camera pulls back to reveal a pair of dirty hands examining a lottery ticket. Underneath the arm is a bundle wrapped in old newspapers. A losing ticket is torn up, and the pieces are scattered on the street. Only then, as Dobbs turns and walks through the crowded marketplace, panhandling unsuccessfully, are we permitted to see the rest of the

The Treasure of the Sierra Madre. A bargain is struck: The framing suggests the central role (and the solidity) of Howard.

person. In just a few shots Huston has characterized Dobbs as a loser, an impoverished outcast trying to exist on luck and handouts.

Huston expands two scenes from the early pages of the novel to develop the positive sides of Dobb's character: Dobbs's attempt to collect the earnings owed to him by McCormick and the formation of his partnership with Curtin. In the first of these, McCormick starts a fight with Dobbs and Curtin, while buying them drinks. After a brutal battle (which has no basis in the novel), Dobbs and Curtin beat McCormick senseless on the floor, and Dobbs removes McCormick's wallet from his jacket pocket. Counting aloud, Dobbs takes what McCormick owes them and drops the rest of the money (a sizable amount) on his recumbent form. Although Dobbs clearly has the potential for violence and a propensity to talk to himself (which will be developed later as madness overtakes him), he also seems basically honest, taking only what belongs to him.

Dobbs's generosity becomes evident near the beginning of the film when he offers Curtin a cigarette, another incident without basis in the novel. This quality is affirmed when Dobbs shares the proceeds from his lottery ticket with Curtin, thus enabling him to join the partnership. By emphasizing Dobb's positive qualities early in the film, Huston makes the corrosive effects of gold on him even more pronounced.

Dobbs's attitude toward money is established as Huston shows us how Dobbs spends what cash he does have. He begs three times from the man in the white suit. With the first handout, Dobbs buys a meal and more cigarettes. Huston combines this scene with the one from the book where Dobbs purchases a fraction of yet another lottery ticket, which he knows he cannot afford. Dobbs spends his second handout on a haircut. The shot of him proudly examining his slicked down hair in the barber shop mirror emphasizes his egocentricity. With his third handout Dobbs sets off in pursuit of a prostitute, but he pauses on the way to ask another American for money. These scenes immediately establish the system of values by which Fred C. Dobbs operates.

Dobbs's disintegration begins early in the film and is developed with much greater detail than in the novel. We have already noticed how Dobbs counts McCormick's money aloud. Later, in the Mexican hills, Dobbs complains to himself about having to go into the village for provisions. He is suspicious and resentful, and so Curtin goes instead, after commenting to Howard on Dobbs's habit of mumbling to himself. Dobbs talks to himself constantly after his attempted murder of Curtin. In the novel Traven writes: " 'Maybe,' he was thinking, 'I didn't bump him off at all. Perhaps he only staggered and dropped to the ground without being hit. Let's figure that out. How is it?' " In the film Huston transforms these thoughts into a monologue that, in addition to conveying information, emphasizes Dobbs's rapidly disintegrating mind.

For Huston dialogue is an important means of characterization. Some conversations are taken directly from the book (although usually abridged),

The Treasure of the Sierra Madre. What Dobbs might have been: The Man in the White Suit (John Huston, the director).

and others are created from the omniscient third-person narration Traven employs. The following passage is a good example of the transformation of narration into dialogue. Traven's narrator speculates on how Dobbs can make money:

> Even if Dobbs had had three pesos to buy the outfit, bootblacking was out, for he could not be a bootblack here among the natives. No white had ever tried to run around here shouting: "Shine, mister?" He would rather die. A white may sit on a bench in the plaza in rags, three-fourths starved; he may beg and humiliate himself before another white; he may even commit burglary or other crimes . . . But should he happen to shine shoes in the street, or beg from a native anything but water . . . then he would sink below the lowest native and would die from starvation.

In the film these observations become a conversation between Dobbs and Curtin, which characterizes them by revealing their attitudes toward the subject, rather than the narrator's.

The power struggle between Dobbs and Curtin that follows Howard's departure is developed in part through framing. We have already noticed

framing used to convey balance and equality, and here it suggests supremacy. Dobbs is at first alone in the frame, and when he is joined by Curtin he
dominates the frame by being in the right foreground. Dobbs is almost always
closest to us, except for over-the-shoulder shots (from behind Curtin), where
he dominates by facing us. At the end of the sequence, he is again alone in
the frame. In this way Curtin's relative weakness is underlined.

Nearly half the film occurs at night, and Huston uses lighting very effectively, especially to stress the sinister aspects of Dobbs's personality. When
Dobbs awakens Curtin and seizes him by the hair, the side lighting emphasizes Dobbs's power over Curtin and makes Dobbs appear satanic. After his
attempted murder of Curtin (which, like Dobbs's later murder by the bandits,
takes place off camera), Dobbs sits behind the flames of the bonfire that separate him from the camera. The flames seem to rise higher and higher as
Dobbs lies down and the camera lowers with him. The flickering light on his
face suggests his insanity, and finally the flames appear to engulf the entire
screen. Metaphorically, Dobbs is in hell, and the cinematic trope renders this
effectively.

The next morning Dobbs awakens and begins worrying about Curtin's
corpse. Here Dobbs's mental confusion is depicted physically, as he darts to
and fro, stumbling and continually talking to himself. The moving camera
underlines this effect. Although it is daylight, Dobbs's face is now in shadows. He literally doesn't know which way to turn, and his disorientation is
emphasized as Huston dissolves to the tranquil, bucolic setting where Howard is relaxing in a hammock. The juxtaposition of frenzy and repose perfectly characterizes the two men at this point.

Huston also develops Dobbs's character by expanding the role of the
bandit with the golden sombrero who becomes Dobbs's nemesis. The bandit
is first seen leading the attack on the train carrying Dobbs, Curtin, and Howard south (the dramatization of a story related by Lacaud in the novel). As the
Federales drive the bandits away, Dobbs comments, "Sure wish I'd got him,"
an understatement of rather colossal proportions. When the prospectors are
attacked in their camp by bandits, again the figure with the golden sombrero
leads them. In the novel Curtin crouches in a foxhole and keeps the bandit
at bay, but Huston has Dobbs confront the bandit at close range. The bandit
is the darker side of Dobbs's own personality, and if Dobbs appears victorious at this moment, it is only because he has the support of Howard, Curtin, and Cody (as Lacaud is called in the film). After his attempted murder of
Curtin, Dobbs confronts his nemesis for the last time. In Traven's novel
Dobbs meets "three ragged tramps" quite by chance: "As he [Dobbs] returned the water-bag to the saddle, he heard somebody say: *'Tiene un cigaro,
hombre?* Have you got a cigarette?' " Huston makes this into a suspenseful
encounter with the self. Exhausted and out of water, Dobbs is stumbling
across the desert with his burros when he comes upon a waterhole. Dobbs
pushes the burros aside and plunges his face into the murky water. As the
pool clears, he sees in the water the reflection of the glittering golden som-

The Treasure of the Sierra Madre. What Dobbs has become: The Man in the Gold Hat.

brero of the Mexican bandit. Then Dobbs turns and observes its owner standing above him on the rim of the waterhole. The viewer immediately identifies the bandit and the bandit recognizes Dobbs, but Dobbs is the last to understand and it is then too late. He is destroyed by the man who exemplifies the darkest aspects of his own self.

For much of the remainder of the film, Huston relies entirely on visuals to tell his story. The three bandits argue in Spanish over the division of

Dobb's goods, showing that they, too, are afflicted by greed. After discarding the bags of gold, they ride into town to sell the burros and the hides. The Indians are suspicious and check the brand marks, which we had seen being carefully copied into registers earlier in the film. The denouement is perfectly clear, whether or not we understand the Spanish being spoken. The bandits are taken into custody, asked to dig their graves, and then executed on the spot.

Howard and Curtin hear the shots as they ride into town. Unlike the book, where they finally find a few sacks of gold, the film leaves them with nothing—nothing, that is, except what they have become in the course of their experiences. As in the novel, they are at first dismayed and then laugh at the irony of fate. Howard decides to return with the Indians, and Curtin plans to go north to fulfill a childhood dream. Both have earned their rewards by their actions, just as Dobbs has earned his. Growth and fulfillment, or disintegration and destruction—these are the themes of Huston's powerful film. The final shot, an empty bag impaled on a small cactus, shows how elusive humanity's false dreams can be.

The Treasure of the Sierra Madre

Production Credits

Director	John Huston
Producer	Henry Blanke
Screenplay by	John Huston
Based on the novel by	B. Traven
Director of Photography	Ted McCord, A.S.C.
Art Director	John Hughes
Film Editor	Owen Marks
Assistant Director	Dick Mayberry
Music by	Max Steiner
Orchestrations by	Murray Cutter

USA. 1948. 126 minutes. Black and white.

Cast

Dobbs	Humphrey Bogart
Howard	Walter Huston
Curtin	Tim Holt
Cody	Bruce Bennett
McCormick	Barton MacLane
Gold Hat	Alfonso Bedoya
Mexican boy	Robert Blake
White Suit	John Huston
Flophouse bum	Jack Holt

Further Reading

Beja, Morris. *Film and Literature*. New York: Longman, 1979.
Houston, John. *An Open Book*. New York: Knopf, 1980.
Kaminsky, Stuart. *John Huston: Maker of Magic*. Boston: Houghton Mifflin Co., 1978.
_____. "Gold Hat, Gold Fever, Silver Screen." In *The Modern American Novel and the Movies*. Gerald Peary and Roger Shatzkin, Eds. New York: Frederick Ungar, 1978.
Madsen, Axel. *John Huston*. Garden City, New York: Doubleday, 1978.
Miller, Gabriel. *Screening the Novel: Rediscovered American Fiction in Film*. New York: Frederick Ungar, 1980.
Naremore, James, ed. *The Treasure of the Sierra Madre*. Madison, Wisconsin: The University of Wisconsin Press, 1979.
Nolan, William F. *John Huston: King Rebel*. Los Angeles: Sherbourne Press, 1965.
Pratley, Gerald. *The Cinema of John Huston*. South Brunswick and New York: A. S. Barnes and Co., 1977.

 # Macbeth

Successful artists transform the limitations of their medium into strengths. Nowhere is this more clear than in *Macbeth,* where Shakespeare convincingly chronicles the decline and disintegration of a man of great potential who, in spite of the vilest of deeds, maintains the sympathy of the audience until the very end. In developing Macbeth's character, Shakespeare turns the physical limitations of the Elizabethan stage and the restriction of the drama's length to his advantage. Film is free of such restrictions, and the natural tendency of a director is to open up a play when adapting it to film. In the case of *Macbeth,* however, such an expansion would have far-reaching consequences in terms of our reaction to the plight of Macbeth. The delicate balance between the disintegration of Macbeth and our sympathy for him depends on the limitations of Shakespeare's play. In Roman Polanski's *Macbeth* (1972), these confines are removed, and compensatory means of characterization must be created.

In his essay on the development of character in *Macbeth,* Wayne Booth analyzed the situation as follows: How does one take a good man, full of the "milk of human kindness," and transform him into a crude murderer who continues to command our sympathies?[1] It is difficult enough to show the convincing moral breakdown of a character, but it is nearly impossible to create sympathy for someone who performs atrocities.

[1]Wayne Booth, "Shakespeare's Tragic Villain," in *Shakespeare's Tragedies,* ed. Laurence Lerner, (Baltimore: Penguin Books, 1963), pp. 180–191.

First, as Booth notes, if the character's fall is to be tragic, we must believe in his goodness as well as his importance. One way of establishing these qualities in Macbeth would be to show him in action, performing deeds that raise him in our esteem. But the drama is too short, so instead Shakespeare presents testimony to Macbeth's earlier acts of greatness. In the second scene, Macbeth is enthusiastically praised by the Captain and then by the King, who is surely a reliable source of information. As if this were not enough, we have the supporting evidence of Macbeth's wife, and that could be more convincing than the "unimpeachable testimony of a wicked character deploring goodness?"[2]

The remarks of others are an important means of establishing Macbeth's character, but Shakespeare also gives us insight into Macbeth's mind as it vacillates between action and inaction. Immediately after Macbeth has been made Thane of Cawdor, he reflects upon the witches' prophecy:

> This supernatural soliciting
> Cannot be ill, cannot be good. If ill,
> Why hath it given me earnest of success,
> Commencing in a truth? I am Thane of Cawdor.
> If good, why do I yield to that suggestion
> Whose horrid image doth unfix my hair,
> And make my seated heart knock at my ribs,
> Against the use of nature? Present fears
> Are less than horrible imaginings.
> My thought, whose murder yet is but fantastical,
> Shakes so my single state of man, that function
> Is smothered in surmise, and nothing is
> But what is not. (I, iii, 130–142)

Here is a man with considerable potential for goodness and an acute sensitivity to the nature of his situation, which he is able to articulate with clarity and grace. Later, he contemplates the enormity of attempting to assassinate the King. The speech in which he decries the vileness of the crime creates sympathy for him:

> . . . He's here in double trust;
> First, as I am his kinsman, and his subject,
> Strong both against the deed; then, as his host,
> Who should against his murderer shut the door,
> Not bear the knife myself. (I, vii, 12–16)

Macbeth proceeds to characterize the goodness of Duncan, thus making the nature of the deed all the more abhorrent. Yet, as he does this, we are moved by his plight and marvel at his understanding of his own moral dilemma.

Not only is it difficult to establish Macbeth's character in a drama of

[2]Ibid., p. 182.

such limited scope, but it is equally hard to chronicle moral decline. Shakespeare's problem is complicated by the necessity of maintaining our sympathy for Macbeth while making his downfall believable. Here he uses the limitations of the drama to his advantage.

Consider the events of the drama. Duncan is the first character to be murdered by Macbeth, and yet the murder itself occurs offstage. Moreover, Shakespeare purposely limits our knowledge of Duncan. We do not know him intimately, and hence, although the crime horrifies us, the loss we experience is not personal. Shakespeare does not focus our attention on the act, but on the remorse of Macbeth that follows it.

The murder of Banquo presents greater difficulties because we have come to know him better. We have seen him act, we have heard others speak about him, and we have heard his innermost thoughts. In addition, he is murdered onstage, before our eyes. But Macbeth does not perform the deed himself; his accomplices slay Banquo at some distance from the castle. Moreover, Banquo has been shown to be a threat to Macbeth. Once again, the emphasis shifts quickly from the crime to Macbeth's remorse, as he suffers at the banquet.

The final act of carnage—the slaughter of Lady Macduff and her children—is the most gruesome of all. The horror of the massacre is underscored by the tender scene between Lady Macduff and her son, which precedes the killing. They are fully realized characters, and we are outraged by their murder. Yet, Macbeth is far away when it happens. He has given the command, nothing more. When we do return to Dunsinane, we witness another scene of remorse, this time Lady Macbeth's.

Each murder, then, is followed by a scene of suffering and guilt, so that we are concerned finally with the effects of the crimes on Macbeth rather than with the atrocities themselves. Our attitude toward Macbeth depends as much on what is not shown as on what is shown. Rather than condemn him as a murderous villain, we feel sorrow for the extraordinary loss involved in his decline.

Roman Polanski's adaptation of *Macbeth* is very much a film of the seventies, reflecting a renewed interest in magic and witchcraft and a graphic treatment of violence. Both of these elements can be found in Shakespeare's play, but not to the extent that Polanski employs them. Much of the violence of Shakespeare's play occurs offstage, and we have just examined some of the reasons for this. Polanski depicts the murders in detail and uses the resources of cinemascope and color to emphasize the carnage of the battlefield. The magical aspects are also expanded, particularly in the elaborate witches' mass, consisting of a gaggle of naked hags, who confront Macbeth when he seeks their advice for a second time. Having chosen to expand Shakespeare's drama, Polanski is faced with obvious problems in view of the ways Shakespeare uses its limitations to develop Macbeth's character. How can Polanski retain our sympathy and admiration for a character who becomes increasingly steeped in gore?

Polanski is aware of this problem, and his solutions are of considerable interest. Just as Kurosawa radically altered the moral universe in which his Macbeth (Washizu) operated, so has Polanski. To begin with, Polanski's world is one in which violence is the norm and witchcraft is commonplace. The film opens with the three witches performing a ceremony on the beach, before going their separate ways. It is not Macbeth alone who will seek their advice and comfort: They are recognized by all and sought out by many. Fog fills the screen as the witches depart, and the credits appear. Harsh sounds of a raging battle slowly increase in volume. After the completion of the credits, the fog lifts, and we see a soldier being brutally bludgeoned to death. The violence seems at first gratuitous, but, coupled with the sorcery of the first scene, it helps to establish the dominant values of the film.

Not only does Polanski depict a brutal and bloodthirsty age, but Macbeth also becomes for him an embodiment of these values. These values are evident in the sequence that culminates in the murder of the King. Polanski expands the sequence of the banquet, adding musicians on the balcony (evoking a painting by Brueghel) and entertainment provided by the young Fleance, who sings, in angelic innocence, a lyric of Chaucer's while his father looks on proudly. The King dances with Lady Macbeth, and toasts are drunk to all. As a result, both the King and Fleance are individualized far more than in Shakespeare's play, and the subsequent attempts on their lives repel us even more. Not only that, but Polanski shows us Macbeth stabbing the King while the latter lies defenseless in bed. Macbeth continues the

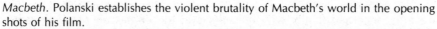

Macbeth. Polanski establishes the violent brutality of Macbeth's world in the opening shots of his film.

equivocation evident in his earlier soliloquy: He stands before the King's bed with knife in hand, unable to act. The King awakens, sees Macbeth, realizes instantly what is happening, and tries to call out. His crown rolls to the floor, and Macbeth plunges the knife in repeatedly, finally twisting it in the jugular vein, from which blood spurts.

The killing of Banquo is less bloody (although the thud of the ax as it hits his back makes a gruesome sound), but Banquo and his son have been more fully characterized than the King was. Moreover, while Polanski underlines Macbeth's hypocrisy by showing him affectionately patting Fleance before the boy rides out with his father, he also dramatizes a nightmare of Macbeth's in which Fleance takes Macbeth's crown and places it upon his own head,

Macbeth. Polanski uses the limitless space of film to distance the bludgeoning of Banquo from Macbeth

Macbeth. Macbeth's surrogate, Ross.

while Banquo laughs appreciatively. The dream continues with Fleance threatening Macbeth by holding an arrow to his throat, thus making Banquo appear to be a genuine threat to Macbeth. The presence of the third murderer, unspecified in Shakespeare's play but identified here, also shifts some of the responsibility from Macbeth. This murderer is Ross, who aids in the planning and execution of the deed and is developed by Polanski as a surrogate for Macbeth's evil side.

Ross plays an even more central role in the most grisly sequence of the film: the rape and massacre of Macduff's wife, family, and servants. Ross is present at the beginning of the scene in Shakespeare's play, but there is no suggestion that he is at all connected with the subsequent happenings. Polanski shows him participating in the children's game of blind-man's bluff and then taking leave of Lady Macduff. As Ross rides out of the castle, he opens the doors to let the cutthroats in. The scene that follows between Lady Macduff and her son becomes highly suspenseful, given our knowledge that the killers are present in the castle. Polanski has eliminated the messenger who warns Lady Macduff to flee. Instead, the lovely domestic scene is interrupted by screams and then by the rude entrance of the killers. Before the sequence is over, the castle is in flames, the children slaughtered, and the women raped.

Polanski's Ross exemplifies *the* duplicitous politician, who changes sides when it is expedient to do so. It is Ross who greets Macbeth with the news that he is Thane of Cawdor. Banquo's aside ("What can the devil speak true?") takes on a double meaning in Polanski's film. Throughout, as we have seen, Ross assists Macbeth in the implementation of his atrocities. He supports Macbeth from the time he becomes Thane of Cawdor. He is present at the investiture of Macbeth and is the first to cry, "All Hail Macbeth, King of Scotland." He aids Macbeth with his crimes, eventually deserting him only when he feels that Macbeth has failed to recognize his merits by passing him over for promotion to Thane. Ross's reasons for joining Malcolm and Macduff are purely personal; he has been slighted, and, no less importantly, he only backs a winner. Near the conclusion of the film, it will be Ross who places the crown on Malcolm's head and proclaims, "Hail, King of Scotland," as he had done earlier with Macbeth. Ross operates in a political world where all values are relative, and he personifies the baser instincts of Macbeth himself. In our eyes he becomes associated with the crimes as much as Macbeth. In fact, Polanski attempts to retain our sympathy for Macbeth by associating the worst of his activities with Ross.

We are also moved by a sense of loss as we witness the physical disintegration of Macbeth and Lady Macbeth. By the end, Macbeth's behavior has become coarse and animalistic; his physical appearance is unruly. Lady Macbeth, too, has degenerated. Toward the end of the film, Polanski has her reread the letter from her husband, and the contrast between the youthful, vibrant, sensual woman of the early scenes and this crazed, unkempt figure is striking.

Like a cornered animal, Macbeth singlehandedly tries to oppose the forces besieging the castle; we cannot help admiring him for his sheer bravado. Everyone has fled. When Siward enters the great hall, Macbeth sits alone on the throne in a pose of defiance. Polanski emphasizes Macbeth's strength and deformed greatness as he fights with Siward and later Macduff. Macbeth also spares Macduff's life, and this increases our respect for him. As he repeats the words of the witches' prophecy, Macduff explains his birth and sets on Macbeth again. Finally, Macbeth falters and Macduff beheads him. The tyrant has been deposed, and Malcolm is made king.

But order is not restored, as it was in Shakespeare's play. First, we remain suspicious of Ross, who has eagerly changed sides, and who, we know, will do so again if it benefits him. More ominous still is Donalbain's action. Throughout he has been characterized as a shifty, devious person, with a weasel-like countenance and a marked limp, racked by jealousy for his attractive, successful brother. The last shots of the film show him hobbling off across a rain-swept landscape to seek out the witches in their coven. In a world where betrayal and deception are commonplace, the stability that has been regained is fragile and precarious.

Polanski has opened up the world of Shakespeare, but not without a realization of the ways this affects the characterization of Macbeth. To compensate, he has embodied in Ross the darker aspects of Macbeth's personality. And he has made Macbeth's lust for power and duplicitous actions seem less repulsive in a world where treachery is the norm. If there are no exemplary figures in that dark world, Polanski seems to ask, how can we condemn Macbeth?

Macbeth

Production Credits

Director	Roman Polanski
Producer	Andrew Braunsberg
Screenplay by	Roman Polanski, Kenneth Tynan
Based on the play by	William Shakespeare
Director of Photography	Gilbert Taylor
Art Directors	Wilfred Shingleton, Fred Carter
Film Editor	Alastair McIntyre
Music by	Third Ear Band

USA. 1971. 120 minutes. Color

Cast

Macbeth	Jon Finch
Lady Macbeth	Francesca Annis
Ross	John Stride
Banquo	Martin Shaw
Duncan	Nicholas Selby
Malcolm	Stephen Chase
Donalbain	Paul Shelley
MacDuff	Terence Bayler
Young Witch	Noelle Rimmington
Blind Witch	Maisie McFarquhar
First Witch	Elsie Taylor
Lady MacDuff	Diane Fletcher

Doctor	Richard Pearson
Porter	Sidney Bromley
First Murderer	Michael Balfour
Second Murderer	Andrew McCulloch

Further Reading

Berlin, Normand. "*Macbeth:* Polanski and Shakespeare." *Literature/Film Quarterly,* 1, No. 4 (Fall 1973), 291–98.

Grossvogel, David I. "When the Stain Won't Wash: Polanski's *Macbeth.*" *Diacritics: A Review of Contemporary Criticism,* 2, No. 2 (1972), 46–51.

Jorgens, Jack J. *Shakespeare on Film.* Bloomington: Indiana University Press, 1977.

Kael, Pauline. "Killers and Thieves." In *Deeper Into Movies.* Boston: Little, Brown and Co., 1973.

Mullin, Michael. "*Macbeth* on Film." *Literature/Film Quarterly,* 1, No. 4 (Fall 1973), 332–42.

Reddington, John. "Film, Play and Idea." *Literature/Film Quarterly,* 1, No. 4 (Fall 1973), 367–71.

Rothwell, Kenneth S. "Roman Polanski's *Macbeth:* Golgotha Triumphant." *Literature/Film Quarterly,* 1, No. 1 (Winter 1973), 71–75.

Tynan, Kenneth. *The Sound of Two Hands Clapping.* New York: Holt, Rinehart and Winston, 1975.

 # Jules and Jim

François Truffaut's *Jules and Jim* is one of the most self-conscious of cinematic adaptations. In adapting Henri-Pierre Roché's semi-autobiographical novel of the same name, Truffaut has created a work that brilliantly captures the spirit and ambiance of its source. The film illuminates Truffaut's relationship with Roché and incorporates two of Truffaut's abiding passions: books and films.

When Truffaut was still a young critic dreaming of making his own movies, he discovered the novel in a Paris bookstall and mentioned it in his review of another film. As a result, Roché wrote Truffaut, and a lengthy correspondence began. One of the subjects of their letters was the possibility of Truffaut's adapting *Jules and Jim.* However, two other projects intervened: Truffaut's first short film, *Les Mistons* (1957), and then his own work of autobiographical fiction, *The Four Hundred Blows* (1959). Roché was enthusiastic about *Les Mistons* but died before the release of *The Four Hundred Blows.*

Several years later, Truffaut succeeded in filming *Jules and Jim.* In his adaptation of this novel, Truffaut pays homage to his relationship with Roché through his development of the principal characters. Jules, Jim, and Catherine grow out of a wide range of sources—their counterparts in Roché's novel, qualities drawn from minor characters in the novel, and allusions to films and incidents in Truffaut's own life—and they are delineated with an encyclopedic range of cinematic devices. Although Truffaut's film is closely related to Roché's novel, it clearly bears Truffaut's personal imprint.

A clue to the filmmaker's intentions lies in the story Jim recounts to Jules and Albert in the second half of the film. The story is about a soldier who briefly meets a young woman on a train and begins a correspondence with her. Through a lengthy exchange of letters, their relationship becomes increasingly intimate; they decide to marry. Then, suddenly, the soldier receives a head wound in combat. The day before the armistice, he dies in the hospital, without ever seeing the young woman again.

To many viewers this story seems irrelevant, and yet it is central to an understanding of Truffaut's movie. The incident is based on the letters of Guillaume Apollinaire, who was the soldier, to Madeleine Pagès, the young woman. An accomplished poet and friend of painters, in addition to being a prodigious correspondent, Guillaume Apollinaire exemplifies the prewar period of artistic ferment. His story, as Truffaut presents it, leads us in two directions: inward to the world of the film, and outward to Truffaut's personal experience.

The incident is changed in one significant respect: Truffaut has the soldier die before being reunited with the woman, and thus, his dreams are never tested by reality. Apollinaire did die from a war wound, but he had severed his relationship with Madeleine Pagès and was married to a woman he had met during his convalescence. By altering the story, Truffaut creates a strong parallel to his own relationship with Roché: like the soldier in Jim's anecdote, Roché died before he could see the dreams of his correspondence realized.

Throughout the film Truffaut identifies Jim with Roché and Jules with himself. Jim remains close to Roché's characterization of him in the novel, but Truffaut makes him, rather than Jules, the novelist. Jules is no longer Jewish nor nearly as neurotic as the suicidal character of Roché's creation. Jules shares Truffaut's fascination with language and, at crucial moments in the film, finds expressions of his own emotions in literary sources (such as Baudelaire and Goethe). Jules's fantasy about writing a novel with insects as characters (and the profusion of metaphors in the second half of the film comparing Catherine to an insect) reflects the fact that Truffaut himself produced a film on the sex life of insects—for none other than the son of Henri-Pierre Roché.

Catherine's character has undergone the greatest change. While Roché's Kate is German, Truffaut has made Catherine French to align her more closely with Jim. Throughout the film she identifies with Napoleon and therefore *La France*. The many women of different nationalities who surround Jules and Jim in the novel have been dropped, and Catherine's role has been made correspondingly larger. Incidents involving deleted characters (e.g., the burning of the letters or the translation of Goethe's poem) have been transferred to Catherine. Whereas in the novel two women represent "sacred love [and] profane love" to Jim, Truffaut's Catherine is both sacred and profane, "a woman," in Jules's words, "we all love . . . and whom all men desire." She speaks the first words in the film and, in a sense, the final word as well, since her song ("Le Tourbillon") echoes in Jules's head as the movie ends.

Although Truffaut has simplified Roché's novel, he has retained much of its language. Truffaut's love of words nearly equals his love of film, and here his fidelity to Roché is considerable. Indirect discourse becomes direct speech, and important speeches, like incidents, are transferred from deleted characters to one of the principals or to the narrator. It is a tribute to Truffaut's skill of characterization that his characters remain consistent.

The presence of Roché's narrator becomes much more obtrusive in the film than it was in the novel. The narrator distances us from the action and makes us continually aware of the artifice involved in the storytelling. His is a frequent voice in the film, summarizing action, providing transitions, and giving us access to the thoughts of Jules and Jim.

Truffaut is faithful to the general outlines of Roché's novel, but he condenses, selects, and even adds, all the while developing the material in a very personal way. The initial encounter between Jules, Jim, and Catherine is taken from Roché's novel, but Truffaut makes significant alterations and additions.

The discovery of Catherine becomes symptomatic of the confusion of art and life that pervades the lives of the protagonists. The sequence opens in Albert's Paris apartment, where Jules and Jim have gathered to view a slide show. Truffaut spent his own childhood in darkened cinemas, and it is appropriate that he should have Jules and Jim discover their ideal woman in a similar environment. Her model is revealed through the successive refinements of different artistic media: the photographic reproduction (slide) of an "imitation" (statue) of a woman dead for many centuries. As spectators we experience this with them through yet another medium, film. To heighten our awareness of the distances involved here, and to emphasize the element of artifice, Truffaut has the second half of the sequence entirely narrated. Jules and Jim pursue this statue at once; Truffaut dissolves directly from the slide of the statue in Albert's apartment to a shot of Jules and Jim on the island, and the juxtaposition substantiates our feelings of their impetuosity. Then, through a subjective camera, we participate in their exploration of the terrain until the statue is located. A series of shots of the statue recapitulates the shots in Albert's apartment, while the narrator assures us that if ever they met such a statue "they would follow it."

Truffaut adds an important scene before the meeting with Catherine. Jules and Jim are boxing in a gymnasium. Jim offers to read from his novel that, it becomes clear, is quite autobiographical. Jules listens intently and then declares that he would like to translate it into German. In Roché's novel, Jules is writing fiction but without the autobiographical intent of this scene. Truffaut makes Jim the novelist to identify him with Roché; the novel he reads from resembles nothing more than *Jules and Jim*. Jules, like Truffaut, chooses to "translate" the work of his friend from one language (or medium) to another. Their activities here contribute to their own characterizations but also illuminate the life of their creator and his problems in the making of this film.

For the first meeting with Catherine, Truffaut transfers a restaurant scene from early in the novel to Jules's apartment. As three women descend a flight of steps, the camera lingers on Catherine's face. Here is the actualization of the ideal the two men have discovered in art. A series of close-ups duplicates the earlier shots of the statue, which duplicated the slides in Albert's apartment. Once again, the viewer participates in their discovery. To strengthen the visual parallels, the narrator comments on the likeness, noting that "the occasion took on a dreamlike quality." The scene is a perfect fusion of the literary and the purely cinematic.

Truffaut's adaptation of Roché's novel strongly reflects his relationship with Roché, but it is personal for other reasons as well. Through his use of cinematic allusions and through an extraordinary variety of cinematic techniques, Truffaut presents the viewer with a cross section of some of the films in his life, including: *Une Partie de Compagne* (1936), in the early shot of Jules and Jim rowing with two women on the river; Welles's *Citizen Kane* (1941), in the sequence at the theater as well as in the use of musical themes identified with characters; Ophuls's *La Rond* (1950), in the scene before the mirror when Jim and Catherine spend a night at a hotel before his return to France; Chaplin's *The Kid* (1921), in Catherine's masquerade; Hitchcock's *Under Capricorn* (1949), in the use of the moving camera when Catherine tries to seduce Jules after she has taken Jim for her lover; and Hitchcock's *Shadow of a Doubt,* with the superstition of the hat on the bed. Moreover, there is a production still accompanying both the French and English editions of the filmscript showing Truffaut directing in a costume that recalls D. W. Griffith, just as within the film there is a painting of Jules as Mozart. And Jules, as he is leaving the Cinéma des Ursulines with Catherine, pauses momentarily before a 1928 cover from the French periodical *Du Cinéma,* an important predecessor of *Cahiers du Cinéma,* which helped support Truffaut as a young critic. Truffaut has lived his life in and through films, and *Jules and Jim* chronicles some of these privileged moments.

The tribute to Chaplin builds on separate incidents in Roché's novel: Catherine's masquerade and her foot race with Jules and Jim. Truffaut combines an homage to *The Kid*, by dressing Catherine like "the kid," with an homage to its creator, by giving her a mustache like Chaplin himself. In addition, the music helps evoke the period of the great silent films. The scene captures Catherine's need to dramatize and to masquerade. But with all its

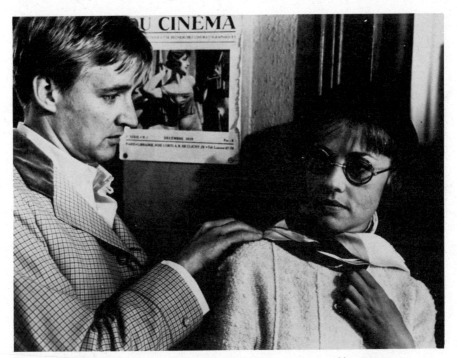

Jules and Jim. A cinematic homage to Truffaut's own roots as a film critic.

gaiety, the scene is filled with ominous undertones. The setting contrasts markedly with the early shots of Jules and Jim frolicking over a bridge in the countryside, where the simple, pastoral beauty of nature was an appropriate metaphor for their relationship. Here the trio passes a barred fence and then enters a totally enclosed industrial bridge with iron girders and chain-link fencing, suggesting confinement and entrapment. Catherine's behavior sub-stantiates the feeling created by the *mise en scène*.

    Catherine's first leap into the Seine foreshadows her suicide near the end of the film. Here, too, Truffaut takes significant liberties with his text and in-corporates several important homages. Truffaut prefaces the sequence with an original scene at a theatrical performance to which Jim has invited Jules and Catherine. At the conclusion of the play, Catherine claps with enthusi-asm and persistence, recalling a similar scene in *Citizen Kane*. The three leave the theater, and Catherine states the reasons for the heroine's appeal in terms that define her perfectly: "She wants to be free. She invents her life at every moment." Catherine identifies with the liberated heroines of Ibsen and Strindberg, an identification that also points to her propensity to dramatize. And that is exactly what she does in the scene that follows. Jules and Jim pay little attention to her and instead discuss the play in a cerebral manner, with Jules quoting Baudelaire on the nature of women. To regain their attention,

Jules and Jim. A metaphoric use of setting.

Catherine takes a dramatic jump. Truffaut has provided a motivation for Catherine's action that is lacking in the novel; it is both a protest against the crippling intellectualism of Jules and the personal neglect accompanying it. Roché's woman calls for help after jumping, but Truffaut's Catherine manages extremely well on her own. By this gesture she succeeds in becoming once again the focus of their attention and in inspiring Jim to attempt to capture this magnificent action in a drawing. Truffaut's characters continually make art out of the materials of their lives and model their lives on works of art.

Truffaut's love of film also reveals itself in his use, within *Jules and Jim*, of actual footage from earlier films. Old clips of Paris, for example, add an important note of authenticity to his period of recreation. The war, which plays a negligible role in Roché's novel, looms large in Truffaut's film; the numerous war scenes mark a decisive break between the gaiety of prewar Paris and the more somber life that follows. Truffaut stretches this footage to the dimensions of his wide screen and projects silent clips at sound speed; as a result the images become distorted, and the movement of the figures appears mechanized. Not only does this increase our sense of distance from the war, but it also becomes a telling comment on the futility of the combat.

In the period before the war, time seems to stand still. Characteristically, Jules records the passage of time with an hourglass, whose form remains the same while the sands shift from one side to another. Neither he nor Jim appears to age during the more than twenty years chronicled by the film. Jim is living with Gilberte and still thinking of getting married, as he was when the film began. Jules attends the cremation in the same striped suit he had worn on his first outing with Jim and Catherine. Jules and Jim live for art and thus seem to be eternally young, as Roché must have appeared to Truffaut. Only Catherine expresses a fear of aging, and her appearance gradually alters from one of romantic lushness to Nazi severity in the more slowly paced second half of the film. Truffaut signals the passage of time not only by changes in his characters' appearances but by the presence of works of art that transcend time. Chief among these are Picasso's paintings, which can be dated only by the time of their creation. Other time signals are the films we see within this film—the newsreels of the war and the burning of the books.

Jules and Jim make creation a part of their daily lives: In his novel Jim attempts to capture his early experiences with Jules; Jules sketches the woman he loves on a café table; Jim observes Catherine's first plunge into the Seine and desires to make a drawing of it. Catherine shares their continual need to shape the incidents of their lives into anecdotal stories, and few films contain as many narrated stories as this one. But while it is salutary to transform the materials of one's life into works of art, there is a danger in doing the reverse. Jules and Jim's discovery of Catherine is a good example of this, and Catherine herself aspires to model her entire life after works of art. In Roché's novel Catherine keeps a diary and later achieves some success as a writer and illustrator. Truffaut eliminates this aspect of her creativity and instead shows her attempting to make her life a work of art. Albert's song "Le Tourbillon" ("The Whirlwind") is both about her and characteristically performed by her; it is a perfect summation of her enticing and capricious nature. But Catherine realizes that her life, however artful, is evanescent, and she seeks to overcome this transience by having a child with Jim.

Within the world of the film, none of the characters succeeds in fixing the flux of his or her life in art; yet the aspirations of each are realized by the work of Roché and then Truffaut. Though we have no way of evaluating Roché's fidelity to his own experience, Truffaut does adhere to the contours of Roché's story and is quite faithful to the book's language. He also honors his relationship with Roché by creating a strong parallel in Jules's relationship with Jim. Truffaut's characters are composites of many sources, and his film finally resembles a series of reflecting mirrors: a semi-autobiographical film creating a work of art out of a semiautobiographical novel that creates a work of art out of the lives of the author's friends, who themselves are engaged in the same process. Jules and Jim is an affirmation of the powers of art to immortalize experience, and it joins the august company of those timeless works that Truffaut has incorporated into it.

Jules and Jim

Production Credits

Director	François Truffaut
Producer	Carrosse Films and S.E.D.I.F.
Screenplay by	François Truffaut, Jean Gruault
Based on the novel by	Henri-Pierre Roché
Director of Photography	Raoul Coutard
Film Editor	Claudine Bouche
Assistant Directors	Georges Pellegrin, Robert Bober
Music by	George Delerue
Song	"Le Tourbillon," words and music by Boris Bassiak

France. 1962. 105 minutes. Black & white.

Cast

Catherine	Jeanne Moreau
Jules	Oscar Werner
Jim	Henri Serre
Gilberte	Vanna Urbino
Albert	Boris Bassiak
Sabine	Sabine Haudepin
Thérèse	Marie Dubois
Albert's friend	Danielle Bassiak
And the voice of	Michel Subor

Further Reading

DeNitto, Dennis and William Herman. *Film and the Critical Eye*. New York: Macmillan Publishing Co., 1975.

Eidsvik, Charles. *Cineliteracy: Film Among the Arts*. New York: Horizon Press, 1978.

Greenspun, Roger. "Elective Affinities: Aspects of *Jules et Jim*." *Sight and Sound*, 32, No. 2 (Spring 1963), 78–82.

Insdorf, Annette. *Francois Truffaut*. Boston: Twayne Publishers, 1978.

Kael, Pauline. "*Jules and Jim*." In *I Lost It at the Movies*. Boston: Little, Brown and Co., 1965.

Kauffmann, Stanley. "*Jules and Jim*." In *A World on Film: Criticism and Comment*. New York: Harper & Row, 1966.

Monaco, James. *The New Wave: Truffaut, Godard, Chabrol, Rohmer, Rivette*. New York: Oxford University Press, 1976.

Truffaut, Francois. *Jules and Jim* [filmscript]. tr. Nicholas Fry. New York: Frederick Ungar, 1984.

5

Point of View

Introduction

There was once upon a time a woman who was a real witch and had two daughters, one ugly and wicked, and this one she loved because she was her own daughter, and one beautiful and good, and this one she hated, because she was her step-daughter.

So begins one of the many fairy tales collected by the Grimm brothers. The narration is simple, and we are aware at once of the presence of a teller relating the tale. The choice of narrator is extremely important since it determines both how the story will be told and consequently which story will be told. In the example given above, the narrator stands outside the world of the story and tells us *about* the witch and her two daughters. Already in the opening sentence he makes value judgments (one daughter is "ugly and wicked" and the other is "beautiful and good"), which control our response to the rest of the story. The narration continues:

The step-daughter once had a pretty apron, which the other fancied so much that she became envious, and told her mother that she must and would have that apron. "Be quiet, my child," said the old woman, "and you shall have it. Your step-sister has long deserved death, tonight when she is asleep I will come and cut her head off. Only be careful that you are at the far-side of the bed, and push her well to the front."

The stepsister overhears this conversation, and arranges things much to the surprise of her evil stepmother. But imagine how differently this material would be presented if the stepsister were telling the story? Or the witch? Or the ugly sister? Each would explain the circumstances and motivations differently, and the choice of narrator would determine which emotions (fear, sadness, joy) would be evoked in the reader. In short, the story would reflect the bias of the narrator, and each version would be very different from the present one.

A limited but useful classification of point of view can be made on the basis of the pronouns used by the narrator. The above example, from "Sweetheart Roland," is narrated in the third person (the narrator employs the pronouns "He," "she," and "they") by a narrator who possesses complete knowledge of the characters. He understands their motivations and actions and can explain these freely while manipulating the characters in any way he likes. Such a narration is called third-person omniscient or unlimited point of view, and it is noted for its flexibility. A further distinction among omniscient narrators is useful: A narrator may either be intrusive or impersonal. The intrusive narrator of "Sweetheart Roland" evaluates his characters as he presents them; an impersonal narrator would describe without making judgments. Although intrusive narrators may be more common in older works of fiction, they are certainly not unknown in modern fiction. In *The Treasure of Sierra Madre*, the third-person omniscient narrator frequently makes political and sociological evaluations of actions. Early in the novel, the three protagonists discuss whether or not to register their claims. The narrator comments:

> The discussion about the registration of their claim brought comprehension of their changed standing in life. With every ounce more of gold possessed by them they left the proletarian class and neared that of the property holders, the well-to-do middle class . . .
>
> Those who up to this time had been considered by them as their proletarian brethren were now enemies against whom they had to protect themselves. As long as they had owned nothing of value, they had been slaves to their hungry bellies, slaves to those who had the means to fill their bellies. All this was changed now.
>
> They had reached the first step by which man became the slave of his property.

None of the three men would be likely to entertain such thoughts. Instead, these observations seem attributable to the omniscient narrator, who conceives of the men's actions within a greater context (in this case, political) than they are capable of doing. In fact, we are likely to attribute these views to the "implied author," as we call the consciousness that controls every aspect of the novel.

More common in modern fiction is the unintrusive or impersonal narrator, who describes or shows actions and characters without explicitly judging them. This is the "dramatic method" because it most nearly resembles the method of a play, where we maintain an objective point of view as spectators and judge characters solely on the basis of their actions and words. Characters are developed by "showing" rather than by "telling." The individual testimonies of the characters in Akutagawa's "In the Woods" are extreme examples of this method. Akutagawa presents no descriptions of characters or setting, only the commentaries of each character. Ernest Hemingway is well known for his objective style of narration. Compare the opening of his story, "A Clean, Well Lighted Place" with the opening of "Sweetheart Roland:"

> It was late and every one had left the cafe except an old man who sat in the shadow the leaves of the tree made against the electric light. In the day time the street was dusty, but at night the dew settled the dust and the old man liked to sit late because he was deaf and now at night it was quiet and he felt the difference.

The scene is established with neutral description, and we are barely aware of a narrative presence. The narrator has nearly achieved the formulation given us by Stephen Dedalus, in James Joyce's *A Portrait of the Artist as a Young Man*, where he is described as "invisible, refined out of existence, indifferent, paring his fingernails."

Omniscient narrators can enter their works and address the reader directly, or intrude through commentary or editorializing. Or they can remain aloof from their works, so that the reader is hardly aware of their existence. But a third-person narrator need not be omniscient: He or she may have a very limited perspective. The narrator still refers to characters as "he," "she," or "they" but identifies with one character, and his or her knowledge is restricted to what the chosen character is capable of knowing or feeling. Third-person restricted or limited narration is a technique Henry James refined in his later novels, where the protagonists (described in the third person) became "centers of consciousness," through whom we are introduced to the world. This point of view is called third person restricted or limited narration.

Third-person narration is the most frequently employed in film, and all the modes discussed above apply to film as well. Actions can be presented impersonally in a film, as in a drama, or the omniscient narrator can shape our responses through composition, camera angle, lighting, and so on. Film can also excel in the limited point of view, where one character clearly presents a consciousness through which the entire film is filtered. Such a presentation is employed by Antonioni in *Blow-up*.

The other principal narrative voice in fiction is first person, where the "I" narrates. Here authors are restricted to the vocabulary of their own chosen protagonists, and can report only what the protagonist knows and is capable of understanding firsthand. The story is presented directly and hence gains an immediacy over the third-person limited narrator. Although the implied author cannot intervene and comment upon the narrator, he or she can make us aware, through dramatic irony, of the narrator's limitations.

First-person narrators can be classified further by their degree of partici-pation in the stories they are narrating. Here, as in third-person narration, the narrator may be the protagonist, like Meursault in *The Stranger,* or a minor character, like Nick Carraway in *The Great Gatsby.* Or the narrator may merely be an observer.

There are many ways of presenting first-person narration: in the form of a story, told by the narrator ("The Loneliness of the Long-Distance Runner"); in the form of a diary or journal (as in Miranda's diary in *The Collector);* through letters; in the form of a legal testimony ("In the Woods"); or through the thoughts of the protagonist, to name but a few. Some of these forms heighten the sense of immediacy, and some appear more realistic than the others.

A story can, of course, be told through multiple points of view. "In the Woods" presents the first-person narrations of a number of participants. Each narration is self-enclosed, presenting its own view of the events without com-menting on the other presentations. Readers must make their own evalua-tions. In *The Collector* Fowles balances Miranda's temporally oriented diary against Freddy's retrospective account, part of which is written before his dis-covery of her diary, and part afterward. The reader weighs each account against the other. *The Turn of the Screw* begins with a narration that "frames" the rest of the novel (and hence is called a frame narration), by pro-viding a context for our assessment of the veracity of the governess' narra-tion. These examples are but a few of the many possibilities that exist for a writer.

In respect to point of view, film is closer to short stories and novels than to drama since it permits a range of possibilities concerning narration. We have already examined cinematic presentations of third-person point of view, but first-person point of view is equally possible. The subjective shot or point of view shot is commonly accepted as a correlative for the field of vision of given characters: What we see represents what they see through their own eyes. But this is only one way of presenting a first-person point of view in film. The classic example of consistent use of subjective shots to reproduce the first-person point of view is Robert Montgomery's *Lady in the Lake* (1946), an adaptation of the novel by Raymond Chandler. Here the protagonist is seen only in reflection because his eyes are the camera lens. Subjective shots can lead to ludicrous awkwardnesses, as when someone steps forward to em-brace the camera or to throw a fist toward it. A similar use of subjective cam-era in Delmer Daves's *Dark Passage* (1947) is more plausible since the pro-tagonist is an escaped convict trying to remain concealed. In general, we see through his eyes until he has had an operation to change his appearance, at which point the narration shifts to omniscient, and we see this narrator as well. Thus, the subjective shots function thematically.

In its awkward self-consciousness, a consistent use of subjective shots in a film resembles more an equally rare technique in fiction: second-person narration. Consider the opening lines of Michel Butor's *La Modification* *(trans. A Change of Heart,* 1958):

> Standing with your left foot on the grooved brass sill, you try in vain with your right shoulder to push the sliding door a little wider open.
> You edge your way in through the narrow opening, then you lift up your suitcase of bottle-green grained leather . . .

We accept this awkwardness as a convention in literature and before too many pages we are accustomed to it. But in film the consistent use of the subjective shot is jarring. The analogy between the camera lens and the human eye breaks down because of the continual awkwardness it creates.

Just as in a dream we see ourselves part of an unfolding drama, so in film first-person narrators can be included in what they narrate. There are many ways of indicating that they are the narrators: by voice-overs, by dissolves, and by identification of them with the scene being presented. In *Citizen Kane* each friend or acquaintance narrates his version of Kane's past, and the narrator is included in the visual field of the narration. Each presentation is colored by the narrator's bias. Subjective distortions are even more apparent in *Rashomon,* where each participant has a great deal at stake personally. Here too the testimonies are dramatized and show the narrator interacting with the others. The point of view, however, remains clearly first person.

Two additional narrative strategies that transcend individual point of view should be mentioned here. The first of these is the self-conscious narrator, who shares the problems of creating a work with readers. Such a narrator is the protagonist of "Blow-up," for whom the process of capturing an experience in words becomes the subject of his story. The same struggle to tell a story preoccupies the narrator of "The Loneliness of the Long-Distance Runner." In both cases the narrator appears to represent attitudes we associate with the implied author, but we should never confuse the two. The narrator is always a fictional creation.

A second narrative strategy that transcends point of view is the fallible or unreliable narrator. Critical disagreement over *The Turn of the Screw* revolves in part around the question of the reliability of the governess. Are we meant to believe the story she tells us? As we have already observed, distortion occurs in all subjective testimony. Narrators need not be any more reliable than anyone else.

Clearly, the selection of narrator is crucial for the writer and for the filmmaker. A filmmaker must weigh the strengths and weaknesses of each potential narrator and then make the choice that best suits his or her purpose. By being aware of the infinite possibilities available to the author or filmmaker, the reader or viewer can more fully weigh the implications of the final choice.

Additional Recommended Films

Une Femme Douce (A Gentle Woman, 1969), directed by Robert Bresson, based on a short story by Dostoevski. The short story is available in paperback.

The Great Gatsby (1974), directed by Jack Clayton, based on the novel by F. Scott Fitzgerald. The novel is available in paperback.

Great Expectations (1941), directed by David Lean, based on the novel by Charles Dickens. The novel is available in paperback.

See Also:

The Member of the Wedding (Chapter 3)
The Collector (Chapter 5)
Blow-up (Chapter 6)
The Loneliness of the Long-Distance Runner (Chapter 6)
The Fallen Idol (Chapter 7)
All The King's Men
Tom Jones

 # The Innocents

In the "Preface" to the New York edition of *The Turn of the Screw* (1908), Henry James refers to his novella as "an amusette to catch those not easily caught." Yet until 1934, when Edmund Wilson published his essay, "The Ambiguity of Henry James," most readers seem to have been caught by James. On the whole, early readers believed the governess when she said that there were ghosts striving to possess and corrupt Flora and Miles, the two innocent children in her care. Edmund Wilson argued, however, that the governess was a "neurotic case of sex repression" whose tormented reaction to her purely subjective hallucinations resulted in the breakdown of Flora and the death of Miles. Since the publication of Wilson's essay, commentators have argued ceaselessly about the reliability of the governess's testimony and the meaning of the story as a whole. Are the ghosts real, or are they merely figments of the imagination of the governess? Are the children possessed or in danger of being possessed by the ghosts, and is the struggle of the governess therefore heroic? Is the story a tale of corruption or an allegory of the fall from innocence?

   The continuing debate over the many possible interpretations of the story is made possible by James's choice of the governess as the narrator. Although the governess' story comprises most of the novella, James prefaces it with a frame narration that creates a realistic background, making it appear to be a "found manuscript." The anonymous first-person narrator of this chapter introduces Douglas, an acquaintance at whose home ghost stories are being told by a group assembled around the hearth on Christmas Eve. Douglas confesses that he has a tale that will make the others pale by comparison. Interest is aroused by Douglas' cryptic comments, and suspense is created by his delay in procuring the manuscript, for the tale, we learn, had been recorded by a participant. This delay gives Douglas an opportunity to testify to the good character of the author of the manuscript. As a result, we are prepared to accept her story as accurate. If, however, as Edmund Wilson suggests, we begin to question her sanity, the horror of the tale no longer results from the sight of innocent children being corrupted by evil spirits, but from their destruction at the hands of an obsessed and deranged woman. When viewed in this light, the details of the story achieve a new significance.

The governess is by her own admission inexperienced, having led a sheltered existence as the daughter of a country parson. This is her first position, and she has accepted it at the urging of a most persuasive bachelor with whom she falls in love and about whom she fantasizes continually while at Bly. Her paramount desire is to please him, and her story becomes in one sense a self-justifying autobiography. She views her life at Bly initially as a sort of fairy tale located in a "castle of romance inhabited by a rosy sprite, such a place as would somewhere . . . take all colour out of story-books and fairy tales." The uncle is like a handsome young prince, whose appearance she is dreaming of when suddenly she sees the first specter on the tower whom she later identifies—with the promptings of Mrs. Grose—as Peter Quint. At the time she is admittedly fatigued, having spent the preceding nights in restless sleep. In fact, all her visions occur at moments of physical and psychological distress. When she sees Quint for the second time, she has recently received "disturbing letters from home." Because the governess is telling the story, we have only her words on which to judge her actions and those of others. And these words have been the subject of critical debate that continues to flourish, with articles and books arguing all sides.[1]

Jack Clayton entered this debate in 1962 with his adaptation of James's story, entitled *The Innocents*. The first problem confronting Clayton as a director was the question of point of view. As we have seen, there are two aspects of this in the novella: the consistent first-person point of view of the story, which limits the perspective to experiences, feelings, and knowledge of the governess; and the frame narration that provides a testimony to her good character and establishes a realistic basis for the story. Clayton has avoided both the literal treatment of first-person point of view in film—where the camera consistently duplicates the eye of the narrator through subjective shots—and the framing device of the prefatory chapter. Instead, Clayton begins his film with a darkened screen and the sound of a child's voice singing. Although the song appears to be quite innocent, it later suggests an associa-

[1]A good collection of critical opinion is presented in the Norton Critical Edition of *The Turn of the Screw* (New York, 1966).

tion between Flora, who is singing it, and Miss Jessel. Moreover, the song occurs in the film before each of the governess's visions. By having this theme precede the film, Clayton underlines the subjective nature of our experience as viewers, for we too are about to witness a vision, and that vision is *The Innocents*. Then, from the left of the darkened screen a pair of clasped hands appears, as we hear the sounds of birds accompanied by a muffled weeping. A woman's face in profile enters the frame and a voice-over narration begins: "All I want to do is save the children . . . not destroy them . . . More than anything I love the children, more than anything . . . They need affection, love, someone to whom they can belong." The credits accompany this, and when they are completed there is a slow dissolve to a different setting. A male voice gradually becomes audible, as a handsome man addresses the unidentified woman of the opening: "May I ask you a somewhat personal question? Do you have an imagination?" When she replies in the affirmative, he qualifies his question by noting: "Truth is very seldom understood by any but very imaginative persons . . ." This qualification also applies to the viewer of the film. The language of the interview is continually charged with meaning on different levels. Several lines from the governess's opening voice-over narration are repeated, thus creating a psychological connection between the two scenes. The uncle's remarks have sexual undertones and often resemble a proposal of marriage. Clayton makes this interview (merely mentioned in the prefatory chapter of the story) play an important thematic role in the film. But the interview is also important structurally: By presenting the body of the film as a flashback, Clayton has given his work a circular structure. The film begins exactly where it ends. Hence, the film constitutes the governess's recollections of all that has happened, told at the instant of Miles's death. Because of our identification with the governess, and because of the objective nature of film as a medium, we tend to forget that we are viewing her subjective vision. Clayton exploits the ambiguity of this situation to full measure. We share the visions of the governess with her and want to believe them. But through the use of the flashback, the subjectivity of the entire film has been established.

Clayton, then, strives to retain the ambiguity of James's story. At the same time, Clayton heightens the sexuality of James's drama. Miss Giddens (as he calls James's anonymous governess) is characterized as a woman whose repressed sexuality leads directly to hysteria. But Clayton also provides realistic explanations for her first visions in order to encourage our identification with her. Upon her arrival at Bly, Miss Giddens steps down from the carriage and walks to the mansion so that she can more fully appreciate the grandiose setting. Before meeting anyone, she hears a high-pitched voice calling "Flora" three times in succession. We too hear the voice and consequently become more sure of it with each repetition, although no source is evident. Almost immediately thereafter, Miss Giddens encounters Flora, who is standing at the edge of a large pond. Flora is thus associated with the pond (in fact, we see her reflection before we see her body), and the pond is identified with the mysterious voice summoning Flora, and later with Miss Jessel.

Reflective surfaces (water, glass, mirrors) play an important role in Clayton's film. A good example occurs early in the film and reveals Miss Giddens's strong jealousy of her predecessor: After being introduced to Mrs. Grose at the front door, Miss Giddens enters the house, and the camera tracks steadily with her in a lenghty shot that conveys her sense of wonder and amazement. Miss Giddens pauses before a vase of white roses. As she touches the petals, they fall to the table. (Is this an innocent occurrence, or the first example of her destructive touch? In spite of Mrs. Grose's reassuring words that it happens all the time, it seems to happen only to Miss Giddens, and all too frequently.) Miss Giddens then steps into the next room and pauses before a mirror; as she stares at her reflection, she inquires about Miss Jessel. Her posture before the mirror suggests a relationship with her predecessor that is later reinforced by her increasing resemblance to Miss Jessel in dress and appearance.

The depiction of jealousy, both in Miss Giddens's feelings for her predecessor and between the children, is just one aspect of the general heightening of sexual tensions in the film. Miss Giddens's visions in the film, while no less ambiguous than in the novel, also have a sexual side to them. Her first vision of Peter Quint on the tower unites the dominant symbols of the film—flowers, statues, ponds, and towers—all of which carry strong sexual connotations.

In the story the governess is strolling on the grounds alone, fantasizing that "it would be as charming as a charming story suddenly to meet someone." That "someone" is clearly the children's uncle, about whom she thinks constantly. In the film, however, she is out cutting roses, an activity that connects her with Flora (whose name evokes the Roman goddess of springtime and flowers) and the uncle (who wears a white rose in his lapel when interviewing her for the position). She parts the foliage to reveal a statue of a cherubic child, whose outstretched fingers clutch the severed hands of an adult. Such a statue could be found at Bly, but it is unsettling and in retrospect seems like a horrifying omen (the child grasping an adult who is no longer there). Clayton cuts to a close-up of the statue as a dark beetle suddenly issues from the mouth; our unease is confirmed by the sense of corruption this evokes. Miss Giddens steps back, and Flora's mysterious song suddenly stops. In fact, all natural sounds cease as Miss Giddens stares up into the blinding sun. She drops her roses and scissors (significantly, into a circular pond at her feet) and turns to look toward the tower. Although nearly blinded by the sun, she sees the figure of a man on top of the tower. The vision lasts a brief moment before she turns away, and normal sounds return as she walks toward the house. She pauses and stares again toward the tower. Clayton cuts to a point-of-view shot of pigeons, flying in slow motion, near the top of the tower. She looks away and strides toward the house, then decides (unlike the story) to explore the tower. She mounts the steps and discovers none other than Miles on top, caressing the pigeons that light on his arms and shoulders. To her inquiries about the man she has seen, Miles answers, "I've been quite alone," adding that "I expect you imagined it." After Miles makes several flirtatious remarks about Miss Giddens's appearance, the scene concludes.

Thus, Clayton, unlike James, provides a realistic basis for the vision (perhaps it was only Miles on the tower?). He also suggests connections between Miles and Peter Quint, both through the shots of the statue that precede the vision and through Miles's manliness (and hence his sexuality), as well as hinting at the possibility of Miles's being possessed.

Similar connections are made in the sequence that culminates with Peter Quint's appearance at the window. At the end of a long day, Miss Giddens agrees to permit the children to play hide and seek anywhere they like in the house. They scurry upstairs, leaving her below. We know that something is going to occur, and Clayton quickly builds suspense. Miss Giddens ascends the stairs and turns down a long narrow corridor. The rapid tracking of the camera behind her heightens the tension. Clayton suddenly cuts to a close-up of Miss Giddens as she exclaims, "Anna?" and follows this with a point-of-view shot of a woman in black crossing the landing. We are surprised and wonder what we have seen. But before we can assess the meaning of these shots, we hear the children's voices calling, "Miss Giddens," which prompts her to pass the landing and hasten up the stairs toward the attic. She slowly opens the attic door, and a bobbing head is seen across the room. Because of the distortion of perspective, we are unable to judge its size. The head appears lifelike, and the effect is most disconcerting. Miss Giddens enters the room and approaches it, recognizing (as we then do) that it is only a doll. As she reaches it, she knocks something onto the floor. A music box opens, revealing a ballerina moving as the tune we have now come to identify with Flora and Miss Jessel begins to play. Next to the ballerina is a locket with a man's face under the cracked glass. Miss Giddens has found what she has been unconsciously searching for throughout the house: Miss Jessel and Peter Quint. Before we can reflect on this discovery, the door creaks and a hand appears; we are relieved when it is *only* Miles. He embraces Miss Giddens, but his embrace becomes a stranglehold, and she implores him to stop: "You're hurting me," she says, words we later hear in her nightmare, where they are associated with Miss Jessel's plea to Peter Quint during lovemaking. Flora enters the room and interrupts the embrace. Now it is Miss Giddens's turn to hide, and as she leaves, Miles and Flora lean on the rocking horse and begin to count. The horse evokes Miles's earlier riding scene, and his association with Quint.

Miss Giddens quickly descends the staircase and crosses the drawing room, brushing against a vase of roses. Again the petals fall ominously to the ground. She hides behind a window curtain and then realizes that her feet are exposed and pulls them back to conceal herself more fully. She glances nervously through the window and sees a figure. Our discomfort is assuaged as we realize it is only a statue. But just as we have relaxed our guard, another vision is superimposed on the first: Peter Quint appears framed in the windowpane, as he was behind the glass of the locket. Is the vision of Peter Quint a projection of Miss Giddens's fear and horror, as though she were looking into a mirror? When the vision passes she steps outside and, finding

The Innocents. Merriment or demonic possession?

no one, turns back to the house. For a moment her reflection is superimposed on that of Mrs. Grose, who has heard the noise and come to see what is happening. We observe the fear on her face as well. Miss Giddens confronts her with the news, describing the man in detail and identifying him with the face she has seen in the locket. She then hastens back to the staircase to find and save the children. As Miss Giddens pauses on the first landing, Mrs. Grose informs her with fear in her voice that Peter Quint is dead! Clayton cuts immediately to a low angle shot of the children standing on a higher landing behind the railing and laughing at the sight of Miss Giddens below. Their laughter could be that of innocent children discovering the object of their search, but the juxtaposition of the shot with Mrs. Grose's comment, in addition to the way the shot is composed and lit, all suggest otherwise.

Again, Clayton has given a realistic basis for the vision while at the same time maintaining the ambiguity of the situation. The effect is to strengthen audience identification with the governess early in the film. While the later visions become increasingly subjective, they are *filmed* in a more objective manner. The vision of Miss Jessel across the pond lacks a realistic explanation, and the "evidence" of the tear in the schoolroom is rather questionable. But once the identification has been established, we tend to accept what we *see*, particularly when we see Miss Jessel in over-the-shoulder shots, which heighten the objectivity. This is one of the strengths of film as a medium, and Clayton uses it to full advantage throughout. Thus, he succeeds in maintaining a tenuous balance between an immediately objective presentation and the subjectivity of the entire film. Although Clayton has heightened the sexuality of the situation, this does not undercut the possibility of the ghosts' being real. As Clayton noted at the time of making the film:

> To regard Miss Giddens as just another frustrated woman is too pat. . . . There may be that element, but I also believe that she saw the ghosts. You could always take the story two ways. You could, for instance, say that any sensitive person who enters a strange house may have disturbing intuitions that arise in part from the environment, in part from the depths of his own character. This is what I love about the story: there is nothing black and white about it: it's full of question marks and possibilities. I don't want, you know, to say absolutely what the picture means. There should be an area of uncertainty; that's what I think James intended. I want the audience to exercise its intelligence.[2]

By a skillful manipulation of point of view, and by working against the realistic nature of film as a medium, Clayton has created a film that forces the audience "to exercise its intelligence." Moreover, Clayton has set traps for his viewers that rival those set by James sixty years earlier.

[2]*Show*, January 1962 (Vol. II, No. 1), p. 30.

The Innocents

Production Credits

Director	Jack Clayton
Producer	Jack Clayton
Screenplay by	Truman Capote, William Archibald
Based on the novella	
"The Turn of the Screw" by	Henry James
Director of Photography	Freddie Francis
Film Editor	James Clark
Music by	Georges Auric

Great Britain. 1961. 99 minutes. Black & white.

Cast

Miss Giddens	Deborah Kerr
Mrs. Grose	Megs Jenkins
Uncle	Michael Redgrave
Miles	Martin Stephens
Flora	Pamela Franklin

Further Reading

Allen, Jeanne Thomas. "*The Turn of the Screw* and *The Innocents:* Two Types of Ambiguity." In *The Classic American Novel and the Movies.* Eds. Gerald Peary and Roger Shatzkin. New York: Frederick Ungar, 1977.

Houston, Penelope. "*The Innocents.*" *Sight and Sound,* 30, No. 3 (Summer 1961), 114–115.

———. "*The Innocents.*" *Sight and Sound,* 31, No. 1 (Winter 1962), 39–40.

Kael, Pauline. "*The Innocents.*" In *I Lost It at the Movies.* Boston: Little, Brown and Co., 1965.

Kauffmann, Stanley. "*The Innocents.*" In *A World on Film: Criticism and Comment.* New York: Harper & Row, 1966.

Palmer, James. W. "Cinematic Ambiguity: James's *The Turn of the Screw* and Clayton's *The Innocents.*" *Literature/Film Quarterly,* 5, No. 3 (Summer 1977), 198–215.

The Collector

In *The Collector* John Fowles juxtaposes two accounts of the abduction and death of a beautiful young woman, one narrated by the kidnapper and the other by the woman herself. Freddie Clegg, the psychopathic abductor, tells his story in a very matter-of-fact manner, with a limited vocabulary accurately reflecting his narrow understanding of the world. He is not an introspective person, and he remains totally unaware of the extent or severity of his own problems. Fowles presents Freddie's version of the events first. We see him planning and then executing his crime. Freddie also has the last word, in two brief chapters, where he comments on Miranda's death and later on his discovery of her diary.

Miranda's diary, a chronicle of her thoughts and experiences while in captivity, forms the central part of Fowles's novel. Unlike Freddie, whose account is obsessively devoted to a description of his daily life with Miranda, Miranda uses her diary to record her reflections on past relationships, on the nature of her art, and on her future. Her narrative is written retrospectively, a day at a time, and as a result we are able to follow her development easily. She displays a perceptive self-awareness and a capacity for growth during her confinement as she re-examines her personal goals and her relationships with others. Indeed, horrible though her experience with Freddie is, she clearly benefits from it and becomes a better person. Through her diary, we come to know her intimate thoughts and to care for her and admire her. This makes our sense of loss at her death considerable.

We never feel this intimacy with Freddie. His narration is also written retrospectively, but from a greater distance in time and from a much greater emotional distance. Hints are dropped from the opening pages of his account that the situation will turn out badly for Miranda. Because of this, the hope and optimism she displays in her diary seem pathetic. Her rich interior life remains entirely hidden from Freddie throughout the first part of the narration. When, after her death, he discovers her diary, he concludes from it that "she never loved me, she only thought of herself and the other man all the time." Thus, her diary provides him with a way of justifying his behavior.

Point of view is employed by Fowles as an important means of characterization. The two narrations contrast significantly in style, diction, and levels of self-awareness. Not only are we able to balance two versions of the story against each other, but we are also able to assess Freddie's reading of Miranda's journal. Fowles thus enables the reader to achieve an understanding of the complexity of the situation and a sympathetic involvement with that situation that would be impossible with either a single first-person narrator or an omniscient narrator.

In his adaptation of the novel, William Wyler chooses not to preserve two distinct points of view. He creates sympathetic portrayals of both characters but goes to great lengths to prevent complete identification with either. An examination of several sequences will demonstrate how Wyler achieves this balance.

The film opens with a long high-angle shot of a green field. Freddie enters the field from the right, a small and fragile figure with a butterfly net in his hand. He stalks a butterfly across the field and into a wooded area where he succeeds in capturing it. Through the sequence of shots, Wyler brings us closer and closer to Freddie, culminating with an extreme close-up of Freddie's hands removing the butterfly from the net and placing it in a glass jar, which encloses it for his observation.

Thus, the sequence of shots (extreme long shot to extreme close-up) duplicates the movement from freedom to entrapment, which the film as a whole chronicles. Freddie rises with the jar and net in his hands and looks to his left; the camera pans left to reveal an imposing house with a *For Sale* sign on the gate. He climbs the gate and slowly walks around the house. Once again the camera pans left, as though an unknown force were pulling both Freddie and the viewer. The camera reveals an extension of the house, with a cellar door. Freddie steps onto a low wall and gingerly approaches the basement. (This is the first of many instances of his childlike behavior, and it rather endears him to us.) He advances toward the basement and pushes hard on the door. Until this point we have viewed him objectively, and, as the door yields to his weight, we expect to have a subjective shot of the basement. Instead, Wyler cuts to a low-angle shot from the other side of the basement, so that we view Freddie's entrance objectively. Freddie crosses this room, advances to a second door, and pushes it open, and once again Wyler cuts to a low-angle shot from the other side of the room. The camera tracks slowly to the left as Freddie stands in the doorway staring with wonder. Through its movement the objective camera expresses Freddie's sense of amazement and perhaps even the vacancy that will soon be filled. As Freddie slowly leaves the basement, he is shot in close-up with low lighting, making him suddenly appear sinister. He walks back around the house, and Wyler holds a long low-angle shot of him leaning slightly against the wall. His angular posture, enforced by the strong diagonals of the house behind him, make him appear unbalanced before he has uttered a word. Then, for the first time in the film, we hear Freddie's thoughts in a voice-over. They communicate orally what Wyler has already expressed visually: Freddie's derangement and, more specifically, his plan to capture Miranda as he has just caught a butterfly. Wyler uses voice-overs very sparingly in this film, but rather than making us identify with Freddie, the cold calculating tones of his voice increase our estrangement from him.

It is rather simple to prevent identification with a character like Freddie, but less so with as attractive a character as Miranda. Because of the voice-over, we know that something is going to happen, and the sequence that culminates with Miranda's being chloroformed is very suspenseful. We are fearful for Miranda, but we do not identify with her, in part because we know so little about her. But, through his adroit manipulation of point of view, Wyler maintains this distance even as we come to know each character better.

This handling of point of view is apparent in the scene where the two characters are brought together for the first time at Freddie's house. The scene begins with Freddie carefully carrying Miranda down to the basement. As he turns on the light, we see in an instant that the room has been completely transformed since the last time we viewed it. As Freddie places Miranda on the bed, we are reminded of the caution and care he exercised earlier with the butterfly. After arranging her hair and delicately pulling her skirt over her knees, Freddie removes her shoes and covers her with a comforter. He departs through the double doors, locking each one carefully, and then enters the kitchen. After removing his jacket, he plunges his head under the cold water of the kitchen tap. As he stares dreamily through the window, there is a crash of thunder and rain begins to fall. Freddie dashes outside and frolics exuberantly in the downpour. As he dances about and then sinks onto his back in the driving rain, we experience a sense of exhilaration with him that is both childlike and sexual.

At this hour of triumph, Freddie's thoughts return to the moment when he discovered he had won the money that made his present situation possible. His flashback is in black and white: a perfect expression of the way he views the world. We see him being humiliated, both by his co-workers in the bank and then by his aunt, whom he has told (because he is embarrassed by her lower-class vulgarity) never to visit him at work. This scene contrasts strikingly with the earlier scene of Miranda in the bar, surrounded by friends who respect and admire her. These two scenes provide the only basis for our understanding of how each character reacts with others, and they also contrast with the characters' present solitude. Wyler dissolves from Freddie's flashback to a shot of him recumbent on the grass with his head on the right of the frame. He then cuts immediately to a shot of Miranda on the bed, her head on the left. Later, after she has arisen, she stands at the sink and splashes cold water on her face as if to ask if it can be true. The parallel visuals and the parallel actions (the first of many) suggest a relationship, as yet undefined, between Freddie and Miranda. Our growing perception of this relationship makes identification with either character difficult.

Miranda's awakening is viewed with an objectivity as harsh as our initial view of Freddie. After a brief shot of the ceiling, the camera holds a long close-up of her as she stares around the room with horror. We await a cut to another point-of-view shot, but it never comes; instead, the camera continues to study her face. The glowing red of the heater casts a sinister light over the room. Finally, she arises and pounds desperately on the door. When there is no response, she begins to examine the contents of the room. Although we never view the room through her eyes, we share her sense of discovery. She first notices the impersonal necessities (toothbrush, hairbrush, toilet) and then those objects that make her realize that this prison has been created for her alone: the art books, and especially the drawers filled with clothes in her favorite colors. The fan on the bookcase indicates that her residency may last into the summer (it is only May). Just as she is holding up a dress to check the size, there is a knock on the door. The spectator shares her apprehension: What will this madman do next? As the door opens, Wyler cuts to a low-angle shot from a corner of the basement. The top of the door is obscured, so that Freddie descends into the frame and we see his face last. This is not

The Collector. The unexpected: An attentive young man whose mastery is established by the low-angle shot.

how Miranda sees him (he would be entirely visible once the door was opened); rather, the shot is an objective evocation of the emotions she would have experienced (suspense, fear, apprehension). We expect a psychotic sex maniac and are surprised to discover a courteous young man, dressed in his best Sunday suit, who, as he carefully balances a breakfast tray, says, "I hope you slept well . . ." Wyler keeps us off balance by constantly confounding our expectations.

As a result, Wyler prevents our identification with either character while maintaining our sympathies for both. Nowhere is this more apparent than in the sequence involving Miranda's first bath. Here Wyler puts us in a most difficult position: We sympathize with Freddie and to a certain extent participate in his voyeurism. At the same time, we want Miranda to escape. Yet when that possibility is present, we have mixed feelings about it. Let us consider these points separately.

Film is a medium that makes voyeurs of us all. We are able to invade a character's privacy with moral and legal impunity. In the bath scene, Wyler encourages us to share Freddie's voyeuristic desires. As Miranda examines the bathroom and then begins to undress, Freddie engages her in what at first appears to be a frivolous conversation, until the viewer realizes that in fact he is questioning her about her sex life. Freddie is obsessed with her sexuality, and yet he is so repressed that he can deal with it only indirectly, as in this conversation. Finally, Miranda silences Freddie, and Wyler cuts to a low-angle shot of him seated like a pouting child, visibly frustrated as he listens to Miranda splashing in the tub. However, the viewer has achieved what Freddie longs to do: to observe Miranda as she undresses and bathes. There are limitations to what we see, of course, and Wyler teases us so that we can understand Freddie's frustration more fully.

From the objective shot of Freddie suffering because he has been unable to see what we have just seen, Wyler cuts to an exterior shot. A car stops outside, and a man strides purposefully toward the house. Neither Freddie nor Miranda is aware of the visitor, and Wyler quickly builds suspense around this fact. The bell rings and Freddie panics. He dashes into the bathroom as Miranda screams. A fierce struggle ensues as Freddie attempts to keep Miranda immobile and quiet. Wyler cuts between the frenzied movement in the bathroom and the tranquility outside the house. Receiving no response, the man strolls toward the lit basement, pauses on the steps, and calls down. Our ambivalence toward him is strengthened here because he is shown to be an intruder, probing into Freddie's secrets. Freddie comes to the window and for a moment Wyler holds a long shot with the visitor in the lower left-hand corner and Freddie in the upper right. After a tense pause, Freddie calls from the window and the man returns to the door. At first his conversation seems quite threatening, and we are relieved when he introduces himself as a neighbor. Our relief is a measure of our identification with Freddie. Although the neighbor logically represents the possibility of freedom

for Miranda, Wyler handles the scene in such a way that we become apprehensive for Freddie, and we sympathize with his social awkwardness, as
when he mistakes his neighbor's outstretched hand for a handshake. Wyler
manipulates us so that finally we want the man to leave.

Normally, in a suspenseful scene, we wish to warn the victim because
we want the victim to be saved. But who is the victim here?: Miranda, certainly; but also Freddie. This fact becomes apparent when Miranda turns on
the tap, and we watch the water rising and overflowing, as the neighbor below discourses on the "priest hole." Each time he starts to leave we breathe
a sigh of relief. Finally, the water begins to cascade over the landing, and the
neighbor mounts the stairs. Freddie hurries to cut him off and prevent him
from entering the bathroom. Freddie's violence in tightening Miranda's bonds
almost alienates us, but Wyler recovers the balance with the neighbor's humorous departure. When Freddie returns to the bathroom, Wyler cuts to a
shot from the lower corner of the room, so that Freddie enters the frame in a
manner identical to his first entrance into the basement. Here, too, we expect
something horrible to happen. Instead, Freddie's reaction to Miranda is a
mixture of tenderness and frustration. Once again Wyler has defeated our expectations and, in so doing, has prevented our simple identification with one
of the characters.

Throughout this film we observe a refusal on Wyler's part to show the
action through the point of view of either character. In fact, there is a striking
absence of point-of-view shots in the film. Each time we expect one, Wyler
cuts to an objective shot, and our identification with the character is frustrated. As a result, Wyler maintains our sympathies for each of his characters
more fully, and just as he stresses the resemblances between Freddy and Miranda (by parallel shots and parallel actions), so he also stresses the affinities
between them and us.

The Collector

Production Credits

Director	William Wyler
Producers	Jud Kinberg, John Kohn
Screenplay by	Stanley Mann, John Kohn
Based on the novel by	John Fowles
Director of Photography	Robert Surtees (Hollywood); Robert Krasker (England)
Art Director	John Stoll
Film Editor	Robert Swink
Music by	Maurice Jarre

Great Britain & USA. 1965. 119 minutes. Color.

Cast

Freddie Clegg	Terence Stamp
Miranda Grey	Samantha Eggar
Aunt Annie	Mona Washbourne
Neighbor	Maurice Dallimore

Further Reading

Anderegg, Michael A. *William Wyler*. Boston: Twayne Publishers, 1979.
Corbett, Thomas. "Film and the Book: A Case Study of *The Collector*." *English Journal*, 57, No. 3 (March 1968), 328–333.
Kauffmann, Stanley. "*The Collector*." In *A World of Film: Criticism and Comment*. New York: Harper & Row, 1966.

Rashomon

In the Author's Acknowledgements for *My Mother/My Self* (1978), Nancy Friday speaks of the patterns of mother-daughter relationships she had expected to find on the basis of her extensive interviews: "I was looking for clarification. I discovered Rashomon." Friday elaborates: "Mother: 'I very carefully prepared my daughter for menstruation.' Daughter: 'My mother told me nothing.' Two versions of the same story, different and yet the same . . .'"[3]

Rashomon may be the only example of a foreign film whose title has become a word in English, a word that now expresses the subjectivity of an individual's point of view. In Japanese Rashomon is the name of the largest of the gates in Kyoto, the ancient capital of Japan. Ryunosuke Akutagawa (1892–1927) used it as the title of a short story in which the action occurred at this location, and Akira Kurosawa set his film of the same name there, though it was largely based on another story by Akutagawa, "In the Woods."

"In the Woods" presents the testimonies of seven characters concerning a robbery, rape, and possible murder. Each character speaks as though responding to questions posed by the police commissioner. These characters, who represent a microcosm of Japanese society, have varying degrees of involvement in the crime: a woodcutter, who had seen the dead body of the raped woman's samurai husband; a Buddhist priest, who had observed the couple traveling on the road; the policeman who had captured the rapist; the aged mother of the rape victim; Tajomaru, the robber, rapist, and possibly also the murderer; the wife; and the dead husband, whose story is narrated

---

[3]Nancy Friday, *My Mother/My Self* (New York: Delacorte Press, 1978), p. xiv.

through a medium. Each of these characters presents his or her testimony to us directly, without comment on the confessions of the others. Thus, readers are placed in the role of the police commissioner and forced to sift among the testimonies and judge them for themselves.

For his adaptation, Kurosawa has deleted the mother, whose version adds little to the story, and has altered the presentation of the stories significantly. The film takes place after the testimonies have been given, and thus, the viewer is not present at the trial. Two of the witnesses, the woodcutter and the priest, seek shelter during a rainstorm at the Rashomon gate, an appropriate symbol of the decaying institutions and ideals that confront them. There the witnesses ponder the meaning of what they have heard, their perplexity stems in part from a discovery we too make during the film: Each participant or witness has related a different version of the events. We learn this through the recollections of the priest and woodcutter rather than, as in the story, the characters' own testimonies. Only the woodcutter's testimony is presented to us directly. The other testimonies are distorted by being presented secondhand.

The woodcutter and the priest seem compelled to discuss the events because of their horror and their confusion. At the outset the woodcutter knows (or at least thinks he knows) what has happened, but the priest is genuinely confused. They are joined at the gate by a commoner, as he is designated in the film, who inquires about the event in order to pass the time until the downpour ceases. He initially functions as a catalyst whose presence encourages the others' recollections. The woodcutter speaks first and repeats the story he had told the day before at the police station. In fact, when the sequence ends, Kurosawa cuts to the police station, where we see the woodcutter finishing his tale. He has been the first to testify at the station, and no one else is present in the shot, so his testimony (unlike the others') was probably heard by no one but the commissioner. We tend to believe him because his story is dramatized before the others' and because it is presented directly.

Next, the priest relates what he saw. His story is a flashback (his view of the couple on the road, before the crime occurred) within another flashback (his testimony at the police station). The importance of the priest lies in his participation at the trial. He witnesses the other testimonies (although not the event itself) and can comment upon them impartially.

The police agent who has captured Tajomaru is the third to testify, and through him we begin to understand how a testimony can be distorted by the needs of the teller. The agent boasts of how he captured the "notorious bandit." But Tajomaru interrupts the police agent with vociferous objections, unlike in the short story, where each testimony is self-enclosed. Tajomaru claims that he would still be free if he had not drunk from a poisoned spring, which made him ill. Such a statement, of course, cannot be verified, and it is the first indication of the role subjectivity plays in the film.

Tajomaru testifies next, and he begins by noting that since his death is imminent, he is free to tell the truth. However, he still has his self-image and his reputation to protect, and he enhances both in his retelling of the events. His is the longest (twenty minutes) and most complete version of what happened, beginning with his seeing the couple as they pass him on the road, through his deception of the husband, rape of the wife, and killing of the husband. Throughout, Tajomaru emphasizes his total control of the situation and his innate superiority to the couple, though he is below them socially. The husband is foolish and greedy and easily deceived. The wife is a "spitfire," a woman full of fight and energy, and thus worthy of Tajomaru's seduction. After the seduction, he engages (with the wife's encouragement) in combat with the husband, which Kurosawa depicts as the most heroic of encounters, accompanied by martial music on the soundtrack. Although the samurai husband fights valiantly, crossing swords with Tajomaru twenty-three times, he is finally defeated. However, as Tajomaru is about the thrust the sword into the fallen body of the husband, the camera (shooting across the husband toward Tajomaru) tilts up, thereby eliminating the husband from the frame. Kurosawa purposely does not show the one event (as opposed to attitude) about which the participants will present conflicting testimony.

At the end of Tajomaru's version, the woodcutter declares that it is "a lie." "They're all lies," he states. "Tajomaru's confession, the woman's story—they're lies!" We wonder how he can be so certain, since at the conclusion of his own testimony he had declared that he did not witness the rape or murder. In fact, he is lying himself (for reasons we later discover) and projecting his own duplicity onto others.

Rashomon. Tajomaru's point of view: The wife proves herself to be worthy of his attention.

The next testimony, the wife's, is told secondhand like Tajomaru's story: The priest is merely repeating what the wife had confessed at the police station, even though Kurosawa dramatizes it. The wife begins her story after the rape. In all versions, this event is followed by a conversation between the wife and Tajomaru, which the husband observes from a distance. According to the wife, Tajomaru divulges his identity and boasts of his prowess. Then, after jeering at the couple, he leaves them to their fate. She is filled with shame and receives no consolation from her husband, who views her with disgust. She removes her dagger from the ground and advances toward him. Finally, she lunges toward her husband, as though possessed. Since he is off screen, we see nothing more. The wife faints, and when she awakens she finds her husband slumped on the ground with the dagger in his chest.

Kurosawa cuts from her story back to the gate, and by this time the commoner too is beginning to be confused. How was the husband killed? And what was the nature of the conversation following the rape? The commoner voices our own questions.

Another set of answers is provided by the dead husband, whose version of the events is presented to us through the testimony of a medium. He begins his story after the attack and interprets the conversation between his wife

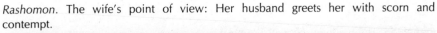

Rashomon. The wife's point of view: Her husband greets her with scorn and contempt.

and Tajomaru as Tajomaru attempts to console the wife. However, given the distance at which this conversation takes place, it is very unlikely that the husband could have heard it. Then he views her face from afar and concludes that "never, in all of our life together, had I seen her more beautiful." His own desires and projections influence his observations (as do those of both his wife and Tajomaru in their confessions). At this point his wife turns to Tajomaru and, pointing in her husband's direction, screams : "Kill him, kill him!" Tajomaru then rejects the wife and flings her upon the ground: "What do you want me to do? Kill her? [or] Let her go?" he asks the husband. The wife flees, and Tajomaru cuts the husband's bonds before leaving. After a long period of reflection, the husband takes his wife's dagger and plunges it into his chest. We watch him sink downward, before Kurosawa cuts to the medium, whose fall completes the husband's. This is the first time we have seen the sword or dagger actually penetrate the husband. However, although this version of the events is told with the greatest clarity, it is actually the furthest removed from the teller: The woodcutter and/or the priest are telling the commoner what they had been told by a medium who purported to be speaking for a man now dead!

This version, in addition to adding a new viewpoint, serves another function: It suggests the woodcutter's involvement. The medium concludes

Rashomon. The medium recounts the husband's version: A deceitful wife.

her narration by noting that "I lay quietly in this stillness. Then someone seemed to approach me. Softly, gently. Who could it have been? Then someone's hand grasped the dagger and drew it out." This scene is shot in medium close-up, and thus, the two observers in the rear—the woodcutter and the priest—are closer to us than in previous scenes in the courtyard. As the medium mentions the withdrawal of the dagger, the woodcutter blinks his eye nervously. Then the medium falls forward to the ground, leaving the woodcutter in center frame. Kurosawa holds this shot for fifty-nine seconds (thus making it one of the longest shots in the film), so that we will establish a connection between the medium's words and the woodcutter. Kurosawa then cuts to the gate; the commoner and the priest are seated, while the woodcutter paces back and forth several times before denying the story. But now it is clear that he lied earlier. Was it simply, as he says, so that he would not become involved? Or was it to conceal the fact that he had stolen the dagger?

The woodcutter presents his second version of the events, beginning (as had everyone but Tajomaru) with the conversation after the rape. Interestingly, his is the only version to be told without music. Does this reflect the veracity of his version or merely the fact that he is addressing us directly? Tajomaru promises to reform if only the woman will have him, and we see him pleading with her in a way Tajomaru himself would never have acknowledged. The samurai husband, when released, refuses to fight. Seeing that the husband no longer wants his wife diminishes Tajomaru's interest in her, until she calls them cowards and goads them into fighting each other. In contrast to Tajomaru's recollection of the fight, the woodcutter's version is an unheroic and realistic struggle, the two men fighting for their lives like animals. The struggle concludes with Tajomaru's victory, and the woodcutter corroborates Tajomaru's story about how it was accomplished. But once again, when the sword is about to be plunged downward, the camera tilts up so that we do not see the husband actually being killed. There is no way, in fact, that we can be sure how, or by whose hand, the husband died. All participants have their own reasons for narrating the story as they do, and hence, we are left with four irreconcilable versions. They agree on the initial deception of the husband and on the rape, but on little else.

The woodcutter is shocked at how much these stories differ from what he thinks he has seen himself, without acknowledging that he too is capable of distorting the facts. The priest is distressed by what he has witnessed and heard, but the commoner accepts the confusion as an affirmation of the duplicity and the debased nature of humankind. The film thus far has enabled the woodcutter and the priest to relive their experiences both directly, as they were involved in the action, and secondarily, through the confessions at the police station. Like the audience, the commoner has been introduced to these stories for the first time.

At the end of his film, Kurosawa creates a situation that enables these characters to demonstrate how, if at all, they have been changed by what they have witnessed and participated in. For the first time, we see an extended action occurring in the present. The commoner behaves in a manner that would confirm the dismal view of humanity expressed by the priest at the beginning of the film. During the film, the commoner has made kindling out of the Rashomon gate, and so has shown that he has no respect for tradition or history; by stealing the clothes of the newly discovered baby, he shows that he has no respect for the future either. *Rashomon* came out of a war-torn nation, and nowhere is this more evident than in this final episode where the rays of sunshine that greet the woodcutter's positive decision coincide with Oriental music, heard for the first time in the film. The encounter has changed the woodcutter, who now is able to accept responsibility for another without thinking of himself. By direct and vicarious experience, Kurosawa suggests, we can profit and move forward. Now the priest, heartened at last, and the woodcutter bow to each other in Japanese fashion. Clutching the future in his hands, the woodcutter strides forward with the crumbling ruins of the past behind him.

Clearly, the word *Rashomon* no longer refers to the setting of the film, nor to the burden of history the gate represented, nor even to Kurosawa's optimistic conclusion. Instead, it refers to the extreme subjectivity with which an event—any event—will necessarily be viewed by those who participate in it. By his extraordinary manipulation of point of view, Kurosawa demonstrates that there are as many versions of an event as there are participants: The "truth" lies in a recognition of this fact rather than in the superiority of any one version.

Rashomon

Production Credits

Director	Akira Kurosawa
Producer	Jingo Minoru (later titles: Produced by Masaichi Nagata)
Screenplay by	Shinobu Hashimoto and Akira Kurosawa
Based on "Rashomon" and "In the Woods" by	Ryunosuke Akutagawa
Director of Photography	Kazuo Miyagawa
Art Director	So Matsuyama
Music by	Fumio Hayasaka

Japan. 1950. 88 minutes. Black & white.

Cast

Tajomaru, the bandit	Toshiro Mifune
Takehiro, the samurai	Masayuki Mori

Masago, his wife	Machiko Kyo
The woodcutter	Takashi Shimura
The priest	Minoru Chiaki
The commoner	Kichijiro Ueda
The police agent	Daisuke Kato
The medium	Fumiko Homma

Further Reading

Beja, Morris. *Film and Literature*. New York: Longman, 1979.

Bellone, Julius, ed. *Renaissance of the Film*. New York: Collier Books, 1970.

Cook, David A. *A History of Narrative Film*. New York: W. W. Norton and Co., 1981.

DeNitto, Dennis and William Herman. *Film and the Critical Eye*. New York: Macmillan Publishing Co., 1975.

Kauffmann, Stanley. *Living Images*. New York: Harper & Row, 1975.

Kurosawa, Akira. *Rashomon: A Film*. New York: Grove Press, 1969.

McVay, Douglas. "The Rebel in a Kimono." *Films and Filming*, 7, No. 10 (July 1961), 9–101.

Richie, Donald. *The Films of Akira Kurosawa*. Berkeley: University of California Press, 1970.

_____. *Focus on Rashomon*. Englewood Cliffs, New Jersey: Prentice-Hall, 1972.

Rashōmon
Akutagawa Ryūnosuke

Translated from the Japanese by Virginia Marcus

At dusk the servant huddled under the eaves of Rashōmon Gate waiting for the rain to stop. A lone cricket clung to one of the thick, weather-beaten pillars of the gate, where the red paint had begun to peel off. The man sat by himself under the towering structure. Rashōmon Gate stood on busy Sujaku Street, and a person might expect to find others in their sedge hats or court caps seeking shelter from the storm. Yet tonight no one else ventured into sight.

In the late twelfth century, Kyōto had been plagued by one disaster after another—earthquakes, tornadoes, fires, famines—and the damage throughout the city had reached untold proportions. Historical records tell how people smashed Buddhist icons and piled the gilded or lacquered pieces by the roadside to be sold for firewood. Because the entire city lay in ruins, no one gave much thought to the repair of Rashōmon Gate. The dilapidated structure soon became a haven for wild animals and thieves, and eventually people took to dumping unclaimed bodies there. The place had a forbidding air to it, and no one dared to go near the gate after sundown.

But crows flocked to Rashōmon Gate. During the day they made a racket as they swarmed around the rooftiles. At dusk, when they flew against the glowing sunset, they could be taken for black seeds scattered in the wind. No doubt they came to peck at the corpses abandoned in the gate's loft.

Today, however, not a single crow flew overhead. Perhaps it was already too late in the day. Their white droppings were splattered over the stone steps, now crumbling and overgrown with tall weeds. The servant, dressed in a worn, blue kimono, sat on the top step and picked at the large pimple on his right cheek. All the while he stared aimlessly out into the rain.

I said that he was waiting for a break in the rain, but in fact this man had nowhere to go. Ordinarily, he would return to his master's house, but he had been dismissed a few days before. The city of Kyōto had fallen into unprecedented decline, and the dismissal of a faithful servant was little more than a tiny tremor in this unsettled age.

No, the man was not really waiting for the rain to stop. The truth is that he was stranded in the downpour. He had no idea where to turn. And to make matters worse, the rain, which had begun late in the afternoon and showed no signs of letting up, had considerably disheartened him. The servant naturally turned to thoughts of his future. "It's hopeless. What can I do?" he wondered, half-listening to the rain beating down on the road. The rains pelting Rashōmon Gate bore in with a roar. As evening descended, a low cloud, dark and foreboding, loomed heavily above the corner rooftiles.

The servant had little time to decide a course of action. He would soon die of hunger and be found by the roadside or next to a dirt wall. He would be thrown among the corpses in the loft like a stray dog. When he thought things over, he kept arriving at the same conclusion. He had no choice. He had to do something—except that something meant stealing in order to stay alive. This was the only way out, he knew, but somehow he could not bring himself to do it.

He sneezed loudly and picked his listless body off the ground. As the cold night air fell on the city and the wind whipped around the pillars in the darkness, he longed for the warmth of a fire. The lone cricket had by now left its perch on the red pillar.

The man looked around and then drew his head down, pulling the collar of his blue kimono up over his thin underclothes until it was tight around his neck. "If only I could find a hideaway, a shelter from the storm," he thought. And at that moment, he spotted a large red ladder leading up to the loft. It occurred to him that anyone he might find up there would be dead. He lifted his straw sandal onto the bottom rung, checking that the sword at his side stayed in place. He inched his way up as stealthily as a cat and held his breath. Midway up the ladder, he looked above him. A ray of light shone faintly on his bearded face, on the side where red pus was oozing from the pimple on his cheek. The only thing he expected to find up there was a pile of bodies. But, when he climbed higher, it struck him that someone had lit a fire. There it was—a flickering yellow light playing among the cobwebs that hung from every corner of the ceiling. What kind of madman would light a fire in the loft of Rashōmon Gate on such a rainy night?

Quiet as a lizard, he moved up the steep ladder until he reached the top. He crouched down, craned his neck and peered inside the room, fighting off his fear. Corpses were indeed strewn about the loft, just as he had heard. The fire illuminated a smaller area than he had first thought. He could not begin to count the bodies lying there. Although barely able to see, he peered through the darkness. He managed to distinguish the men from the women. Some were naked, others clothed. Could these lifeless clay dolls, sprawled on the floor with mouths agape and arms thrown about, have once been living human beings? The firelight shone dimly on their chests and shoulders. The dark recesses of their bodies remained totally hidden in shadow. Like the deaf and dumb, they lay forever silent.

The room reeked of decaying flesh. The servant instinctively brought his hand to his nose, but a moment later he let it down, disregarding the stench. The scene was so terrifying that he had lost his sense of smell. He saw before him an old woman holding a torch and crouching down among the dead. She was short and thin, and she had the face of a monkey. She wore a crimson kimono. Her gaze was fixed upon one of the bodies. It would be that of a woman, judging from the long hair.

More horrified than curious, the man gasped for breath. His hair actually stood on end. The old woman, having wedged her torch between the floorboards, now held the head that she had been staring at. Then, like a monkey grooming its young, she began to pull out one long strand of hair after another. Each one seemed to lift right out of the head.

With every hair she plucked, the man's fear gradually subsided. But, at the same time, he began to feel an intense hatred for this old woman. To put it more accurately, a growing aversion to all manner of evil slowly welled up inside him. If at this moment he were to weigh the merits of stealing or starving to death, as he had done under the gate, he would have chosen death without any hesitation. Like the old woman's torch thrust between those slats, he was burning with hatred.

Naturally, he had no way of knowing why this woman was removing the hair of the dead. He was not sure, then, if he should condemn her. Nevertheless, this fiendish act on a stormy night atop Rashōmon Gate was inexcusable. He had, of course, already forgotten that only a few minutes earlier he himself had made up his mind to become a thief.

Summoning all his strength, he lifted himself off the ladder and suddenly sprang into the loft. With sword in hand, he landed in front of the woman. Needless to say, she was frightened out of her wits. She jumped to her feet as swiftly as an arrow. Stumbling over the bodies, she ran for the ladder, but he blocked her path.

"You witch!" he shouted. "Where do you think you're going?"

When she tried to shove him aside, he held her back, not letting her escape. In the sea of corpses the two silently grappled with each other, but the old woman was no match for him. He wrenched her arm, all skin and bones like a scrawny chicken, and threw her down.

"Now out with it! What have you been up to? If you don't tell me, I'll . . ." He let go of her, then brandished his sword, thrusting the silver blade in front of her face. She did not utter a word. As if mute, she remained silent, her hands trembling and her shoulders shaking as she gasped for breath. Her gaping expression made it look as though her eyes would pop out of her head. When it finally occurred to him that the woman's life was in his hands, the fiery venom in his heart began to cool. A wave of satisfaction and complacency washed over him, now that he had acted so decisively. Looking down at the old crone, he spoke less roughly.

"I'm not the police. I'm only passing through, and I happened to come by this gate. I won't tie you up. I wouldn't do anything like that. Just tell me what you're doing up here."

The old woman opened her eyes still wider and stared at him. They were the beady red eyes of a bird of prey. Her shrivelled mouth seemed to be joined to her nose, and she moved her lips as though chewing on something. Her Adam's apple, sharp and pointed, bobbed up and down her skinny neck. Between gasps he could make out a rasping, crow-like voice coming from somewhere deep in her throat. "I pull their hair . . . I pull it . . . to make wigs."

The man was disappointed. He had not expected such a banal response. His hatred returned, only this time he controlled it. The old woman doubtless knew what he was thinking. Holding the hair that she had plucked from the corpse, she let out a croaking sound. "It's terrible, I know," she mumbled, "plucking hair from the dead. But they wouldn't mind—I'm sure of it. This woman here used to cut up snakes and palm them off as dried fish to the palace guards. If the plague hadn't killed her, she'd still be doing business. The guards used to buy all she had, they thought it was so good. She didn't do anything wrong. She would have starved to death otherwise. She had no choice. What I do isn't wrong, either. I'd die of hunger if I didn't do this. I can't help it. I know the woman would forgive me."

So went the old lady's explanation. The man remained calm as he listened to her, sword in hand. With his free hand, he kept digging at the festering pimple on his right cheek. The woman's words gave him the courage he had lacked under the gate. True, he had dared to climb up to the loft, but now he felt a different kind of boldness. Whether to steal or not—the question no longer troubled him. He now knew that he would not starve to death.

"Really?" he asked her sarcastically when she had finished talking. "Is that so?" He stepped toward her. His right hand stopped picking at his cheek and grabbed the woman by the collar. "Then you won't blame me for robbing you!" he said with clenched teeth. "Otherwise I'd starve to death, too."

Within seconds he had ripped off her kimono. She clung to his leg, but he kicked her violently and flung her onto the pile of corpses. It was only a few steps to the ladder. With her crimson kimono under his arm, he sped down the steps and into the depths of the night.

The old woman looked as though she had fallen down dead, but before long she managed to lift herself up from the pile of bodies. Groping her way by the light of the torch, she grumbled and moaned as she crawled over to the ladder. She stared below, her short white hair falling in her face. Only the pitch black night, empty and void, awaited her.

As for the servant, his whereabouts were never discovered.

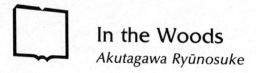

In the Woods
Akutagawa Ryūnosuke

Translated from the Japanese by Virginia Marcus

The Woodcutter's Account to the Commissioner

That's right. I'm the one who found the body. I discovered it this morning in a grove up in the mountains. I was going into the backwoods to cut cedar, the way I always do.

Where? In a deserted bamboo grove about six-hundred yards from the Yamashina post road. Cedar saplings were also growing among the bamboo. The dead man was lying on his back, and he had on a light blue kimono and one of those soft caps they wear in Kyōto. True, there was only one wound, but it was from a sword thrust right through the chest. The fallen leaves by the body were stained dark red from the blood.

No, he had stopped bleeding by then. The wound looked as though it had dried up. I remember there was a horsefly sitting right on it—must not have heard me coming.

Did I find the weapon? No, nothing. But I did come across a rope under one of the cedars. Oh yes, and a comb. Nothing else, just a rope and a comb. I tell you, he must have put up a good fight, though. The underbrush was completely trampled.

Was there a horse nearby? A horse couldn't get into that thicket. It was too far off the beaten path.

• • •

The Itinerant Priest's Account to the Commissioner

I'm certain I saw the dead man yesterday.

What time? Around noon, on the road that goes from Sekiyama to Ya-mashina. A woman was riding a horse and he was walking beside her. They were going toward Sekiyama. The woman had on a veil, so I couldn't see what she looked like. I did notice what she was wearing, though. It was one of those layered kimonos, maroon with a blue lining. The horse was light-colored with a clipped mane.

Its height? Do I think it was about four feet? Well, being a Buddhist priest, I don't pay much attention to that sort of thing. It's hard to say.

The man? He had a long sword at his side and was carrying a bow and arrows. There were some twenty arrows—military ones, I think—in his black quiver. I do remember that much about him.

Who could have dreamed that such a thing would happen? Truly, our lives are as fleeting as the dew, as ephemeral as a flash of lightning. What an awful thing to have happened. I'm simply at a loss for words.

• • •

The Policeman's Account to the Commissioner

The man I arrested? Why, he's the famous thief, Tajōmaru. I found him lying on the stone bridge at Awataguchi, moaning away. He must have fallen off his horse.

The time? Yesterday, around eight o'clock at night. The last time I tried to nab him, he had on that same blue kimono and his sword was unsheathed and ready for battle. Yesterday, though, he also had a bow and arrows.

You say they belonged to the dead man? Well, then, Tajōmaru has to be the murderer. All these things—the bow wrapped in leather, the black quiver and the seventeen military arrows with hawk feathers—these were all probably the dead man's.

Yes, that's right. A light-colored horse with a clipped mane. I'm sure it was the hand of fate that threw him from that animal. It was grazing by the roadside not far from the bridge. Its long tether was just hanging there.

He's one of the thieves who roam the streets of Kyōto, all right, but he's also known to go after women. They say he's the one who killed the court lady and the young girl last fall. They were making a visit to the Toribe Temple and were found murdered in the mountains behind the statue of Binzuru. If Tajōmaru did kill this man, then who knows what became of the woman on the horse? I know this is none of my business, but please find out what happened to her.

• • •

The Mother's Account to the Commissioner

Yes, the deceased was married to my daughter. But he wasn't from Kyōto. His name is Kanazawa Takehiro, a samurai from a city in Wakasa. He was twenty-six years old.

No, he had no enemies to speak of. He was a kind and gentle man.

My daughter? Her name is Masago. She's nineteen and as headstrong as any man. Takehiro was the only man she had ever been with. She has a darkish complexion and a small, oval face with a mole near the corner of her left eye.

They set out for Wakasa yesterday. Why did this terrible thing have to happen? What on earth has become of her? The death of my son-in-law is bad enough, but my daughter . . . I'll never get over it. Please. I'm an old woman. I beg you. Please search every corner of these woods. This thief, this Tajōmaru—he is a despicable man. Not only Takehiro, but my daughter, too . . . (She could not be understood through her tears.)

• • •

Tajōmaru's Confession

I killed him, but I didn't kill her.

Then where is she? I have no idea. Look, it won't do you any good to torture me. I can't tell you something I don't know. I have nothing to hide from you.

I met up with those two yesterday, just past noon. I saw the woman's face for a brief second when the wind caught her veil. All I got was a glimpse, though. But, I tell you, she had the face of an angel. I knew right then I had to have her, even if it meant killing him.

Killing someone is not the big thing you make it out to be. Not for me at least. If I'm going to get the woman, the man has to be done away with. But, unlike you, I use a real weapon to kill with. You have no need for swords. You murder with your money and power. You make people think you're so concerned about them, with your fancy talk, and then you go in for the kill. No blood gets spilled. No one dies. But, still, you've ruined them. Who's the real villain here—me or you? (He snickered at them.)

I didn't want to kill that man. I would've been happy enough just to have her. I had planned to do it without killing him, but I couldn't do anything on the Yamashina road. Luring them into the woods was easy, though. After I got in good with them, I told them I had dug up some swords and mirrors from an old grave and buried them for safekeeping in a mountain thicket. If they wanted anything, I would let it go cheap. The man grew more and more interested. Ah! the power of greed. In less than an hour, the couple had turned their horse onto the mountain path.

When we reached a thicket, I told them to go in and see for themselves. The man was itching to get his hands on the goods, so he was more than willing. The woman, though, wouldn't get off the horse. She said she'd stay behind. And it was no wonder, considering that dense grove. Actually, things turned out exactly the way I planned. The two of us went into the thicket while the woman waited.

After about fifty yards, the bamboo trees opened up onto a small grove of cedars. I couldn't have asked for a better place. While we were making our way through the underbrush, I told him that the stuff was buried under one of the cedars. He headed straight for the young, spindly trees. The bamboo had begun to thin out and we could see the clump of cedars. As soon as we got there, I pounced on him. He may have been a tough samurai, armed with his swords, but this time he was caught off guard. I had him tied to a tree in no time.

What did I use for a rope? Fortunately, we thieves always carry a rope. You never know when you might have to jump over a wall or something. Anyway, all I had to do now was gag him with bamboo leaves so that he couldn't yell.

When I was done with him, I went back to the woman. I told her the man had suddenly taken sick and she should go to him. She fell for it, all right. She removed her hat and let me lead her by the hand into the woods. The minute she saw him tied to the tree, she pulled out a dagger from her breast pocket. I never saw such a violent woman. She could have stabbed me in the side if I hadn't been careful. I dodged her, but she came at me with a vengeance. She was a real tigress, but no one fools with Tajōmaru. Somehow or other, without drawing my sword, I managed to knock the dagger out of her hand. If a woman is unarmed, it doesn't matter how strong she is. At last I made her give in to me. I had my way with her, and I didn't have to kill the man. My plan was working.

That's right, at this point I hadn't killed him. Nor was I planning to. I was about to make my getaway, leaving the woman sprawled on the ground crying, when suddenly she grabbed my arm like someone possessed. I could barely figure out what she was saying through her screams. She said that one of us had to die—either me or the husband, that she couldn't bear having the two of us know what'd been done to her. Panting for breath, she promised to go with the one who survived. Then and there I knew I wanted to kill the man. (He spoke excitedly in an ominous tone.)

You must think I'm ruthless and cruel. But you didn't see her face. If you could have only seen the gleam in her eyes! The moment I looked into those eyes I knew I had to have her for my wife. Lightning could have struck me dead—I didn't care. I would make her mine. She was the only thing I could think about. But you're wrong if you think it was lust that drove me to do it. If that's all it was, I would have kicked her down and then run off. And I wouldn't have stained my sword with his blood. But the minute I saw her face there in the dark of the bushes I knew that I couldn't leave without killing the man.

I wanted to do this thing right, so I untied him and told him to put up a good fight. (The rope that you found under the cedar is the one I forgot to get rid of.) The man turned pale as death and drew his sword. Without a word, he lunged at me in a rage. Of course I don't have to tell you what happened. The twenty-third slash of my sword went right through his chest. The twenty-third cut, mind you. This still amazes me. He's the only person who's ever lasted for more than twenty blows. (The man smiled cheerfully.)

When he fell to the ground, I lowered my bloody weapon and returned for the woman. But who would have guessed it? She'd disappeared. Where could she have gone? Not a trace of her. She wasn't in the cedar grove and she wasn't in the bamboo brush. I tried listening for her, but all I heard were the man's dying gasps. She probably ran through the thicket for help after we started fighting. That's when it dawned on me that my own life might be in danger. I grabbed the man's sword and his bow and arrows and ran back to the mountain road. There's no point in telling you what happened after that. Before I reached Kyōto, though, I had gotten rid of the sword.

So that's my story. I'm ready to take my punishment. I suppose my head will hang on the prison gate for everyone to see. (He seemed quite pleased with himself.)

•　•　•

The Woman's Confession at Kiyomizu Temple

After the man in the blue kimono raped me, he glared at my husband, who was tied to the tree, and sneered at him. That grin must have driven my husband mad. He squirmed and writhed in anguish, but the ropes only cut deeper and deeper into his flesh. Without thinking, I headed to his side, but I stumbled and before I could get to him the man kicked me down. It was at that moment that I saw the strange glint in my husband's eyes. There's no way to describe the look. When I think of it, I can't stop trembling. He couldn't speak, but his expression told me everything. He wasn't angry, or sad. No, that ice-cold glare was full of nothing but contempt for me. The man had kicked me down, but that's not what made me scream like a madwoman and eventually pass out. It was the daggers in my husband's eyes.

When I came to, the man had disappeared. My husband was the only one there, still tied to the base of the tree. I managed to pick myself up from the fallen leaves, and I looked my husband straight in the eye. There was no change. An icy venom still lurked in his glare. Shame, desperation, anger—I can't tell you what I was feeling at that moment. I staggered to my feet and went over to him.

"I can't be with you after what's happened," I told him. "I've made up my mind to die. But . . . but I want you to die with me. I've been disgraced and you saw everything. I can't leave you behind like this."

My earnest plea fell on deaf ears. He only stared at me with disgust. It was all I could do to contain my anguish. I went to look for my husband's sword. The thief no doubt took it, along with the bow and arrows. I couldn't find it anywhere. But luckily my dagger had fallen on the ground.

"Die with me. Let me take your life," I said again, brandishing the blade. "Then I'll put an end to mine."

He finally tried to move his lips, but, gagged as he was with bamboo leaves, not a word came out of his mouth. Even so, it suddenly came to me that he was trying to say "Kill me!" He still had a look of loathing in his eyes. What happened next was like a nightmare. I plunged the dagger through his blue kimono and into his chest.

I must have fainted again, because when I finally looked over to my husband, still bound to the tree, he had already breathed his last. The setting sun shone down upon his pale face through the cedars in the bamboo grove. As I untied him, I tried to hold back my tears.

And . . . and then what did I do? I don't have the strength to go on with this . . . In any case, I didn't have it in me to commit suicide, though believe me I tried. I tried slitting my throat, and, when that didn't work, I tried drowning myself in the pond at the foot of the mountains. But it was no good. I couldn't. This shame will be with me as long as I live. (She smiled wanly.) I'm sure even the compassionate Kannon, Goddess of Mercy though she be, would turn her back on such a worthless human being. I was raped by that thief; I murdered my husband. How can I go on? How can I . . . (She burst into tears.)

• • •

The Dead Man's Account Told Through a Medium

The thief had raped my wife and was sitting next to her trying to console her. I couldn't talk of course. I was tied to the tree, but any number of times I signalled to her with my eyes. I wanted to tell her not to believe a word he says, that it's all lies. But she only sat in the bamboo grass looking down at her lap in despair. Somehow she seemed to be listening to him. I was seething with jealousy, but the thief had a way with words.

"It only happened once, but you're unclean now," he told her. "So how can you go on being with him? How about becoming my wife? Wouldn't that be better than staying with him? I was violent with you only because I love you."

How could he dare to say such things! My wife lifted her head up as if she were in a trance. I had never seen her so beautiful. But what did this beautiful wife of mine say to the thief, there in front of her own husband tied to a tree? My soul may wander in this black wilderness, but I still writhe with anger and hatred every time I recall her words. "I'll go wherever you go," she said. "Please take me with you." (A long pause.)

That wasn't her only crime. If that had been all, I wouldn't be suffering so in this land of darkness. This is what happened.

My wife held the thief's hand as if in a daze. She was about to leave the woods with him when suddenly she grew pale and pointed at me under the cedar tree. Half-crazed, she screamed, "Kill him! If he lives, I can't go with you. Kill him!" Even now I can hear the echo of her words gathering momentum like a windstorm and hurling me into the depths of this black abyss.

Never had I heard such loathsome words. I could hardly believe they came from a human being. Has anyone ever heard such a cursed voice? Anyone? (He suddenly broke out with a sneer.) Even the thief was taken aback when he heard her. "Kill him!" she screamed, clutching his arm. He stared at her and seemed unable to answer, or so I thought. But, before I knew it, he kicked her to the ground and stood calmly with his arms folded. He turned to me. "Tell me what I should do with her. Kill her? Or let her live? Just nod yes or no. Kill her?" When I heard this, I wanted to forgive him for his crime. (Again, a long pause.)

While I was trying to decide whether he should kill her or not, she screamed and ran deeper into the woods. He darted after her but couldn't even manage to grasp hold of her billowing sleeves. All I could do was watch this nightmare.

After my wife escaped, the thief picked up my sword and bow and arrows. When he cut me free, he mumbled something about how *his* life was at stake now. Then he ran out of the woods and disappeared. Afterwards, all was still. No, that's not true. I could hear someone crying. As I untied the rope, I strained my ears only to realize that the sound I heard was coming from me. I was sobbing. (For the third time, a long pause.)

At last I lifted my exhausted body from the ground. Below, glistening at my feet, was the dagger my wife had dropped. I picked it up and plunged it into my chest. A bloody lump rose in my throat, but there was no pain. A numbing chill spread through me, and then a hush fell over the woods. How peaceful it was—not a single bird chirping in the sky above. A faint ray of sunlight shone dimly on the treetops, but it soon disappeared as darkness fell. I could no longer see the bamboo trees and the cedars. As I lay on the ground, a tomblike quiet flooded over me.

Shortly after, someone came sneaking over to my side. I tried to see who it was, but darkness had already closed in on me. Whoever it was gently pulled the dagger out of my chest. A clot of blood, thick and slimy, gushed up into my mouth again. Ever since, I have been engulfed in the darkness of this shadowy abyss.

6

The World of Inner Experience

Introduction

In our discussion of point of view, we observed that novelists developed fictional techniques in the late nineteenth century that enabled implied authors to disappear from their work. This occurred both in the development of first-person narration and in those third-person narrations that were either limited or objective. At the same time, attempts were being made to understand more fully the world of inner experience and to express it with as much detail as could be used to portray the objective world. Could the world of dreams, fantasies, and recollections become as central to a fictional work as the external world of objects and actions?

Feelings and thoughts had been depicted in the earliest fictional works, but they had not been presented directly. Rather, they had been conveyed through set speeches or allegory or through the intervention of an omniscient narrator. The following passage from *The Treasure of the Sierra Madre* is typical of a simple depiction of thoughts:

> "Maybe," he was thinking, "I didn't bump him off at all. Perhaps he only staggered and dropped to the ground without being hit. Let's figure that out. How was it?

These thoughts occur in the form of an overheard speech, as though the character were talking to himself. To the extent that they are conveyed in an ordered and logical form, they resemble another convention, the soliloquy, examples of which abound in *Macbeth*. In both the overheard speech and the soliloquy, thoughts are reported rather than dramatized. A similar but more complex presentation can be cited from D. H. Lawrence's *Women in Love*. Mrs. Critch is discussing Gerald with Birkin, and she tells him that she wishes Gerald had a friend.

> Birkin looked down into her eyes, which were blue, and watching heavily. He could not understand them. "Am I my brother's keeper?" he said to himself, almost flippantly.
>
> Then he remembered, with a slight shock, that that was Cain's cry. And Gerald was Cain, if anybody. Not that he was Cain, either, although he had slain his brother. There was such a thing as pure accident, and the consequences did not attach to one, even though one had killed one's brother in such wise. Gerald as a boy had accidentally killed his brother. What then? Why seek to draw a brand and a curse across the life that had caused the accident? A man can live by accident, and die by accident. Or can he not? Is every man's life subject to pure accident, it is only the race, the genus, the species, that has a universal reference? Or is this not true, is there no such thing as pure accident? Has everything that happens a universal significance? Has it? Birkin, pondering as he stood there, had forgotten Mrs. Critch, as she had forgotten him.

Here we have a much more vivid sense of a mind at work, being drawn from one idea to the next, from one question to the next, as the consciousness withdraws from conversation into reverie. Although present, the omniscient narrator is less evident than in the preceding passage, and the thought processes are considerably more intricate.

With increasingly varied possibilities of point of view and the advancements in psychological research, modern authors have begun to develop ways of presenting thoughts in an unmediated way to the reader. We have discussed the dramatic method of characterization ("showing") where characters are allowed to perform without the intrusive commentary of an author. Suppose, then, that we could not only see characters interacting before us, but that we could also penetrate the minds of those characters and have access to their most private thoughts, feelings, and dreams? Perhaps we could even experience the workings of their minds, like psychoanalysts who listen to their patients "free associate" from one thought, feeling, or idea to another. Modern novelists have invented ways of presenting thoughts so realistically that we seem to be experiencing them directly.

Many names have been coined to cover this presentation of thoughts. The psychologist William James, brother of the novelist, adopted the term "stream of consciousness" to describe how the mind works, and his terminology has come to refer to a passage in a fictional work that gives the appearance of being the unmediated flow of thoughts through a character's mind. This flow of thoughts, of course, has been carefully chosen and organized by the author, but it must appear to be a random selection. James Joyce perfected this technique in *Ulysses* (1922), from which the following example is cited:

> Pineapple rock, lemon platt, butterscotch. A sugarsticky girl shovelling scoopfuls of creams for a christian brother. Some school treat. Bad for their tummies. Lozenge and comfit manufacturer to His Majesty the King. God. Save. Our. Sitting on his throne, sucking red jujubes white.

These words are the thoughts of Leopold Bloom as he wanders through the Dublin streets shortly after noon, his mind on food. He passes Graham Lemon's candy store and sees (or perhaps only remembers) three different candies. Through the window he observes a young clerk waiting on a priest. He then remembers eating candy as a child and recalls the stern remonstrance of an adult ("Bad for their tummies"). The advertisement (probably a sign in the window), "Lozenge and comfit manufacturer to His Majesty the King," reminds him of the national anthem, as well as a child's song or jingle. These observations and memories are presented in the form of Bloom's apparently random thoughts. Thus, this technique conveys information while characterizing the way Bloom's mind moves from one association to another.

Another term for the subjective thought process is internal monologue, often used interchangeably with stream of consciousness. However, the term monologue has theatrical associations and does not sufficiently convey the notion of flux that characterizes stream of consciousness. The term is more appropriately applied to a relatively ordered thought process, similar to the soliloquy. Camus employs such a technique in *The Stranger:*

> Nothing, nothing had the least importance, and I knew quite well why . . . From the dark horizon of my future a sort of slow, persistent breeze had been blowing toward me, all of my life long, from the years that were to come. And on its way that breeze had leveled out all the ideas that people tried to foist on me in the equally unreal years I then was living through . . .

These reflections are closer to those of Birkin than to those of Bloom. The principal differences result from the choice of point of view: Camus presents us Meursault's thoughts directly, without the presence of an omniscient narrator. However, they lack the appearance of the randomness that characterizes Bloom's thoughts and hence are more appropriately considered as an internal monologue.

Clearly, film excels in the presentation of external details: The most complex settings and objects can be presented in an instant, and our attention can be directed to whatever part of that scene is important through lighting, camera position, or camera movement. But how can film penetrate the mind and show us even the simplest thoughts or feelings?

In our discussion of point of view, we considered the ways film can present a subjective point of view, whether in the first person or the third person. Once the visual field of the film becomes identified with a narrator's perspective, thoughts and feelings can be expressed by the way in which the narrator experiences the world. Subjectivity can be indicated by what and how the narrator sees and hears. As we observed earlier, the narrator's participation in what he or she sees does not invalidate the subjectivity of that vision. Film can dramatize dreams or reveries in which the narrator plays a role. This is equally evident in nondreamlike states. Music is used in Visconti's film *The Stranger* to depict the mental state of Meursault, just as the insistent ticking of clocks in *High Noon* characterizes the feelings of Will Kane. In *Blow-up*, Antonioni employs a limited third-person narration: We know no more about the characters or events than the photographer does. We understand his thoughts and feelings by the way he experiences the world: through visual composition, through colors, through sound and, in the darkroom sequence, by watching his mind in action. Thoughts can also be revealed through subjective cutaway shots; suddenly the director cuts to a shot that is clearly not an event occurring simultaneously but rather the visualization of a thought occurring in the mind of the protagonist, a technique used by Richardson at the end of *The Loneliness of the Long-Distance Runner*. Narrators can also express their thoughts verbally, through a voice-over such as Visconti uses in *The Stranger*. Film can present thought processes like dreams—which are visual—and with brevity and clarity. As we saw in the opening shots of *Citizen Kane*, the camera can move with impunity through the objective world and enter the world of inner experience, in spite of the *No Trespassing* signs that frequently confront it.

Additional Recommended Films

This Sporting Life (1963), directed by Lindsay Anderson, based on the novel by David Storey. The novel is available in paperback.

Ulysses (1977), directed by Joseph Strick, based on the novel by James Joyce. The novel is available in paperback.

Deliverance (1972), directed by John Boorman, based on the novel by James Dickey. The novel is available in paperback.

See Also:

The Collector (Chapter 5)
The Innocents (Chapter 5)
The Fallen Idol (Chapter 7)
The Throne of Blood (Chapter 7)
Women in Love (Chapter 7)
The Rocking-Horse Winner (Chapter 8)
Great Expectations
The Trial

The Loneliness of the Long-Distance Runner

"The Loneliness of the Long-Distance Runner" is a young delinquent's story of his refusal to conform to the values of his oppressors. Smith, Alan Sillitoe's seventeen-year-old narrator, tells his story retrospectively, as he looks back on the events preceding his confinement at a Borstal and tries to understand them. While training for a track meet at the Borstal, he discovers that running promotes thinking and that his real life is internal. The story is Smith's attempt to articulate these thoughts and feelings and to act upon them.

The story has a three-part structure. In the first part of the story, Smith relates how he came to be in the Borstal and then, in the second part, he tells about his home life before being locked up. Smith's language is that of an uneducated teenager, self-consciously groping to express himself. He is well aware of the difficulties of writing and mentions them often: "I can't tell you much about what it was like there," he states at one point about life in the Borstal, "because I haven't got the hang of describing buildings or saying how many crumby chairs and slatted windows make a room." In fact, he minimizes physical description and instead tries to express his feelings and thoughts, most of which have occurred to him while running.

Although Smith speaks of how running promotes thinking and of the liberated feeling he experiences while running, the demonstration of this remains for the third part of the story. This section is devoted to the race, and Sillitoe enters Smith's mind to reveal his thoughts. Sillitoe effectively manipulates stream of consciousness throughout part three. By showing us the thoughts that flash through Smith's head, like "magic lantern slides," Sillitoe enables us to understand the workings of Smith's mind. Tony Richardson's greatest challenge in filming the story is to capture the thought processes that come to constitute the most significant aspect of Smith's life.

Richardson begins his film, *The Loneliness of the Long-Distance Runner* (1962), with shots of Smith jogging along a road during a practice session at the Borstal. The camera tracks behind him, and we hear him musing on the importance of running and particularly on the "loneliness of the long-distance runner." We understand that Smith thinks as he runs, even before the credits are shown, and we learn what his attitude toward running is. Then Richardson cuts to Smith's arrival at the Borstal; life there is shown as a flashback, within which there are the additional flashbacks to the material covered in the second part of the story. We catch up to the present only near the end of the film, when Smith is training for the big race.

Voice-overs are a conventional way of presenting a character's thoughts, and Richardson employs them at the beginning of his film to reveal Smith's thoughts while running. The other means Richardson uses are considerably more innovative and rely on an effective counterpoint of sound and image.

There are two long sequences of Smith training for the race, neither of which has any dialogue, yet Smith's feelings about what he is doing are conveyed perfectly. The first of these is Smith's initial run without supervision. The headmaster comes out to watch the boys training and, as a demonstration of his trust in Smith, he asks him to run the course alone. Mr. Craig, one of the masters, opens the gate, and Smith cautiously walks out. From Smith's point of view, we see Craig closing and locking the gate, and then a reverse angle shot shows Smith on the other side looking through the bars. For just an instant, we wonder if he is going to run. Then Richardson cuts to an extreme high-angle shot (taken from the school's watchtower), and a trumpet begins to play a syncopated jazz tune. The abrupt cut creates an immediate sense of liberation, perfectly paralleling Smith's feelings. A sequence of shots taken with a moving camera follows, first of the winter sky and then of the barren tree branches whirling above. Finally, the camera tilts down to reveal Smith in the distance, running toward it. The shots, we realize, have not been from Smith's point of view, but rather are correlatives for his feelings. The camera continues to track steadily, and Smith approaches. With ecstatic movements, he stretches toward the sky and soaks up the winter sun. Richardson cuts again from shots of Smith to a sequence of the sky and trees, finally returning to Smith. Then, as the camera tracks parallel to him, he runs away from it, only to return and move away again, becoming smaller and smaller. This freedom of movement in relation to the camera reflects his state of mind. Richardson then cuts to a medium shot of Smith as he slides down a slope on his back and stares contentedly at a spinning sky. Lying on the slope, Smith remembers the shopping spree that followed his father's death. The transition Richardson employs here (a series of enlarging stars) resembles something out of a television commercial, which is appropriate, given the context. Throughout the film Richardson avoids using dissolves to introduce Smith's flashbacks, since for Smith the past is immediately accessible.

An exuberant feeling of liberation is only one of Smith's responses to running, as the second running sequence demonstrates. Richardson manages a carefully modulated change of mood between the sequences. The first ends, as we noted, with Smith's remembrance of the shopping spree with his family, which is a very quickly paced sequence. The family returns home, where they are joined by Mrs. Smith's boyfriend. Smith's mother passes him some bills, which he reluctantly takes, and then, in a somber mood, he mounts the stairs to his father's room. In the darkness he lights the corner of a one pound note and stares silently as it burns. Richardson holds the shot to emphasize Smith's thoughtfulness and sensitivity before cutting to his being awakened for his early morning run.

The treatment of this run emphasizes Smith's isolation rather than his sense of freedom. He sits alone on his bed dressing, while the camera surveys the sleeping forms that line the walls. Finally, he rises, walks down the corridor to the door, exits into the cold morning air, and experiences the feeling of being the "first man in the world":

> I feel like the first man because I've hardly got a stitch on and am sent against the frozen fields in a shimmy and shorts . . . frozen stiff, with nothing to get me warm except a couple hours' long-distance running before breakfast, not even a slice of bread-and-sheepdip.

Richardson underlines Smith's solitude by shooting him in profile on a very low horizon. The slow, even tracking shots (in marked contrast to the frantic movements of the earlier sequence) emphasize the tranquility and harmony of Smith's situation. He moves through the misty winter landscape with grace and control. As Smith runs along a pond, Richardson tilts the camera down to show his reflection in the water and then cuts to Smith preparing to go away with his friend Mike and their two girlfriends. That recollection, too, is a moment of harmony, consonant with his running experience.

The final race suggests other ways in which film can communicate thoughts. In the story Sillitoe has Smith remark on how the guards at the Borstal "can't make an X-ray of our guts to find out what we're telling ourselves." But that is exactly what a film can do. The "magic lantern slides" that fill Smith's head as he runs are the stuff films are made of.

As he runs in the film, Smith's thoughts are far more complex than those he has in the story. During the race he reviews all the significant events in his life before and after coming to the Borstal. In the early stages of the race, these thoughts are infrequent and of sufficiently long duration for the viewer to comprehend fully the significance of the recollection. Most of the shots range from twenty-five to thirty-five frames, and they are interspersed with shots of the race. In counterpoint to these images is a montage of sounds from Smith's past. Of central importance, as in the story, is the example of his father. But many other forces are pulling on Smith as well—his girlfriend, pressures of family life, and demands of authority figures. As the race progresses, the internal rhythm of this sequence speeds up. The final dozen flashbacks are no longer than eight or nine frames each; they would be incomprehensible without the context provided by the rest of the movie. The meaning of the images is not derived by the immediate context but by the recollections they stir in us, the viewers. Richardson can speed up the rhythm because we recognize the images on repeated viewing. By the end of the race, Smith seems to be bombarded by thoughts that have a very direct influence on his behavior. In the story Smith tells us at the outset that he intends to lose the race. In the film we are not sure until the race itself. In fact, all the other boys at the Borstal believe Smith to be "the governor's blue-eyed boy" and fully expect him to win. Richardson shows the forces shaping

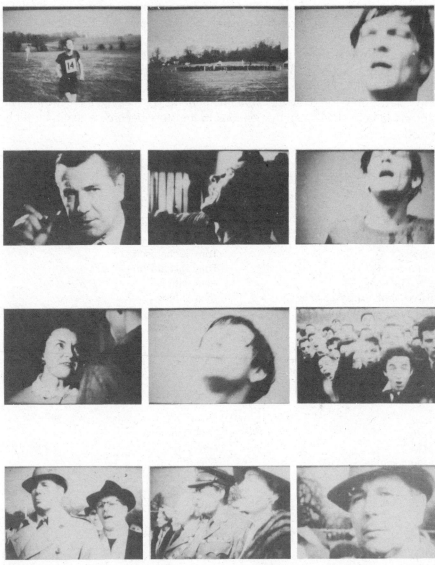

The Loneliness of the Long-Distance Runner. Past and present mingle like a series of magic lantern slides.

Smith's behavior as he is struggling to make a decision. He has been running all his life: Richardson has suggested this earlier by cutting from Smith running from the detective who finds the stolen money to a shot of Smith running the course at the Borstal. Now, to achieve his own identity, Smith must stop running. Richardson emphasizes the enormity of this action by very briefly freezing the image of the crowd cheering him on, just as, at the very end of the film, he freezes Smith at work dismantling gasmasks. In a work so dependent on motion, moments of stasis become powerful statements.

Richardson conveys the relationship between Smith's running and his thinking very effectively in a medium where motion can be shown, rather than merely described. By carefully creating a context for Smith's thoughts early in the film, Richardson is able to convey to us the associations that rapidly fill Smith's mind at the very moment he is making a decision. The "magic lantern slides" Smith mentions in the story become a reality in Richardson's film.

The Loneliness of the Long-Distance Runner

Production Credits

Director	Tony Richardson
Producer	Tony Richardson
Screenplay by	Alan Sillitoe
Based on the short story by	Alan Sillitoe
Director of Photography	Walter Lassally
Film Editor	Antony Gibbs
Music by	John Addison

Great Britain. 1962. 103 minutes. Black & white.

Cast

Colin	Tom Courtenay
Mike	James Bolam
Colin's mother	Avis Bunnage
Borstal headmaster	Michael Redgrave
Public school runner	James Fox

Further Reading

Di Marco, V., J. Harrington and E. P.Walz. *Frames of Reference: Essays on the Rhetoric of Film.* Dubuque, Iowa: Kendall/Hunt Publishing Co., 1972.

Harcourt, Peter. "I'd Rather Be Like I Am: Some Comments on *The Loneliness of the Long-Distance Runner." Sight and Sound,* 32 (Winter 1962–63), 16–19.

Kael, Pauline. "How the Long-Distance Runner Throws the Race." In *I Lost It at the Movies.* Boston: Little, Brown and Co., 1965.

Kauffmann, Stanley. *"The Loneliness of the Long-Distance Runner."* In *A World on Film: Criticism and Comment.* New York: Harper & Row, 1966.

Maynard, Richard A. *Literature of the Screen: Identity.* New York: Scholastic Book Services, 1974.

Quirk, Eugene F. "Social Class as Audience: Sillitoe's Story and Screenplay *The Loneliness of the Long-Distance Runner.*" *Literature/Film Quarterly*, 9, No. 3 (1981), 161–71.

Rollins, Janet Buck. "Novel [*sic*] into Film: *The Loneliness of the Long-Distance Runner.*" *Literature/Film Quarterly*, 9, No. 3 (1981), 172–88.

The Loneliness of the Long-Distance Runner

Allan Sillitoe

As soon as I got to Borstal they made me a long-distance cross-country runner. I suppose they thought I was just the build for it because I was long and skinny for my age (and still am) and in any case I didn't mind it much, to tell you the truth, because running had always been made much of in our family, especially running away from the police. I've always been a good runner, quick and with a big stride as well, the only trouble being that no matter how fast I run, and I did a very fair lick even though I do say so myself, it didn't stop me getting caught by the cops after that bakery job.

You might think it a bit rare, having long-distance cross-country runners in Borstal, thinking that the first thing a long-distance cross-country runner would do when they set him loose at them fields and woods would be to run as far away from the place as he could get on a bellyful of Borstal slumgullion—but you're wrong, and I'll tell you why. The first thing is that them bastards over us aren't as daft as they most of the time look, and for another thing I'm not so daft as I would look if I tried to make a break for it on my long-distance running, because to abscond and then get caught is nothing but a mug's game, and I'm not falling for it. Cunning is what counts in this life, and even that you've got to use in the slyest way you can; I'm telling you straight: they're cunning, and I'm cunning. If only 'them' and 'us' had the same ideas we'd get on like a house on fire, but they don't see eye to eye with us and we don't see eye to eye with them, so that's how it stands and how it will always stand. The one fact is that all of us are cunning, and because of this there's no love lost between us. So the thing is that they know I won't try to get away from them: they sit there like spiders in that crumbly manor house, perched like jumped-up jackdaws on the roof, watching out over the drives and fields like German generals from the tops of tanks. And even when I jog-trot on behind a wood and they can't see me anymore they know my sweeping-brush head will bob along that hedge-top in an hour's time and that I'll report to the bloke on the gate. Because when on a raw and frosty morning I get up at five o'clock and stand shivering my belly off on the stone floor and all the rest still have another hour to snooze before the bells go, I slink downstairs through all the corridors to the big outside door with a permit running-card in my fist, I feel like the first and last man on the world, both at once, if you can believe what I'm trying to say. I feel like the first man because I've hardly got a stitch on and am sent against the frozen fields in a shimmy and shorts—even the first poor bastard dropped on to the earth in midwinter knew how to make a suit of leaves, or how to skin a pterodactyl for a topcoat. But there I am, frozen stiff, with nothing to get me warm except a couple of hours' long-distance running before breakfast, not even a slice of bread-and-sheepdip. They're training me up fine for the big sports day when all the pig-faced snotty-nosed dukes and ladies—who can't add two and two together and would mess themselves like loonies if they didn't have slavies to beck-and-call—come and make speeches to us about sports being just the thing to get us leading an honest life and keep our itching finger-ends off them shop locks and safe handles and hairgrips to open gas meters. They give us a bit of blue ribbon and a cup for a prize after we've shagged ourselves out running or jumping, like race horses, only we don't get so well looked-after as race horses, that's the only thing.

So there I am, standing in the doorway in shimmy and shorts, not even a dry crust in my guts looking out at frosty flowers on the ground. I suppose you think this is enough to make me cry? Not likely. Just because I feel like the first bloke in the world wouldn't make me bawl. It makes me feel fifty times better than when I'm cooped up in that dormitory with three hundred others. No, it's sometimes when I stand there feeling like the *last* man in the world that I don't feel so good. I feel like the last man in the world because I think that all those three hundred sleepers behind me are dead. They sleep so well I think that every scruffy head's kicked the bucket in the night and I'm the only one left, and when I look out into the bushes and frozen ponds I have the feeling that it's going to get colder and colder until everything I can see, meaning my red arms as well, is going to be covered with a thousand miles of ice, all the earth, right up to the sky and over every bit of land and sea. So I try to kick this feeling out and act like I'm the first man on earth. And that makes me feel good, so as soon as I'm steamed up enough to get this feeling in me, I take a flying leap out of the doorway, and off I trot.

I'm in Essex. It's supposed to be a good Borstal, at least that's what the governor said to me when I got here from Nottingham. "We want to trust you while you are in this establishment," he said, smoothing out his newspaper with lily-white workless hands, while I read the big words upside down: *Daily Telegraph*. "If you play ball with us, we'll play ball with you." (Honest to God, you'd have thought it was going to be one long tennis match.) "We want hard honest work and we want good athletes," he said as well. "And if you give us both these things you can be sure we'll do right by you and send you back into the world an honest man." Well, I could have died laughing, especially when straight after this I hear the barking sergeant-major's voice calling me and two others to attention and marching off us like we was Grenadier Guards. And when the governor kept saying how 'we' wanted you to do this, and 'we' wanted you to do that, I kept looking round for the other blokes, wondering how many of them there was. Of course, I knew there were thousands of them, but as far as I knew only one was in the room. And there *are* thousands of them, all over the poxeaten country, in shops, offices, railway stations, cars, houses, pubs—In-law blokes like you and them, all on the watch for Outlaw blokes like me and us—and waiting to 'phone for the coppers as soon as we make a false move. And it'll always be there, I'll tell you that now, because I haven't finished making all my false moves yet, and I dare say I won't until I kick the bucket. If the In-laws are hoping to stop me making false moves they're wasting their time. They might as well stand me up against a wall and let fly with a dozen rifles. That's the only way they'll stop me, and a few million others. Because I've been doing a lot of thinking since coming here. They can spy on us all day to see if we're pulling our puddings and if we're working good or doing our 'athletics' but they can't make an X-ray of our guts to find out what we're telling ourselves. I've been asking myself all sorts of questions, and thinking about my life up to now. And I like doing all this. It's a treat. It passes the time away and don't make Borstal seem half so bad as the boys in our street used to say it was. And this long-distance running lark is the best of all, because it makes me think so good that I learn things even better than when I'm on my bed at night. And apart from that, what with thinking so much while I'm running I'm getting to be one of the best runners in the Borstal. I can go my five miles round better than anybody else I know.

So as soon as I tell myself I'm the first man ever to be dropped into the world, and as soon as I take that first flying leap out into the frosty grass of an early morning when even birds haven't the heart to whistle, I get into thinking, and that's what I like. I go my rounds in a dream, turning at lane or footpath corners without knowing I'm turning, leaping brooks without knowing they're there, and shouting good morning to the early cow-milker without seeing him. It's a treat, being a long-distance runner, out in the world by yourself with not a soul to make you bad-tempered or tell you what to do or that there's a shop to break and enter a bit back from the next street. Sometimes I think that I've never been so free as during that couple of hours when I'm trotting up the path out of the gates and turning by that bare-faced, big-bellied oak tree at the lane end. Everything's dead, but good, because it's dead before coming alive, not dead after being alive. That's how I look at it. Mind you, I often feel frozen stiff at first. I can't feel my hands or feet or flesh at all, like I'm a ghost who wouldn't know the earth was under him if he didn't see it now and again through the mist. But even though some people would call this frost-pain suffering if they wrote about it to their mams in a letter, I don't, because I know that in half an hour I'm going to be warm, that by the time I get to the main road and am turning on to the wheatfield footpath by the bus stop I'm going to feel as hot as a potbellied stove and as happy as a dog with a tin tail.

It's a good life, I'm saying to myself, if you don't give in to coppers and Borstal-bosses and the rest of them bastard-faced In-laws. Trot-trot-trot. Puff-puff-puff. Slap-slap-slap go my feet on the hard soil. Swish-swish-swish as my arms and side catch the bare branches of a bush. For I'm seventeen now, and when they let me out of this—if I don't make a break and see that things turn out otherwise—they'll try to get me in the army, and what's the difference between the army and this place I'm in now? They can't kid me, the bastards. I've seen the barracks near where I live, and if there weren't swaddies on guard outside with rifles you wouldn't know the difference between their high walls and the place I'm in now. Even though the swaddies come out at odd times a week for a pint of ale, so what? Don't I come out three mornings a week on my long-distance running, which is fifty times better than boozing. When they first said that I was to do my long-distance running without a guard pedalling beside me on a bike I couldn't believe it; but they called it a progressive and modern place, though they can't kid me because I know it's just like any other Borstal, going by the stories I've heard, except that they let me trot about like this. Borstal's Borstal no matter what they do; but anyway I moaned about it being a bit thick sending me out so early to run five miles on an empty stomach, until they talked me round to thinking it wasn't so bad—which I knew all the time—until they called me a good sport and patted me on the back when I said I'd do it and that I'd try to win them the Borstal Blue Ribbon Prize Cup For Long Distance Cross Country Running (All England). And now the governor talks to me when he comes on his rounds, almost as he'd talk to his prize race horse, if he had one.

"All right, Smith?" he asks.

"Yes, sir," I answer.

He flicks his grey moustache: "How's the running coming along?"

"I've set myself to trot round the grounds after dinner just to keep my hand in, sir," I tell him.

The pot-bellied pop-eyed bastard gets pleased at this: "Good show. I know you'll get us that cup," he says.

And I swear under my breath: "Like boggery, I will." No, I won't get them that cup, even though the stupid tash-twitching bastard has all his hopes in me. Because what does his barmy hope mean? I ask myself. Trot-trot-trot, slap-slap-slap, over the stream and into the wood where it's almost dark and frosty-dew twigs sting my legs. It don't mean a bloody thing to me, only to him, and it means as much to him as it would mean to me if I picked up the racing paper and put my bet on a hoss I didn't know, had never seen, and didn't care a sod if I ever did see. That's what it means to him. And I'll lose that race, because I'm not a race horse at all, and I'll let him know it when I'm about to get out—if I don't sling my hook even before the race. By Christ I will. I'm a human being and I've got thoughts and secrets and bloody life inside me that he doesn't know is there, and he'll never know what's there because he's stupid. I suppose you'll laugh at this, me saying the governor's a stupid bastard when I know hardly how to write and he can read and write and add-up like a professor. But what I say is true right enough. He's stupid, and I'm not, because I can see further into the likes of him than he can see into the likes of me. Admitted, we're both cunning, but I'm more cunning and I'll win in the end even if I die in gaol at eighty-two, because I'll have more fun and fire out of my life than he'll ever get out of his. He's read a thousand books I suppose, and for all I know he might even have written a few, but I know for a dead cert, as sure as I'm sitting here, that what I'm scribbling down is worth a million to what he could ever scribble down. I don't care what anybody says, but that's the truth and can't be denied. I know when he talks to me and I look into his army mug that I'm alive and he's dead. He's as dead as a doornail. If he ran ten yards he'd drop dead. If he got ten yards into what goes on in my guts he'd drop dead as well—with surprise. At the moment it's dead blokes like him as have the whip-hand over blokes like me, and I'm almost dead sure it'll always be like that, but even so, by Christ, I'd rather be like I am—always on the run and breaking into shops for a packet of fags and a jar of jam—than have the whip-hand over somebody else and be dead from the toe nails up. Maybe as soon as you get the whip-hand over somebody you do go dead. By God, to say that last sentence has needed a few hundred miles of long-distance running. I could no more have said that at first than I could have took a million-pound note from my back pocket. But it's true, you know, now I think of it again, and has always been true, and always will be true, and I'm surer of it every time I see the governor open that door and say Good-morning lads.

As I run and see my smoky breath going out into the air as if I had ten cigars stuck in different parts of my body I think more on the little speech the governor made when I first came. Honesty. Be honest. I laughed so much one morning I went ten minutes down in my timing because I had to stop and get rid of the stitch in my side. The governor was so worried when I got back late that he sent me to the doctor's for an X-ray and heart check. Be honest. It's like saying: Be dead, like me, and then you'll have no more pain of leaving your nice slummy house for Borstal or prison. Be honest and settle down in a cosy six pounds a week job. Well, even with all this long-distance running I haven't yet been able to decide what he means by this, although I'm just about beginning to—and I don't like what it means. Because after all my thinking I found that it adds up to something that can't be true about me, being born and brought up as I was. Because another thing people like the governor will never understand is that I *am* honest, that I've never been anything else but honest, and that I'll always be honest. Sounds funny. But it's true because I know what honest means according to me and he only knows what it means according to him. I think my honesty is the only sort in the world, and he thinks his is the only sort in the world as well. That's why this dirty great walled-up and fenced-up manor house in the middle of nowhere has been used to coop-up blokes like me. And if I had the whip-hand I wouldn't even bother to build a place like this to put all the cops, governors, posh whores, penpushers, army officers, Members of Parliament in; no, I'd stick them up against a wall and let them have it, like they'd have done with blokes like us years ago, that is, if they'd ever known what it means to be honest, which they don't and never will so help me God Almighty.

I was nearly eighteen months in Borstal before I thought about getting out. I can't tell you much about what it was like there because I haven't got the hang of describing buildings or saying how many crumby chairs and slatted windows make a room. Neither can I do much complaining, because to tell you the truth I didn't suffer in Borstal at all. I gave the same answer a pal of mine gave when someone asked him how much he hated it in the army. "I didn't hate it," he said. "They fed me, gave me a suit, and pocket-money, which was a bloody sight more than I ever got before, unless I worked myself to death for it, and most of the time they wouldn't let me work but sent me to the dole office twice a week." Well, that's more or less what I say. Borstal didn't hurt me in that respect, so since I've got no complaints I don't have to describe what they gave us to eat, what the dorms were like, or how they treated us. But in another way Borstal does something to me. No, it doesn't get my back up, because it's always been up, right from when I was born. What it does do is show me what they've been trying to frighten me with. They've got other things as well, like prison and, in the end, the rope. It's like me rushing up to thump a man and snatch the coat off his back when, suddenly, I pull up because he whips out a knife and lifts it to stick me like a pig if I come too close. That knife is Borstal, clink, the rope. But once you've seen the knife you learn a bit of unarmed combat. You have to, because you'll never get that sort of knife in your own hands, and this unarmed combat doesn't amount to much. Still, there it is, and you keep on rushing up to this man, knife or not, hoping to get one of your hands on his wrist and the other on his elbow both at the same time, and press back until he drops the knife.

You see, by sending me to Borstal they've shown me the knife, and from now on I know something I didn't know before: that it's war between me and them. I always knew this, naturally, because I was in Remand Homes as well and the boys there told me a lot about their brothers in Borstal, but it was only touch and go then, like kittens, like boxing-gloves, like dobbie. But now that they've shown me the knife, whether I ever pinch another thing in my life again or not, I know who my enemies are and what war is. They can drop all the atom bombs they like for all I care: I'll never call it war and wear a soldier's uniform, because I'm in a different sort of war, that they think is child's play. The war they think is war is suicide, and those that go and get killed in war should be put in clink for attempted suicide because that's the feeling in blokes' minds when they rush to join up or let themselves be called up. I know, because I've thought how good it would be sometimes to do myself in and the easiest way to do it, it occurred to me, was to hope for a big war so's I could join up and get killed. But I got past that when I knew I already was in a war of my own, that I was born into one, that I grew up hearing the sound of 'old soldiers' who'd been over the top at Dartmoor, half-killed at Lincoln, trapped in no-man's-land at Borstal, that sounded louder than any Jerry bombs. Government wars aren't my wars; they've got nowt to do with me, because my own war's all that I'll ever be bothered about. I remember when I was fourteen and I went out into the country with three of my cousins, all about the same age, who latter went to different Borstals, and then to different regiments, from which they soon deserted, and then to different gaols where they still are as far as I know. But anyway, we were all kids then, and wanted to go out to the woods for a change, to get away from the roads of stinking hot tar one summer. We climbed over fences and went through fields, scrumping a few sour apples on our way, until we saw the wood about a mile off. Up Colliers' Pad we heard another lot of kids talking in high-school voices behind a hedge. We crept up on them and peeped through the brambles, and saw they were eating a picnic, a real posh spread out of baskets and flasks and towels. There must have been about seven of them, lads and girls sent out by their mams and dads for the afternoon. So we went on our bellies through the hedge like crocodiles and surrounded them, and then dashed into the middle, scattering the fire and batting their tabs and snatching up all there was to eat, then running off over Cherry Orchard fields into the wood, with a man chasing us who'd come up while we were ransacking their picnic. We got away all right, and had a good feed into the bargain, because we'd been clambed to death and couldn't wait long enough to get our chops ripping into them thin lettuce and ham sandwiches and creamy cakes.

Well, I'll always feel during every bit of my life like those daft kids should have felt before we broke them up. But they never dreamed that what happened was going to happen, just like the governor of this Borstal who spouts to us about honesty and all that wappy stuff don't know a bloody thing, while I know every minute of my life that a big boot is always likely to smash any nice picnic I might be barmy and dishonest enough to make for myself. I admit that there've been times when I've thought of telling the governor all this so as to put him on his guard, but when I've got as close as seeing him I've changed my mind, thinking to let him either find out for himself or go through the same mill as I've gone through. I'm not hard-hearted (in fact I've helped a few blokes in my time with the odd quid, lie, fag, or shelter from the rain when they've been on the run) but I'm boggered if I'm going to risk being put in the cells just for trying to give the governor a bit of advice he don't deserve. If my heart's soft I know the sort of people I'm going to save it for. And any advice I'd give the governor wouldn't do him the least bit of good; it'd only trip him up sooner than if he wasn't told at all, which I suppose is what I want to happen. But for the time being I'll let things go on as they are, which is something else I've learned in the last year or two. (It's a good job I can only think of these things as fast as I can write with this stub of pencil that's clutched in my paw, otherwise I'd have dropped the whole thing weeks ago.)

By the time I'm half-way through my morning course, when after a frost-bitten dawn I can see a phlegmy bit of sunlight hanging from the bare twigs of beech and sycamore, and when I've measured my half-way mark by the short-cut scrimmage down the steep bush-covered bank and into the sunken lane, when still there's not a soul in sight and not a sound except the neighing of a piebald foal in a cottage stable that I can't see, I get to thinking the deepest and daftest of all. The governor would have a fit if he could see me sliding down the bank because I could break my neck or ankle, but I can't not do it because it's the only risk I take and the only excitement I ever get, flying flat-out like one of them pterodactyls from the 'Lost World' I once heard on the wireless, crazy like a cut-balled cockerel, scratching myself to bits and almost letting myself go but not quite. It's the most wonderful minute because there's not one thought or word or picture of anything in my head while I'm going down. I'm empty, as empty as I was before I was born, and I don't let myself go, I suppose, because whatever it is that's farthest down inside me don't want me to die or hurt myself bad. And it's daft to think deep, you know, because it gets you nowhere, though deep is what I am when I've passed this half-way mark because the long-distance run of an early morning makes me think that every run like this is a life—a little life, I know—but a life as full of misery and happiness and things happening as you can ever get really around yourself— and I remember that after a lot of these runs I thought that it didn't need much know-how to tell how a life was going to end once it had got well started. But as usual I was wrong, caught first by the cops and then by my own bad brain, I could never trust myself to fly scot-free over these traps, was always tripped up sooner or later no matter how many I got over to the good without even knowing it. Looking back I suppose them big trees put their branches to their snouts and gave each other the wink, and there I was whizz- ing down the bank and not seeing a bloody thing.

II

I don't say to myself: "You shouldn't have done the job and then you'd have stayed away from Borstal"; no, what I ram into my runner-brain is that my luck had no right to scram just when I was on my way to making the coppers think I hadn't done the job after all. The time was autumn and the night foggy enough to set me and my mate Mike roaming the streets when we should have been rooted in front of the telly or stuck to a plush posh seat at the pictures, but I was restless after six weeks away from any sort of work, and well you might ask me why I'd been bone-idle for so long because normally I sweated my thin guts out on a milling-machine with the rest of them, but you see, my dad died from cancer of the throat, and mam collected a cool five hundred in insurance and benefits from the factory where he'd worked, "for your bereave- ment," they said, or words like that.

Now I believe, and my mam must have thought the same, that a wad of crisp blue-back fivers ain't a sight of good to a living soul unless they're flying out of your hand into some shopkeeper's till, and the shopkeeper is passing you tip-top things in exchange over the counter, so as soon as she got the money, mam took me and my five brothers and sisters out to town and got us dolled-up in new clothes. Then she ordered a twenty-one-inch telly, a new car- pet because the old one was covered with blood from dad's dying and wouldn't wash out, and took a taxi home with bags of grub and a new fur coat. And do you know—you wain't believe me when I tell you—she'd still near three hundred left in her bulging handbag the next day, so how could any of us go to work after that? Poor old dad, he didn't get a look in, and he was the one who'd done the suffering and dying for such a lot of lolly.

Night after night we sat in front of the telly with a ham sandwich in one hand, a bar of chocolate in the other, and a bottle of lemonade between our boots, while mam was with some fancy-man upstairs on the new bed she'd ordered, and I'd never known a family as happy as ours was in that couple of months when we'd got all the money we needed. And when the dough ran out I didn't think about anything much, but just roamed the streets—looking for another job, I told mam—hoping I suppose to get my hands on another five hundred nicker so's the nice life we'd got used to could go on and on for ever. Because it's surprising how quick you can get used to a different life. To begin with, the adverts on the telly had shown us how much more there was in the world to buy than we'd ever dreamed of when we'd looked into shop windows but hadn't seen all there was to see because we didn't have the money to buy it with anyway. And the telly made all these things seem twenty times better than we'd ever thought they were. Even adverts at the cinema were cool and tame, because now we were seeing them in private at home. We used to cock our noses up at things in shops that didn't move, but suddenly we saw their real value because they jumped and glittered around the screen and had some pasty-faced tart going head over heels to get her nail-polished grabbers on to them or her lipstick over them, not like the crumby adverts you saw on posters or in newspapers as dead as doornails; these were flickering around loose, half-open packets and tins, making you think that all you had to do was finish opening them before they were yours, like seeing an unlocked safe through a shop window with the man gone away for a cup of tea without thinking to guard his lolly. The films they showed were good as well, in that way, because we couldn't get our eyes unglued from the cops chasing the rob-bers who had satchel-bags crammed with cash and looked like getting away to spend it—until the last moment. I always hoped they would end up free to blow the lot, and could never stop wanting to put my hand out, smash into the screen (it only looked a bit of rag-screen like at the pictures) and get the copper in a half-nelson so's he'd stop following the bloke with the money-bags. Even when he'd knocked off a couple of bank clerks I hoped he wouldn't get nabbed. In fact when I wished more than ever he wouldn't because it meant the hot-chair if he did, and I wouldn't wish that on anybody no matter what they'd done, because I'd read in a book where the hot-chair worn't a quick death at all, but that you just sat there scorching to death until you were dead. And it was when these cops were chasing the crooks that we played some good tricks with the telly, because when one of them opened his big gob to spout about getting their man I'd turn the sound down and see his mouth move like a goldfish or mackerel or a minnow mimicking what they were sup-posed to be acting—it was so funny the whole family nearly went into fits on the brand-new carpet that hadn't yet found its way to the bedroom. It was the best of all though when we did it to some Tory telling us about how good his government was going to be if we kept on voting for them—their slack chops rolling, opening and bumbling, hands lifting to twitch moustaches and touching their buttonholes to make sure the flower hadn't wilted, so that you could see they didn't mean a word they said, especially with not a murmur coming out because we'd cut off the sound. When the governor of the Borstal first talked to me I was reminded of those times so much that I nearly killed myself trying not to laugh. Yes, we played so many good stunts on the box of tricks that man used to call us the Telly Boys, we got so clever at it.

My pal Mike got let off with probation because it was his first job—anyway the first they ever knew about—and because they said he would never have done it if it hadn't been for me talking him into it. They said I was a menace to honest lads like Mike—hands in his pockets so that they looked stone-empty, head bent forward as if looking for half-crowns to fill 'em with, a ripped jersey on and his hair falling into his eyes so that he could go up to women and ask them for a shilling because he was hungry—and that I was the brains behind the job, the guiding light when it came to making up anybody's mind, but I swear to God I worn't owt like that because really I ain't got no more brains than a gnat after hiding the money in the place I did. And I—being cranky like I am—got sent to Borstal because to tell you the honest truth I'd been to Remand Homes before—though that's another story and I suppose if ever I tell it it'll be just as boring as this one is. I was glad though that Mike got away with it, and I only hope he always will, not like silly bastard me.

So on this foggy night we tore ourselves away from the telly and slammed the front door behind us, setting off up our wide street like slow tugs on a river that'd broken their hooters, for we didn't know where the housefronts began what with the perishing cold mist all around. I was snatched to death without an overcoat: mam had forgotten to buy me one in the scrummage of shopping, and by the time I thought to remind her of it the dough was all gone. So we whistled 'The Teddy Boys Picnic' to keep us warm, and I told myself that I'd get a coat soon if it was the last thing I did. Mike said he thought the same about himself, adding that he'd also get some brand-new glasses with gold rims, to wear instead of the wire frames they'd given him at the school clinic years ago. He didn't twig it was foggy at first and cleaned his glasses every time I pulled him back from a lamp-post or car, but when he saw the lights on Alfreton Road looking like octopus eyes he put them in his pocket and didn't wear them again until we did the job. We hadn't got two ha-pennies between us, and though we weren't hungry we wished we'd got a bob or two when we passed the fish and chip shops because the delicious sniffs of salt and vinegar and frying fat made our mouths water. I don't mind telling you we walked the town from one end to the other and if our eyes worn't glued to the ground looking for lost wallets and watches they was swivelling around house windows and shop doors in case we saw something easy and worth nipping into.

Neither of us said as much as this to each other, but I know for a fact that that was what we was thinking. What I don't know—and as sure as I sit here I know I'll never know—is which of us was the first bastard to latch his peepers on to that baker's backyard. Oh yes, it's all right me telling myself it was me, but the truth is that I've never known whether it was Mike or not, because I do know that I didn't see the open window until he stabbed me in the ribs and pointed it out. "See it?" he said.

"Yes," I told him, "so let's get cracking."

"But what about the wall though?" he whispered, looking a bit closer.

"On your shoulders," I chipped in.

His eyes were already up there: "Will you be able to reach?" It was the only time he ever showed any life.

"Leave it to me," I said, ever-ready. "I can reach anywhere from your ham-hock shoulders."

Mike was a nipper compared to me, but underneath the scruffy draught-board jersey he wore were muscles as hard as iron, and you wouldn't think to see him walking down the street with glasses on and hands in pockets that he'd harm a fly, but I never liked to get on the wrong side of him in a fight because he's the sort that don't say a word for weeks on end—sits plugged in front of the telly, or reads a cowboy book, or just sleeps—when suddenly BIFF—half kills somebody for almost nothing at all, such as beating him in a race for the last Football Post on a Saturday night, pushing in before him at a bus stop, or bumping into him when he was day-dreaming about Dolly-on-the-Tub next door. I saw him set on a bloke once for no more than fixing him in a funny way with his eyes, and it turned out that the bloke was cockeyed but nobody knew it because he'd just that day come to live in our street. At other times none of these things would matter a bit, and I suppose the only reason why I was pals with him was because I didn't say much from one month's end to another either.

He puts his hands up in the air like he was being covered with a Gatling-Gun, and moved to the wall like he was going to be mowed down, and I climbed up him like he was a stile or step-ladder, and there he stood, the palms of his upshot maulers flat and turned out so's I could step on 'em like they was the adjustable jack-spanner under a car, not a sound of a breath nor the shiver of a flinch coming from him. I lost no time in any case, took my coat from between my teeth, chucked it up to the glass-topped wall (where the glass worn't too sharp because the jags had been worn down by years of accidental stones) and was sitting astraddle before I knew where I was. Then down the other side, with my legs rammed up into my throat when I hit the ground, the crack coming about as hard as when you fall after a high para-chute drop, that one of my mates told me was like jumping off a twelve-foot wall, which this must have been. Then I picked up my bits and pieces and opened the gate for Mike, who was still grinning and full of life because the hardest part of the job was already done. "I came, I broke, I entered," like that clever-dick Borstal song.

I didn't think about anything at all, as usual, because I never do when I'm busy, when I'm draining pipes, looting sacks, yaling locks, lifting latches, forc-ing my bony hands and lanky legs into making something move, hardly feeling any lungs going in-whiff and out-whaff, not realizing whether my mouth is clamped tight or gaping, whether I'm hungry, itching from scabies, or whether my flies are open and flashing dirty words like muck and spit into the late-night final fog. And when I don't know anything about all this then how can I honest-to-God say I think of anything at such times? When I'm wondering what's the best way to get a window open or how to force a door, how can I be thinking or have anything on my mind? That's what the four-eyed white-smocked bloke with the note-book couldn't understand when he asked me questions for days and days after I got to Borstal; and I couldn't explain it to him then like I'm writing it down now; and even if I'd been able to maybe he still wouldn't have caught on because I don't know whether I can understand it myself even at this moment, though I'm doing my best you can bet.

So before I knew where I was I was inside the baker's office watching Mike picking up that cash box after he'd struck a match to see where it was, wearing a tailor-made fifty-shilling grin on his square crew-cut nut as his paws closed over the box like he'd squash it to nothing. "Out," he suddenly said, shaking it so's it rattled. "Let's scram."

"Maybe there's some more," I said, pulling half a dozen drawers out of a rollertop desk.

"No," he said, like he'd already been twenty years in the game, "this is the lot," patting his tin box, "this is it."

I pulled out another few drawers, full of bills, books and letters. "How do you know, you loony sod?"

He barged past me like a bull at a gate. "Because I do."

Right or wrong, we'd both got to stick together and do the same thing. I looked at an ever-loving babe of a brand-new typewriter, but knew it was too traceable, so blew it a kiss, and went out after him. "Hang on," I said, pulling the door to, "we're in no hurry."

"Not much we aren't," he says over his shoulder.

"We've got months to splash the lolly," I whispered as we crossed the yard, "only don't let that gate creak too much or you'll have the narks tuning-in."

"You think I'm barmy?" he said, creaking the gate so that the whole street heard.

I don't know about Mike, but now I started to think, of how we'd get back safe through the streets with that money-box up my jumper. Because he'd clapped it into my hand as soon as we'd got to the main road, which might have meant that he'd started thinking as well, which only goes to show how you don't know what's in anybody else's mind unless you think about things yourself. But as far as my thinking went at that moment it wasn't up to much, only a bit of fright that wouldn't budge not even with a hot blow-lamp, about what we'd say if a copper asked us where we were off to with that hump in my guts.

"What is it?" he'd ask, and I'd say: "A growth." "What do you mean, a growth, my lad?" he'd say back, narky like. I'd cough and clutch myself like I was in the most tripe-twisting pain in the world, and screw my eyes up like I was on my way to the hospital, and Mike would take my arm like he was the best pal I'd got. "Cancer," I'd manage to say to Narker, which would make his slow punch-drunk brain suspect a thing or two. "A lad of your age?" So I'd groan again, and hope to make him feel a real bully of a bastard, which would be impossible, but anyway: "It's in the family. Dad died of it last month, and I'll die of it next month by the feel of it." "What, did he have it in the guts?" "No, in the throat. But it's got me in the stomach." Groan and cough. "Well, you shouldn't be out like this if you've got cancer, you should be in the hospital." I'd get ratty now: "That's where I'm trying to go if only you'd let me and stop asking so many questions. Aren't I, Mike?" Grunt from Mike as he unslung his cosh. Then just in time the copper would tell us to get on our way, kind and considerate all of a sudden, saying that the outpatient department of the hospital closes at twelve, so hadn't he better call us a taxi? He would if we liked, he says, and he'd pay for it as well. But we tell him not to bother, that he's a good bloke even if he is a copper, that we know a short cut anyway. Then just as we're turning a corner he gets it into his big batchy head that we're going the opposite way to the hospital, and calls us back. So we'd start to run . . . if you can call all that thinking.

Up in my room Mike rips open that money-box with a hammer and chisel, and before we know where we are we've got seventy-eight pounds fifteen and fourpence ha'penny *each* lying all over my bed like tea spread out on Christmas Day: cake and trifle, salad and sandwiches, jam tarts and bars of chocolate: all shared and shared alike between Mike and me because we believed in equal work and equal pay, just like the comrades my dad was in until he couldn't do a stroke anymore and had no breath left to argue with. I thought how good it was that blokes like that poor baker didn't stash all his cash in one of the big marble-fronted banks that take up every corner of the town, how lucky for us that he didn't trust them no matter how many millions of tons of concrete or how many iron bars and boxes they were made of, or how many coppers kept their blue pop-eyed peepers glued on to them, how smashing it was that he believed in money-boxes when so many shopkeepers thought it old-fashioned and tried to be modern by using a bank, which wouldn't give a couple of sincere, honest, hardworking, conscientious blokes like Mike and me a chance.

Now you'd think, and I'd think, and anybody with a bit of imagination would think, that we'd done as clean a job as could ever be done, that, with the baker's shop being at least a mile from where we lived, and with not a soul having seen us, and what with the fog and the fact that we weren't more than five minutes in the place, that the coppers should never have been able to trace us. But then, you'd be wrong, I'd be wrong, and everybody else would be wrong, no matter how much imagination was diced out between us.

Even so, Mike and I didn't splash the money about, because that would have made people think straightaway that we'd latched on to something that didn't belong to us. Which wouldn't do at all, because even in a street like ours there are people who love to do a good turn for the coppers, though I never know why they do. Some people are so mean-gutted that even if they've only got tuppence more than you and they think you're the sort that would take it if you have half the chance, they'd get you put inside if they saw you ripping lead out of a lavatory, even if it weren't their lavatory—just to keep their tuppence out of your reach. And so we didn't do anything to let on about how rich we were, nothing like going down town and coming back dressed in brand-new Teddy boy suits and carrying a set of skiffle-drums like another pal of ours who'd done a factory office about six months before. No, we took the odd bobs and pennies out and folded the notes into bundles and stuffed them up the drainpipe outside the door in the backyard. "Nobody'll ever think of looking for it there," I said to Mike. "We'll keep it doggo for a week or two, then take a few quid a week out till it's all gone. We might be thieving bastards, but we're not green."

Some days later a plain-clothes dick knocked at the door. And asked for me. I was still in bed, at eleven o'clock, and had to unroll myself from the comfortable black sheets when I heard mam calling me. "A man to see you," she said. "Hurry up, or he'll be gone."

I could hear her keeping him at the back door, nattering about how fine it had been but how it looked like rain since early this morning—and he didn't answer her except to snap out a snotty yes or no. I scrambled into my trousers and wondered why he'd come—knowing it was a copper because 'a man to see you' always meant just that in our house—and if I'd had any idea that one had gone to Mike's house as well at the same time I'd have twigged it to be because of that hundred and fifty quid's worth of paper stuffed up the drainpipe outside the back door about ten inches away from that plain-clothed copper's boot, where mam still talked to him thinking she was doing me a favour, and I wishing to God she'd ask him in, though on second thoughts realizing that that would seem more suspicious than keeping him outside, because they know we hate their guts and smell a rat if they think we're trying to be nice to them. Mam wasn't born yesterday, I thought, thumping my way down the creaking stairs.

I'd seen him before: Borstal Bernard in nicky-hat, Remand Home Ronald in rowing-boat boots, Probation Pete in a pitprop mackintosh, three-months clink in collar and tie (all this out of a Borstal skiffle-ballad that my new mate made up, and I'd tell you it in full but it doesn't belong in this story), a 'tec who'd never had as much in his pockets as that drainpipe had up its jackses. He was like Hitler in the face, right down to the paint-brush tash, except that being six-foot tall made him seem worse. But I straightened my shoulders to look into his illiterate blue eyes—like I always do with any copper.

Then he started asking me questions, and my mother from behind said: "He's never left that television set for the last three months, so you've got nowt on him, mate. You might as well look for somebody else, because you're wasting the rates you get out of my rent and the income-tax that comes out of my pay-packet standing there like that"—which was a laugh because she'd never paid either to my knowledge, and never would, I hoped.

"Well, you know where Papplewick Street is, don't you?" the copper asked me, taking no notice of mam.

"Ain't it off Alfreton Road?" I asked him back, helpful and bright.

"You know there's a baker's half-way down on the left-hand side, don't you?"

"Ain't it next door to a pub, then?" I wanted to know.

He answered me sharp: "No, it bloody well ain't." Coppers always lose their tempers as quick as this, and more often than not they gain nothing by it. "Then I don't know it," I told him, saved by the bell.

He slid his big boot round and round on the doorstep. "Where were you last Friday night?" Back in the ring, but this was worse than a boxing match.

I didn't like him trying to accuse me of something he wasn't sure I'd done. "Was I at that baker's you mentioned? Or in the pub next door?"

"You'll get five years in Borstal if you don't give me a straight answer," he said, unbuttoning his mac even though it was cold where he was standing.

"I was glued to the telly, like mam says," I swore blind. But he went on and on with his looney questions: "Have you got a television?"

The things he asked wouldn't have taken in a kid of two, and what else could I say to the last one except: "Has the aerial fell down? Or would you like to come in and see it?"

He was liking me even less for saying that. "We know you weren't listening to the television set last Friday, and so do you, don't you?"

"P'raps not, but I was *looking* at it, because sometimes we turn the sound down for a bit of fun." I could hear mam laughing from the kitchen, and I hoped Mike's mam was doing the same if the cops had gone to him as well.

"We know you weren't in the house," he said, starting up again, cranking himself with the handle. They always say 'We' 'We', never 'I' 'I'—as if they feel braver and righter knowing there's a lot of them against only one.

"I've got witnesses," I said to him. "Mam for one. Her fancy-man, for two. Ain't that enough? I can get you a dozen more, or thirteen together, if it was a baker's that got robbed."

"I don't want no lies," he said, not catching on about the baker's dozen. Where do they scrape cops up from anyway? "All I want is to get from you where you put that money."

Don't get mad, I kept saying to myself, don't get mad—hearing mam setting out cups and saucers and putting the pan on the stove for bacon. I stood back and waved him inside like I was a butler. "Come and search the house. If you've got a warrant."

"Listen, my lad," he said, like the dirty bullying jumped-up bastard he was. "I don't want too much of your lip, because if we get you down to the Guildhall you'll get a few bruises and black-eyes for your trouble." And I knew he wasn't kidding either, because I'd heard about all them sort of tricks. I hoped one day though that him and all his pals would be the ones to get the black-eyes and kicks; you never knew. It might come sooner than anybody thinks, like in Hungary. "Tell me where the money is, and I'll get you off with probation."

"What money?" I asked him, because I'd heard that one before as well.

"You know what money."

"Do I look as though I'd know owt about money?" I said, pushing my fist through a hole in my shirt.

"The money that was pinched, that you know all about," he said. "You can't trick me, so it's no use trying."

"Was it three-and-eightpence ha'penny?" I asked.

"You thieving young bastard. We'll teach you to steal money that doesn't belong to you."

I turned my head around: "Mam," I called out, "get my lawyer on the blower, will you?"

"Clever, aren't you?" he said in a very unfriendly way, "but we won't rest until we clear all this up."

"Look," I pleaded, as if about to sob my socks off because he'd got me wrong, "it's all very well us talking like this, it's like a game almost, but I wish you'd tell me what it's all about, because honest-to-God I've just got out of bed and here you are at the door talking about me having pinched a lot of money, money that I don't know anything about."

He swung around now as if he'd trapped me, though I couldn't see why he might think so. "Who said anything about money? I didn't. What made you bring money into this little talk we're having?"

"It's you," I answered, thinking he was going barmy, and about to start foaming at the chops, "you've got money on the brain, like all policemen. Baker's shops as well."

He screwed his face up. "I want an answer from you: where's that money?"

But I was getting fed-up with all this. "I'll do a deal."

Judging by his flash-bulb face he thought he was suddenly on to a good thing. "What sort of a deal?"

So I told him: "I'll give you all the money I've got, one and fourpence ha'penny, if you stop this third-degree and let me go in and get my breakfast. Honest, I'm clambed to death. I ain't had a bite since yesterday. Can't you hear my guts rollin'?"

His jaw dropped, but on he went, pumping me for another half hour. A routine check-up, as they say on the pictures. But I knew I was winning on points.

Then he left, but came back in the afternoon to search the house. He didn't find a thing, not a French farthing. He asked me questions again and I didn't tell him anything except lies, lies, lies, because I can go on doing that forever without batting an eyelid. He'd got nothing on me and we both of us knew it, otherwise I'd have been down at the Guildhall in no time, but he kept on keeping on because I'd been in a Remand Home for a high-wall job before; and Mike was put through the same mill because all the local cops knew he was my best pal.

When it got dark me and Mike were in our parlour with a low light on and the telly off, Mike taking it easy in the rocking chair and me slouched out on the settee, both of us puffing a packet of Woods. With the door bolted and curtains drawn we talked about the dough we'd crammed up the drainpipe. Mike thought we should take it out and both of us do a bunk to Skegness or Cleethropes for a good time in the arcades, living like lords in a boarding house near the pier, then at least we'd both have had a big beano before getting sent down.

"Listen, you daft bleeder," I said, "we aren't going to get caught at all, *and* we'll have a good time, later." We were so clever we didn't even go out to the pictures, though we wanted to.

In the morning old Hitler-face questioned me again, with one of his pals this time, and the next day they came, trying as hard as they could to get something out of me, but I didn't budge an inch. I know I'm showing off when I say this, but in me he'd met his match, and I'd never give in to questions no matter how long it was kept up. They searched the house a couple of times as well, which made me think they thought they really had something to go by, but I know now that they hadn't, and that it was all buckshee speculation. They turned the house upside down and inside out like an old sock, went from top to bottom and front to back but naturally didn't find a thing. The copper even poked his face up the front-room chimney (that hadn't been used or swept for years) and came down looking like Al Jolson so that he had to swill himself clean at the scullery sink. They kept tapping and pottering around the big aspidistra plant that grandma had left to mam, lifting it up from the table to look under the cloth, putting it aside so's they could move the table and get at the boards under the rug—but the big headed stupid ignorant bastards never once thought of emptying the soil out of the plant pot, where they'd have found the crumpled-up money-box that we'd buried the night we did the job. I suppose it's still there, now I think about it, and I suppose mam wonders now and again why the plant don't prosper like it used to—as if it could with a fistful of thick black tin lapped around its guts.

The last time he knocked at our door was one wet morning at five minutes to nine and I was sleep-logged in my crumby bed as usual. Mam had gone for work that day so I shouted for him to hold on a bit, and then went down to see who it was. There he stood, six-feet tall and sopping wet, and for the first time in my life I did a spiteful thing I'll never forgive myself for: I didn't ask him to come in out of the rain, because I wanted him to get double pneumonia and die. I suppose he could have pushed by me and come in if he'd wanted, but maybe he'd got used to asking questions on the doorstep and didn't want to be put off by changing his ground even though it was raining. Not that I don't like being spiteful because of any barmy principle I've got, but this bit of spite, as it turned out, did me no good at all. I should have treated him as a brother I hadn't seen for twenty years and dragged him in for a cup of tea and a fag, told him about the picture I hadn't seen the night before, asked him how his wife was after her operation and whether they'd shaved her moustache off to make it, and then sent him happy and satisfied out by the front door. But no, I thought, let's see what he's got to say for himself now.

He stood a little to the side of the door, either because it was less wet there, or because he wanted to see me from a different angle, perhaps having found it monotonous to watch a bloke's face always telling lies from the same side. "You've been identified," he said, twitching raindrops from his tash. "A woman saw you and your mate yesterday and she swears blind you are the same chaps she saw going into that bakery."

I was dead sure he was still bluffing, because Mike and I hadn't even seen each other the day before, but I looked worried. "She's a menace then to innocent people, whoever she is, because the only bakery I've been in lately is the one up our street to get some cut-bread on tick for mam."

He didn't bite on this. "So now I want to know where the money is"—as if I hadn't answered him at all.

"I think mam took it to work this morning to get herself some tea in the canteen." Rain was splashing down so hard I thought he'd get washed away if he didn't come inside. But I wasn't much bothered, and went on: "I remember I put it in the telly-vase last night—it was my only one-and-three and I was saving it for a packet of tips this morning—and I nearly had a jibbering black fit just now when I saw it had gone. I was reckoning on it for getting me through today because I don't think life's worth living without a fag, do you?"

I was getting into my stride and began to feel good, twigging that this would be my last pack of lies, and that if I kept it up for long enough this time I'd have the bastards beat: Mike and me would be off to the coast in a few weeks time having the fun of our lives, playing at penny football and latching on to a couple of tarts that would give us all they were good for. "And this weather's no good for picking-up fag-ends in the street," I said, "because they'd be sopping wet. Course, I know you could dry 'em out near the fire, but it don't taste the same you know, all said and done. Rainwater does summat to 'em that don't bear thinkin' about: it turns 'em back into hoss-tods without the taste though."

I began to wonder, at the back of my brainless eyes, why old copper-lugs didn't pull me up sharp and say he hadn't got time to listen to all this, but he wasn't looking at me anymore, and all my thoughts about Skegness went bursting to smithereens in my sludgy loaf. I could have dropped into the earth when I saw what he'd fixed his eyes on.

He was looking at *it,* an ever-loving fiver, and I could only jabber: "The one thing is to have some real fags because new hoss-tods is always better than stuff that's been rained on and dried, and I know how you feel about not being able to find money because one-and-three's one-and-three in anybody's pocket, and naturally if I see it knocking around I'll get you on the blower tomorrow straightaway and tell you where you can find it."

I thought I'd go down in a fit: three green-backs as well had been washed down by the water, and more were following, lying flat at first after their fall, then getting tilted at the corners by wind and rainspots as if they were alive and wanted to get back into the dry snug drainpipe out of the terrible weather, and you can't imagine how I wished they'd be able to. Old Hitler-face didn't know what to make of it but just kept staring down and down, and I thought I'd better keep on talking, though I knew it wasn't much good now.

"It's a fact, I know, that money's hard to come by and half-crowns don't get found on bus seats or in dustbins, and I didn't see any in bed last night because I'd 'ave known about it, wouldn't I? You can't sleep with things like that in the bed because they're too hard, and anyway at first they're. . . ." It took Hitler-boy a long time to catch on; they were beginning to spread over the yard a bit, reinforced by the third colour of a ten-bob note, before his hand clamped itself on to my shoulder.

III

The pop-eyed potbellied governor said to a pop-eyed potbellied Member of Parliament who sat next to his pop-eyed potbellied whore of a wife that I was his only hope for getting the Borstal Blue Ribbon Prize Cup For Long Distance Cross Country Running (All England), which I was, and it set me laughing to myself inside, and I didn't say a word to any potbellied pop-eyed bastard that might give them real hope, though I knew the governor anyway took my quietness to mean he'd got that cup already stuck on the bookshelf in his office among the few other mildewed trophies.

"He might take up running in a sort of professional way when he gets out," and it wasn't until he'd said this and I'd heard it with my own flap-tabs that I realized it might be possible to do such a thing, run for money, trot for wages on piece work at a bob a puff rising bit by bit to a guinea a gasp and retiring through old age at thirty-two because of lace-curtain lungs, a football heart, and legs like varicose beanstalks. But I'd have a wife and car and get my grinning long-distance clock in the papers and have a smashing secretary to answer piles of letters sent by tarts who'd mob me when they saw who I was as I pushed my way into Woolworth's for a packet of razor blades and a cup of tea. It was something to think about all right, and sure enough the governor knew he'd got me when he said, turning to me as if I would at any rate have to be consulted about it all: "How does this matter strike you, then, Smith, my lad?"

A line of potbellied pop-eyes gleamed at me and a row of goldfish mouths opened and wiggled gold teeth at me, so I gave them the answer they wanted because I'd hold my trump card until later. "It'd suit me fine sir," I said.

"Good lad. Good show. Right spirit. Splendid."

"Well," the governor said, "get that cup for us today and I'll do all I can for you. I'll get you trained so that you whack every man in the Free World." And I had a picture in my brain of me running and beating everybody in the world, leaving them all behind until only I was trot-trotting across a big wide moor alone, doing a marvellous speed as I ripped between boulders and reed-clumps, when suddenly: CRACK! CRACK!—bullets that can go faster than any man running, coming from a copper's rifle planted in a tree, winged me and split my gizzard in spite of my perfect running, and down I fell.

The potbellies expected me to say something else. "Thank you, sir," I said.

Told to go, I trotted down the pavilion steps, out on to the field because the big cross-country was about to begin and the two entries from Gunthorpe had fixed themselves early at the starting line and were ready to move off like white kangaroos. The sports ground looked a treat: with big tea-tents all around and flags flying and seats for families—empty because no mam or dad had known what opening day meant—and boys still running beats for the hundred yards, and lords and ladies walking from stall to stall, and the Borstal Boys Brass Band in blue uniforms; and up on the stands the brown jackets of Hucknall as well as our own grey blazers, and then the Gunthorpe lot with shirt sleeves rolled. The blue sky was full of sunshine and it couldn't have been a better day, and all of the big show was like something out of Ivanhoe that we'd seen on the pictures a few days before.

"Come on, Smith," Roach the sports master called to me, "we don't want you to be late for the big race, eh? Although I dare say you'd catch them up if you were." The others cat-called and grunted at this, but I took no notice and placed myself between Gunthorpe and one of the Aylesham trusties, dropped on my knees and plucked a few grass blades to suck on the way around. So the big race it was, for them, watching from the grandstand under a fluttering Union Jack, a race for the governor, that he had been waiting for, and I hoped he and all the rest of his pop-eyed gang were busy placing big bets on me, hundred to one to win, all the money they had in their pockets, all the wages they were going to get for the next five years, and the more they placed the happier I'd be. Because there was a dead cert going to die on the big name they'd built for him, going to go down dying with laughter whether it choked him or not. My knees felt the cool soil pressing into them, and out of my eye's corner I saw Roach lift his hand. The Gunthorpe boy twitched before the signal was given; somebody cheered too soon; Medway bent forward; then the gun went, and I was away.

We went once around the field and then along a half-mile drive of elms, being cheered all the way, and I seemed to feel I was in the lead as we went out by the gate and into the lane, though I wasn't interested enough to find out. The five-mile course was marked by splashes of whitewash gleaming on gateposts and trunks and stiles and stones, and a boy with a waterbottle and bandage-box stood every half-mile waiting for those that dropped out or fainted. Over the first stile, without trying, I was still nearly in the lead but one; and if any of you want tips about running, never be in a hurry, and never let any of the other runners know you are in a hurry even if you are. You can always overtake on long-distance running without letting the others smell the hurry in you; and when you've used your craft like this to reach the two or three up front then you can do a big dash later that puts everybody else's hurry in the shade because you've not had to make haste up till then. I ran to a steady jog-trot rhythm, and soon it was so smooth that I forgot I was running, and I was hardly able to know that my legs were lifting and falling and my arms going in and out, and my lungs didn't seem to be working at all, and my heart stopped that wicked thumping I always get at the beginning of a run. Because you see I never race at all; I just run, and somehow I know that if I forget I'm racing and only jog-trot along until I don't know I'm running I always win the race. For when my eyes recognize that I'm getting near the end of the course—by seeing a stile or cottage corner—I put on a spurt, and such a fast big spurt it is because I feel that up till then I haven't been running and that I've used up no energy at all. And I've been able to do this because I've been thinking; and I wonder if I'm the only one in the running business with this system of forgetting that I'm running because I'm too busy thinking; and I wonder if any of the other lads are on to the same lark, though I know for a fact that they aren't. Off like the wind along the cobbled footpath and rutted lane, smoother than the flat grass track on the field and better for thinking because it's not too smooth, and I was in my element that afternoon knowing that nobody could beat me at running but intending to beat myself before the day was over. For when the governor talked to me of being honest when I first came in he didn't know what the word meant or he wouldn't have had me here in this race, trotting along in shimmy and shorts and sunshine. He'd have had me where I'd have had him if I'd been in his place: in a quarry breaking rocks until he broke his back. At least old Hitler-face the plain-clothes dick was honester than the governor, because he at any rate had had it in for me and I for him, and when my case was coming up in court a copper knocked at our front door at four o'clock in the morning and got my mother out of bed when she was paralytic tired, reminding her she had to be in court at dead on half past nine. It was the finest bit of spite I've ever heard of, but I would call it honest, the same as my mam's words were honest when she really told that copper what she thought of him and called him all the dirty names she'd ever heard of, which took her half an hour and woke the terrace up.

I trotted on along the edge of a field bordered by the sunken lane, smelling green grass and honeysuckle, and I felt as though I came from a long line of whippets trained to run on two legs, only I couldn't see a toy rabbit in front and there wasn't a collier's cosh behind to make me keep up the pace. I passed the Gunthorpe runner whose shimmy was already black with sweat and I could just see the corner of the fenced-up copse in front where the only man I had to pass to win the race was going all out to gain the half-way mark. Then he turned into a tongue of trees and bushes where I couldn't see him anymore, and I couldn't see anybody, and I knew what the loneliness of the long-distance runner running across country felt like, realizing that as far as I was concerned this feeling was the only honesty and realness there was in the world and I knowing it would be no different ever, no matter what I felt at odd times, and no matter what anybody else tried to tell me. The runner behind me must have been a long way off because it was so quiet, and there was even less noise and movement than there had been at five o'clock of a frosty winter morning. It was hard to understand, and all I knew was that you had to run, run, run, without knowing why you were running, but on you went through fields you didn't understand and into woods that made you afraid, over hills without knowing you'd been up and down, and shooting across streams that would have cut the heart out of you had you fallen into them. And the winning post was no end to it, even though crowds might be cheering you in, because on you had to go before you got your breath back, and the only time you stopped really was when you tripped over a tree trunk and broke your neck or fell into a disused well and stayed dead in the darkness forever. So I thought: they aren't going to get me on this racing lark, this running and trying to win, this jog-trotting for a bit of blue ribbon, because it's not the way to go on at all, though they swear blind that it is. You should think about nobody and go your own way, not on a course marked out for you by people holding mugs of water and bottles of iodine in case you fall and cut yourself so that they can pick you up—even if you want to stay where you are—and get you moving again.

On I went, out of the wood, passing the man leading without knowing I was going to do so. Flip-flap, flip-flap, jog-trot, jog-trot, crunchslap-crunchslap, across the middle of a broad field again, rhythmically running in my greyhound effortless fashion, knowing I had won the race though it wasn't half over, won it if I wanted it, could go on for ten or fifteen or twenty miles if I had to and drop dead at the finish of it, which would be the same, in the end, as living an honest life like the goveror wanted me to. It amounted to: win the race and be honest, and on trot-trotting I went, having the time of my life, loving my progress because it did me good and set me thinking which by now I liked to do, but not caring at all when I remembered that I had to win this race as well as run it. One of the two, I had to win the race or run it, and I knew I could do both because my legs had carried me well in front—now coming to the short cut down the bramble bank and over the sunken road—and would carry me further because they seemed made of electric cable and easily alive to keep on slapping at those ruts and roots, but I'm not going to win because the only way I'd see I come in first would be if winning meant that I was going to escape the coppers after doing the biggest bank job of my life, but winning means the exact opposite, no matter how they try to kill or kid me, means running right into their white-gloved wall-barred hands and grinning mugs and staying there for the rest of my natural long life of stone-breaking anyway, but stone-breaking in the way I want to do it and not in the way they tell me.

Another honest thought that comes is that I could swing left at the next hedge of the field, and under its cover beat my slow retreat away from the sports ground winning post. I could do three or six or a dozen miles across the turf like this and cut a few main roads behind me so's they'd never know which one I'd taken; and maybe on the last one when it got dark I could thumb a lorry-lift and get a free ride north with somebody who might not give me away. But no, I said I wasn't daft didn't I? I won't pull out with only six months left, and besides there's nothing I want to dodge and run away from; I only want a bit of my own back on the In-laws and Potbellies by letting them sit up there on their big posh seats and watch me lose this race, though as sure as God made me I know that when I do lose I'll get the dirtiest crap and kitchen jobs in the months to go before my time is up. I won't be worth a trepp'ny-bit to anybody here, which will be all the thanks I get for being honest in the only way I know. For when the governor told me to be honest it was meant to be in his way not mine, and if I kept on being honest in the way he wanted and won my race for him he'd see I got the cushiest six months still left to run; but in my own way, well, it's not allowed, and if I find a way of doing it such as I've got now then I'll get what-for in every mean trick he can set his mind to. And if you look at it in my way, who can blame him? For this is war—and ain't I said so?—and when I hit him in the only place he knows he'll be sure to get his own back on me for not collaring that cup when his heart's been set for ages on seeing himself standing up at the end of the afternoon to clap me on the back as I take the cup from Lord Earwig or some such chinless wonder with a name like that. And so I'll hit him where it hurts a lot, and he'll do all he can to get his own back, tit for tat, though I'll enjoy it most because I'm hitting first, and because I planned it longer. I don't know why I think these thoughts are better than any I've ever had, but I do, and I don't care why. I suppose it took me a long time to get going on all this because I've had no time and peace in all my bandit life, and now my thoughts are coming pat and the only trouble is I often can't stop, even when my brain feels as if it's got cramp, frostbite and creeping paralysis all rolled into one and I have to give it a rest by slap-dashing down through the brambles of the sunken lane. And all this is another upper-cut I'm getting in first at people like the governor, to show how—if I can—his races are never won even though some bloke always comes unknowingly in first, how in the end the governor is going to be doomed while blokes like me will take the pickings of his roasted bones and dance like maniacs around his Borstal's ruins. And so this story's like the race and once again I won't bring off a winner to suit the governor; no, I'm being honest like he told me to, without him knowing what he means, though I don't suppose he'll ever come in with a story of his own, even if he reads this one of mine and knows who I'm talking about.

I've just come up out of the sunken lane, kneed and elbowed, thumped and bramble-scratched, and the race is two-thirds over, and a voice is going like a wireless in my mind saying that when you've had enough of feeling good like the first man on earth of a frosty morning, and you've known how it is to be taken bad like the last man on earth on a summer's afternoon, then you get at last to being like the only man on earth and don't give a bogger about either good or bad, but just trot on with your slippers slapping the good dry soil that at least would never do you a bad turn. Now the words are like coming from a crystal-set that's broken down, and something's happening inside the shell-case of my guts that bothers me and I don't know why or what to blame it on, a grinding near my ticker as though a bag of rusty screws is loose inside me and I shake them up every time I trot forward. Now and again I break my rhythm to feel my left shoulder-blade by swinging a right hand across my chest as if to rub the knife away that has somehow got stuck there. But I know it's nothing to bother about, that more likely it's caused by too much thinking that now and again I take for worry. For sometimes I'm the greatest worrier in the world I think (as you twigged I'll bet from me having got this story out) which is funny anyway because my mam don't know the meaning of the word so I don't take after her; though dad had a hard time of worry all his life up to when he filled his bedroom with hot blood and kicked the bucket that morning when nobody was in the house. I'll never forget it, straight I won't, because I was the one that found him and I often wished I hadn't. Back from a session on the fruit-machines at the fish-and-chip shop, jingling my three-lemon loot to a nail-dead house, as soon as I got in I knew something was wrong, stood leaning my head against the cold mirror above the mantelpiece trying not to open my eyes and see my stone-cold clock—because I knew I'd gone as white as a piece of chalk since coming in as if I'd been got at by a Dracula-vampire and even my penny-pocket winnings kept quiet on purpose.

Gunthorpe nearly caught me up. Birds were singing from the briar ledge, and a couple of thrushies flew like lightning into some thorny bushes. Corn had grown high in the next field and would be cut down soon with scythes and mowers; but I never wanted to notice much while running in case it put me off my stroke, so by the haystack I decided to leave it all behind and put on such a spurt, in spite of nails in my guts, that before long I'd left both Gunthorpe and the birds a good way off; I wasn't far now from going into that last mile and a half like a knife through margarine, but the quietness I suddenly trotted into between two pickets was like opening my eyes under-water and looking at the pebbles on a stream bottom, reminding me again of going back that morning to the house in which my old man had croaked, which is funny because I hadn't thought about it at all since it happened and even then I didn't brood much on it. I wonder why? I suppose that since I started to think on these long-distance runs I'm liable to have anything crop up and pester at my tripes and innards, and now that I see my bloody dad be-hind each grass-blade in my barmy runner-brain I'm not so sure I like to think and that it's such a good thing after all. I choke my phlegm and keep on run-ning anyway and curse the Borstal-builders and their athletics—flappity-flap, slop-slop, crunch-slap-crunchslap-crunchslap—who've maybe got their own back on me from the bright beginning by sliding magic-lantern slides into my head that never stood a chance before. Only if I take whatever comes like this in my runner's stride can I keep on keeping on like my old self and beat them back; and now I've thought on this far I know I'll win, in the crunchslap end. So anyway after a bit I went upstairs one step at a time not thinking anything about how I should find dad and what I'd do when I did. But now I'm making up for it by going over the rotten life mam led him ever since I can remember, knocking-on with different men even when he was alive and fit and she not caring whether he knew it or not, and most of the time he wasn't so blind as she thought and cursed and roared and threatened to punch her tab, and I had to stand up to stop him even though I knew she deserved it. What a life for all of us. Well, I'm not grumbling, because if I did I might just as well win this bleeding race, which I'm not going to do, though if I don't lose speed I'll win it before I know where I am, and then where would I be?

Now I can hear the sportsground noise and music as I head back for the flags and the lead-in drive, the fresh new feel of underfoot gravel going against the iron muscles of my legs. I'm nowhere near puffed despite that bag of nails that rattles as much as ever, and I can still give a big last leap like gale-force wind if I want to, but everything is under control and I know now that there ain't another long-distance cross-country running runner in England to touch my speed and style. Our doddering bastard of a governor, our half-dead gan-grened gaffer is hollow like an empty petrol drum, and he wants me and my running life to give him glory, to put in him blood and throbbing veins he never had, wants his potbellied pals to be his witness as I gasp and stagger up to his winning post so's he can say: "My Borstal gets that cup, you see, I win my bet, because it pays to be honest and try to gain the prizes I offer to my lads, and they know it, have known it all along. They'll always be honest now, because I made them so." And his pals will think: "He trains his lads to live right, after all; he deserves a medal but we'll get him made a Sir"—and at this very moment as the birds come back to whistling I can tell myself I'll never care a sod what any of the chinless spineless In-laws think or say. They've seen me and they're cheering now and loudspeakers set around the field like ele-phant's ears are spreading out the big news that I'm well in the lead, and can't do anything else but stay there. But I'm still thinking of the Out-law death my dad died, telling the doctors to scat from the house when they wanted him to finish up in hospital (like a bleeding guinea-pig, he raved at them). He got up in bed to throw them out and even followed them down the stairs in his shirt though he was no more than skin and stick. They tried to tell him he'd want some drugs but he didn't fall for it, and only took the pain-killer that mam and I got from a herb-seller in the next street. It's not till now that I know what guts he had, and when I went into the room that morning he was lying on his stomach with the clothes thrown back, looking like a skinned rabbit, his grey head resting just on the edge of the bed, and on the floor must have been all the blood he'd had in his body, right from his toe-nails up, for nearly all of the lino and carpet was covered in it, thin and pink.

And down the drive I went, carrying a heart blocked up like Boulder Dam across my arteries, the nail-bag clamped down tighter and tighter as though in a woodwork vice, yet with my feet like birdwings and arms like tal-

ons ready to fly across the field except that I didn't want to give anybody that
much of a show, or win the race by accident. I smell the hot dry day now as
I run towards the end, passing a mountain-heap of grass emptied from cans
hooked on to the fronts of lawnmowers pushed by my pals; I rip a piece of
tree-bark with my fingers and stuff it in my mouth, chewing wood and dust
and maybe maggots as I run until I'm nearly sick, yet swallowing what I can
of it just the same because a little birdie whistled to me that I've got to go on
living for at least a bloody sight longer yet but that for six months I'm not
going to smell that grass or taste that dusty bark or trot this lovely path. I hate
to have to say this but something bloody-well made me cry, and crying is a
thing I haven't bloody-well done since I was a kid of two or three. Because
I'm slowing down now for Gunthorpe to catch me up, and I'm doing it in a
place just where the drive turns in to the sportsfield—where they can see what
I'm doing, especially the governor and his gang from the grandstand, and I'm
going so slow I'm almost marking time. Those on the nearest seats haven't
caught on yet to what's happening and are still cheering like mad ready for
when I make that mark, and I keep on wondering when the bleeding hell Gunthorpe behind me is going to nip by on to the field because I can't hold this
up all day, and I think Oh Christ it's just my rotten luck that Gunthorpe's
dropped out and that I'll be here for half an hour before the next bloke comes
up but even so, I say, I won't budge, I won't go for that last hundred yards if
I have to sit down cross-legged on the grass and have the governor and his
chinless wonders pick me up and carry me there, which is against their rules
so you can bet they'd never do it because they're not clever enough to break
the rules—like I would be in their place—even though they are their own. No,
I'll show him what honesty means if it's the last thing I do, though I'm sure
he'll never understand because if he and all them like him did it'd mean they'd
be on my side which is impossible. By God I'll stick this out like my dad stuck
out his pain and kicked them doctors down the stairs: if he had guts for that
then I've got guts for this and here I stay waiting for Gunthorpe or Aylesham
to bash that turf and go right slap-up against that bit of clothes-lines stretched
across the winning post. As for me, the only time I'll hit that clothes-line will
be when I'm dead and a comfortable coffin's been got ready on the other side.
Until then I'm a long-distance runner, crossing country all on my own no matter how bad it feels.

The Essex boys were shouting themselves blue in the face telling me to
get a move on, waving their arms, standing up and making as if to run at that
rope themselves because they were only a few yards to the side of it. You
cranky lot, I thought, stuck at that winning post, and yet I knew they didn't
mean what they were shouting, were really on my side and always would be,
not able to keep their maulers to themselves, in and out of cop-shops and
clink. And there they were now having the time of their lives letting themselves go in cheering me which made the governor think they were heart and
soul on his side when he wouldn't have thought any such thing if he'd had a
grain of sense. And I could hear the lords and ladies now from the grandstand,

and could see them standing up to wave me in: "Run!" they were shouting in their posh voices. "Run!" But I was deaf, daft and blind, and stood where I was, still tasting the bark in my mouth and still blubbing like a baby, blubbing now out of gladness that I'd got them beat at last.

Because I heard a roar and saw the Gunthorpe gang throwing their coats up in the air and I felt the pat-pat of feet on the drive behind me getting closer and closer and suddenly a smell of sweat and a pair of lungs on their last gasp passed me by and went swinging on towards that rope, all shagged out and rocking from side to side, grunting like a Zulu that didn't know any better, like the ghost of me at ninety when I'm heading for that fat upholstered coffin. I could have cheered him myself: "Go on, go on, get cracking. Knot yourself up on that piece of tape." But he was already there, and so I went on, trot-trotting after him until I got to the rope, and collapsed, with a murderous sounding roar going up through my ears while I was still on the wrong side of it.

It's about time to stop; though don't think I'm not still running, because I am, one way or another. The governor at Borstal proved me right; he didn't respect my honesty at all; not that I expected him to, or tried to explain it to him, but if he's supposed to be educated then he should have more or less twigged it. He got his own back right enough, or thought he did, because he had me carting dustbins about every morning from the big full-working kitchen to the garden-bottoms where I had to empty them; and in the after-noon I spread out slops over spuds and carrots growing in the allotments. In the evenings I scrubbed floors, miles and miles of them. But it wasn't a bad life for six months, which was another thing he could never understand and would have made it grimmer if he could, and it was worth it when I look back on it, considering all the thinking I did, and the fact that the boys caught on to me losing the race on purpose and never had enough good words to say about me, or curses to throw out (to themselves) at the governor.

The work didn't break me; if anything it made me stronger in many ways, and the governor knew, when I left, that his spite had got him nowhere. For since leaving Borstal they tried to get me in the army, but I didn't pass the medical and I'll tell you why. No sooner was I out, after that final run and six-months hard, that I went down with pleurisy, which means as far as I'm con-cerned that I lost the governor's race all right, and won my own twice over, because I know for certain that if I hadn't raced my race I wouldn't have got this pleurisy, which keeps me out of khaki but doesn't stop me doing the sort of work my itchy fingers want to do.

I'm out now and the heat's switched on again, but the rats haven't got me for the last big thing I pulled. I counted six hundred and twenty-eight pounds and am still living off it because I did the job all on my own, and after it I had the peace to write all this, and it'll be money enough to keep me going until I finish my plans for doing an even bigger snatch, something up my sleeve I wouldn't tell to a living soul. I worked out my systems and hiding-places while pushing scrubbing-brushes around them Borstal floors, planned my outward life of innocence and honest work, yet at the same time grew perfect in the razor-edges of my craft for what I knew I had to do once free; and what I'll do again if netted by the poaching coppers.

In the meantime (as they say in one or two books I've read since, useless though because all of them ended on a winning post and didn't teach me a thing) I'm going to give this story to a pal of mine and tell him that if I do get captured again by the coppers he can try and get it put into a book or something, because I'd like to see the governor's face when he reads it, if he does, which I don't suppose he will; even if he did read it though I don't think he'd know what it was all about. And if I don't get caught the bloke I give this story to will never give me away; he's lived in our terrace for as long as I can remember, and he's my pal. That I do know.

The Stranger

In *The Stranger* (1942) Albert Camus has created a character who exists from day to day, finding little meaning in life. Meursault, Camus's protagonist, leads a depressingly ordinary life as a clerk in a small firm in Algiers. His chief pleasures are sensual, and his intellectual life is nonexistent. Two occurrences disturb his routine: the death of his mother, and his "accidental" killing of an Arab. Meursault must stand trial for the killing, but as a Frenchman living under colonial rule in Algiers, it seems unlikely that he will be severely punished. As legal proceedings unroll, however, it becomes evident that Meursault is not being tried for murder but rather for being a "stranger," or outsider, whose emotional detachment at the time of his mother's death poses a threat to the social values of the community.

One of the tasks confronting Camus is to create in his readers a sense of the void Meursault experiences, and he achieves this through his narrative style. Meursault tells his own story, so we expect a highly subjective presentation. Instead, Meursault appears disturbingly objective:

> Mother died today. Or, maybe, yesterday; I can't be sure. The telegram from the Home says: YOUR MOTHER PASSED AWAY. FUNERAL TOMORROW: DEEP SYMPATHY. Which leaves the matter doubtful; it could have been yesterday.

The content of this opening paragraph could hardly be more personal or potentially moving; yet Meursault seems untouched by his mother's death. He fixes upon a relatively insignificant detail: the day of her death. This concern is puzzling to the reader since neither "today" nor "yesterday" is related to any temporal context. In fact, Meursault doesn't even know the age of his mother at the time of her death, and he seems equally unconcerned with how she died.

As we soon discover, Meursault matter-of-factly records events, sights, and physical sensations, but he rarely comments on them or tries to understand them. He talks about an important moment as he might discuss the weather. Consider, for example, his reflections on his mother's burial:

> And I can remember the look of the church, the villagers in the street, the red geraniums on the graves, Perez's fainting fit—he crumbled up like a rag doll—the tawny-red earth patterning on Mother's coffin, the bits of white roots mixed up with it; then more people, voices, the wait outside a cafe for the bus, the rumble of the engine and my little thrill of pleasure when we entered the first brightly lit streets of Algiers. . . .

As this example shows, Meursault employs a limited and largely descriptive vocabulary with few adjectives. His use of a simile here is extremely unusual. In general, his thoughts and recollections are presented in a uniformly dispassionate manner, with no analysis. As one critic has pointed out, Meursault avoids the language of causality.[1] Instead of *thus* or *because,* we find *and* or *then*. Consequently, events are presented as discontinuous occurrences, succeeding one another without forming any pattern. In this way, Camus conveys to us the experience of the absurd.

Another striking aspect of Meursault's language is his frequent use of indirect discourse. The novel abounds in conversations, and many of them are presented indirectly, which robs them of their immediacy. Moreover, these conversations are internalized without being accompanied by the narrator's reflections. The use of indirect discourse is most striking when Meursault recounts his relationship with Marie. In spite of the physical closeness they quickly achieve, Meursault remains removed from her emotionally. After Marie has spent the night at his apartment, Meursault comments:

> When she laughed I wanted her again. A moment later she asked me if I loved her. I said that sort of question had no meaning, really; but I suppose I didn't. She looked sad for a bit, but when we were getting our lunch ready she brightened up and started laughing. . . .

By placing Marie's question in indirect discourse, Camus creates a distance between the reported conversation and his reader, while underlining Meursault's own lack of involvement. Meursault's frequent recourse to a flat retelling of a conversation suggests his estrangement and general lack of interaction with others.

Camus believed that language can distort our perception of reality. Meursault's behavior before shooting the Arab expresses that belief. As Meursault walks down the beach for the final time, leaving his friends behind, his

---

[1] John Cruickshank, *Albert Camus and the Literature of Revolt* (London: Oxford University Press, 1959, p. 155). I am indebted to this work in my discussion of the novel.

perceptions of the setting and situation change. Suddenly he resorts to figurative language (note the abundance of tropes in this cluster of paragraphs and the relative absence of them elsewhere in the novel), which incorrectly describes the experience and thus distorts it. Meursault wrongly concludes that he is being attacked and pulls the trigger in self-defense. His language has betrayed him.

Camus thus relies on a subtle use of language to convey Meursault's mental processes and to display Meursault's attitudes toward experience. Visconti's challenge is to find cinematic equivalents for this literary technique. In addition, Visconti must make Meursault's passivity, detachment, and boredom interesting to the viewer.

Visconti has altered the structure of the story by beginning his film with a scene from the opening of Part II of Camus's work. This alteration creates immediate interest in Meursault's plight and makes all of Part I of the novel a flashback in the film. By transforming this material into a recollection, Visconti causes Meursault to appear even further removed from us.

The opening shots of Visconti's film show Meursault in handcuffs, being led down a corridor, and the first stages of his interrogation follow at once. Questions immediately occur to the viewer: Why is this man a prisoner?

The Stranger. Visconti continually contrasts overcrowded interiors (as in this opening shot) and expansive exteriors.

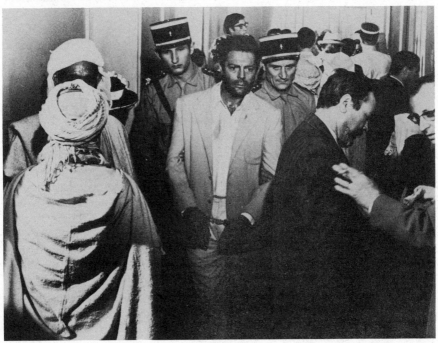

What is his crime, which, in interrogation, he deems to be a "simple" one? Visconti cuts from the interrogation room to a long shot of Meursault running to catch a bus. The contrast between the opening scene, in the restricted and enclosed corridors and offices of the police station, and the brilliantly lit and expansive landscape of Algiers is striking. Like Meursault the viewer is caught between sea and sky and can feel the oppressive heat that makes Meursault drowsy. Meursault takes a seat on the bus and appears to doze, as the opening words of the novel are recited in a voice-over narration. The juxtaposition between these words and the interrogation proves to be significant since Meursault's crime, in the eyes of the jurors, is related to the death of his mother.

Voice-over narration is but one of the verbal means Visconti employs to articulate Meursault's ideas. He also uses voice-overs to convey indirect discourse, which results in a greater sense of estrangement than that achieved in the novel. A good example occurs in the scene on the quay. Typically, Visconti cuts to this brilliantly lit exterior from a scene of darkness and confinement, thus emphasizing the extremes in Meursault's life. Meursault and Marie stroll on the quay, part of the large crowd out for a walk. In fact, this couple rarely find themselves alone, whether on the beach, in a darkened movie theater, or even at Meursault's apartment. The presence of others always intrudes. Visconti shoots the scene through a telephoto lens, which flattens the space and minimizes their privacy by creating a greater sense of crowding.

Meursault begins by reflecting (in a voice-over) on how Marie had come to pick him up at the office, and how they had crossed the city on foot. Then he notes, "The women were beautiful. And I asked Marie if she had noticed them. She said to me, Yes, she had, and that she understood." This indirect discourse, spoken by Meursault in a voice-over as Marie walks at his side, suggests that they are incapable of communicating. Finally, Marie breaks the silence by asking Meursault directly: "Would you like to marry me?" "No, it doesn't matter to me", he replies, "If you want to, we can do it." "But do you love me?" she asks. "No," he replies, "I don't think so. No. But if you want to, we can get married." After another brief and cryptic exchange, Meursault withdraws into the world of indirect discourse and comments in a voice-over: "She said I was strange. . . . That doubtless she loved me because of that. . . ." The language here shifts from voice-over narration, to voice-over indirect discourse, to direct discourse (dialogue), back to voice-over indirect discourse, and finally to voice-over narration. A moment of human contact occurs in the middle of the scene, but the casual utterances of the dialogue undercut Marie's most personal questions ("Would you like to marry me?") spoken in the most public of places. The distance between them could hardly be shown more effectively or economically.

Like Camus, Visconti minimizes transitions that link events, thus creating a sense of discontinuity and ellipsis. For example, the funeral sequence ends with Perez, Meursault's mother's friend, fainting in the sun. Visconti cuts to a shot of the sun, and then to the beach, where Meursault is spending his Saturday. The brilliant sun connects the two scenes visually, but there is absolutely no logical connection between them, merely a temporal one. Significantly, the court will try to establish a connection since the judge and jurors cannot accept such discontinuity.

Even within a carefully delineated time sequence, there is little sense of causality. Consider, for example, the way Meursault spends his Sunday. In the novel Camus carefully describes the crowds who pass, and conveys a sense of duration through the changes in the street life, as Meursault watches passively. Visconti captures all these details, even down to the physical characteristics of the passersby. But Visconti's Meursault is even more withdrawn than Camus'. At one point Camus' character exchanges a greeting with a member of a soccer team who is returning from a match. Visconti's protagonist remains withdrawn and silent: The bars on the balcony behind which he sits seal him off as surely as the prison bars later will. Time passes and Meursault exists, nothing more.

Meursault's lack of involvement is felt even more strongly when in the presence of others. We have noticed it in his relationship with Marie, and it

The Stranger. Meursault's isolation behind the bars of his balcony.

is equally evident in the scene on the beach that precedes his killing the Arab.

In Visconti's film, two forces contribute to Meursault's action: the sun and the drowsiness induced by the alcohol that accompanied his meal. Earlier, at his mother's funeral, Meursault suffered from the oppressive heat and the brilliant rays of the sun. In the scene at Raymond's apartment that culminated with Meursault composing the letter for Raymond, the effects of alcohol on his state were apparent. Now, as Meursault walks along the beach in the midday sun, these forces again take their toll. He is drowsy and lags behind Raymond and Masson. When Raymond and Masson encounter the Arabs and begin to fight, Meursault watches passively. The three return to the house, and Raymond and Masson leave to seek help from a doctor. Visconti cuts to a close-up of Marie, looking distracted and worried, and then cuts to a two shot of her and Meursault. Visconti slowly zooms in on Meursault until Marie is excluded from the frame. The shot perfectly conveys Meursault's isolation.

When Raymond returns, he tells Meursault that he is going to seek revenge for his wound, and the two of them go back to the beach. This time Raymond takes a revolver. They find the Arabs seated by a rushing stream, one of them playing a flute. Raymond wants to kill them in cold blood, but Meursault prevents him. Meursault pockets Raymond's gun, saying that "if he takes out his knife, I'll shoot." They return to the house and prepare to catch the five P.M. bus.

From this point onward, Meursault's actions seem beyond his control. Dazzled by the sun, he descends the steps from the cottage and pauses on the bottom one. The shot aptly expresses his sense of disorientation. The subjective sound we have come to associate with the heat becomes increasingly loud as Meursault wanders down the beach. The huge sky, creating an enormous sense of imbalance, threatens to overwhelm him. He is sweating profusely, and the sun seems unbearably bright. As he arrives at the stream, the sounds of the heat cease and are replaced by the natural (although amplified) sound of the flowing water, supported by a steady rhythmical sound like a heartbeat. Meursault appears blinded by the sun, and a zoom shot conveys his sudden perception of the Arab who had stabbed Raymond. The Arab pulls his knife, and the reflection of the sun from the knife blade slashes Meursault across his face. He pulls the trigger. Visconti immediately cuts to a shot of the sun. Then, in a visual synecdoche that impersonalizes the action, Visconti gives us a close-up of the hand clutching the gun and squeezing the trigger four more times: "And each successive shot was another loud, fateful rap on the door of my undoing." This is the first verbalization of Meursault's state of mind since leaving the cottage. Visconti then cuts to a high-angle extreme long shot, which aptly conveys the "benign indifference of the universe."

Visconti succeeds here in making Meursault's behavior explicable to us, although certainly not to those who will judge him. As we observe Meursault's trial and incarceration, we share his sense of life's absurdity. Visconti facilitates this by making us privy to Meursault's innermost reflections and observations. After experiencing the workings of Meursault's mind, we too confront the void that engulfs him.

The Stranger

Production Credits

Director	Luchino Visconti
Producer	Dino De Laurentiis
Screenplay by	Luchino Visconti, Suso Cecchi D'Amico, Georges Conchon
Based on the novel by	Albert Camus
Director of Photography	Giuseppe Rotunno
Art Director	Mario Garbuglia
Film Editor	Ruggero Mastoianni
Assistant Directors	Rinaldo Ricci, Albino Cocchi
Music by	Piero Piccioni

Italy/France/Algiers. 1967. 104 minutes. Color

Cast

Meursault	Marcello Mastroianni
Marie Cardona	Anna Karina
Examining Magistrate	Georges Wilson
Defence Counsel	Bernard Blier
Director of Home	Jacques Herlin
Raymond Sintes	Georges Géret
Employer	Jean-Pierre Zola
Masson	Mimmo Palmara
Mme. Masson	Angela Luce
Priest	Bruno Cremer
Judge	Pierre Bertin
Emanuel	Marc Laurent
Prosecutor	Alfred Adam
Lawyer	Vittorio Duse
Salamano	Joseph Maréchal
1st Arab	Saada Cheritel
2nd Arab	Mohamed Ralem
3rd Arab	Brahim Hadjadj

Further Reading

Kauffmann, Stanley. "The Stranger." In *Figures of Light: Film Criticism and Comment*. New York: Harper & Row, 1971.
Nowell-Smith, Geoffrey. *Luchino Visconti*. New York: Viking Press, 1973.

Simon, John. "The Stranger". In *Movies Into Film: Film Criticism, 1967–1970*. The Dial Press, 1971.

Wagner, Geoffrey. *The Novel and the Cinema*. Rutherford, New Jersey: Fairleigh Dickinson University Press, 1975.

 # Blow-Up

Julio Cortázar's short story, "Blow-Up," might appear to be an unlikely source for a feature film since much of the action occurs within the mind of the protagonist. The story concerns a man's struggle to describe a scene he has photographed. Cortázar's interest lies less in the subject of his protagonist's photograph than in the process of capturing that subject in two different media—still photography and language—and in exploring the differences between them. In comparing the two means of expression, Cortázar is able to question the relationship between a finished work of art and the materials of which it is made.

The story's protagonist, Roberto Michel, observes an encounter between a young boy and a woman in a park. He begins to fabricate a biography for the boy. Gradually he realizes that the meaning of the scene is eluding him, so he decides to try to remedy this by preserving the moment in another medium: photography. However, in preparing to take his photograph, he frames the action aesthetically, thereby excluding a man sitting in a car who turns out to have been an important figure in the drama. Thus, his artistic demands cause him to distort the situation. In addition, his own presence with the camera disturbs the scene he is trying to photograph objectively. Seated in his apartment with the blown-up photograph on the wall before him, Roberto must confront these issues in order to understand what he has seen.

This search for understanding forms the basis for Cortázar's story. But there is an additional challenge for the protagonist: How to narrate the story of these discoveries. Roberto addresses this problem in the opening paragraph:

> It'll never be known how this has to be told, in the first person or in the second, using the third person plural or continually inventing modes that will serve for nothing. If one might say: I will see the moon rose, or: we hurt me at the back of my eyes, and especially: you the blond woman was the clouds that race before my your his our yours their faces. What the hell.

The problem of narration is similar to the problems Roberto faced as a photographer when he took the picture he now wants to discuss. He had to select a point of view, and this eliminated characters and objects from his frame.

He knew then that the point of view in still photography, as in fiction, determines which story ("my your his our yours their") will be told. He also found it impossible to remain objective; he had created a story about his subjects before even snapping the shutter. Moreover, as he took his picture and froze a moment in time, so he inevitably participated in that scene and altered it forever.

As we read the story, Roberto, who is a translator by profession, is seated at his typewriter. Mounted on the wall opposite him, at the identical distance (ten feet) that had separated him from the actual scene, is a blow-up of the photograph, which distracts him as he tries to concentrate on the document he is translating. He finds himself continually looking up from his typewriter at the picture, and he gradually perceives a resemblance between his "enlargement of 32 × 28" and a movie screen. As he stares at the picture, it comes to life. The photograph becomes a window to a world of fantasy and imagination, a blank sky through which clouds are continually passing and upon which fantasies can be projected. The incident he witnessed earlier recurs. Like a moviegoer, he now is unable to influence the action, unable to call out and warn the boy. In order to understand completely what is happening, he must add the temporal dimension (which he associates with his typewriter) to the spatial dimension (which he associates with his camera). Only then can he comprehend the scene taking place before him.

Roberto's dual roles as translator and photographer symbolize the problems that confront Antonioni as adaptor of this story. As translators search for equivalents to an expression in another language, they become acutely aware of the limitations of their own languages. Still photography is like translation in that it changes a living subject, situation, or scene into a frozen moment. Film projects such frozen moments twenty-four times per second and hence creates the illusion of movement. Such transformations are at the heart of the problems of adaptation.

As we have seen, the focus of Cortázar's story is on the protagonist's mental processes. Antonioni's *Blow-up* is a film with relatively little dialogue, yet we learn as much about the workings of the mind of Antonioni's protagonist as we do about Cortázar's. The film, like the story, is a tale of discoveries, and although the stimuli are external, the process is internal.

One way Antonioni characterizes the mental state of his protagonist is through a sophisticated use of color. Early in the film, the photographer drives from his studio to an antique shop he is considering purchasing. Just before leaving his studio, he is approached by two teenage girls who want to be photographed. Although he contemptuously dismisses them, they follow him outside to his car. He reserves his most scathing comment for the color of a purse one of them carries, and then races his Rolls Royce away from the curb. The two girls run to the corner after him and stand against a building covered with brilliant red tiles. The jarring color is an appropriate correlative for the photographer's mental state. Antonioni holds the shot of the girls and then cuts back to the photographer, filming him through his car windshield as he adjusts his radio and mimes the words of a song. Antonioni then cuts to a profile shot of the photographer and tracks with him as he drives through the streets. He passes several blocks of bright red buildings that finally give way to a more harmonious blue. All the buildings have been painted according to Antonioni's specifications. The series of colors perfectly and unobtrusively communicates the photographer's state of mind, as his agitation finally gives way to tranquility. Then the colors cease and he drives through a desolate area of new concrete buildings. Above him in one shot is the mysterious sign that will later dominate the landscape of the park. The internal rhythm of the shots (the speed of his driving) and the external rhythm (created by editing) slow down as he approaches his destination. The music gradually ceases as well. Finally, the photographer arrives at the antique shop, as two effeminate men stroll past with a pair of poodles. The photographer's discomfort at their presence is communicated by the extreme oblique-angle shot of the antique shop. (We are not surprised when he later comments on the men over his car telephone.) Throughout the entire sequence, Antonioni has deftly expressed the thoughts and feelings of his protagonist without once resorting to language.

In Cortázar's story, the blow-up enables Roberto Michel to compare the medium of his own story (language) with another medium (still photography).

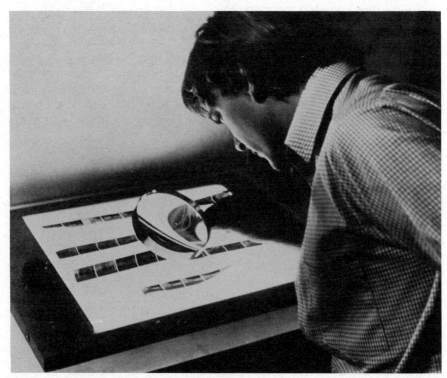

Blow-up. With optical magnification, the individual shots begin to take on significance.

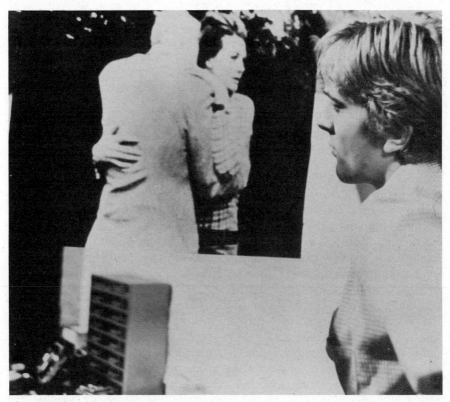

Blow-up. The "blow-up" makes the photographer's involvement possible.

Antonioni creates an equally self-reflective work in which the blow-up illuminates the nature of cinema as a medium.

The blow-up scene is one of visual discovery, where language is of little importance. The photographer's interest in his negatives has been piqued by the woman's compelling desire to retrieve them. Since she wants the film so badly, he reasons, it must have value (the same logic later applies to his attempts to obtain the neck of Jeff Beck's guitar). He enters the darkroom and begins to develop the roll of film. We see him study the strips with a magnifying glass and mark certain shots for enlargement. He prepares the enlargements, develops them, and hangs them on the wall of his studio. Two in particular seem significant, and he places them side by side: One is a long shot of the woman leading the man by the arm; in the other they are embracing. The camera pans from the photo on the left to the one on the right, zooming in while panning, and then back to the left, zooming in again. Antonioni has described the two shots in his script:

> A sense of utter peacefulness emanates from both photographs. But the GIRL'S behaviour is not entirely natural: the effort she is making to drag

the MAN across to the other side of the field. And more than that, as she is embracing the MAN, she seems to be looking with a strangely tense expression at something out of the picture.[2]

The camera movement here (pan and zoom) suggests the photographer's gradual personal involvement in his art. In the park he was a disinterested voyeur who "shot" the couple from (among other places) a position identical to the actual killer's: behind the picket fence. Having observed the situation both with his naked eye and through his camera, he concluded that he understood what he saw, and he later said the photograph of the scene in the park was a perfect tranquil ending for the book of photos he is preparing. (In fact, Antonioni's own collection of photographs—the film Blow-Up—ends with a tranquil scene in the same park.) In Cortázar's story the third party was excluded from the picture for aesthetic reasons and only drawn into the scene by the photographer's act of taking the picture. At this point Antonioni's photographer is unaware of the presence of a third party: He believes he has intruded on a pastoral scene of beauty. Now, as he studies the enlargements, he slowly becomes involved in his subject. He steps back from the two blow-ups, and Antonioni cuts to a shot of the photographer from the other side of the photos. Seen through the opaque prints, he appears to be a part of what he is examining. He then enlarges the second picture again and hangs it on the wall. Like him, we are trying to understand what is placed before us. After studying the pictures further, he makes another enlargement and then blows up all of the photographs and arranges them on his walls sequentially. He is still puzzled. Suddenly he remembers the telephone number the woman has given him. He dashes to the phone and dials, but finds that she has given him a wrong number. We observe him through a Plexiglas sheet as he telephones. Behind him are expanses of white walls with simple black decorations. The blank decor metaphorically expresses his failure to connect with the outside world.

The photographer returns to examine the photographs again and then enters the darkroom to make another blow-up. This time he enlarges the shot of the bushes, toward which the woman seems to be looking. The enlargement reveals the possible outline of a face in the bushes, and below that what appears to be a pistol with a silencer. He steps back to examine the entire sequence. The camera moves from one shot to another, and we discover—with the photographer—that the meaning resides not in any individual shot but in the sequence as a whole. He has discovered the art of cinematography.

Antonioni emphasizes this discovery by having the movie camera lead us from one still photograph to another without ever cutting back to the photographer. As we relive the event through another medium (still photography), we gradually become aware of the sound of the wind, which signifies the

[2]Michelangelo Antonioni, Blow-Up (New York: Frederick Ungar, 1984), p. 79.

photographer's total absorption and imaginative participation in his art. The sound is purely subjective. The photographer has achieved an understanding, and he returns to the telephone to communicate it to his friend Ron. This time, however, he passes a brightly colored poster and carries the phone to a window, beside which he stands while talking. In sharp contrast with his earlier call, he establishes contact with the outside world, which the camera set-up emphasizes.

At this point the photographer is interrupted by the teenage girls, who return to be photographed. Instead, the three of them engage in sexual play. Afterward, the photographer sits on the floor and looks with fresh eyes at the photos before him. He sees something that had gone unnoticed before: a body. He dismisses the girls, makes a blow-up of the area beneath the tree, and studies the photograph. He is not sure, however, so he leaves his studio and drives to the park to verify the existence of the body with his naked eye.

Throughout this sequence, Antonioni has enabled us to participate in the intellectual discoveries of his protagonist. One of his discoveries is the significance of context, a discovery many of the subplots of the film reaffirm. An object (or a single photograph) has meaning only in context. Once taken out of context (like the objects in the antique shop), it becomes something else. The photographer also comes to understand how he shapes the reality he photographs, much like Cortázar's protagonist. By sharing these discoveries with us, Antonioni permits us to make them ourselves.

In the final sequence of the film, our involvement in this process reaches a culmination, as the photographer participates in a reality whose corporeal existence cannot be confirmed. He returns to the park with his camera. It is early morning, and the body whose existence he had verified the night before with his own eyes (but not with his camera) no longer lies beneath the bush. The park is deserted and as quiet as on the previous afternoon. Suddenly a jeepload of the costumed students we saw at the opening of the film descend on the tennis court. A man and a woman mime a game of singles, without racquet or balls, as the rest of the crowd watches, their heads turning to observe the imaginary ball as it passes from one side of the net to the other.

The photographer, too, becomes a spectator, observing solitarily from an extreme end of the court. After a lengthy volley, the woman playing on his end of the court misses the ball. As she fetches it, her eyes make contact with his. Once this happens, the camera begins following the ball over the net, indicative of the photographer's growing involvement. After a few minutes of play, the ball is hit out of the court, and the camera follows it to a spot on the field beyond the photographer. The female player gestures to him. He steps back, puts down his camera, picks up the imaginary ball and tosses it back into the court. Antonioni holds a close-up on the photographer as he observes the game. Imperceptibly at first, and then more and more clearly, we hear a tennis ball being hit from one side of the court to the other while we continue to watch the face of the photographer. The sound is purely subjective, like the sound of the wind that filled the photographer's studio as he

Blow-up. The photographer begins to observe without his camera.

studied the blow-up, and it connotes his acceptance of a reality he cannot confirm with his eyes. Antonioni does not permit us to see the tennis court again, for this would dispel the illusion. The photographer glances down, and almost before we can question the sound Antonioni cuts to a high-angle long shot of him in the field of green grass. He bends over and retrieves his camera. As the music comes on, the photographer disappears before our eyes, leaving nothing but an empty field of green on which the final credits appear.

Throughout the film we have shared the subjective world of the photographer, and now Antonioni is asking us to question the "reality" of what we have just seen. The photographer is gone: Did he ever exist? This question, of course, is the same the photographer himself posed when he returned to the park in the light of morning to verify the existence of the corpse. The question is central to our experience of any work of art.

Blow-Up

Production Credits

Director	Michelangelo Antonioni
Producer	Carlo Ponti
Screenplay by	Michelangelo Antonioni, Tonino Guerra

English dialogue in collaboration * with*	Edward Bond
Based on a short story by	Julio Cortázar
Director of Photography	Carlo Di Palma
Art Director	Assheton Gorton
Film Editor	Frank Clarke
Assistant Director	Claude Watson
Music by	Herbert Hancock; "Stroll On" featured by The Yardbirds

Great Britain. 1966. 111 minutes. Color

Cast

Thomas	David Hemmings
The Girl (Jane)	Vanessa Redgrave
Patricia	Sarah Miles
Painter	John Castle
Ron	Peter Bowles
Models	Verushka, Jill Kennington, Peggy Moffitt, Rosaleen Murray, Ann Norman, Melanie Hampshire
Teenagers	Jane Birkin, Gillian Hills
Antique Dealer	Harry Hutchinson
Antique Shop Owner	Susan Broderick
Fashion Editor	Mary Khal
Jane's Lover	Ronan O'Casey
Receptionist	Tsai Chin
Tennis Players	Julian Chagrin, Claude Chagrin

Further Reading

Antonioni, Michelangelo. *Blow-up* [filmscript]. New York: Frederick Ungar, 1984.

Cameron, Ian and Robin Wood. *Antonioni*. New York: Praeger, 1971.

Eidsvik, Charles. *Cineliteracy: Film Among the Arts*. New York: Horizon Press, 1978.

Huss, Roy, ed. *Focus on Blow-up*. Englewood Cliffs, New Jersey: Prentice-Hall, Inc., 1971.

Isaacs, Neil D. "The Triumph of Artifice." In *Modern European Filmmakers and the Art of Adaptation*. Eds. Andrew S. Horton and Joan Magretta. New York: Frederick Ungar, 1981.

Kael, Pauline, "Tourist in the City of Youth." In *Kiss Kiss Bang Bang*. Boston: Little, Brown and Co., 1968.

Kauffmann, Stanley. "A Year with *Blow-up*—Some Notes." In *Figures of Light: Film Criticism and Comment*. New York: Harper & Row, 1971.

Blow-Up

Julio Cortázar

It'll never be known how this has to be told, in the first person or in the second, using the third person plural or continually inventing modes that will serve for nothing. If one might say: I will see the moon rose, or: we hurt me at the back of my eyes, and especially: you the blond woman was the clouds that race before my your his our yours their faces. What the hell.

Seated ready to tell it, if one might go to drink a bock over there, and the typewriter continue by itself (because I use the machine), that would be perfection. And that's not just a manner of speaking. Perfection, yes, because here is the aperture which must be counted also as a machine (of another sort, a Contax I.I.2) and it is possible that one machine may know more about another machine than I, you, she—the blond—and the clouds. But I have the dumb luck to know that if I go this Remington will sit turned to stone on top of the table with the air of being twice as quiet that mobile things have when they are not moving. So, I have to write. One of us all has to write, if this is going to get told. Better that it be me who am dead, for I'm less compromised than the rest; I who see only the clouds and can think without being distracted, write without being distracted (there goes another, with a grey edge) and remember without being distracted, I who am dead (and I'm alive, I'm not trying to fool anybody, you'll see when we get to the moment, because I have to begin some way and I've begun with this period, the last one back, the one at the beginning, which in the end is the best of the periods when you want to tell something).

All of a sudden I wonder why I have to tell this, but if one begins to wonder why he does all he does do, if one wonders why he accepts an invitation to lunch (now a pigeon's flying by and it seems to me a sparrow), or why when someone has told us a good joke immediately there starts up something like a tickling in the stomach and we are not at peace until we've gone into the office across the hall and told the joke over again; then it feels good immediately, one is fine, happy, and can get back to work. For I imagine that no one has explained this, that really the best thing is to put aside all decorum and tell it, because, after all's done, nobody is ashamed of breathing or of putting on his shoes; they're things that you do, and when something weird happens, when you find a spider in your shoe or if you take a breath and feel like a broken window, then you have to tell what's happening, tell it to the guys at the office or to the doctor. Oh, doctor, every time I take a breath . . . Always tell it, always get rid of that tickle in the stomach that bothers you.

And now that we're finally going to tell it, let's put things a little bit in order, we'd be walking down the staircase in this house as far as Sunday, November 7, just a month back. One goes down five floors and stands then in the Sunday in the sun one would not have suspected of Paris in November, with a large appetite to walk around, to see things, to take photos (because we were photographers, I'm a photographer). I know that the most difficult thing is going to be finding a way to tell it, and I'm not afraid of repeating myself. It's going to be difficult because nobody really knows who it is telling it, if I am I or what actually occurred or what I'm seeing (clouds, and once in a while a pigeon) or if, simply, I'm telling a truth which is only my truth, and then is the truth only for my stomach, for this impulse to go running out and to finish up in some manner, with, this, whatever it is.

We're going to tell it slowly, what happens in the middle of what I'm writing is coming already. If they replace me, if, so soon, I don't know what to say, if the clouds stop coming and something else starts (because it's impossible that this keep coming, clouds passing continually and occasionally a pigeon), if something out of all this . . . And after the "if" what am I going to put if I'm going to close the sentence structure correctly? But if I begin to ask questions, I'll never tell anything, maybe to tell would be like an answer, at least for someone who's reading it.

Roberto Michel, French-Chilean, translator and in his spare time an amateur photographer, left number 11, rue Monsieur-le-Prince Sunday November 7 of the current year (now there're two small ones passing, with silver linings). He had spent three weeks working on the French version of a treatise on challenges and appeals by José Norberto Allende, professor at the University of Santiago. It's rare that there's wind in Paris, and even less seldom a wind like this that swirled around corners and rose up to whip at old wooden venetian blinds behind which astonished ladies commented variously on how unreliable the weather had been these last few years. But the sun was out also, riding the wind and friend of the cats, so there was nothing that would keep me from taking a walk along the docks of the Seine and taking photos of the Conservatoire and Sainte-Chapelle. It was hardly ten o'clock, and I figured that by eleven the light would be good, the best you can get in the fall; to kill some time I detoured around by the Isle Saint-Louis and started to walk along the quai d'Anjou, I stared for a bit at the hôtel de Lauzun, I recited bits from Apollinare which always get into my head whenever I pass in front of the hôtel de Lauzun (and at that I ought to be remembering the other poet, but Michel is an obstinate beggar), and when the wind stopped all at once and the sun came out at least twice as hard (I mean warmer, but really it's the same thing), I sat down on the parapet and felt terribly happy in the Sunday morning.

One of the many ways of contesting level-zero, and one of the best, is to take photographs, an activity in which one should start becoming an adept very early in life, teach it to children since it requires discipline, aesthetic education, a good eye and steady fingers. I'm not talking about waylaying the lie like any old reporter, snapping the stupid silhouette of the VIP leaving number 10 Downing Street, but in all ways when one is walking about with a camera, one has almost a duty to be attentive, to not lose that abrupt and happy rebound of sun's rays off an old stone or the pigtails-flying run of a small girl going home with a loaf of bread or a bottle of milk. Michel knew that the photographer always worked as a permutation of his personal way of seeing the world as other than the camera insidiously imposed upon it (now a large cloud is going by, almost black), but he lacked no confidence in himself, knowing that he had only to go out without the Contax to recover the keynote of distraction, the sight without a frame around it, light without the diaphragm aperture or 1/250 sec. Right now (what a word, *now*, what a dumb lie) I was able to sit quietly on the railing overlooking the river watching the red and black motorboats passing below without it occurring to me to think photographically of the scenes, nothing more than letting myself go in the letting go of objects, running immobile in the stream of time. And then the wind was not blowing.

After, I wandered down the quai de Bourbon until getting to the end of the isle where the intimate square was (intimate because it was small, not that it was hidden, it offered its whole breast to the river and the sky), I enjoyed it, a lot. Nothing there but a couple and, of course, pigeons; maybe even some of those which are flying past now so that I'm seeing them. A leap up and I settled on the wall, and let myself turn about and be caught and fixed by the sun, giving it my face and ears and hands (I kept my gloves in my pocket). I had no desire to shoot pictures, and lit a cigarette to be doing something; I think it was that moment when the match was about to touch the tobacco that I saw the young boy for the first time.

What I'd thought was a couple seemed much more now a boy with his mother, although at the same time I realized that it was not a kid and his mother, and that it was a couple in the sense that we always allegate to couples when we see them leaning up against the parapets or embracing on the benches in the squares. As I had nothing else to do, I had more than enough time to wonder why the boy was so nervous, like a young colt or a hare, sticking his hands into his pockets, taking them out immediately, one after the other, running his fingers through his hair, changing his stance, and especially why was he afraid, well, you could guess that from every gesture, a fear suffocated by his shyness, an impulse to step backwards which he telegraphed, his body standing as if it were on the edge of flight, holding itself back in a final, pitiful decorum.

All this was so clear, ten feet away—and we were alone against the parapet at the tip of the island—that at the beginning the boy's fright didn't let me see the blond very well. Now, thinking back on it, I see her much better at that first second when I read her face (she'd turned around suddenly, swinging like a metal weathercock, and the eyes, the eyes were there), when I vaguely understood what might have been occurring to the boy and figured it would be worth the trouble to stay and watch (the wind was blowing their words away and they were speaking in a low murmur). I think that I know how to look, if it's something I know, and also that every looking oozes with mendacity, because it's that which expels us furthest outside ourselves, without the least gurantee, whereas to smell, or (but Michel rambles on to himself easily enough, there's no need to let him harangue on this way). In any case, if the likely inaccuracy can be seen beforehand, it becomes possible again to look;

perhaps it suffices to choose between looking and the reality looked at, to strip things of all their unnecessary clothing. And surely all that is difficult besides.

As for the boy I remember the image before his actual body (that will clear itself up later), while now I am sure that I remember the woman's body much better than the image. She was thin and willowy, two unfair words to describe what she was, and was wearing an almost-black fur coat, almost long, almost handsome. All the morning's wind (now it was hardly a breeze and it wasn't cold) had blown through her blond hair which pared away her white, bleak face—two unfair words—and put the world at her feet and horribly alone in front of her dark eyes, her eyes fell on things like two eagles, two leaps into nothingness, two puffs of green slime. I'm not describing anything, it's more a matter of trying to understand it. And I said two puffs of green slime.

Let's be fair, the boy was well enough dressed and was sporting yellow gloves which I would have sworn belonged to his older brother, a student of law or sociology; it was pleasant to see the fingers of the gloves sticking out of his jacket pocket. For a long time I didn't see his face, barely a profile, not stupid—a terrified bird, a Fra Filippo angel, rice pudding with milk—and the back of an adolescent who wants to take up judo and has had a scuffle or two in defense of an idea or his sister. Turning fourteen, perhaps fifteen, one would guess that he was dressed and fed by his parents but without a nickel in his pocket, having to debate with his buddies before making up his mind to buy a coffee, a cognac, a pack of cigarettes. He'd walk through the streets thinking of the girls in his class, about how good it would be to go to the movies and see the latest film, or to buy novels or neckties or bottles of liquor with green and white labels on them. At home (it would be a respectable home, lunch at noon and romantic landscapes on the walls, with a dark entry-way and a mahogany umbrella stand inside the door) there'd be the slow rain of time, for studying, for being mama's hope, for looking like dad, for writing to his aunt in Avignon. So that there was a lot of walking the streets, the whole of the river for him (but without a nickel) and the mysterious city of fifteen-year-olds with its signs in doorways, its terrifying cats, a paper of fried potatoes for thirty francs, the pornographic magazine folded four ways, a sol-itude like the emptiness of his pockets, the eagerness for so much that was incomprehensible but illumined by a total love, by the availability analogous to the wind and the streets.

This biography was of the boy and of any boy whatsoever, but this par-ticular one now, you could see he was insular, surrounded solely by the blond's presence as she continued talking with him. (I'm tired of insisting, but two long ragged ones just went by. That morning I don't think I looked at the sky once, because what was happening with the boy and the woman ap-peared so soon I could do nothing but look at them and wait, look at them and . . .) To cut it short, the boy was agitated and one could guess without too much trouble what had just occurred a few minutes before, at most half-an-hour. The boy had come onto the tip of the island, seen the woman and thought her marvelous. The woman was waiting for that because she was there waiting for that, or maybe the boy arrived before her and she saw him from one of the balconies or from a car and got out to meet him, starting the conversation with whatever, from the beginning she was sure that he was going to be afraid and want to run off, and that, naturally, he'd stay, stiff and sullen, pretending experience and the pleasure of the adventure. The rest was easy because it was happening ten feet away from me, and anyone could have gauged the stages of the game, the derisive, competitive fencing; its major attraction was not that it was happening but in foreseeing its denouement. The boy would try to end it by pretending a date, an obligation, whatever, and would go stumbling off disconcerted, wishing he were talking with some assurance, but naked under the mocking glance which would follow him until he was out of sight. Or rather, he would stay there, fascinated or simply incapable of taking the initiative, and the woman would begin to touch his face gently, muss his hair, still talking to him voicelessly, and soon would take him by the arm to lead him off, unless he, with an uneasiness beginning to tinge the edge of desire, even his stake in the adventure, would rouse himself to put his arm around her waist and to kiss her. Any of this could have happened, though it did not, and perversely Michel waited, sitting on the railing, making the settings almost without looking at the camera, ready to take a picturesque shot of a corner of the island with an uncommon couple talking and looking at one another.

Strange how the scene (almost nothing: two figures there mismatched in their youth) was taking on a disquieting aura. I thought it was I imposing it, and that my photo, if I shot it, would reconstitute things in their true stupidity. I would have liked to know what he was thinking, a man in a grey hat sitting at the wheel of a car parked on the dock which led up to the footbridge, and whether he was reading the paper or asleep. I had just discovered him because people inside a parked car have a tendency to disappear, they get lost in that wretched, private cage stripped of the beauty that motion and danger give it. And nevertheless, the car had been there the whole time, forming part (or deforming that part) of the isle. A car: like saying a lighted streetlamp, a park bench. Never like saying wind, sunlight, those elements always new to the skin and the eyes, and also the boy and the woman, unique, put there to change the island, to show it to me in another way. Finally, it may have been that the man with the newspaper also became aware of what was happening and would, like me, feel that malicious sensation of waiting for everything to happen. Now the woman had swung around smoothly, putting the young boy between herself and the wall, I saw them almost in profile, and he was taller, though not much taller, and yet she dominated him, it seemed like she was hovering over him (her laugh, all at once, a whip of feathers), crushing him just by being there, smiling, one hand taking a stroll through the air. Why wait any longer? Aperture at sixteen, a sighting which would not include the horrible black car, but yes, that tree, necessary to break up too much grey space . . .

I raised the camera, pretended to study a focus which did not include them, and waited and watched closely, sure that I would finally catch the revealing expression, one that would sum it all up, life that is rhythmed by movement but which a stiff image destroys, taking time in cross section, if we do not choose the essential imperceptible fraction of it. I did not have to wait long. The woman was getting on with the job of handcuffing the boy smoothly, stripping from him what was left of his freedom a hair at a time, in an incredibly slow and delicious torture. I imagined the possible endings (now a small fluffy cloud appears, almost alone in the sky), I saw their arrival at the house (a basement apartment probably, which she would have filled with large cushions and cats) and conjectured the boy's terror and his desperate decision to play it cool and to be led off pretending there was nothing new in it for him. Closing my eyes, if I did in fact close my eyes, I set the scene: the teasing kisses, the woman mildly repelling the hands which were trying to undress her, like in novels, on a bed that would have a lilac-colored comforter, on the other hand she taking off his clothes, plainly mother and son under a milky yellow light, and everything would end up as usual, perhaps, but maybe everything would go otherwise, and the initiation of the adolescent would not happen, she would not let it happen, after a long prologue wherein the awkwardnesses, the exasperating caresses, the running of hands over bodies would be resolved in who knows what, in a separate and solitary pleasure, in a petulant denial mixed with the art of tiring and disconcerting so much poor innocence. It might go like that, it might very well go like that; that woman was not looking for the boy as a lover, and at the same time she was dominating him toward some end impossible to understand if you do not imagine it as a cruel game, the desire to desire without satisfaction, to excite herself for someone else, someone who in no way could be that kid.

Michel is guilty of making literature, of indulging in fabricated unrealities. Nothing pleases him more than to imagine exceptions to the rule, individuals outside the species, not-always-repugnant monsters. But that woman invited speculation, perhaps giving clues enough for the fantasy to hit the bullseye. Before she left, and now that she would fill my imaginings for several days, for I'm given to ruminating, I decided not to lose a moment more. I got it all into the view-finder (with the tree, the railing, the eleven-o'clock sun) and took the shot. In time to realize that they both had noticed and stood there looking at me, the boy surprised and as though questioning, but she was irritated, her face and body flat-footedly hostile, feeling robbed, ignominiously recorded on a small chemical image.

I might be able to tell it in much greater detail but it's not worth the trouble. The woman said that no one had the right to take a picture without permission, and demanded that I hand her over the film. All this in a dry, clear voice with a good Parisian accent, which rose in color and tone with every phrase. For my part, it hardly mattered whether she got the roll of film or not, but anyone who knows me will tell you, if you want anything from me, ask nicely. With the result that I restricted myself to formulating the opinion that not only was photography in public places not prohibited, but it was looked upon with decided favor, both private and official. And while that was getting said, I noticed on the sly how the boy was falling back, sort of actively backing up though without moving, and all at once (it seemed almost incredible) he turned and broke into a run, the poor kid, thinking that he was walking off and in fact in full flight, running past the side of the car, disappearing like a gossamer filament of angel-spit in the morning air.

But filaments of angel-spittle are also called devil-spit, and Michel had to endure rather particular curses, to hear himself called meddler and imbecile, taking great pains meanwhile to smile and to abate with simple movements of his head such a hard sell. As I was beginning to get tired, I heard the car door slam. The man in the grey hat was there, looking at us. It was only at that point that I realized he was playing a part in the comedy.

He began to walk toward us, carrying in his hand the paper he had been pretending to read. What I remember best is the grimace that twisted his mouth askew, it covered his face with wrinkles, changed somewhat both in location and shape because his lips trembled and the grimace went from one side of his mouth to the other as though it were on wheels, independent and involuntary. But the rest stayed fixed, a flour-powdered clown or bloodless man, dull dry skin, eyes deepset, the nostrils black and prominently visible, blacker than the eyebrows or hair or the black necktie. Walking cautiously as though the pavement hurt his feet; I saw patent-leather shoes with such thin soles that he must have felt every roughness in the pavement. I don't know why I got down off the railing, nor very well why I decided to not give them the photo, to refuse that demand in which I guessed at their fear and coward-ice. The clown and the woman consulted one another in silence: we made a perfect and unbearable triangle, something I felt compelled to break with a crack of a whip. I laughed in their faces and began to walk off, a little more slowly, I imagine, than the boy. At the level of the first houses, beside the iron footbridge, I turned around to look at them. They were not moving, but the man had dropped his newspaper; it seemed to me that the woman, her back to the parapet, ran her hands over the stone with the classical and absurd ges-ture of someone pursued looking for a way out.

What happened after that happened here, almost just now, in a room on the fifth floor. Several days went by before Michel developed the photos he'd taken on Sunday; his shots of the Conservatoire and of Sainte-Chapelle were all they should be. Then he found two or three proof-shots he'd forgotten, a poor attempt to catch a cat perched astonishingly on the roof of a rambling public urinal, and also the shot of the blond and the kid. The negative was so good that he made an enlargement; the enlargement was so good that he made one very much larger, almost the size of a poster. It did not occur to him (now one wonders and wonders) that only the shots of the Conservatoire were worth so much work. Of the whole series, the snapshot of the tip of the island was the only one which interested him; he tacked up the enlargement on one wall of the room, and the first day he spent some time looking at it and remembering, that gloomy operation of comparing the memory with the gone reality; a frozen memory, like any photo, where nothing is missing, not even, and especially, nothingness, the true solidifier of the scene. There was the woman, there was the boy, the tree rigid above their heads, the sky as sharp as the stone of the parapet, clouds and stones melded into a single substance and inseparable (now one with sharp edges is going by, like a thunderhead). The first two days I accepted what I had done, from the photo itself to the enlargement on the wall, and didn't even question that every once in a while I would interrupt my translation of José Norberto Allende's treatise to encounter once more the woman's face, the dark splotches on the railing. I'm such a jerk; it had never occurred to me that when we look at a photo from the front, the eyes reproduce exactly the position and the vision of the lens; it's these things that are taken for granted and it never occurs to anyone to think about them. From my chair, with the typewriter directly in front of me, I looked at the photo ten feet away, and then it occurred to me that I had hung it exactly at the point of view of the lens. It looked very good that way; no doubt, it was the best way to appreciate a photo, though the angle from the diagonal doubtless has its pleasures and might even divulge different aspects. Every few minutes, for example when I was unable to find the way to say in good French what José Norberto Allende was saying in very good Spanish, I raised my eyes and looked at the photo; sometimes the woman would catch my eye, sometimes the boy, sometimes the pavement where a dry leaf had fallen admirably situated to heighten a lateral section. Then I rested a bit from my labors, and I enclosed myself again happily in that morning in which the photo was drenched, I recalled ironically the angry picture of the woman demanding I give her the photograph, the boy's pathetic and ridiculous flight, the entrance on the scene of the man with the white face. Basically, I was satisfied with myself; my part had not been too brilliant, and since the French have given the gift of the sharp response, I did not see very well why I'd chosen to leave without a complete demonstration of the rights, privileges and prerogatives of citizens. The important thing, the really important thing was having helped the kid to escape in time (this in case my theorizing was correct, which was not sufficiently proven, but the running away itself seemed to show it so). Out of plain meddling, I had given him the opportunity finally to take advantage of his fright to do something useful; now he would be regretting it, feeling his honor impaired, his manhood diminished. That was better than the attentions of a woman capable of looking as she had looked at him on that island. Michel is something of a puritan at times, he believes that one should not seduce someone from a position of strength. In the last analysis, taking that photo had been a good act.

Well, it wasn't because of the good act that I looked at it between paragraphs while I was working. At that moment I didn't know the reason, the reason I had tacked the enlargement onto the wall; maybe all fatal acts happen that way, and that is the condition of their fulfillment. I don't think the almost-furtive trembling of the leaves on the tree alarmed me, I was working on a sentence and rounded it out successfully. Habits are like immense herbariums, in the end an enlargement of 32×28 looks like a movie screen, where, on the tip of the island, a woman is speaking with a boy and a tree is shaking its dry leaves over their heads.

But her hands were just too much. I had just translated: "In that case, the second key resides in the intrinsic nature of difficulties which societies . . ."— when I saw the woman's hand beginning to stir slowly, finger by finger. There was nothing left of me, a phrase in French which I would never have to finish, a typewriter on the floor, a chair that squeaked and shook, fog. The kid had ducked his head like boxers do when they've done all they can and are waiting for the final blow to fall; he had turned up the collar of his overcoat and seemed more a prisoner than ever, the perfect victim helping promote the catastrophe. Now the woman was talking into his ear, and her hand opened again to lay itself against his cheekbone, to caress and caress it, burning it, taking her time. The kid was less startled than he was suspicious, once or twice he poked his head over the woman's shoulder and she continued talking, saying something that made him look back every few minutes toward that area where Michel knew the car was parked and the man in the grey hat, carefully eliminated from the photo but present in the boy's eyes (how doubt that now) in the words of the woman, in the woman's hands, in the vicarious presence of the woman. When I saw the man come up, stop near them and look at them, his hands in his pockets and a stance somewhere between disgusted and demanding, the master who is about to whistle in his dog after a frolic in the square, I understood, if that was to understand, what had to happen now, what had to have happened then, what would have to happen at that moment, among those people, just where I had poked my nose in to upset an established order, interfacing innocently in that which had not happened, but which was now going to happen, now was going to be fulfilled. And what I had imagined earlier was much less horrible than the reality, that woman, who was not there by herself, she was not caressing or propositioning or encouraging for her own pleasure, to lead the angel away with his tousled hair and play the tease with his terror and his eager grace. The real boss was waiting there, smiling petulantly, already certain of the business; he was not the first to send a woman in the vanguard, to bring him the prisoners manacled with flowers. The rest of it would be so simple, the car, some house or another, drinks, stimulating engravings, tardy tears, the awakening in hell. And there was nothing I could do, this time I could do absolutely nothing. My strength had been a photograph, that, there, where they were taking their revenge on me, demonstrating clearly what was going to happen. The photo had been taken, the time had run out, gone; we were so far from one another, the abusive act had certainly already taken place, the tears already shed, and the rest conjecture and sorrow. All at once the order was inverted, they were alive, moving, they were deciding and had decided, they were going to their future; and I on this side, prisoner of another time, in a room on the fifth floor, to not know who they were, that woman, that man, and that boy, to be only the lens of my camera; something fixed, rigid, incapable of intervention. It was horrible, their mocking me, deciding it before my impotent eye, mocking me, for the boy again was looking at the flour-faced clown and I had to accept the fact that he was going to say yes, that the proposition carried money with it or a gimmick, and I couldn't yell for him to run, or even open the road to him again with a new photo, a small and almost meek intervention which would ruin the framework of drool and perfume. Everything was going to resolve itself right there, at that moment; there was like an immense silence which had nothing to do with physical silence. It was stretching it out, setting itself up. I think I screamed, I screamed terribly, and that at that exact second I realized that I was beginning to move toward them, four inches, a step, another step, the tree swung its branches rhythmically in the foreground, a place where the railing was tarnished emerged from the frame, the woman's face turned toward me as though surprised, was enlarging, and then I turned a bit, I mean that the camera turned a little, and without losing sight of the woman, I began to close in on the man who was looking at me with the black holes he had in place of eyes, surprised and angered both, he looked, wanting to nail me onto the air, and at that instant I happened to see something like a large bird outside the focus that was flying in a single swoop in front of the picture, and I leaned up against the wall of my room and was happy because the boy had just managed to escape, I saw him running off, in focus again, sprinting with his hair flying in the wind, learning finally to fly across the island, to arrive at the footbridge, return to the city. For the second time he'd escaped them, for the second time I was helping him to escape, returning him to his precarious paradise. Out of breath, I stood in front of them; no need to step closer, the game was played out. Of the woman you could see just maybe a shoulder and a bit of the hair, brutally cut off by the frame of the picture; but the man was directly center, his mouth half open, you could see a shaking black tongue, and he lifted his hands slowly, bringing them into the foreground, an instant still in perfect focus, and then all of him a lump that blotted out the island, the tree, and I shut my eyes, I didn't want to see any more, and I covered my face and broke into tears like an idiot.

Now there's a big white cloud, as on all these days, all this untellable time. What remains to be said is always a cloud, two clouds, or long hours of a sky perfectly clear, a very clean, clear rectangle tacked up with pins on the wall of my room. That was what I saw when I opened my eyes and dried them with my fingers: the clear sky, and then a cloud that drifted in from the left, passed gracefully and slowly across and disappeared on the right. And then another, and for a change sometimes, everything gets grey, all one enormous cloud, and suddenly the splotches of rain cracking down, for a long spell you can see it raining over the picture, like a spell of weeping reversed, and little by little, the frame becomes clear, perhaps the sun comes out, and again the clouds begin to come two at a time, three at a time. And the pigeons once in a while, and a sparrow or two.

7

Figurative Discourse: Metaphor, Simile, Synecdoche, and Metonymy

Introduction

Whenever we speak or write figuratively, we use words in ways that modify or extend their literal sense. Most of us do this every day without being aware of it. As I write, it is raining cats and dogs outside; but, in fact, the only cats and dogs visible are those sleeping on my study floor. Comparisons like "raining cats and dogs" (which means "raining furiously like cats and dogs fighting"), or "dumb as an ox," or "happy as a lark" have become clichés. When Jonathan Swift invented the expression "raining cats and dogs" in 1728, it was striking because of its novelty. The comparison enabled readers to conceive of rainfalls (and cats and dogs) in new ways.

Comparison is the method of two types of figurative language, simile and metaphor. Any comparison that uses "like" or "as" is called a simile. A direct comparison is called a metaphor. Both similes and metaphors transfer attributes from one subject to another in order to suggest new ways of perceiving something. It is customary to speak of the subject of the metaphor or simile as the tenor and the thing being compared as the vehicle. When, for example, the narrator of D. H. Lawrence's story "The Rocking Horse Winner" comments that "the voices in the house suddenly went mad, like a chorus of frogs on a spring evening," he is forcing us to consider these "voices" (the tenor) in an entirely new light. Already he has personified the house (an inanimate object) by giving it a human characteristic (a voice), and in the context of the story this comparison is very unsettling. Now, by a simile that characterizes these voices not as human but as a mindless "chorus of frogs" (the vehicle) gone "mad," Lawrence makes the situation all the more frightening.

Simile and metaphor are the most common types of figurative language (or tropes as they are also called), but in fact nearly two hundred and fifty tropes have been catalogued by rhetoricians. Many of these tropes occur rarely, and the distinctions between them are often slight. Let us consider two other types of tropes important in both literature and film: synecdoche and metonymy, both of which involve the substitution of one idea for a closely related one. In the most common form of synecdoche, a part stands for the whole, or the whole for a part. For example, the command, "All hands on deck" does not literally mean what it says: the hands, which on board ship once did most of the work, are substituted for the entire person. Similarly, a slang term for automobile is "wheels:" a part represents the whole. An example of the whole being substituted for a part occurs when we speak of a policeman as "the law." In metonymy, a word is applied to something else with which it is closely associated. The "voice of the house" in Lawrence's story is a metonymy for the voice of the parents who own the house. Similarly, when newspaper reporters speak of "The White House," they are using a metonymy for its current inhabitant and his policies.

Figurative language is particularly important in literature, but, as the above examples indicate, it plays a role in daily conversation as well. What these tropes—metaphor, simile, synecdoche, and metonymy—have in common is the transference of meaning from one area to another. This transfer is their method; let us consider more examples in order to understand their function better.

As we noted in Chapter 4, tropes can be a powerful tool for characterization. Tropes may, of course, tell us more about the speaker than about the things being compared. When Philip joins Baines and his girlfriend for tea in "The Basement Room," the narrator—expressing the point of view of the little boy—remarks: "The afternoon was broken, the cake was like dry bread in the throat. The girl left them at once . . . like a blunt icicle in her white mackintosh she stood in the doorway with her back to them, then melted into the afternoon." In all these examples, the vehicles represent the viewpoints of a child. Philip barely comprehends the effect of his intrusion, so he expresses it in terms he does understand. The tropes tell us more about him than about "the afternoon," "the cake," or "the girl." Similarly, the protagonist of *The Collector* often compares people or feelings to his passion for butterfly collecting ("Seeing her always made me feel like I was catching a rarity . . ."), and here as well we learn more about him than about the objects he is describing. However, with an omniscient narrator the tenor of the trope becomes illuminated by the comparison, as when the narrator of *Jules and Jim* speaks of "the whirlwind that was Kate . . ." Our focus here remains on Kate, and our perception of her is enhanced by the comparison. In a concise metaphor (which Truffaut expands into the song, "The Whirlwind"), Pierre-Roché has captured many of Kate's qualities: her impetuosity, her violence, her changeability, and her unpredictability. In *Women in Love* Birkin often views Ursula in terms of fire imagery. The frequent use of figurative language enriches both their characters, as in the following observations (made by the omniscient narrator, who at this point is entering Birkin's consciousness):

> He looked up at her. He saw her face strangely enkindled, as if suffused from within by a powerful fire. His soul was arrested in wonder. She was enkindled in her own living fire.

A hundred pages later Birkin experiences this again:

> He stood smiling in frustration and amusement and irritation and admiration and love. She was so quick, and so lambent, like a discernible fire, and so vindictive, and so rich in her dangerous sensitiveness.

"The fire of passion" has become a cliché, and yet Lawrence invests this image with new life in these lines and thereby heightens the emotional intensity considerably.

Shakespeare is a master of figurative language, and we need turn no further than to *Macbeth* for copious examples. The first speech of any length in the play is the captain's. He reports to the King on the scene of battle from which he has just come:

> Doubtful it stood;
> As two spent swimmers, that do cling together
> And choke their art. The merciless Macdonwald
> (Worthy to be a rebel, for to that
> The multiplying villanies of nature
> Do swarm upon him) from the western isles
> Of Kernes and Gallowglasses is supplied;
> And Fortune, on his damned quarrel smiling,
> Show'd like a rebel's whore: but all's too weak;
> For brave Macbeth (well he deserves that name),
> Disdaining Fortune, with his brandish'd steel,
> Which smok'd with bloody execution,
> Like Valour's minion, carv'd out his passage,
> Till he fac'd the slave,
> Which ne'er shook hands, nor bade farewell to him,

> Till he unseam'd him from the nave to the chops,
> And fix'd his head upon our battlements.

Were we to remove the tropes from this passage, very little would remain. The tropes enable the captain to describe the situation intensely and with great economy.

The passage begins with a simile that introduces the elements of fatigue ("spent"), helplessness ("cling together"), and thwarted power. By contrast, Macdonwald, the antagonist, is described in terms that make him seem all-powerful: He is "merciless" and "worthy to be a rebel" with the support of countless traitors. These traitors are described in vivid and denigrating terms: with metonymy, as "villainies of nature" who "multiply" and "swarm" (both verbs suggest insects) and as "Kernes and Gallowglasses" (Irish foot soldiers and horsemen). Even Fortune, personified here, is on the traitor's side, for she smiles on Macdonwald "like a rebel's whore," and the simile suggests that this fickle lady has her price. The strength of Macdonwald's position heightens the suspense, as we hang on each word of the captain, awaiting the outcome. Then "brave Macbeth" is introduced: This is the first mention of him, and the epithet "brave" will remain with us as we witness his disintegration. Macbeth's confrontation with Macdonwald is depicted in graphic terms, enhanced by the metonymy "brandished steel" (for sword). Macbeth's courage is expressed through another personification: He becomes "valour's minion," the darling (minion) of valour, a personified abstraction. In addition to presenting Macbeth's abstract characteristics in a striking manner, this personification is set in opposition to the earlier personification of Fortune. Fortune is a whore, but Valour remains constant. The brutal carnage of the ensuing struggle is clearly and vigorously evoked, but at the same time the figurative language distances us from it. Macbeth's killing of Macdonwald is described with a metaphor (the verb, "unseamed") and two examples of synecdoche, "nave" (navel) for stomach, and "chops" for head. The final gruesome line, however, is without figurative adornment, and it clearly prefigures Macbeth's own fate.

The passage from Macbeth demonstrates the emotional intensity and the compactness of presentation that can be gained with the use of tropes. Since this is the captain's only appearance, his speech can be said to function primarily for exposition rather than characterization. Macbeth's language, however, both conveys information and develops his character. Through his soliloquies we are given access to his thoughts. His power to create language remains one of the sources of his fascination for us. After hearing the news of his wife's death, Macbeth turns aside and utters what are perhaps the most famous words in the play:

> To-morrow, and to-morrow, and to-morrow,
> Creeps in this petty pace from day to day,
> To the last syllable of recorded time;
> And all our yesterdays have lighted fools

The way to dusty death. Out, out, brief candle!
Life's but a walking shadow; a poor player,
That struts and frets his hour upon the stage,
And then is heard no more: it is a tale
Told by an idiot, full of sound and fury,
Signifying nothing.

At the heart of this passage is an extended comparison between life and a candle. Without analyzing the tropes here in as much detail as in the preceding passage, we can note the resonances of this comparison: For the momentary duration of its burning, a candle provides illumination and heat in the darkness; it is preceded and followed by darkness; it can be snuffed out at any moment; and if left to burn, it becomes smaller and smaller, until finally nothing is left. In addition, a candle is a common, everyday object of little worth. The other vehicles also emphasize the insubstantiality and insignificance of life, and they do so with a remarkable economy and concreteness. Not the least of the effects communicated by these tropes, and by those discussed above, is the pleasure they give to the reader or listener perceiving new likenesses between dissimilar things.

Filmmakers also have the desire to communicate insight and pleasure through the comparison of dissimilar objects, and they have discovered a number of imaginative ways of creating cinematic tropes that do just this. One of the first means used was editing, the immediate proximity of any two pictures suggesting a relationship between them. Sergei Eisenstein suggested that one could do more than merely compare the two things being juxtaposed. Instead, the components of the juxtaposition, like the hieroglyphs of a Chinese ideogram, could result in something entirely new, an idea greater than the sum of its parts. Since the early discussions of V. I. Pudovkin and Sergei Eisenstein, it has become apparent that film, like prose, can present a wider range of tropes than metaphors and similes. Film abounds in synecdoches: We see a hand enter the frame, and we assume it is attached to a body. Often, synecdoches suggest the fragmentation of a personality, as when we see the gigantic lips in *Citizen Kane* mouthing the word "rosebud," or a distancing effect, as when Meursault pulls the trigger in *The Stranger*. Visual objects also lend themselves naturally to metonymy and personification. Clearly, editing is but one way of creating tropes. Virtually any film technique, including composition, lighting, camera position, and framing, can be used figuratively. In addition, several tropes created in this manner can exist simulataneously in a film. For the filmmaker, as for the writer, tropes are an important means of enabling us to view the world in new and different ways.

Additional Recommended Films

The Servant (1963), directed by Joseph Losey, based on the novella by Robert Maugham. The novella is out of print, but the script is available in paperback.

Death in Venice (1971), directed by Luchino Visconti, based on the short story by
Thomas Mann. The story is available in paperback.

A Clockwork Orange (1971), directed by Stanley Kubrick, based on the novel by Anthony Burgess. The novel is available in paperback.

See Also:

Rashomon (Chapter 5)
The Innocents (Chapter 5)
The Rocking-Horse Winner (Chapter 8)
Fellini Satyricon (Chapter 8)

Great Expectations
The Trial

The Throne of Blood

Akira Kurosawa's *The Throne of Blood* (1957) is thought by some critics and
directors to be the best version of *Macbeth* on film and one of the most successful cinematic adaptations of Shakespeare.[1] On first consideration this
would seem unlikely, for the rich cadences of Shakespeare's English are missing entirely, the setting has been shifted to medieval Japan, and the action of
the play has been greatly simplified. However, Kurosawa has created a
highly cinematic version of *Macbeth*, which succeeds as a distillation of the
original.

There is relatively little dialogue in Kurosawa's film, and many of the
conflicts in Shakespeare's play have been internalized by making the external
world an objectification of the protagonist's mind. Thus, Kurosawa's film
abounds in tropes, most of which have their source in Shakespeare's verse.

The film's opening shots reveal the ruins of a fortress shrouded in fog
and mist. A chorus, adopted from the tradition of the Noh drama, intones a
moral lesson offscreen:

> Behold within this place
> Now desolated, stood
> Once a might fortress,
> Here lived a proud warrior
> Murdered by ambition . . .
> His spirit walks still
> Vain pride, then as now,
> Will lead ambition to the kill.

[1]Roger Manvell cites the praise of Grigori Kozintsev, Peter Hall, and Peter Brook in his
Shakespeare and the Film (New York: Praeger, 1971), p. 107.

Kurosawa creates a circular structure for his drama by beginning and ending with this same scene. The story of Macbeth becomes a flashback, with the outcome known from the first scene. Instead of opening his drama as Shakespeare does with a concrete embodiment of evil (the three witches), Kurosawa stresses the futility of man's ambitions amidst a general setting of decay and dissolution. The fog, here associated with destruction, will later become a metaphor for the protagonist's state of mind.

Kurosawa pans and cuts through the mists until the fortress comes into view. Within the fortress, the established rulers are formally seated on a platform, receiving news of the battles raging offscreen. Because of the opening, we know that the supremacy of the rulers cannot last. Time is compressed through a series of wipes, moving from left to right, in the direction from which the horsemen enter the fortress. Kurosawa's choice of transitions throughout the film is significant: Dissolves and fades are used very sparingly; most of the transitions are cuts or wipes, suggesting, as Donald Richie has pointed out, that choices within this world are an unequivocal either/or.[2] Kurosawa also shows a preference for full shots over close-ups. Many filmmakers will dolly or cut to a close-up in a moment of emotional tension: Kurosawa usually does just the opposite here. His full shots often reveal both cause and effect as well as create a sense of audience estrangement.[3]

While the commanders ponder their alternatives within the fortress, one suggests: "Place our men in the forest . . . it is a natural labyrinth . . . and the enemy will lose themselves." A series of riders bring news, concluding with the report that Washizu (Macbeth) and Miki (Banquo) have been victorious. With a reverse wipe, Washizu and Miki are shown on horseback in the forest. The direction of the wipe is unsettling, as it disrupts the visual rhythm of the film. This ominous omen is the first of many connected with Washizu.

The sequence that follows gives proof to the assertion that "the forest is a labyrinth" and demonstrates that this labyrinth is the mind of Washizu. Kurosawa employs the forest as the embodiment of Washizu's thoughts: As one critic has noted, the "encounter with the forest is a headlong plunge into the self."[4] To control the castle one must control the forest: The implications of this situation become clearer as the film proceeds.

The forest is given a supernatural quality by the lightning, the gnarled forms of the trees, and the eerie sounds emanating from it. At first Washizu and Miki are certain that they can traverse the forest, but they gradually realize that they are lost. At Washizu's suggestion, they use their weapons in an attempt to break the spell of the forest. They ride frantically in what appears to be a maze as they keep returning to the spot they had just left. The folly of their earlier confidence is readily apparent, and the forest seems to

---

[2]Donald Richie, *The Films of Akira Kurosawa* (Berkeley: University of California Press, 1973), p. 120. Richie is wrong when he states, "There are no fades, no dissolves, nothing soft, nothing flowing, nothing amorphous," but his general point is a good one.

[3]Ibid., p. 121.

[4]J. Blumenthal, "*Macbeth* into *Throne of Blood*," *Sight and Sound*, 34 (Autumn 1965), 191.

The Throne of Blood. A confrontation with the self.

be laughing mockingly at them. As they hurry confusedly through the heavy growth, a hut materializes before them, and they stop abruptly. Kurosawa has placed the sorceress in the heart of the forest, appropriate since she articulates Washizu's innermost desires. Trapped within himself, he is seeking a way out: The spirit provides him with one. As she sits within her hut spinning, the sorceress chants about the vain ambitions of mankind and then utters a short prophecy for each of the men before disappearing upward into the mist. Washizu has confronted his hidden thoughts, and he is visibly shaken.

Neither Washizu nor Miki quite knows what to make of the prophecy, and the mood and pace of the film are markedly different after they leave the site of the spirit's hut. Like spectral figures in a ghostly landscape, they wander slowly through a heavy fog. Uncertainty and hesitation have replaced the aggressive defiance shown earlier, and conversation is sparse. Finally, the outlines of the fortress appear in the distance. They dismount from their horses, sit at opposite sides of the frame with the fortress between them, and discuss the prophecy. Miki states: "We dream of what we wish. Who would not want to be lord of a mighty castle?" As they voice their thoughts, the fog lifts and the fortress becomes increasingly visible. Doubts are eradicated and motives are illuminated: The movement of the fog becomes a perfect visualization of Washizu's state of mind.

Not only do the fog and mist indicate Washizu's thoughts, but also the animal world mirrors the equilibrium or disequilibrium in the human world. There is ample precedent for this in Shakespeare's play, but Kurosawa provides additional examples and gives each an ambivalent meaning. Shakespeare has the natural world respond after the killing of the king: As Macbeth returns from the king's chamber, he asks: "Didst thou not hear a noise?" Lady Macbeth replies: "I heard the owl scream and the crickets cry." In *The Throne of Blood* crows caw before the king is murdered, and thus, they function as an omen. Washizu is distressed and interprets their sounds as evil. His wife, however, explains them differently. "The throne is yours," she states boldly. This is not the first time Washizu has been warned by birds. The screeching in the forest seems ominous to Washizu and Miki; they believe the sounds to be the voice of the spirit entrapping them there. But the birds also lead them to the prophecy of the sorceress. At the end of the film, the birds return, as Washizu sits with his counselors discussing the defense of the castle. There is a natural explanation for their presence here, although it is not known to the men within the castle: The forest is being cut down, and the birds are thus put to flight. The birds disturb Washizu's counselors, but he remains confident and interprets them as a positive sign. The meaning of

The Throne of Blood. The natural order is disturbed.

an omen seems to be in the eye of the beholder, reflecting Washizu's confidence or uncertainty at that moment. For the audience, however, all the omens are negative.

The actions of horses also function as a correlative to the natural order, and here too, Kurosawa elaborates on Shakespeare's text. In their ride together through the forest, the horses of Washizu and Miki become supernatural creatures, through Kurosawa's use of lighting and accelerated movements. The horses seem possessed, as are their owners. Later, after the king's murder, his horses break loose and run wild, as they are reported to have done in *Macbeth:*

> And Duncan's horses—a thing most strange and certain—
> Beauteous, and swift, the minions of their race,
> Turned wild in nature, broke their stall, flung out,
> Contending 'gainst obedience, as they would
> Make war with mankind. (II, iv, 14–18)

The frenzied activity of the horses contrasts markedly with the moment of stasis preceding it (Washizu and Asaji retiring for the night). Kurosawa develops this analogue further with Miki's horse, whose behavior foreshadows Miki's own impending demise. The sequence begins with a group of soldiers speculating on the possibility of Washizu having an heir. Washizu and Asaji are then seen inside discussing the same subject. Washizu acknowledges his indebtedness to Miki and suggests that he make Miki's son his heir. Washizu's wife confronts him with the news, which startles him as much as it shocks the viewer: "I am with child," she declares. Kurosawa immediately cuts to the courtyard, where Miki's horse is running wild. The abrupt juxtaposition of these two shots creates a cinematic simile: The wild horse is a perfect embodiment of Washizu's response to his wife's declaration. Miki then tells his son of the prophecy. The son is skeptical and views the horse's behavior as an evil omen. He urges his father to refrain from riding that afternoon, but Miki assures him that all is well. They saddle up and depart. Kurosawa cuts to the battlements. It is night time, and we overhear the same soldiers discoursing on recent events. Their conversation is interrupted by the distant sounds of a horse's hooves, which gradually become louder and louder. Finally, Miki's horse gallops into the courtyard with its empty saddle. The soldiers look uneasy, and we know that the omen has been fulfilled. However, it is double-edged: not only has Miki been killed, but also Asaji's child will die within her.

Thus, Kurosawa develops objectifications of Washizu's mind in the natural world (the fog and the forest) and in the animal world (the behavior of birds and horses). He also develops important parallels between characters, which function metaphorically. Noriyasu, the king, is not the upright ruler of Shakespeare's play. Instead, he is deceptive, treacherous, and willing to go to any lengths to maintain his power. When Washizu explains the prophecy to his wife and expresses his hesitancy to act on it, she reminds him that the king "murdered his own master to get where he is." Washizu becomes more and more like Kuniharu, and the parallels are developed through matching scenes, such as the moment when Washizu meets with his counselors on the eve of the battle as Kuniharu had done earlier.

Strong parallels are also created between Asaji and the sorceress in the forest. Both understand Washizu's lust for power, and both articulate his hidden desires. After persuading her husband to kill the king, Asaji takes the potion to the soldiers. As she steps into the doorway, she disappears into a dark void, just as the witch had disappeared after her prophecy. Asaji, too, has become a supernatural creature. In both cases, the parallels are strengthened by the circular structure of Kurosawa's film, which suggests that history repeats itself endlessly.

Kurosawa's conclusion to *The Throne of Blood* is in keeping with his earlier development of the forest as a metaphor of Washizu's mind. When Washizu returns to the forest for a clarification of the prophecy, the spirit tells him to fear only the forest moving. The rest of the prophecy in Macbeth is eliminated to strengthen the presentation of Washizu as a man torn from within. In spite of the apparent weakness of his situation at the end, he remains supremely confident, rallying his men as they try to flee from the fortress. He mounts the battlements and boasts of the prophecy, which, in his eyes, makes him invincible. He had earlier told his counselors that "We will

The Throne of Blood. Washizu: Destroyed from within.

conquer the enemy": What he does not yet perceive is that he himself is the enemy. Finally, the forest begins to move, in what is one of the most strikingly beautiful of the many extraordinary images in Kurosawa's film. Washizu's own soldiers turn their weapons in his direction, creating with their arrows another labyrinth from which there is no escape. The enemy *is* within, and so Washizu is destroyed not by external forces but by his own men. As he sinks to the ground with arrows piercing him on all sides, his men draw back, astonished by the superhuman exertion of his will. The fog begins to rise, and Kurosawa cuts to the soldiers besieging the castle. They will soon be victorious, but this is unimportant. Instead of showing us the restoration of order with which *Macbeth* concludes, Kurosawa cuts to the images of desolation and waste with which his own film began. This is the inevitable result of man's relentless struggle for power.

The *Throne of Blood* is an unusual example of cultural transmission and dramatic expansion. Kurosawa minimizes the role of language and instead creates a striking series of tropes, which heighten our understanding of the protagonist and alter our perceptions of the world in which he lives.

The Throne of Blood
Also called The Castle of the Spider's Web

Production Credits

Director	Akira Kurosawa
Producers	Shojiro Motoki, Akira Kurosawa
Screenplay by	Shinobu Hashimoto, Ryuzo Kikushima, Hideo Oguni, Akira Kurosawa
Based on "Macbeth" by	William Shakespeare
Director of Photography	Asakazu Nakai
Art Directors	Yoshiro Muraki, Kohei Ezaki
Music by	Masaru Sato

Japan. 1957. 105 minutes. Black and white.

Cast

Taketoki Washizu (Macbeth)	Toshiro Mifune
Asaji, his wife (Lady Macbeth)	Isuzu Yamada
Yoshiaki Miki, his friend (Banquo)	Minoru Chiaki
Yoshiteru, Miki's son (Fleance)	Akira Kubo
Kuniharu Tsuzuki (Duncan)	Takamaru Sasaki
Kunimaru, Kuniharu's son (Malcolm)	Yoichi Tachikawa
Noriyasu Odagura	Takashi Shimura
Witch	Chieko Naniwa

Further Reading

Bazerman, Charles. "Time in Play and Film: *Macbeth* and *Throne of Blood.*" *Literature/Film Quarterly,* 5, No. 4 (Fall 1977), 333–38.

Blumenthal, J. "*Macbeth* into *Throne of Blood.*" *Sight and Sound,* 34 (Autumn 1965), 190–95.

Gerlach, John. "Shakespeare, Kurosawa, and Macbeth: A Response to J. Blumenthal." *Literature/Film Quarterly,* 1, No. 4 (Fall 1973), 352–59.

Jorgens, Jack J. *Shakespeare on Film.* Bloomington: Indiana University Press, 1977.

Kinder, Marsha. "*Throne of Blood:* A Morality Dance." *Literature/Film Quarterly,* 5, No. 4 (Fall 1977), 339–45.

Manvell, Roger. *Shakespeare and the Film.* New York: Praeger, 1971.

Richie, Donald. *The Films of Akira Kurosawa.* Berkeley: University of California Press, 1970.

Tyler, Parker. *Classics of the Foreign Film: A Pictorial Treasury.* New York: The Citadel Press, 1962.

Zambrano, Ana Laura. "*Throne of Blood:* Kurosawa's *Macbeth.*" *Literature/Film Quarterly,* 2, No. 3 (Summer 1974), 262–74.

The Fallen Idol

The Fallen Idol (1948), based on Graham Greene's short story, "The Basement Room," was Carol Reed's first collaboration with Greene, who wrote the screenplay, and it resulted in one of Reed's finest films. Through an imaginative use of cinematic tropes, *The Fallen Idol* brilliantly captures the feelings of a little boy confronted for the first time with the complexities of the adult world. Reed and Greene succeed in creating a range of visual equivalents for the figurative language of the story, and their solutions suggest a great deal about the possibilities and limitations of each medium.

"The Basement Room" records the transformation of Philip Lane from a joyful, innocent seven-year-old into an embittered old man. Philip is left for a fortnight in the care of his parents' butler and housekeeper, Baines and Mrs. Baines. In less than two days he discovers the hatred that exists between the couple, learns that Baines has a girlfriend (although he remains confused about their relationship), and witnesses an argument between the couple that culminates with Baines accidentally pushing his wife downstairs and killing her. Philip is unprepared for any of this, and although he loves Baines, he refuses to protect him. Consequently, the police arrest Baines, and Philip retreats from life, eschewing the responsibilities and duplicities that for him have come to characterize the adult world.

The boy's story is told in retrospect by an omniscient narrator. The presentation is chronological, interrupted by a series of flash-forwards that ends with the boy's death as an old man and keeps his ultimate fate constantly before us. Greene desires to maintain a tension in his story between the innocent child and the withdrawn old man that precludes the use of a first person narrator. However, to convey the perspective of the child, Greene employs diction and figurative language suggesting a child's outlook. For example, adults are usually referred to as "grown-ups," and a distinction is made between "their world" and "yours." Significant characters and events are often described in terms of a child's fears, principally the fear of the dark, the fear of being alone, and the fear of strangers. Mrs. Baines is consistently characterized by this language. She becomes so closely connected with the world of nightmares that we are not surprised when she is transformed into the wicked witch. This transformation occurs after she has learned from Philip about Baines's girlfriend. She pretends to leave the house for a short trip, and that night as Philip dozes off he discovers "the inevitable terrors of sleep . . . a bleeding head lay on the kitchen table in a basket, and the Siberian wolves crept closer. He was bound hand and foot and couldn't move; they leapt round him breathing heavily; he opened his eyes and Mrs. Baines was there, her grey untidy hair in threads over his face, her black hat askew." His worst fears have been confirmed, as his bad dreams have become a reality.

This nightmare world is largely the world of the adults ("their world"), and Mrs. Baines characterizes just a part of it. The central conflict in the story is between this world and the world of the child. Philip cannot understand what he discovers in "the basement room," and so he retreats to the safety of his nursery. His final refusal to aid Baines is tantamount to a rejection of the adult world. Baines moves easily in both worlds, and his mobility is at once a source of his attraction for Philip and a reason for Philip's ultimate betrayal of him.

Philip fears a confusion of the two worlds, and this is precisely what happens when Mrs. Baines returns to the house at night, awakens him, and begins searching for her husband and his lover. The two worlds, once distinct, collide so rapidly that Philip is unprepared to cope with the results: "The whole house had been turned over to the grown-up world; he wasn't safe in the night nursery; their passions had flooded it." His last refuge has been invaded and he must flee. Never again can he feel safe in the house now that his territory has been desecrated.

In all the above examples, Greene characterizes Baines and Mrs. Baines as Philip sees them, by using figurative language that evokes Philip's point of view. Greene also employs figurative language for anything Philip cannot quite understand, as with the "passion" cited above. Emotions beyond his ken thus become reduced to his perspective. This is precisely what happens when Philip interrupts Baines and his girlfriend in the tea shop. He sees them through the window and tries to surprise them by imitating Mrs. Baines's piercing cry: "Baines!" Although Philip has meant no harm by this, the couple is understandably shocked, and Greene expresses this shock not in their terms but in Philip's: "Baines was the first to recover and trace the voice, but that didn't make things as they were. The sawdust was spilled out of the afternoon; nothing you did could mend it." The irrevocability of Philip's action (which he cannot fully comprehend) is compared to something he knows well. By drawing on the child's diction for his figurative language, Greene is able to give a concrete sense of the immense fear elicited in Philip by the conflict between his own world and the mysterious world of the adults, while maintaining the tension between Philip as a young boy and as an old man.

In the film Reed and Greene have deleted the flash-forwards and expanded the action to focus on the boy's brief encounter with the world and the question of Baines's innocence or guilt. The deletion has significant consequences, for without the flash-forwards it becomes possible to adopt a modified first-person point of view for the story. In fact, Reed and Greene have chosen to do just this. We view much of the action through the eyes of Phillipe (as he is called in the film, where he is the son of a French-speaking ambassador in London), and from his perspective the adult world seems awesome and overpowering.

One way Greene distinguishes between the two worlds noted above is in spatial terms, in the contrast between "the basement room" of the servants and Philip's own nursery. In the film Reed has capitalized on these distinctions. The house becomes an enormous embassy, with three levels above ground and one below. The ground floor is the "public" level, containing reception rooms, a dining room, and a library, while the upper floors are for the family, with the nursery on the very top. Phillipe is first seen on the top floor, peering through an iron railing at Baines, who is emptying ashtrays on the ground floor. Baines performs the chore with an exaggerated shuffle for Phillipe's benefit, thereby combining the two worlds. A warm bond clearly exists between them, and this contrasts sharply with Phillipe's formal relationship to his own father. The latter is about to leave to fetch Phillipe's mother from the hospital where she has spent the previous eight months. Phillipe remains frozen on his level as his father departs: They speak across an enormous space that characterizes their isolation from each other. In fact, Reed consistently uses space figuratively: The same vastness separating Phillipe from his father is duplicated at the end of the film when his mother returns. She purposefully bustles into the embassy, calling out a greeting while Phillipe hesitantly descends the vast staircase. The conclusion is certainly not happy, but it is very much in keeping with Reed's predilection for equivocal endings.

The bars that separate Phillipe from the rest of the house in the opening scene are employed figuratively throughout the film. There are hints of this in the story: Early, when Philip has been forbidden by Mrs. Baines from going for a walk with her husband, he turns to Baines "for help and only intercepted hate; the sad hopeless hate of something behind bars" (the hate here is directed toward Mrs. Baines, not Philip). There is also a railing on the basement steps: Phillipe peers through it when Baines speaks to his wife about the possibility of a separation. The bars isolate Phillipe and shelter him from their emotions. The most developed use of bars occurs during the sequence at the zoo, which expands the brief reference to this outing in the story. Phillipe, Baines, and Julie (Baines's girlfriend) strive to enjoy an uneasy freedom at the zoo, while the caged animals romp without restraint. At one point Phillipe pauses before a cage where monkeys are copulating, and he innocently asks, "What are they doing?" The scene is a cruel reminder of the contrast between the animals' freedom and their own. Later, Phillipe offers food to a moving object behind bars, only to discover that it is a man exiting from a restroom, looking quite puzzled by Phillipe's gesture. We can never forget that the "freedom" the trio enjoys at the zoo is illusory: In fact, they are already encaged. The visual presence of the bars throughout the sequence constantly reminds us of this fact, thus giving the metaphor a duration it could not have in literature.

The sequence at the zoo begins with a brilliant simile created by editing. Baines, thinking that his wife has gone for the day, telephones Julie to arrange for her to meet him and Phillipe at the zoo. Baines is shown in a long shot talking to Julie. Reed cuts to a close-up of Phillipe, who has come downstairs and stopped to listen, as he comprehends the significance of the call. Then he cuts back to the long shot of Baines. Instead of returning to the boy, Reed cuts to a slightly oblique medium shot of Mrs. Baines, huddled in a doorway, also eavesdropping. Reed cuts back to Phillipe, then Baines, then Phillipe; from this he dissolves very quickly to a caged lion, reaching out with its paw and roaring mightily. The lion immediately evokes Mrs. Baines's anger as well as her awesome power over Baines and Phillipe. The simile also functions as a transition from the embassy to the zoo.

The zoo provides other opportunities for visual and aural tropes. Walking with Julie, Phillipe remarks to her about Baines that "the only thing he's afraid of is Mrs. Baines." Reed cuts to a shrieking cockatoo, echoing Mrs. Baines's voice, which has been characterized (in the story) as "the voice in a nightmare." The simile reinforces the continued sense of Mrs. Baines's presence everywhere the trio goes, and suggests that tropes created by editing are most effective when contextual.

Reed manipulates space to delineate relationships between individuals and to characterize their predicaments. This is true of his use of exterior space as well as interior space (the zoo, the embassy). The contrast between Phillipe's two flights through the streets make this apparent. The first occurs at midday before he has any knowledge of Baines's girlfriend. In the story Greene creates a positive sense of unexplored possibilities by concluding the sentence that describes Philip's reaction to leaving the house with a preposition: "it was life he was in the middle of." The film conveys this feeling of limitless choice through loose framing and natural lighting. By contrast, the night scene is bizarrely lit, the lights reflecting on wet empty streets through which the diminished figure of Phillipe furtively darts. Oblique angles and tight framing convey Phillipe's fear and loss of perspective. The streets have

The Fallen Idol. The once-welcome streets have become strange and forbidding.

become an extension of the nightmare world he entered upon being awakened by Mrs. Baines, and he scurries through them like a rat in a maze.

Reed uses framing metaphorically at other crucial moments in the film. For example, tight framing is employed when Phillipe is awakened by Mrs. Baines. Reed cuts from an extreme close-up of Phillipe's motionless face, as a hairpin falls onto the pillow beside him, to an extreme close-up of Mrs. Baines peering down at him: "She was so like the witches of his dreams that he didn't dare to speak." Similarly, tight framing is employed during the inspector's interrogation of Phillipe. Phillipe tries to retreat up the expansive staircase to the safety of his nursery, but the inspector and his assistants encircle him, and the framing becomes tighter and tighter as the questioning becomes increasingly insistent. As the tension mounts, subjective shots of the inspector are seen from an oblique angle, which adds to our perception of Phillipe's discomfort. Finally, Phillipe rises to his feet and Reed cuts to a long shot, thus dissipating the tension as Phillipe speaks to Julie in French. In both sequences the framing aptly suggests Phillipe's entrapment.

Already we have considered some of the ways Reed and Greene create cinematic tropes: through editing, framing, camera angles, and the use of space. But they also develop "sequential metaphors" that bring the worlds of innocence and experience into immediate juxtaposition. None of these sequences is in the story, yet they carry the burden of meaning suggested by the figurative language. One example is the game of hide and seek that Phillipe, Baines, and Julie play on the evening of the day when Mrs. Baines is supposedly absent. In the story they receive Mrs. Baines's letter and are momentarily happy with the news that her return will be delayed, "but you could tell . . . that she [Mrs. Baines] wasn't really away at all; she was there in the basement with them." This vague feeling is actualized in the film. Baines and Julie hurry about the living room, pulling sheets off the chairs Mrs. Baines so carefully covered earlier. Then the chase begins. Suddenly, Reed cuts to a close-up of a woman's high black shoes seen from Phillipe's point of view. This visual synecdoche is much more striking than a full shot would be, and we realize what Phillipe fails to perceive: Mrs. Baines is a participant as well. She is scared off before Phillipe recognizes her, and she is also on the point of being discovered by Baines and Julie when they are surprised by Phillipe. For the viewer, the game has turned serious, as Mrs. Baines's felt presence has become a reality. The suspense is heightened when Phillipe looks through the window from the upper level a few minutes later, recognizes Mrs. Baines, and cries out in horror. But he is too frightened to tell Baines and Julie, and they put him to bed. The sequence is very disconcerting, one that aptly illustrates an observation made in the story: "For if a grown-up could behave so childishly, you were liable too to find yourself in their world."

Another sequence that develops the confrontation between children and grown-ups revolves around the telegram Mrs. Baines sends to her husband. In the story she mails him a letter, and little is made of it except for Philip's silent questioning of its veracity. In the film the telegram is visually important. Phillipe folds it into a glider, and once again, a child's simple game becomes transformed into a momentous act. Phillipe loses the glider and later Baines, fearing its value as evidence against him (he had not told the inspector that Mrs. Baines was presumably away), questions the sleepy child. Phillipe has been drugged by the doctor and cannot remember, so Baines is reassured and returns downstairs. A few minutes later Phillipe stumbles down to the second level, plucks the glider out of a palm tree, and collapses. Baines and the doctor rush to him: Arriving first, the doctor takes the glider from the boy's hand and casually tosses it downward. As Baines watches hopelessly, it slowly drops to the first floor, landing at the inspector's feet. In three short shots the child's world collides with the world of the adults, and Baines becomes involved as a suspect.

These sequences represent yet another way of creating visual equivalents for figurative language. Each is developed as a dramatic expansion of a metaphorical statement: they advance the narrative while developing the contrast between innocence and experience. They are effective because they arise naturally out of the context of the film, a characteristic shared with the other visual tropes considered above.

The Fallen Idol shows some of the ways an inventive director and screenwriter can create cinematic equivalents of figurative language. Although the range of comparisons for visual tropes is perhaps more restricted than in literature, such figures can have a sense of duration impossible in literature, and several can exist simultaneously. Through camera angles, editing, framing, the use of space, and above all, sequences functioning on both narrative and figurative levels, Reed and Greene have created equivalents that enrich film as an art.

The Fallen Idol. A child's game becomes serious.

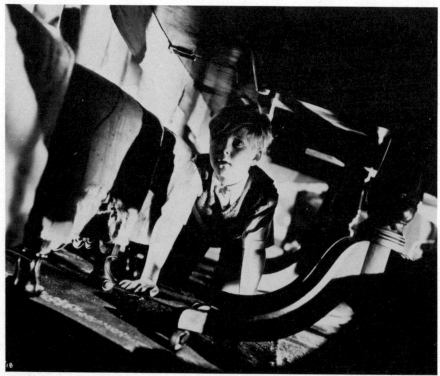

The Fallen Idol

Production Credits

Director	Carol Reed
Producer	Carol Reed
Screenplay by	Graham Greene
Additional dialogue by	Lesley Storm, William Templeton
Based on "The Basement Room"	
by	Graham Greene
Director of Photography	Georges Perinal
Film Editor	Oswald Hafenrichter
Sets by	Vincent Korda
Music by	William Alwyn
Orchestration by	London Film Symphony Orchestra

Great Britain. 1948. 94 minutes. Black & white.

Cast

Baines	Ralph Richardson
Julie	Michele Morgan
Mrs. Baines	Sonia Dresdel
Phillipe	Bobby Henry
Inspector Crowe	Denis O'Dea
Detective Ames	Jack Hawkins
Detective Davis	Geoffrey Keene
Detective Hart	Bernard Lee
Dr. Wilson	John Ruddock
Ambassador	Gerard Heinz
First Secretary	Karel Stepanek
Policeman	Torin Thatcher
Clock Winder	Hay Petrie
Rose	Dora Bryan

Further Reading

Goldstein, R. M. "The Fallen Idol." *Film News*, 33 (September/October 1976), 28.

Phillips, Gene D., *Graham Greene: The Films of his Fiction*. New York: Teachers College Press, 1974.

Zambrano, Ana Laura. "Greene's Visions of Childhood: 'The Basement Room' and *The Fallen Idol*." *Literature/Film Quarterly*, 2, No. 4 (Fall 1974), 324–31.

The Basement Room
Graham Greene

1

When the front door had shut them out and the butler Baines had turned back into the dark heavy hall, Philip began to live. He stood in front of the nursery door, listening until he heard the engine of the taxi die out along the street. His parents were gone for a fortnight's holiday; he was "between nurses," one dismissed and the other not arrived; he was alone in the great Belgravia house with Baines and Mrs. Baines.

He could go anywhere, even through the green baize door to the pantry or down the stairs to the basement living-room. He felt a stranger in his home because he could go into any room and all the rooms were empty.

You could only guess who had once occupied them: the rack of pipes in the smoking-room beside the elephant tusks, the carved wood tobacco jar; in the bedroom the pink hangings and pale perfumes and the three-quarter finished jars of cream which Mrs. Baines had not yet cleared away; the high glaze on the never-opened piano in the drawing-room, the china clock, the silly little tables and the silver: but here Mrs. Baines was already busy, pulling down the curtains, covering the chairs in dust-sheets.

"Be off out of here, Master Philip," and she looked at him with her hateful peevish eyes, while she moved round getting everything in order, meticulous and loveless and doing her duty.

Philip Lane went downstairs and pushed at the baize door; he looked into the pantry, but Baines was not there, then he set foot for the first time on the stairs to the basement. Again he had the sense: this is life. All his seven nursery years vibrated with the strange, the new experience. His crowded busy brain was like a city which feels the earth tremble at a distant earthquake shock. He was apprehensive, but he was happier than he had ever been. Everything was more important than before.

Baines was reading a newspaper in his shirt-sleeves. He said: "Come in, Phil, and make yourself at home. Wait a moment and I'll do the honours," and going to a white cleaned cupboard he brought out a bottle of ginger-beer and half a Dundee cake. "Half-past eleven in the morning," Baines said. "It's opening time, my boy," and he cut the cake and poured out the ginger-beer. He was more genial than Philip had ever known him, more at his ease, a man in his own home.

"Shall I call Mrs. Baines?" Philip asked, and he was glad when Baines said no. She was busy. She liked to be busy, so why interfere with her pleasure?

"A spot of drink at half-past eleven," Baines said, pouring himself out a glass of ginger-beer, "gives an appetite for chop and does no man any harm."

"A chop?" Philip asked.

"Old Coasters," Baines said, "call all food chop."

"But it's not a chop?"

"Well, it might be, you know, cooked with palm oil. And then some paw-paw to follow."

Philip looked out of the basement window at the dry stone yard, the ash-can and the legs going up and down beyond the railings.

"Was it hot there?"

"Ah, you never felt such heat. Not a nice heat, mind, like you get in the park on a day like this. Wet." Baines said, "corruption." He cut himself a slice of cake. "Smelling of rot," Baines said, rolling his eyes round the small basement room, from clean cupboard to clean cupboard, the sense of bareness, of nowhere to hide a man's secrets. With an air of regret for something lost he took a long draught of ginger-beer.

"Why did father live out there?"

"It was his job," Baines said, "same as this is mine now. And it was mine then too. It was a man's job. You wouldn't believe it now, but I've had forty niggers under me, doing what I told them to."

"Why did you leave?"

"I married Mrs. Baines."

Philip took the slice of Dundee cake in his hand and munched it round the room. He felt very old, independent and judicial; he was aware that Baines was talking to him as man to man. He never called him Master Philip as Mrs. Baines did, who was servile when she was not authoritative.

Baines had seen the world; he had seen beyond the railings, beyond the tired legs of typists, the Pimlico parade to and from Victoria. He sat there over his ginger pop with the resigned dignity of an exile; Baines didn't complain; he had chosen his fate; and if his fate was Mrs. Baines he had only himself to blame.

But today, because the house was almost empty and Mrs. Baines was upstairs and there was nothing to do, he allowed himself a little acidity.

"I'd go back tomorrow if I had the chance."

"Did you ever shoot a nigger?"

"I never had any call to shoot," Baines said. "Of course I carried a gun. But you didn't need to treat them bad. That just made them stupid. Why," Baines said, bowing his thin grey hair with embarrassment over the ginger pop, "I loved some of those dammed niggers. I couldn't help loving them. There they'd be, laughing, holding hands; they liked to touch each other; it made them feel fine to know the other fellow was round.

"It didn't mean anything we could understand: two of them would go about all day without loosing hold, grown men; but it wasn't love; it didn't mean anything we could understand."

"Eating between meals," Mrs. Baines said. "What would your mother say, Master Philip?"

She came down the steep stairs to the basement, her hands full of pots of cream and salve, tubes of grease and paste. "You oughtn't to encourage him,

Baines," she said, sitting down in a wicker armchair and screwing up her small ill-humoured eyes at the Coty lipstick, Pond's cream, the Leichner rouge and Cyclax powder and Elizabeth Arden astringent.

She threw them one by one into the wastepaper basket. She saved only the cold cream. "Telling the boy stories," she said. "Go along to the nursery, Master Philip, while I get lunch."

Philip climbed the stairs to the baize door. He heard Mrs. Baines's voice like the voice in a nightmare when the small Price light has guttered in the saucer and the curtains move; it was sharp and shrill and full of malice, louder than people ought to speak, exposed.

"Sick to death of your ways, Baines, spoiling the boy. Time you did some work about the house," but he couldn't hear what Baines said in reply. He pushed open the baize door, came up like a small earth animal in his grey flannel shorts into a wash of sunlight on a parquet floor, the gleam of mirrors dusted and polished and beautified by Mrs. Baines.

Something broke downstairs, and Philip sadly mounted the stairs to the nursery. He pitied Baines; it occurred to him how happily they could live together in the empty house if Mrs. Baines were called away. He didn't want to play with his Meccano sets; he wouldn't take out his train or his soldiers; he sat at the table with his chin on his hands: this is life; and suddenly he felt responsible for Baines, as if he were the master of the house and Baines an ageing servant who deserved to be cared for. There was not much one could do; he decided at least to be good.

He was not surprised when Mrs. Baines was agreeable at lunch; he was used to her changes. Now it was "another helping of meat, Master Philip," or "Master Philip, a little more of this nice pudding." It was a pudding he liked. Queen's pudding with a perfect meringue, but he wouldn't eat a second helping lest she might count that a victory. She was the kind of woman who thought that any injustice could be counterbalanced by something good to eat.

She was sour, but she liked making sweet things; one never had to complain of a lack of jam or plums; she ate well herself and added soft sugar to the meringue and the strawberry jam. The half light through the basement window set the motes moving above her pale hair like dust as she sifted the sugar, and Baines crouched over his plate saying nothing.

Again Philip felt responsibility. Baines had looked forward to this, and Baines was disappointed: everything was being spoilt. The sensation of disappointment was one which Philip could share; knowing nothing of love or jealousy or passion, he could understand better than anyone this grief, something hoped for not happening, something promised not fulfilled, something exciting turning dull. "Baines," he said, "will you take me for a walk this afternoon?"

"No," Mrs. Baines said, "no. That he won't. Not with all the silver to clean."

"There's a forthnight to do it in," Baines said.

"Work first, pleasure afterwards." Mrs. Baines helped herself to some more meringue.

Baines suddenly put down his spoon and fork and pushed his plate away. "Blast," he said.

"Temper," Mrs. Baines said softly, "temper. Don't you go breaking any more things, Baines, and I won't have you swearing in front of the boy. Master Philip, if you've finished you can get down." She skinned the rest of the meringue off the pudding.

"I want to go for a walk," Philip said.

"You'll go and have a rest."

"I will go for a walk."

"Master Philip," Mrs. Baines said. She got up from the table, leaving her meringue unfinished, and came towards him, thin, menacing, dusty in the basement room. "Master Philip, you do as you're told." She took him by the arm and squeezed it gently; she watched him with a joyless passionate glitter and above her head the feet of the typists trudged back to the Victoria offices after the lunch interval.

"Why shouldn't I go for a walk?" But he weakened; he was scared and ashamed of being scared. This was life; a strange passion he couldn't understand moving in the basement room. He saw a small pile of broken glass swept into a corner by the wastepaper basket. He looked to Baines for help and only intercepted hate; the sad hopeless hate of something behind bars.

"Why shouldn't I?" he repeated.

"Master Philip," Mrs. Baines said, "you've got to do as you're told. You mustn't think just because your father's away there's nobody here to—"

"You wouldn't dare," Philip cried, and was startled by Baines's low interjection, "There's nothing she wouldn't dare."

"I hate you," Philip said to Mrs. Baines. He pulled away from her and ran to the door, but she was there before him; she was old, but she was quick.

"Master Philip," she said, "you'll say you're sorry." She stood in front of the door quivering with excitement. "What would your father do if he heard you say that?"

She put a hand out to seize him, dry and white with constant soda, the nails cut to the quick, but he backed away and put the table between them, and suddenly to his surprise she smiled; she became again as servile as she had been arrogant. "Get along with you, Master Philip," she said with glee. "I see I'm going to have my hands full till your father and mother come back."

She left the door unguarded and when he passed her she slapped him playfully. "I've got too much to do today to trouble about you. I haven't covered half the chairs," and suddenly even the upper part of the house became unbearable to him as he thought of Mrs. Baines moving round shrouding the sofas, laying out the dust-sheets.

So he wouldn't go upstairs to get his cap but walked straight out across the shining hall into the street, and again, as he looked this way and looked that way, it was life he was in the middle of.

2

It was the pink sugar cakes in the window on a paper doily, the ham, the slab of mauve sausage, the wasps driving like small torpedoes across the pane that caught Philip's attention. His feet were tired by pavements; he had been afraid to cross the road, had simply walked first in one direction, then in the other. He was nearly home now; the square was at the end of the street; this was a shabby outpost of Pimlico, and he smudged the pane with his nose, looking for sweets, and saw between the cakes and ham a different Baines. He hardly recognized the bulbous eyes, the bald forehead. It was a happy, bold and buc-caneering Baines, even though it was, when you looked closer, a desperate Baines.

Philip had never seen the girl. He remembered Baines had a niece and he thought that this might be her. She was thin and drawn, and she wore a white mackintosh; she meant nothing to Philip; she belonged to a world about which he knew nothing at all. He couldn't make up stories about her, as he could make them up about withered Sir Hubert Reed, the Permanent Secre-tary, about Mrs. Wince-Dudley, who came up once a year from Penstanley in Suffolk with a green umbrella and an enormous black handbag, as he could make them up about the upper servants in all the houses where he went to tea and games. She just didn't belong; he thought of mermaids and Undine; but she didn't belong there either, nor to the adventures of Emil, nor to the Bast-ables. She sat there looking at an iced pink cake in the detachment and mystery of the completely disinherited, looking at the half-used pots of powder which Baines had set out on the marble-topped table between them.

Baines was urging, hoping, entreating, commanding, and the girl looked at the tea and the china pots and cried. Baines passed his handkerchief across the table, but she wouldn't wipe her eyes; she screwed it in her palm and let the tears run down, wouldn't do anything, wouldn't speak, would only put up a silent despairing resistance to what she dreaded and wanted and refused to listen to at any price. The two brains battled over the tea-cups loving each other, and there came to Philip outside, beyond the ham and wasps and dusty Pimlico pane, a confused indication of the struggle.

He was inquisitive and he didn't understand and he wanted to know. He went and stood in the doorway to see better, he was less sheltered than he had ever been; other people's lives for the first time touched and pressed and moulded. He would never escape that scene. In a week he had forgotten it, but it conditioned his career, the long austerity of his life; when he was dying he said, "Who is she?"

Baines had won; he was cocky and the girl was happy. She wiped her face, she opened a pot of powder, and their fingers touched across the table. It occurred to Philip that it would be amusing to imitate Mrs. Baines's voice and call "Baines" to him from the door.

It shrivelled them; you couldn't describe it in any other way; it made them smaller, they weren't happy any more and they weren't bold. Baines was the first to recover and trace the voice, but that didn't make things as they were. The sawdust was spilled out of the afternoon; nothing you did could mend it, and Philip was scared. "I didn't mean . . . " He wanted to say that he loved Baines, that he had only wanted to laugh at Mrs. Baines. But he had discovered that you couldn't laugh at Mrs. Baines. She wasn't Sir Hubert Reed, who used steel nibs and carried a pen-wiper in his pocket; she wasn't Mrs. Wince-Dudley; she was darkness when the night-light went out in a draught; she was the frozen blocks of earth he had seen one winter in a grave-yard when someone said, "They need an electric drill"; she was the flowers gone bad and smelling in the little closet room at Penstanley. There was noth-ing to laugh about. You had to endure her when she was there and forget about her quickly when she was away, suppress the thought of her, ram it down deep.

Baines said, "It's only Phil," beckoned him in and gave him the pink iced cake the girl hadn't eaten, but the afternoon was broken, the cake was like dry bread in the throat. The girl left them at once; she even forgot to take the powder; like a small blunt icicle in her white mackintosh she stood in the doorway with her back to them, then melted into the afternoon.

"Who is she?" Philip asked. "Is she your niece?"

"Oh, yes," Baines said, "that's who she is; she's my niece," and poured the last drops of water on to the coarse black leaves in the teapot.

"May as well have another cup," Baines said.

"The cup that cheers," he said hopelessly, watching the bitter black fluid drain out of the spout.

"Have a glass of ginger pop, Phil?"

"I'm sorry. I'm sorry, Baines."

"It's not your fault, Phil. Why, I could believe it wasn't you at all, but her. She creeps in everywhere." He fished two leaves out of his cup and laid them on the back of his hand, a thin soft flake and a hard stalk. He beat them with his hand: "Today," and the stalk detached itself, "tomorrow, Wednesday, Thursday, Friday, Saturday, Sunday," but the flake wouldn't come, stayed where it was, drying under his blows, with a resistance you wouldn't believe it to possess. "The tough one wins," Baines said.

He got up and paid the bill and out they went into the street. Baines said, "I don't ask you to say what isn't true. But you needn't mention to Mrs. Baines you met us here."

"Of course not," Philip said, and catching something of Sir Hubert Reed's manner. "I understand, Baines." But he didn't understand a thing; he was caught up in other people's darkness.

"It was stupid," Baines said. "So near home, but I hadn't time to think, you see. I'd got to see her."

"Of course, Baines."

"I haven't time to spare," Baines said. "I'm not young. I've got to see that she's all right."

"Of course you have, Baines."

"Mrs. Baines will get it out of you if she can."

"You can trust me, Baines," Philip said in a dry important Reed voice;

and then, "Look out. She's at the window watching." And there indeed she was, looking up at them, between the lace curtains, from the basement room, speculating. "Need we go in, Baines?" Philip asked, cold lying heavy on his stomach like too much pudding, he clutched Baines's arm.

"Careful," Baines said softly, "careful."

"But need we go in, Baines? It's early. Take me for a walk in the park."

"Better not."

"But I'm frightened, Baines."

"You haven't any cause," Baines said. "Nothing's going to hurt you. You just run along upstairs to the nursery. I'll go down by the area and talk to Mrs. Baines." But even he stood hesitating at the top of the stone steps, pretending not to see her where she watched between the curtains. "In at the front door, Phil, and up the stairs."

Philip didn't linger in the hall; he ran, slithering on the parquet Mrs. Baines had polished, to the stairs. Through the drawing-room doorway on the first floor he saw the draped chairs; even the china clock on the mantel was covered like a canary's cage; as he passed it, it chimed the hour, muffled and secret under the duster. On the nursery table he found his supper laid out: a glass of milk and a piece of bread and butter, a sweet biscuit and a little cold Queen's pudding without the meringue. He had no appetite; he strained his ears for Mrs. Baines's coming, for the sound of voices, but the basement held its secrets; the green baize door shut off that world. He drank the milk and ate the biscuit, but he didn't touch the rest, and presently he could hear the soft precise footfalls of Mrs. Baines on the stairs: she was a good servant, she walked softly; she was a determined woman, she walked precisely.

But she wasn't angry when she came in; she was ingratiating as she opened the night nursery door—"Did you have a good walk, Master Philip?"—pulled down the blinds, laid out his pyjamas, came back to clear his supper. "I'm glad Baines found you. Your mother wouldn't have liked your being out alone." She examined the tray. "Not much appetite, have you, Master Philip? Why don't you try a little of this nice pudding? I'll bring you up some more jam for it."

"No, no, thank you, Mrs. Baines," Philip said.

"You ought to eat more," Mrs. Baines said. She sniffed round the room like a dog. "You didn't take any pots out of the wastepaper basket in the kitchen, did you, Master Philip?"

"No." Philip said.

"Of course you wouldn't. I just wanted to make sure." She patted his shoulder and her fingers flashed to his lapel; she picked off a tiny crumb of pink sugar. "Oh, Master Philip," she said, "that's why you haven't any appetite. You've been buying sweet cakes. That's not what your pocket money's for."

"But I didn't," Philip said. "I didn't."

She tasted the sugar with the tip of her tongue.

"Don't tell lies to me, Master Philip. I won't stand for it any more than your father would."

"I didn't. I didn't," Philip said. "They gave it me. I mean Baines," but she had pounced on the word "they." She had got what she wanted; there was no doubt about that, even when you didn't know what it was she wanted. Philip was angry and miserable and disappointed because he hadn't kept Baines's secret. Baines oughtn't to have trusted him; grown-up people should keep their own secrets, and yet here was Mrs. Baines immediately entrusting him with another.

"Let me tickle your palm and see if you can keep a secret." But he put his hand behind him; he wouldn't be touched. "It's a secret between us, Master Philip, that I know all about them. I suppose she was having tea with him," she speculated.

"Why shouldn't she?" he said, the responsibility for Baines weighing on his spirit, the idea that he had got to keep her secret when he hadn't kept Baines's making him miserable with the unfairness of life. "She was nice."

"She was nice, was she?" Mrs. Baines said in a bitter voice he wasn't used to.

"And she's his niece."

"So that's what he said," Mrs. Baines struck softly back at him like the clock under the duster. She tried to be jocular. "The old scoundrel. Don't you tell him I know, Master Philip." She stood very still between the table and the door, thinking very hard, planning something. "Promise you won't tell. I'll give you that Meccano set, Master Philip. . . . "

He turned his back on her; he wouldn't promise, but he wouldn't tell. He would have nothing to do with their secrets, the responsibilities they were determined to lay on him. He was only anxious to forget. He had received already a larger dose of life than he had bargained for, and he was scared. "A 2A Meccano set, Master Philip." He never opened his Meccano set again, never built anything, never created anything, died, the old dilettante, sixty years later, with nothing to show rather than preserve the memory of Mrs. Baines's malicious voice saying good night, her soft determined footfalls on the stairs to the basement, going down, going down.

3

The sun poured in between the curtains and Baines was beating a tattoo on the water-can. "Glory, glory," Baines said. He sat down on the end of the bed and said, "I beg to announce that Mrs. Baines has been called away. Her mother's dying. She won't be back till tomorrow."

"Why did you wake me up so early?" Philip said. He watched Baines with uneasiness: he wasn't going to be drawn in; he'd learnt his lesson. It wasn't right for a man of Baines's age to be so merry. It made a grown person human in the same way that you were human. For if a grown-up could behave so childishly, you were liable too to find yourself in their world. It was enough that it came at you in dreams: the witch at the corner, the man with a knife. So "It's very early," he complained, even though he loved Baines, even though he couldn't help being glad that Baines was happy. He was divided by the fear and the attraction of life.

"I want to make this a long day," Baines said. "This is the best time." He pulled the curtains back. "It's a bit misty. The cat's been out all night. There she is, sniffing round the area. They haven't taken in any milk at 59. Emma's shaking out the mats at 63." He said, "This was what I used to think about on the Coast: somebody shaking mats and the cat coming home. I can see it today," Baines said, "just as if I was still in Africa. Most days you don't notice what you've got. It's a good life if you don't weaken." He put a penny on the washstand. "When you've dressed, Phil, run and get a *Mail* from the barrow at the corner. I'll be cooking the sausages."

"Sausages?"

"Sausages," Baines said. "We're going to celebrate today. A fair bust." He celebrated at breakfast, reckless, cracking jokes, unaccountably merry and nervous. It was going to be a long, long day, he kept on coming back to that: for years he had waited for a long day, he had sweated in the damp Coast heat, changed shirts, gone down with fever, lain between the blankets and sweated, all in the hope of this long day, that cat sniffing round the area, a bit of mist, the mats beaten at 63. He propped the *Mail* in front of the coffee pot and read pieces aloud. He said, "Cora Down's been married for the fourth time." He was amused, but it wasn't his idea of a long day. His long day was the Park, watching the riders in the Row, seeing Sir Arthur Stillwater pass beyond the rails ("He dined with us once in Bo; up from Freetown; he was governor there"), lunch at the Corner House for Philip's sake (he'd have preferred himself a glass of stout and some oysters at the York bar), the Zoo, the long bus ride home in the last summer light: the leaves in the Green Park were beginning to turn and the motors nuzzled out of Berkeley Street with the low sun gently glowing on their wind-screens. Baines envied no one, not Cora Down, or Sir Arthur Stillwater, or Lord Sandale, who came out on to the steps of the Army and Navy and then went back again because he hadn't got anything to do and might as well look at another paper. "I said don't let me see you touch that black again." Baines had led a man's life; everyone on top of the bus pricked their ears when he told Philip all about it.

"Would you have shot him?" Philip asked, and Baines put his head back and tilted his dark respectable manservant's hat to a better angle as the bus swerved round the artillery memorial.

"I wouldn't have thought twice about it. I'd have shot to kill," he boasted, and the bowed figure went by, the steel helmet, the heavy cloak, the down-turned rifle and the folded hands.

"Have you got the revolver?"

"Of course I've got it," Baines said. "Don't I need it with all the burglaries there've been?" This was the Baines whom Philip loved: not Baines singing and carefree, but Baines responsible, Baines behind barriers, living his man's life.

All the buses streamed out from Victoria like a convoy of aeroplanes to bring Baines home with honour. "Forty blacks under me," and there waiting near the area steps was the proper conventional reward, love at lighting-up time.

"It's your niece," Philip said, recognizing the white mackintosh, but not the happy sleepy face. She frightened him like an unlucky number; he nearly told Baines what Mrs. Baines had said; but he didn't want to bother, he wanted to leave things alone.

"Why, so it is," Baines said. "I shouldn't wonder if she was going to have a bite of supper with us." But he said they'd play a game, pretend they didn't know her, slip down the area steps, "and here," Baines said, "we are," lay the table, put out the cold sausages, a bottle of beer, a bottle of ginger pop, a flagon of harvest burgundy. "Everyone his own drink," Baines said. "Run upstairs, Phil, and see if there's been a post."

Philip didn't like the empty house at dusk before the lights went on. He hurried. He wanted to be back with Baines. The hall lay there in quiet and shadow prepared to show him something he didn't want to see. Some letters rustled down, and someone knocked. "Open in the name of the Republic." The tumbrils rolled, the head bobbed in the bloody basket. Knock, knock, and the postman's footsteps going away. Philip gathered the letters. The slit in the door was like the grating in a jeweler's window. He remembered the policeman he had seen peer through. He had said to his nurse, "What's he doing?" and when she said, "He's seeing if everything's all right," his brain immediately filled with images of all that might be wrong. He ran to the baize door and the stairs. The girl was already there and Baines was kissing her. She leant breathless against the dresser.

"This is Emmy, Phil."

"There's a letter for you, Baines."

"Emmy," Baines said, "it's from her." But he wouldn't open it. "You bet she's coming back."

"We'll have supper anyway," Emmy said. "She can't harm that."

"You don't know her," Baines said. "Nothing's safe. Damn it," he said, "I was a man once," and he opened the letter.

"Can I start?" Philip asked, but Baines didn't hear; he presented in his stillness and attention an example of the importance grown-up people attached to the written word: you had to write your thanks, not wait and speak them, as if letters couldn't lie. But Philip knew better than that, sprawling his thanks across a page to Aunt Alice who had given him a doll he was too old for. Letters could lie all right, but they made the lie permanent: they lay as evidence against you; they made you meaner than the spoken word.

"She's not coming back till tomorrow night," Baines said. He opened the bottles, he pulled up the chairs, he kissed Emmy again against the dresser.

"You oughtn't to," Emmy said, "with the boy here."

"He's got to learn," Baines said, "like the rest of us," and he helped Philip to three sausages. He only took one himself; he said he wasn't hungry; but when Emmy said she wasn't hungry either he stood over her and made her eat. He was timid and rough with her; he made her drink the harvest burgundy because he said she needed building up; he wouldn't take no for an answer, but when he touched her his hands were light and clumsy too, as if he were afraid to damage something delicate and didn't know how to handle anything so light.

"This is better than milk and biscuits, eh?"

"Yes," Philip said, but he was scared, scared for Baines as much as for himself. He couldn't help wondering at every bite, at every draught of the ginger pop, what Mrs. Baines would say if she ever learnt of this meal; he couldn't imagine it, there was a depth of bitterness and rage in Mrs. Baines you couldn't sound. He said, "She won't be coming back tonight?" but you could tell by the way they immediately understood him that she wasn't really away at all; she was there in the basement with them, driving them to longer drinks and louder talk, biding her time for the right cutting word. Baines wasn't really happy; he was only watching happiness from close to instead of from far away.

"No," he said, "she'll not be back till late tomorrow." He couldn't keep his eyes off happiness; he'd played around as much as other men, he kept on reverting to the Coast as if to excuse himself for his innocence; he wouldn't have been so innocent if he'd lived his life in London, so innocent when it came to tenderness. "If it was you, Emmy," he said, looking at the white dresser, the scrubbed chairs, "this'd be like a home." Already the room was not quite so harsh; there was a little dust in corners, the silver needed a final polish, the morning's paper lay untidily on a chair. "You'd better go to bed, Phil; it's been a long day."

They didn't leave him to find his own way up through the dark shrouded house; they went with him, turning on lights, touching each other's fingers on the switches; floor after floor they drove the night back; they spoke softly among the covered chairs; they watched him undress, they didn't make him wash or clean his teeth, they saw him into bed and lit his night-light and left his door ajar. He could hear their voices on the stairs, friendly, like the guests he heard at dinner-parties when they moved down to the hall, saying good night. They belonged; wherever they were they made a home. He heard a door open and a clock strike, he heard their voices for a long while, so that he felt they were not far away and he was safe. The voices didn't dwindle, they simply went out, and he could be sure that they were still somewhere not far from him, silent together in one of the many empty rooms, growing sleepy together as he grew sleepy after the long day.

He just had time to sigh faintly with satisfaction, because this too perhaps had been life, before he slept and the inevitable terrors of sleep came round him: a man with a tricolour bat beat at the door on His Majesty's service, a bleeding head lay on the kitchen table in a basket, and the Siberian wolves crept closer. He was bound hand and foot and couldn't move; they leapt round him breathing heavily; he opened his eyes and Mrs. Baines was there, her grey untidy hair in threads over his face, her black hat askew. A loose hair-pin fell on the pillow and one musty thread brushed his mouth. "Where are they?" she whispered. "Where are they?"

4

Philip watched her in terror. Mrs. Baines was out of breath as if she had been searching all the empty rooms, looking under loose covers.

With her untidy grey hair and her black dress buttoned to her throat, her gloves of black cotton, she was so like the witches of his dreams that he didn't dare to speak. There was a stale smell in her breath.

"She's here," Mrs. Baines said; "you can't deny she's here." Her face was simultaneously marked with cruelty and misery; she wanted to "do things" to people, but she suffered all the time. It would have done her good to scream, but she daren't do that: it would warn them. She came ingratiatingly back to the bed where Philip lay rigid on his back and whispered. "I haven't forgotten the Meccano set. You shall have it tomorrow, Master Philip. We've got secrets together, haven't we? Just tell me where they are."

He couldn't speak. Fate held him as firmly as any nightmare. She said, "Tell Mrs. Baines, Master Philip. You love your Mrs. Baines, don't you?" That was too much; he couldn't speak, but he could move his mouth in terrified denial, wince away from her dusty image.

She whispered, coming closer to him, "Such deceit, I'll tell your father. I'll settle with you myself when I've found them. You'll smart; I'll see you smart." Then immediately she was still, listening. A board had creaked on the floor below, and a moment later, while she stooped listening above his bed, there came the whispers of two people who were happy and sleepy together after a long day. The night-light stood beside the mirror and Mrs. Baines could see bitterly there her own reflection, misery and cruelty wavering in the glass, age and dust and nothing to hope for. She sobbed without tears, a dry, breathless sound; but her cruelty was a kind of pride which kept her going; it was her best quality, she would have been merely pitiable without it. She went out of the door on tiptoe, feeling her way across the landing, going so softly down the stairs that no one behind a shut door could hear her. Then there was complete silence again; Philip could move; he raised his knees; he sat up in bed; he wanted to die. It wasn't fair, the walls were down again between his world and theirs; but this time it was something worse than merriment that the grown people made him share; a passion moved in the house he recognized but could not understand.

It wasn't fair, but he owed Baines everything: the Zoo, the ginger pop, the bus ride home. Even the supper called on his loyalty. But he was frightened; he was touching something he touched in dreams: the bleeding head, the wolves, the knock, knock, knock. Life fell on him with savagery: you couldn't blame him if he never faced it again in sixty years. He got out of bed, carefully from habit put on his bedroom slippers, and tiptoed to the door: it wasn't quite dark on the landing below because the curtains had been taken down for the cleaners and the light from the street came in through the tall windows. Mrs. Baines had her hand on the glass door-knob; she was very carefully turning it; he screamed, "Baines, Baines."

Mrs. Baines turned and saw him cowering in his pyjamas by the banisters; he was helpless, more helpless even than Baines, and cruelty grew at the sight of him and drove her up the stairs. The nightmare was on him again and he couldn't move; he hadn't any more courage left for ever; he'd spent it all, had been allowed no time to let it grow, no years of gradual hardening; he couldn't even scream.

But the first cry had brought Baines out of the best spare bedroom and he moved quicker than Mrs. Baines. She hadn't reached the top of the stairs before he'd caught her round the waist. She drove her black cotton gloves at his face and he bit her hand. He hadn't time to think, he fought her savagely like a stranger, but she fought back with knowledgeable hate. She was going to teach them all and it didn't really matter whom she began with; they had all deceived her; but the old image in the glass was by her side, telling her she must be dignified, she wasn't young enough to yield her dignity; she could beat his face, but she mustn't bite; she could push, but she mustn't kick.

Age and dust and nothing to hope for were her handicaps. She went over the banisters in a flurry of black clothes and fell into the hall; she lay before the front door like a sack of coals which should have gone down the area into the basement. Philip saw; Emmy saw; she sat down suddenly in the doorway of the best spare bedroom with her eyes open as if she were too tired to stand any longer. Baines went slowly down into the hall.

It wasn't hard for Philip to escape; they'd forgotten him completely; he went down the back, the servants' stairs because Mrs. Baines was in the hall; he didn't understand what she was doing lying there; like the startling pictures in a book no one had read to him, the things he didn't understand terrified him. The whole house had been turned over to the grown-up world; he wasn't safe in the night nursery; their passions had flooded it. The only thing he could do was to get away, by the back stair, and up through the area, and never come back. You didn't think of the cold, of the need of food and sleep; for an hour it would seem quite possible to escape from people for ever.

He was wearing pyjamas and bedroom slippers when he came up into the square, but there was no one to see him. It was that hour of the evening in a residential district when everyone is at the theatre or at home. He climbed over the iron railings into the little garden: the plane-trees spread their large pale palms between him and the sky. It might have been an illimitable forest into which he had escaped. He crouched behind a trunk and the wolves retreated; it seemed to him between the little iron seat and the tree-trunk that no one would ever find him again. A kind of embittered happiness and self-pity made him cry; he was lost; there wouldn't be any more secrets to keep; he surrendered responsibility once and for all. Let grown-up people keep to their world and he would keep to his, safe in the small garden between the plane-trees. "In the lost childhood of Judas Christ was betrayed"; you could almost see the small unformed face hardening into the deep dilettante selfishness of age.

Presently the door of 48 opened and Baines looked this way and that; then he signalled with his hand and Emmy came; it was as if they were only just in time for a train, they hadn't a chance of saying good-bye; she went quickly by, like a face at a window swept past the platform, pale and unhappy and not wanting to go. Baines went in again and shut the door; the light was lit in the basement, and a policeman walked round the square, looking into the areas. You could tell how many families were at home by the lights behind the first-floor curtains.

Philip explored the garden: it didn't take long: a twenty-yard square of bushes and plane-trees, two iron seats and a gravel path, a padlocked gate at either end, a scuffle of old leaves. But he couldn't stay: something stirred in the bushes and two illuminated eyes peered out at him like a Siberian wolf, and he thought how terrible it would be if Mrs. Baines found him there. He'd have no time to climb the railings; she'd seize him from behind.

He left the square at the unfashionable end and was immediately among the fish-and-chip shops, the little stationers selling Bagatelle, among the accommodation addresses and the dingy hotels with open doors. There were few people about because the pubs were open, but a blowzy woman carrying a parcel called out to him across the street and the commissionaire outside a cinema would have stopped him if he hadn't crossed the road. He went deeper: you could go farther and lose yourself more completely here than among the plane-trees. On the fringe of the square he was in danger of being stopped and taken back: it was obvious where he belonged: but as he went deeper he lost the marks of his origin. It was a warm night: any child in those free-living parts might be expected to play truant from bed. He found a kind of camaraderie even among grown-up people; he might have been a neighbour's child as he went quickly by, but they weren't going to tell on him, they'd been young once themselves. He picked up a protective coating of dust from the pavements, of smuts from the trains which passed along the backs in a spray of fire. Once he was caught in a knot of children running away from something or somebody, laughing as they ran; he was whirled with them round a turning and abandoned, with a sticky fruit-drop in his hand.

He couldn't have been more lost; but he hadn't the stamina to keep on. At first he feared that someone would stop him; after an hour he hoped that someone would. He couldn't find his way back, and in any case he was afraid of arriving home alone; he was afraid of Mrs. Baines, more afraid than he had ever been. Baines was his friend, but something had happened which gave Mrs. Baines all the power. He began to loiter on purpose to be noticed, but no one noticed him. Families were having a last breather on the door-steps, the refuse bins had been put out and bits of cabbage stalks soiled his slippers. The air was full of voices, but he was cut off; these people were strangers and would always now be strangers; they were marked by Mrs. Baines and he shied away from them into a deep class-consciousness. He had been afraid of policemen, but now he wanted one to take him home; even Mrs. Baines could do nothing against a policeman. He sidled past a constable who was directing traffic, but he was too busy to pay him any attention. Philip sat down against a wall and cried.

It hadn't occurred to him that that was the easiest way, that all you had to do was to surrender, to show you were beaten and accept kindness. . . . It was lavished on him at once by two women and a pawnbroker. Another policeman appeared, a young man with a sharp incredulous face. He looked as if he noted everything he saw in pocketbooks and drew conclusions. A woman offered to see Philip home, but he didn't trust her: she wasn't a match for Mrs. Baines immobile in the hall. He wouldn't give his address; he said he was afraid to go home. He had his way; he got his protection. "I'll take him to the station," the policeman said, and holding him awkwardly by the hand (he wasn't married; he had his career to make) he led him round the corner, up the stone stairs into the little bare overheated room where Justice waited.

5

Justice waited behind a wooden counter on a high stool; it wore a heavy moustache; it was kindly and had six children ("three of them nippers like yourself"); it wasn't really interested in Philip, but it pretended to be, it wrote the address down and sent a constable to fetch a glass of milk. But the young constable was interested; he had a nose for things.

"Your home's on the telephone. I suppose," Justice said. "We'll ring them up and say you are safe. They'll fetch you very soon. What's your name, sonny?"

"Philip."

"Your other name."

"I haven't got another name." He didn't want to be fetched; he wanted to be taken home by someone who would impress even Mrs. Baines. The constable watched him, watched the way he drank the milk, watched him when he winced away from questions.

"What made you run away? Playing truant, eh?"

"I don't know."

"You oughtn't to do it, young fellow. Think how anxious your father and mother will be."

"They are away."

"Well, your nurse."

"I haven't got one."

"Who looks after you, then?" That question went home. Philip saw Mrs. Baines coming up the stairs at him, the heap of black cotton in the hall. He began to cry.

"Now, now, now," the sergeant said. He didn't know what to do; he wished his wife were with him; even a policewoman might have been useful.

"Don't you think it's funny," the constable said, "that there hadn't been an inquiry?"

"They think he's tucked up in bed."

"You are scared, aren't you?" the constable said, "What scared you?"

"I don't know."

"Somebody hurt you?"

"No."

"He's had bad dreams," the sergeant said. "Thought the house was on fire, I expect. I've brought up six of them. Rose is due back. She'll take him home."

"I want to go home with you," Philip said: he tried to smile at the constable, but the deceit was immature and unsuccessful.

"I'd better go," the constable said. "It's a woman's job. Tact is what you need. Here's Rose. Pull up your stockings, Rose. You're a disgrace to the Force. I've got a job of work for you." Rose shambled in: black cotton stockings drooping over her boots, a gawky Girl Guide manner, a hoarse hostile voice. "More tarts, I suppose."

"I won't go with her," Philip said. He began to cry again. "I don't like her."

"More of that womanly charm, Rose," the sergeant said. The telephone rang on his desk. He lifted the receiver. "What? What's that?" he said. "Number 48? You've got a doctor?" He put his hand over the telephone mouth. "No wonder this nipper wasn't reported," he said. "They've been too busy. An accident. Woman slipped on the stairs."

"Serious?" the constable asked. The sergeant mouthed at him; you didn't mention the word death before a child (didn't he know? he had six of them), you made noises in the throat, you grimaced, a complicated shorthand for a word of only five letters anyway.

"You'd better go, after all," he said, "and make a report. The doctor's there."

Rose shambled from the stove; pink apply-dapply cheeks, loose stockings. She stuck her hands behind her. Her large morgue-like mouth was full of blackened teeth. "You told me to take him and now just because something interesting . . . I don't expect justice from a man . . ."

"Who's at the house?" the constable asked.

"The butler."

"You don't think," the constable said, "he saw . . . "

"Trust me," the sergeant said, "I've brought up six. I know 'em through and through. You can't teach me anything about children."

"He seemed scared about something."

"Dreams," the sergeant said.

"What name?"

"Baines."

"This Mr. Baines," the constable said to Philip, "you like him, eh? He's good to you?" They were trying to get something out of him; he was suspicious of the whole roomful of them; he said "yes" without conviction because he was afraid at any moment of more responsibilities, more secrets.

"And Mrs. Baines?"

"Yes."

They consulted together by the desk: Rose was hoarsely aggrieved; she was like a female impersonator, she bore her womanhood with an unnatural emphasis even while she scorned it in her creased stockings and her weather-exposed face. The charcoal shifted in the stove; the room was overheated in the mild late summer evening. A notice on the wall described a body found in the Thames, or rather the body's clothes: wool vest, wool pants, wool shirt with blue stripes, size ten boots, blue serge suit worn at the elbows, fifteen and a half celluloid collar. They couldn't find anything to say about the body, except its measurements, it was just an ordinary body.

"Come along," the constable said. He was interested, he was glad to be going, but he couldn't help being embarrassed by his company, a small boy in pyjamas. His nose smelt something, he didn't know what, but he smarted at the sight of the amusement they caused: the pubs had closed and the streets were full again of men making as long a day of it as they could. He hurried through the less frequented streets, chose the darker pavements, wouldn't loiter, and Philip wanted more and more to loiter, pulling at his hand, dragging with his feet. He dreaded the sight of Mrs. Baines waiting in the hall: he knew now that she was dead. The sergeant's mouthings had conveyed that; but she wasn't buried, she wasn't out of sight; he was going to see a dead person in the hall when the door opened.

The light was on in the basement, and to his relief the constable made for the area steps. Perhaps he wouldn't have to see Mrs. Baines at all. The constable knocked on the door because it was too dark to see the bell, and Baines answered. He stood there in the doorway of the neat bright basement room and you could see the sad complacent plausible sentence he had prepared wither at the sight of Philip; he hadn't expected Philip to return like that in the policeman's company. He had to begin thinking all over again; he wasn't a deceptive man; if it hadn't been for Emmy he would have been quite ready to let the truth lead him where it would.

"Mr. Baines?" the constable asked.

He nodded; he hadn't found the right words; he was daunted by the shrewd knowing face, the sudden appearance of Philip there.

"This little boy from here?"

"Yes," Baines said. Philip could tell that there was a message he was trying to convey, but he shut his mind to it. He loved Baines, but Baines had involved him in secrets, in fears he didn't understand. The glowing morning thought, "This is life," had become under Baines's tuition the repugnant memory, "That was life": the musty hair across the mouth, the breathless cruel tortured inquiry, "Where are they," the heap of black cotton tipped into the hall. That was what happened when you loved: you got involved; and Philip extricated himself from life, from love, from Baines, with a merciless egotism.

There had been things between them, but he laid them low, as a retreating army cuts the wires, destroys the bridges. In the abandoned country you may leave much that is dear—a morning in the Park, an ice at a corner house, sausages for supper—but more is concerned in the retreat than temporary losses. There are old people who, as the tractors wheel away, implore to be taken, but you can't risk the rearguard for their sake: a whole prolonged retreat from life, from care, from human relationships is involved.

"The doctor's here." Baines said. He nodded at the door, moistened his mouth, kept his eyes on Philip, begging for something like a dog you can't understand. "There's nothing to be done. She slipped on these stone basement stairs. I was in here. I heard her fall." He wouldn't look at the notebook, at the constable's tiny spidery writing which got a terrible lot on one page.

"Did the boy see anything?"

"He can't have done. I thought he was in bed. Hadn't he better go up? It's a shocking thing. Oh," Baines said, losing control, "it's a shocking thing for a child."

"She's through there?" the constable asked.

"I haven't moved her an inch," Baines said.

"He'd better then—"

"Go up the area and through the hall," Baines said and again he begged dumbly like a dog: one more secret, keep this secret, do this for old Baines, he won't ask another.

"Come along," the constable said. "I'll see you up to bed. You're a gentleman; you must come in the proper way through the front door like the master should. Or will you go along with him, Mr. Baines, while I see the doctor?"

"Yes," Baines said, "I'll go." He came across the room to Philip, begging, begging, all the way with his soft old stupid expression: this is Baines, the old Coaster; what about a palm-oil chop, eh?; a man's life; forty niggers; never used a gun; I tell you I couldn't help loving them: it wasn't what we call love, nothing we could understand. The messages flickered out from the last posts at the border, imploring, beseeching, reminding: this is your old friend Baines; what about an eleven's; a glass of ginger pop won't do you any harm; sausages; a long day. But the wires were cut, the messages just faded out into the enormous vacancy of the neat scrubbed room in which there had never been a place where a man could hide his secrets.

"Come along, Phil, it's bedtime. We'll just go up the steps . . ." Tap, tap, tap, at the telegraph; you may get through, you can't tell, somebody may mend the right wire. "And in at the front door."

"No," Philip said, "no, I won't go. You can't make me go. I'll fight. I won't see her."

The constable turned on them quickly. "What's that? Why won't you go?"

"She's in the hall," Philip said. "I know she's in the hall. And she's dead. I won't see her."

"You moved her then?" the constable said to Baines. "All the way down here? You've been lying, eh? That means you had to tidy up. . . . Were you alone?"

"Emmy," Philip said, "Emmy." He wasn't going to keep any more secrets: he was going to finish once and for all with everything, with Baines and Mrs. Baines and the grown-up life beyond him; it wasn't his business and never, never again, he decided, would he share their confidences and companionship. "It was all Emmy's fault," he protested with a quaver which reminded Baines that after all he was only a child; it had been hopeless to expect help there; he was a child; he didn't understand what it all meant; he couldn't read this shorthand of terror; he'd had a long day and he was tired out. You could see him dropping asleep where he stood against the dresser, dropping back into the comfortable nursery peace. You couldn't blame him. When he woke in the morning, he'd hardly remember a thing.

"Out with it," the constable said, addressing Baines with professional ferocity, "who is she?" just as the old man sixty years later startled his secretary, his only watcher, asking, "Who is she? Who is she?" dropping lower and lower into death, passing on the way perhaps the image of Baines: Baines hopeless, Baines letting his head drop, Baines "coming clean."

Women in Love

Near the end of Ken Russell's *Women in Love*, Gerald and Gudrun and Birkin and Ursula arrive in Switzerland. Gudrun strides across the snow and then stops, stretching her arms exuberantly toward the Matterhorn. In the distance the mountain rises up, an object of beauty and strength, inviting and yet threatening.

So, too, must Russell have contemplated D. H. Lawrence's vast work. The very size of the novel is intimidating, to say nothing of the intricate thought processes and feelings conveyed by Lawrence's highly symbolic prose. The book attempts nothing less than a redefinition of personal and societal relationships, and these are difficult subjects for a filmmaker.

In spite of the length and complexity of Russell's film, it simply cannot begin to capture all the events of Lawrence's novel. Russell himself has commented humorously on this:

> I left a lot of [the book] out because films lasting twenty-four hours are frowned on by distributors and partly . . . because Lawrence simply repeated his theme about the separate-but-united philosophy of love eight times over in different disguises. I thought twice would be enough in the film for most people to get it. When you read a book you put it down and pick it up again, so I guess Lawrence just had to keep reminding his readers of his point, but if you have to condense it into two hours, it's just not on. It's the same with some of his other themes.[5]

A director and a script writer must of course be selective and choose those events that enhance their particular interpretation of the work they are filming. Lawrence develops characters who function within a fully realized land-

---

[5]Quoted in John Baxter, *An Appalling Talent: Ken Russell* (London: Michael Joseph, 1973), pp. 175–176.

scape and whose actions and observations often have a symbolic value. We come to understand their inner lives as fully as we recognize their exterior appearances, but it takes Lawrence many pages to achieve this. Russell has also created realistic characters within a lush physical world, and he has done so with all the economy film provides. In addition, he has found ways of using space metaphorically in order to convey in a visual manner some of the complex ideas of Lawrence's novel.

From the opening shots of the film, the viewer is struck by the way Russell develops new settings for conversations taken from the novel. Ursula and Gudrun's discussion about marriage, for example, with which both works begin, no longer takes place within the bay window of their father's home. Instead, they begin their conversation while walking to the Critch wedding. Russell provides visual confirmation of their comments, as when Gudrun notes that marriage is "more likely to be the end of experience" at the moment they are passing a young couple pushing a baby carriage. Much more significant, however, is the locale where this conversation is continued. They board a bus near their row house and ride to the vicinity of the church. Ursula and Gudrun descend from the bus, and Russell cuts to an extreme long shot of the two sisters hurrying toward the camera through a graveyard overgrown with tall grass. The camera pans right as they walk, zooms back to reveal the wedding party in the foreground of the shot and, by panning right once more, the church where the wedding will take place. Ursula and Gudrun are now in the left of the frame in the extreme background. Having established the two women as spectators, although from afar, Russell begins a series of cross cuts from the churchyard to the groom's home, as people begin to assemble for the wedding. Suspense is created as Russell shows the groom hurrying from his home, and we wonder if he will arrive in time. The other principals of the drama are introduced as they are driven up to the scene. Finally, the groom arrives and pursues his bride to the doors of the church, where they embrace. The others follow them into the church, and Russell cuts back to the graveyard. Gudrun is seated on a gravestone, a piece of straw in her mouth, while Ursula stands in the upper right of the frame leaning on another headstone. As their discussion of marriage continues, Russell cuts to a long shot of Gudrun reclining until she is stretched out on the gravestone. She crosses her hands on her chest, so that she resembles a body lying in state, and solemnly utters to Ursula: "Nothing materializes."

The setting is realistic, and the wedding could have been observed from such a vantage point (although this is not the case in the novel). However, the setting is used metaphorically to shape our attitude toward the topic of discussion: Death and marriage are being compared and that relationship extends beyond the couple who are at that moment pledging their troth.

Settings also function metaphorically in all the lovemaking scenes. The first of these, involving Birkin and Ursula, takes place in the woods the evening of the picnic at Shortlands. Because Russell has deleted many of the earlier incidents involving Birkin and Ursula from the film, the relationship appears to have been consummated rather quickly.

Women in Love. "Nothing materializes": A metaphoric use of setting.

Lawrence describes this encounter as follows:

So they looked down the dark road, then set off again walking towards Beldover. Then suddenly, to show him she was no shallow prude, she stopped and held him tight, hard against her, and covered his face with hard, fierce kisses of passion. In spite of his otherness, the old blood beat up in him.

"Not this, not this," he whimpered to himself, as the first perfect mood of softness and sleep-loveliness ebbed back away from the rushing of passion that came up to his limbs and over his face as she drew him. And soon he was a perfect hard flame of passionate desire for her. Yet in the small core of the flame was an unyielding anguish of another thing. But this also was lost; he only wanted her, with an extreme desire that seemed inevitable as death, beyond question.

Then, satisfied and shattered, fulfilled and destroyed, he went home and away from her, drifting vaguely through the darkness, lapsed into the old fire of burning passion. Far away, far away, there seemed to be a small lament in the darkness. But what did it matter? What did it matter, what did anything matter save this ultimate and triumphant experience of physical passion, that had blazed up anew like a spell of life.

The sequence begins with a tracking shot of long duration as Ursula and Birkin walk through the woods. They are seen in profile, with Ursula on the far side, always slightly in front of Birkin. The background remains an indistinct, dark curtain of vegetation. Our attention is solely on the couple, as they discuss love and death, with particular reference to the couple who have just drowned. Finally, Ursula steps in front of Birkin and arrests their movement. The camera stops tracking. After pausing, Birkin passes Ursula. She touches him provocatively from behind and he responds. The music becomes hallucinatory and the camera quivers constantly, as they grasp at each other's clothes and roll onto the ground. Throughout their lovemaking the camera remains in close, so that we never get a full view of the couple or of their environment. Instead, they appear fragmented and the constant movement of the camera comments metaphorically upon the frenzied nature of their passion. As their ardor abates, Russell cuts to an overhead close-up of the drowned couple, embracing in the mud of the now drained lake. For a moment we are unable to identify them, and then Russell slowly zooms out to a high-angle long shot, as Gerald enters the frame from the left and strides across the lake bed. We can almost feel the mud as he traverses it. Russell cuts to a low-angle close-up of Gerald gazing down at the couple with the intensely blue sky behind him, and then to a shot of the lovers from Gerald's point of view. Russell holds this shot for nearly four seconds, and the absence of camera movement or movement within the shot stands in marked contrast to the frantic activity preceding these shots. Then, in an audacious juxtaposition, Russell cuts from this shot of the dead lovers to a shot of Ursula and Birkin in an identical pose. This cinematic simile reinforces the comparison of love and death from the opening sequence of the film.

Although the camera work suggests the passion and violence of their encounter and the editing develops Lawrence's notion that their "desire . . . seemed inevitable as death," the location underlines the natural, spontaneous quality that characterizes all their lovemaking. Russell has one other scene of Ursula and Birkin making love, and even though this takes place within Birkin's rustic millhouse, Russell depicts it as though it were occurring

Women in Love. Gudrun's bohemian sanctuary.

outside. The scene begins with Birkin bending over Ursula, who is kneeling before the fire. Russell then cuts to an exterior shot of Birkin's naked body floating horizontally down to Ursula, who is rising horizontally to meet him. The setting is a brilliantly lit golden wheat field. The depiction is unrealistic in two ways: they are indoors and not in a wheat field, and secondly, the action is being turned ninety degrees to create a suspended effect. Although this scene clearly depicts the unconventionality of their relationship, one detects a note of irony in Russell's lush presentation.

The metaphoric value of the settings becomes clear when one contrasts the scenes of Gerald and Gudrun making love with the scenes of Ursula and Birkin we have just discussed. It is inconceivable to picture Gerald and Gudrun making love in the settings we have come to associate with Ursula and Birkin. Gerald first comes to Gudrun in her bedroom at her family's home. Her bedroom is a bohemian refuge in a bourgeois setting, set off from the rest of the Brangwen home by the bead curtain hanging in her doorway. The room is cramped and confined and filled with art work that characterizes Gudrun. Russell follows Lawrence's lead in making Gudrun a maternal figure, who offers comfort to Gerald while remaining in control of the situation. As Lawrence notes:

And she, she was the great bath of life, he worshipped her. Mother and substance of all life she was. And he, child and man, received of her and was made whole.

Yet Russell goes even further and indicates that the violence of their passion appears in part to be motivated by Gerald's feelings for his mother, whose image flashes on the screen during their lovemaking in three shots of very short duration. Her haunting presence is clearly conveyed by this cinematic simile in which she is compared to Gudrun.

Russell uses camera movements to express metaphorically the spiritual isolation Gudrun feels in spite of her physical closeness to Gerald. In the novel Lawrence conveys this through physical movement and through his use of figurative language:

> She [Gudrun] disengaged herself softly and rose up a little to look at him. There was a faint light, it seemed to her, in the room. She could just distinguish his features, as he slept the perfect sleep. In this darkness, she seemed to see him so distinctly. But he was far off, in another world. Ah, she could shriek with torment, he was so far off, and perfected, in another world. She seemed to look at him as at a pebble far away under clear dark water . . . He was beautiful, far off, and perfected. They would never be together. Ah, this awful, inhuman distance which would always be interposed between her and the other being! (338–339)

Through his use of dissolves and zooms, Russell renders this distance cinematically. At the conclusion of their lovemaking, Russell fades out and fades in on a close-up of Gudrun's face. The camera zooms out slowly, revealing her and Gerald, and then dissolves to another close-up of her. Russell repeats this combination three times, each time with a different camera position. The combination of zooms and dissolves recalls the first confrontation between Gerald and Gudrun, when he stops her after she has been chasing the cattle. In both instances Russell deftly communicates the figurative distance that separates them now and will keep them forever apart, and he does this entirely through his choice of shots.

Throughout his adaptation of *Women in Love*, Russell makes frequent use of cinematic tropes, and this is one of the means by which he achieves a radical condensation of his source. Through his metaphoric use of settings, camera movement, and editing, Russell attempts to capture the complex relationships Lawrence develops in his richly figurative and symbolic prose.

Women in Love

Production Credits

Director	Ken Russell
Producers	Larry Kramer, Martin Rosen

Screenplay by	Larry Kramer
Based on the novel by	D. H. Lawrence
Director of Photography	Billy Williams
Art Director	Luciana Arrighi
Film Editor	Michael Bradsell
Assistant Director	Jonathan Benson
Music by	Georges Delerue

Great Britain. 1969. 129 minutes. Color.

Cast

Rupert Birkin	Alan Bates
Gerald Crich	Oliver Reed
Gudrun Brangwen	Glenda Jackson
Ursula Brangwen	Jennie Linden
Hermione Roddice	Eleanor Bron
Mr. Crich	Alan Webb
Loerke	Vladek Sheybal
Mrs. Crich	Catherine Wilmer
Winifred Crich	Sarah Nicholls
Laura Crich	Sharon Gurney
Tibby Lupton	Christopher Gable
Mr. Brangwen	Michael Gough
Mrs. Brangwen	Norma Shebeare
Contessa	Nike Arrighi
Minister	James Laurenson
Palmer	Michael Graham Cox
Loerke's friend	Richard Heffer
Maestro	Michael Garratt

Further Reading

Crump, G. B. "*Women in Love:* Novel and Film." *D. H. Lawrence Review*, 4 (1971), 28–41.

Gomez, Joseph. *Ken Russell: The Adaptor as Creator.* London: Frederick Muller, 1976.

——. "Russell's Image of Lawrence's Vision." In *The English Novel and the Movies.* Eds. Michael Klein and Gillian Parker. New York: Frederick Ungar, 1981.

Knoll, Robert F. "*Women in Love.*" *Film Heritage*, 6, No. 4 (Summer 1971), 1–6.

Phillips, Gene D. *Ken Russell.* Boston: Twayne Publishers, 1979.

Weightman, John. "Trifling with the Dead." *Encounter*, 34, No. 1 (January 1970), 50–53.

Zambrano, Ana Laura. "*Women in Love:* Counterpoint on Film." *Literature/Film Quarterly*, 1, No. 1 (January 1973), 46–54.

8

Figurative Discourse: Symbol and Allegory

Introduction

When authors create a symbol or allegory in their works, they extend the meaning of that work beyond the literal level. As we have seen, this is also the function of such other modes of figurative discourse as metaphor, simile, metonymy, and synecdoche. A symbol differs from these tropes by being an object, action, person, or name signifying more than its literal meaning. A symbol is often a concrete expression of something abstract. A symbol can be peripheral and merely reinforce the themes of a work, or be so central as to develop the themes themselves.

A good example of an object that becomes a central symbol is the wooden horse in D. H. Lawrence's short story, "The Rocking-Horse Winner." The horse begins as a child's toy, and while it never ceases to have that function, it gradually takes on complex symbolic meaning. John Steinbeck also makes extensive symbolic use of objects in *The Grapes of Wrath*. Interspersed with the principal narrative is a series of "interchapters," which illuminate the main story in part through symbolic means. In the second of these (Chapter 3), Steinbeck introduces a turtle, whose south-westward movement clearly parallels that of the migrants:

> And over the grass at the roadside a land turtle crawled, turning aside for nothing, dragging his high-domed shell over the grass. His hard legs and

yellow-nailed feet threshed slowly through the grass, not really walking, but boosting and dragging his shell along. . . . His horny beak was partly open, and his fierce, humorous eyes, under brows like fingernails, stared straight ahead.

When, a chapter later, Tom Joad encounters the turtle, the parallels between them are strongly emphasized through the descriptive language:

Joad plodded along, dragging his cloud of dust behind him. A little bit ahead he saw the high-domed shell of a land turtle, crawling slowly along through the dust, its legs working stiffly and jerkily.

The two journeys Steinbeck has been developing separately come together here, as Tom picks up the turtle and carries him for a distance in his pocket. But it is evident from the first description of the turtle (of which we have quoted only a small part) that Steinbeck's reptile is both an actual turtle and the concrete embodiment of the indomitable will and tenacious spirit of the Oakies.

Symbolic objects are not limited to literature. The first word in *Citizen Kane* ("rosebud") creates a mystery that the newspaper reporter struggles to understand throughout the film. He gives up at the conclusion, and only then does the viewer discover that "rosebud" is a sled Kane had owned as a child. But clearly the sled had become a symbol for Kane of all he had once possessed, and then lost. The symbolic meaning of "rosebud" far transcends the literal meaning of the object.

Actions may also have a figurative value. Consider the scene in D. H. Lawrence's *Women in Love* where Ursula and Gudrun watch Gerald race his horse parallel to a train and then control it brutally at the gate until the train passes. Gudrun's reflections on the event emphasize its meaning for her:

Gudrun was as if numbed in her mind by the sense of indomitable soft weight of the man, bearing down into the living body of the horse: the strong, indomitable thighs of the blond man clenching the palpitating body of the mare into pure control; a sort of soft white magnetic domination from the loins and thighs and calves, enclosing and encompassing the mare heavily into unutterable subordination, soft-blood-subordination, terrible.

For Gudrun, the event symbolizes Gerald's physical and sexual power, as we can see by the sexual connotations of her language. Filmmakers could convey such meaning by the way they film the incident (as Ken Russell does), or through a narrative voice like Gudrun's.

Many of the actions in *The Grapes of Wrath* are symbolic. At the conclusion of the novel, Rose of Sharon, who has lost her baby, offers her breast to an aged man dying of hunger:

Her hand moved behind his head and supported it. Her fingers moved gently in his hair. She looked up and across the barn, and her lips came together and smiled mysteriously.

She is performing a physical action that may or may not save the life of the man. But the action itself is less important than what it represents in the context of the entire novel, where it symbolizes the dogged perseverance of the protagonists. *Rashomon* also concludes with a symbolic act: By accepting responsibility for the life of another, the woodcutter demonstrates that he has benefited positively from his recent experience. Moreover, given the historical significance of the Rashomon gate and the immediate historical context of the film, the woodcutter's act can symbolize the hopes of a war-torn nation.

Authors may choose names for characters that symbolize abstract qualities they wish those characters to embody. As Berenice says in *The Member of the Wedding:* " . . . things accumulate around your name." She is speaking of the way an individual's history becomes intertwined with his or her name, but the same is true of historical and mythological connotations of names. In Ken Russell's film of *Women in Love*, Birkin initiates a discussion over the lunch table about the meaning of names: "Peculiar names we all have," he states. "Do you think we have been singled out, chosen for some extraordinary moment in life? Or are we all cursed with the mark of Cain?" The two sisters provide appropriate etymologies: "I'm afraid Ursula was a martyred saint," the older sister notes, to which the younger adds, "Well, in a Norse myth, Gudrun was a sinner who murdered her husband." In Russell's film the names become allusions to specific historical and mythic figures: In Lawrence's novel, they symbolize abstract characteristics that the sisters embody.

The symbol, then, whether a name, object, person, or action can have a multitude of meanings. These meanings are determined either by the context of the work or by reference to our common heritage, in which case they are called public symbols. Examples of public symbols are the cross, which has a symbolic meaning in the Judeo-Christian tradition, or a country's flag, which has a symbolic value for the people it represents. Both private and public symbols can be employed by the filmmaker.

An allegory is a work in which the characters, events, and often even the setting function on several discrete levels at once. Writers of allegories frequently use a well-known story (say from the Bible) or a genre with clearly recognized conventions (such as the western) as a basis for their own work. The meaning of an allegory is often determined by something outside the context of the work. In order to be an allegory, the references to another level of meaning must be continuously employed throughout the work. When John Steinbeck names a character Rose of Sharon, he is making an allusion to *The Song of Solomon* without writing an allegory of this Biblical book. But *The Song of Solomon* itself can be interpreted as an allegory of Christ's love for his church.

Allegories are generally of two types: the political or historical allegory and the allegory of ideas. Characters in the former (whether humans or animals) have parallels in actual historical or contemporary political situations. John Dryden's poem, *Absalom and Achitophel* (1681), employs an Old Testament story to satirize a contemporary political situation. In allegories of ideas, abstractions (virtues, vices, states of mind, etc.) are given concrete embodiments. One of the most famous examples is John Bunyan's *The Pilgrim's Progress* (1678), in which the journey of Christian (both a person and an embodiment of Christianity) is chronicled from the City of Destruction through such places as the Slough of Despond, the Delectable Mountains and Vanity Fair, until he reaches the Celestial City. Along the way, he encounters Worldly Wiseman, Talkative, Pliable, and Sloth, among other characters. Both the settings and the characters function on more than one level consistently, so that two stories are being told at once. Although allegories of ideas are less common today than they once were, Ingmar Bergman's *The Seventh Seal* (1956) and Francis Coppola's *Apocalypse Now* (1979) are modern cinematic examples.

The symbolic and allegorical modes have a long history in literature, painting, sculpture, and dance, and filmmakers have turned to these valuable resources to extend the possibilities of their own work. Because of the literalness of the cinematic image, however, these techniques must be employed with great subtlety. But for the filmmaker who uses them effectively, the result can be a complex and multileveled work.

Additional Recommended Films

Billy Budd (1962), directed by Peter Ustinov, based on the novella by Herman Melville and the play by Louis O. Coxe and Robert Chapman. Both the novella and the play are available in paperback.

The Red Badge of Courage (1951), directed by John Huston, based on the novel by Stephen Crane. The novel is available in paperback.

An Outcast of the Islands (1951), directed by Carol Reed, based on the novel by Joseph Conrad. The novel is available in paperback.

See Also:

The Treasure of the Sierra Madre (Chapter 4)
Rashomon (Chapter 5)
High Noon (Chapter 9)

A Clockwork Orange
Death in Venice
The Servant
Greed
Don't Look Now

The Rocking-Horse Winner

"The Rocking-Horse Winner" was the first of D. H. Lawrence's stories to be made into a movie, and in many respects it posed greater problems than works filmed subsequently. Here Lawrence eschews the realistic mode of his great novels and presents instead a moral fable built on abstract ideas. Abstractions are notoriously difficult to film, even when developed within a realistic setting, yet Anthony Pelissier succeeds admirably in creating visual equivalents for them.

Lawrence's story concerns a young boy whose upper-middle-class parents are living far beyond their means. He discovers that he possesses psychic powers that he believes he can use to bring happiness to the family. Instead, the money he gains by betting on horses feeds his parents' insatiable greed, and the activity of divining winners ultimately destroys him as well.

The opening paragraphs of the story evoke the world of a fairy tale:

> There was a woman who was beautiful, who started with all the advantages, yet she had no luck. She married for love, and the love turned to dust. She had bonny children, yet she felt they had been thrust upon her, and she could not love them. . . .
>
> There was a boy and two little girls. They lived in a pleasant house, with a garden, and they had discreet servants, and felt themselves superior to anyone in the neighborhood.

The words "love" and "luck" stand out, connected by alliteration and their placement in the first paragraph. In large measure the boy's quest is for a "luck" to enable him to win the "love" of his mother. He later confuses "luck" with "lucre," and with this confusion the perimeters of his world, love-luck-money, are established.

The purposeful vagueness of the opening permits the reader to suspend disbelief and enter the world of the story. The protagonists are not named, nor is the setting specified. Greed and urgency for money must seem as real as any of the human characters, and the most effective way of achieving this is by minimizing the specificity of the story. Once the "reality" of these forces has been accepted, everything else can come into greater focus. The voice of the avaricious unnamed mother modulates into the voice of the house:

> Her children were growing up, they would have to go to school. There must be more money, there must be more money. . . . And so the house came to be haunted by the unspoken phrase: *There must be more money! There must be more money!* The children could hear it all the time, although nobody said it aloud.

This secret is the first of many contained by the house, and the boy seeks to combat it with an even greater secret of his own.

The boy, Paul, is given a identity in his first conversation with his mother. Here Paul mistakes "lucre" for "luck," and although his mother explains the difference to him, it is clear that he continues to perceive a relationship between them. He also senses a connection between lucre and his Uncle Oscar, who had first mentioned the word in his presence. After hearing his mother's description of luck, Paul seeks it on his rocking horse, riding the horse with a sort of frenzy, until it finally leads him "to where luck is." Initially, this activity is not connected with horse racing at all but, as W. D. Snodgrass has persuasively argued, is masturbatory and a part of Paul's oedipal relationship with his mother.[1] Paul develops the uncanny ability to discover the winner of a race if only he rides his horse hard enough, but this produces greater avarice in his mother and leads to his own death.

In the film *The Rocking-Horse Winner* (1949), director Anthony Pelissier has a clear challenge to maintain the balance between fable and reality that the story maintains. The script notes that the opening shots are meant to suggest "an Arthur Rackham drawing," but these were cut from the final film. Only the opening shot of the miniature of the house remains, but it is a rather conventional establishing shot. We move immediately to a very realistic setting, as Paul attempts to peek through the window and observe the new gardener-handyman in his quarters. Pelissier has expanded the role of Bassett considerably. He is open and friendly with Paul and immediately shares his interest in horse racing with him. Paul is clearly enjoying himself when his mother appears in the doorway, aloof and immaculately dressed, and summons him away. Pelissier deftly contrasts the warm rapport between Bassett and Paul with the icy formality of Paul's mother.

The roles of the other principal characters are also expanded and given a specificity they lack in the story. Paul's father, Richard, first seen dispensing a few coins to Christmas carolers on the front doorstep, is a compulsive gambler who loses great sums at his club and must be bailed out by his brother-in-law. Nor can he succeed in holding a job for any length of time. The mother is obsessed with spending money to keep up appearances and to acquire new goods, although there is obviously no money to be spent. Like Richard, Oscar is a gambler, yet he is cautious even when he is sure of his bets (as when following Paul's advice) and even though he can afford to lose. He remains highly critical of the life-style of his sister and brother-in-law, yet he supports them financially when necessary.

In the film realistic characters are developed in a real life situation. How then is Pelissier able to create the symbols so important in D. H. Lawrence's story? One means is by the juxtaposition of apparently unrelated scenes that

---

[1]W. D. Snodgrass, "A Rocking-Horse: The Symbol, the Pattern, the Way to Live," The Hudson Review, 11 (Summer, 1958), 191–200. Reprinted in *From Fiction to Film: D. H. Lawrence's "The Rocking-Horse Winner,"* eds. Gerald R. Barrett and Thomas L. Erskine (Encino, California: Dickenson Publishing Co., 1974), pp. 59–68.

illuminate each other by their proximity. The film begins on Christmas eve, and after the Christmas carolers have been paid off and Paul and his sisters put to bed, Richard and Hester Grahame dress for an evening out. Their conversation is exclusively devoted to money and to whether Richard will obtain the new position to which he aspires. As Richard speaks of the possibility of procuring a new job, his wife tells how she will spend the money his increase in salary will bring. She repeats the phrase that will later resound through the house: "We must have more money, Richard. Somehow we've simply just got to have more money, that's all there is to it." After they have left, Paul sneaks downstairs, moving cautiously through the big house, which appears ominous in the darkness. In the living room he finds a large parcel with his name on it, which he carefully probes, attempting to ascertain the contents. Suddenly Pelissier dissolves to the following morning, and Paul is unwrapping the package to discover a rocking horse. The camera pulls back to reveal an ostentatious display of expenditure. We know his parents are pressed for money: How can they afford all this?

In the sequence that follows, by developing two scenes simultaneously, Pelissier suggests a complex relationship between the situation of Paul's parents and the rocking horse. The first scene concerns Paul and Bassett, who carry the rocking horse upstairs, where Bassett gives Paul his first riding lesson. Paul is initially too cautious, and Bassett urges him with a rather heavy irony: "You'll have to go a great deal faster than that or you won't be in time for your own funeral." Such strong encouragement is lacking in the story. Bassett then suggests that the horse may be a source of luck: "And if you speak to him nicely and whisper in his ear there isn't a race he couldn't win for you—and him only half-trying." Paul rocks faster now, and as one critic has noted, "the bars of light on the wall behind indicate cinematically that he is sealing his own imprisonment with the horse which on Christmas morning seems to represent a mode of liberation."[2]

Bassett carries the rocking horse up to the nursery, where Paul remains with his younger sisters and their nurse while their parents argue downstairs with Uncle Oscar about their financial problems. As usual, Hester has the last word: *"There must be more money."* At this point the camera is shooting through the doorway into the room where the three adults are gathered. As Hester speaks she strides toward the door and closes it. The camera pans slowly while the words, "There must be more money," echo up the staircase. Through a montage of shots, Pelissier follows the words up the stairs and down the hallway, through the door leading to the back stairs and up to the nursery. The camera finally enters the nursery, and although the words are now merely a whisper, the two girls look up and cast their eyes in Paul's direction. Paul also listens and stops pushing his horse. He stares in the mouth of the animal, which seems to be uttering, ". . . more money . . . more money," as the picture fades out. A relationship between Paul, his

[2]Joan Mellen, "'The Rocking-Horse Winner' as Cinema," *From Fiction to Film,* p. 217.

rocking horse, and the straitened circumstances of his parents has been established entirely through editing.

Pelissier's treatment of the voice of the house is extremely effective. By having Hester's words as its source, he connects her with the rocking horse, which finally appears to be speaking. Because of its realistic basis, we accept the voice, and in the presentation the basically realistic mode of the movie is extended. When the house talks for a second time, the camera can penetrate the corridors without the stimulus of Hester speaking.

The extension of reality by the introduction of the voice of the house prepares the viewer for Paul's first ride in pursuit of luck, where the strict canons of reality are again violated. The scene begins in the garden, beneath a bright but potentially overcast sky, as Uncle Oscar chats with Hester. The maid interrupts to tell them she is worried about Paul, and after a cut to a shot of him riding his horse, she leads them to the nursery. The two sisters are huddled together, while Paul rocks frantically. As the adults enter the room, thunder is heard, the skies outside darken, and lightning casts an eerie illumination on Paul. Suddenly Pelissier cuts to Paul's point of view, and the camera tilts up and down, simulating the movement of the rocking horse. The camera zooms away from his mother and uncle, and then away from his sisters and nurse. The two zoom shots are reversed, as Paul reenters the real world of the nursery. The shots effectively duplicate Paul's thorough self-absorption when riding "in full tilt" to "where there is luck."

The connection between the rocking horse and luck is made early in the film and is reaffirmed in scenes where Uncle Oscar and Bassett discuss horse racing, and later when Bassett and Paul do the same. Pelissier also reproduces very closely the conversation between Paul and his mother on the subject of luck and money. The setting, not mentioned in the story, dramatically undercuts the conversation in the film. Paul and his mother are out for a walk, and, at her suggestion, they enter an antique shop. She examines a picture with great interest that is later seen on the wall of her home. In spite of her situation, she cannot help desiring one expensive object after another, all the while talking about her impoverished circumstances. The setting forms a perfect counterpoint to the dialogue.

The scene where the house goes wild with voices after Paul's birthday gift to his mother is beautifully rendered in the film. Having already connected Hester's voice with the voice of the house, Pelissier creates a short montage of shots showing her spending money and being involved in the world of high society. Superimposed are shots of Paul rocking with increased zeal and frustration on his horse. The rapid pacing suggests Hester's insatiable obsession with money. The possibility of Paul's ever satisfying her in any way seems remote indeed.

Paul's final ride is another example of Pelissier's use of parallel editing. Paul's mother and father have arrived at a charity ball, and we see them mounting the ornate staircase within the mansion where the dance is to take place. In the parking area before the house, the chauffeurs discuss the upcoming derby, and Bassett ponders with the others the possible winners. Among those mentioned is Malabar, and thus, we are prepared to recognize Paul's eventual discovery. Inside, Paul's mother is uneasy and finally telephones home to see if everything is all right. The nurse assures her that Paul is fine. Paul is then shown listening downstairs in a trancelike state. As he gazes out the window, cloud formations appear in shapes like horses, rising up to the left of the frame. The hallway echoes with the voice of the house and also with the sounds of the racetrack Paul had visited with his Uncle Oscar. As Paul climbs the staircase (an action parallel to his mother's action at the party), voices of the past fill the corridors. Pelissier builds suspense as the viewer waits for something to happen. Paul enters his room and Pelissier cuts back to the ball. Hester's uneasiness finally overcomes her, and she decides to return home. Upon arriving she rushes up the stairs to Paul's room, pausing at the top to listen to the noise of the house. What she hears is very different from what Paul heard earlier; the house is no longer speaking but humming with frenzy. She approaches Paul's room, opens the door, and Pelissier cuts to inside the room, so that we see Hester framed by the doorway as Paul's shadow is cast on the wall. "Paul, what on earth are you doing?" she cries. "It's Malabar!" he shrieks, rocking frantically on his horse. Hester stands frozen in the doorway. Finally, as Paul crashes to the floor, she rushes

The Rocking-Horse Winner. "It's Malabar."

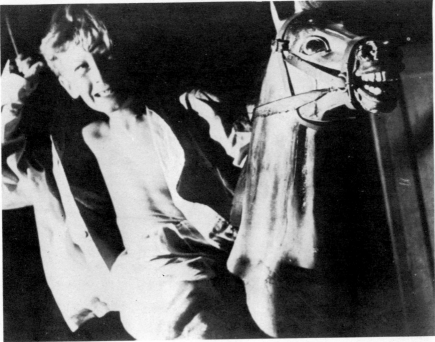

in, and Pelissier cuts to the mocking eyes of the rocking horse. Then Hester bends to pick up Paul, and the picture fades out. The viewer, having earlier participated in Paul's frenzy, here remains caught like Hester and unable to act. The effect is chilling.

Although Pelissier has filmed Paul's deathbed scenes quite close to their treatment in the story, he has felt obliged to add a scene in which Bassett burns the rocking horse and is asked by Hester to burn the money as well. Nothing has prepared the viewer for Hester's change of heart, and Bassett's moralizing is rather too obvious to be effective. In 1949 the ending may have been commercially necessary, but the principal development of the picture is clearly not in this direction. Hester remains condemned, and what follows is anticlimactic.

Pelissier has created a film that faithfully captures one aspect of D. H. Lawrence's story—the destructive pursuit of money by Paul's parents. Paul's own private obsession is more fully explained, although the masturbatory undertones and the suggestions of oedipal love are largely removed. In order to preserve the realistic framework and still have the viewer respond to the symbols of greed and Paul's trances on horseback, Pelissier relies strongly on viewer identification with Paul and on the use of the subjective camera. Although at times he gives the supernatural a realistic basis, this does not diminish the mysterious force of the symbols. *The Rocking-Horse Winner* remains a powerful and disturbing film.

The Rocking-Horse Winner

Production Credits

Director	Anthony Pelissier
Producer	John Mills
Screenplay by	Anthony Pelissier
Based on the short story by	D. H. Lawrence
Director of Photography	Desmond Dickinson
Art Director	Carmen Dillon
Film Editor	John Seabourne
Assistant Director	Robert Asher
Music by	William Alwyn
Orchestration by	Royal Philharmonic Orchestra

Great Britain. 1949. 91 minutes. Black & White.

Cast

Hester Grahame	Valerie Hobson
Paul Grahame	John Howard Davies
Uncle Oscar	Ronald Squire

Bassett	John Mills
Richard Grahame	Hugh Sinclair
Nannie	Susan Richards

Further Reading

Barrett, Gerald R. and Thomas L. Erskine, Eds. *From Fiction to Film: D. H. Lawrence's "The Rocking-Horse Winner."* Encino, California: Dickenson Publishing Co., Inc., 1974.

Becker, Henry. "'The Rocking-Horse Winner': Film as Parable." *Literature/Film Quarterly,* 1, No. 1 (January 1973), 55–63.

Ferlita, Ernest and John R. May. *Film Odyssey.* New York: Paulist Press, 1976.

Goldstein, R. M. *"The Rocking-Horse Winner." Film News* 34 (January/February 1977), 32.

Marcus, F. H. "From Story to Screen." *Media and Methods* 14 (December 1977), 56–58.

Tarrat, Margaret. "An Obscene Undertaking." *Films and Filming,* 17, No. 2 (November 1970), pp. 26–30.

The Rocking-Horse Winner

D. H. Lawrence

There was a woman who was beautiful, who started with all the advantages, yet she had no luck. She married for love, and the love turned to dust. She had bonny children, yet she felt they had been thrust upon her, and she could not love them. They looked at her coldly, as if they were finding fault with her. And hurriedly she felt she must cover up some fault in herself. Yet what it was that she must cover up she never knew. Nevertheless, when her children were present, she always felt the centre of her heart go hard. This troubled her, and in her manner she was all the more gentle and anxious for her children, as if she loved them very much. Only she herself knew that at the centre of her heart was a hard little place that could not feel love, no, not for anybody. Everybody else said of her: "She is such a good mother. She adores her children." Only she herself, and her children themselves, knew it was not so. They read it in each other's eyes.

There were a boy and two little girls. They lived in a pleasant house, with a garden, and they had discreet servants, and felt themselves superior to anyone in the neighbourhood.

Although they lived in style, they felt always an anxiety in the house. There was never enough money. The mother had a small income, and the father had a small income, but not nearly enough for the social position which they had to keep up. The father went into town to some office. But though he had good prospects, these prospects never materialised. There was always the grinding sense of the shortage of money, though the style was always kept up.

At last the mother said: "I will see if I can't make something." But she did not know where to begin. She racked her brains, and tried this thing and the other, but could not find anything successful. The failure made deep lines comes into her face. Her children were growing up, they would have to go to school. There must be more money, there must be more money. The father, who was always very handsome and expensive in his tastes, seemed as if he never *would* be able to do anything worth doing. And the mother, who had a great belief in herself, did not succeed any better, and her tastes were just as expensive.

And so the house came to be haunted by the unspoken phrase: *There must be more money! There must be more money!* The children could hear it all the time, though nobody said it aloud. They heard it at Christmas, when the expensive and splendid toys filled the nursery. Behind the shining modern rocking-horse, behind the smart doll's house, a voice would start whispering: "There *must* be more money! There *must* be more money!" And the children would stop playing, to listen for a moment. They would look into each other's eyes, to see if they had all heard. And each one saw in the eyes of the other two that they too had heard. "There *must* be more money! There *must* be more money!"

It came whispering from the springs of the still-swaying rocking-horse, and even the horse, bending his wooden, champing head, heard it. The big doll, sitting so pink and smirking in her new pram, could hear it quite plainly, and seemed to be smirking all the more self-consciously because of it. The foolish puppy, too, that took the place of the teddy-bear, he was looking so extraordinarily foolish for no other reason but that he heard the secret whisper all over the house: "There *must* be more money!"

Yet nobody ever said it aloud. The whisper was everywhere, and therefore no one spoke it. Just as no one ever says: "We are breathing!" in spite of the fact that breath is coming and going all the time.

"Mother," said the boy Paul one day, "why don't we keep a car of our own? Why do we always use uncle's, or else a taxi?"

"Because we're the poor members of the family," said the mother.

"But why *are* we, mother?"

"Well—I suppose," she said slowly and bitterly, "it's because your father has no luck."

The boy was silent for some time.

"Is luck money, mother?" he asked, rather timidly.

"No, Paul. Not quite. It's what causes you to have money."

"Oh!" said Paul vaguely. "I thought when Uncle Oscar said *filthy lucker*, it meant money."

"*Filthy lucre* does mean money," said the mother. "But it's lucre, not luck."

"Oh!" said the boy. "Then what *is* luck, mother?"

"It's what causes you to have money. If you're lucky you have money. That's why it's better to be born lucky than rich. If you're rich, you may lose your money. But if you're lucky, you will always get more money."

"Oh! Will you? And is father not lucky?"

"Very unlucky, I should say," she said bitterly.

The boy watched her with unsure eyes.

"Why?" he asked.

"I don't know. Nobody ever knows why one person is lucky and another unlucky."

"Don't they? Nobody at all? Does *nobody* know?"

"Perhaps God. But He never tells."

"He ought to, then. And aren't you lucky either, mother?"

"I can't be, if I married an unlucky husband."

"But by yourself, aren't you?"

"I used to think I was, before I married. Now I think I am very unlucky indeed."

"Why?"

"Well—never mind! Perhaps I'm not really," she said.

The child looked at her to see if she meant it. But he saw, by the lines of her mouth, that she was only trying to hide something from him.

"Well, anyhow," he said stoutly, "I'm a lucky person."

"Why?" said his mother, with a sudden laugh.

He stared at her. He didn't even know why he had said it.

"God told me," he asserted, brazening it out.

"I hope He did, dear!" she said, again with a laugh, but rather bitter.

"He did, mother!"

"Excellent!" said the mother, using one of her husband's exclamations.

The boy saw she did not believe him; or rather, that she paid no attention to his assertion. This angered him somewhere, and made him want to compel her attention.

He went off by himself, vaguely, in a childish way, seeking for the clue to 'luck'. Absorbed, taking no heed of other people, he went about with a sort of stealth, seeking inwardly for luck. He wanted luck, he wanted it, he wanted it. When the two girls were playing dolls in the nursery, he would sit on his big rocking-horse, charging madly into space, with a frenzy that made the little girls peer at him uneasily. Wildly the horse careered, the waving dark hair of the boy tossed, his eyes had a strange glare in them. The two girls dared not speak to him.

When he had ridden to the end of his mad little journey, he climbed down and stood in front of his rocking-horse, staring fixedly into its lowered face. Its red mouth was slightly open, its big eye was wide and glassy-bright.

"Now!" he would silently command the snorting steed. "Now, take me to where there is luck! Now take me!"

And he would slash the horse on the neck with the little whip he had asked Uncle Oscar for. He *knew* the horse could take him to where there was luck, if only he forced it. So he would mount again and start on his furious ride, hoping at last to get there. He knew he could get there.

"You'll break your horse, Paul!" said the nurse.

"He's always riding like that! I wish he'd leave off!" said his elder sister Joan.

But he only glared down on them in silence. Nurse gave him up. She could make nothing of him. Anyhow, he was growing beyond her.

One day his mother and his Uncle Oscar came in when he was on one of his furious rides. He did not speak to them.

"Hallo, you young jockey! Riding a winner?" said his uncle.

"Aren't you growing too big for a rocking-horse? You're not a very little boy any longer, you know," said his mother.

But Paul only gave a blue glare from his big, rather close-set eyes. He would speak to nobody when he was in a full tilt. His mother watched him with an anxious expression on her face.

At last he suddenly stopped forcing his horse into the mechanical gallop and slid down.

"Well, I got there!" he announced fiercely, his blue eyes still flaring, and his sturdy long legs straddling apart.

"Where did you get to?" asked his mother.

"Where I wanted to go," he flared back at her.

"That's right son!" said Uncle Oscar. "Don't you stop till you get there. What's the horse's name?"

"He doesn't have a name," said the boy.

"Gets on without all right?" asked the uncle.

"Well, he has different names. He was called Sansovino last week."

"Sansovino, eh? Won the Ascot. How did you know this name?"

"He always talks about horse-races with Bassett," said Joan.

The uncle was delighted to find that his small nephew was posted with all the racing news. Bassett, the young gardener, who had been wounded in the left foot in the war and had got his present job through Oscar Cresswell, whose batman he had been, was a perfect blade of the 'turf'. He lived in the racing events, and the small boy lived with him.

Oscar Cresswell got it all from Bassett.

"Master Paul comes and asks me, so I can't do more than tell him, sir," said Bassett, his face terribly serious, as if he were speaking of religious matters.

"And does he ever put anything on a horse he fancies?"

"Well—I don't want to give him away—he's a young sport, a fine sport, sir. Would you mind asking him himself? He sort of takes a pleasure in it, and perhaps he'd feel I was giving him away, sir, if you don't mind."

Bassett was serious as a church.

The uncle went back to his nephew and took him off for a ride in the car.

"Say, Paul, old man, do you ever put anything on a horse?" the uncle asked.

The boy watched the handsome man closely.

"Why, do you think I oughtn't to?" he parried.

"Not a bit of it! I thought perhaps you might give me a tip for the Lincoln."

The car sped on into the country, going down to Uncle Oscar's place in Hampshire.

"Honour bright?" said the nephew.

"Honour bright, son!" said the uncle.

"Well, then, Daffodil."

"Daffodil! I doubt it, sonny. What about Mirza?"

"I only know the winner," said the boy. "That's Daffodil."

"Daffodil, eh?"

There was a pause. Daffodil was an obscure horse comparatively.

"Uncle!"

"Yes, son?"

"You won't let it go any further, will you? I promised Bassett."

"Bassett be damned, old man! What's he got to do with it?"

"We're partners. We've been partners from the first. Uncle, he lent me my first five shillings, which I lost. I promised him, honour bright it was only between me and him; only you gave me that ten-shilling note I started winning with, so I thought you were lucky. You won't let it go any further, will you?"

The boy gazed at his uncle from those big, hot, blue eyes, set rather close together. The uncle stirred and laughed uneasily.

"Right you are, son! I'll keep your tip private. Daffodil, eh? How much are you putting on him?"

"All except twenty pounds," said the boy. "I keep that in reserve."

The uncle thought it a good joke.

"You keep twenty pounds in reserve, do you, you young romancer? What are you betting, then?"

"I'm betting three hundred," said the boy gravely. "But it's between you and me, Uncle Oscar! Honour bright?"

The uncle burst into a roar of laughter.

"It's between you and me all right, you young Nat Gould," he said, laughing. "But where's your three hundred?"

"Bassett keeps it for me. We're partners."

"You are, are you! And what is Bassett putting on Daffodil?"

"He won't go quite as high as I do, I expect. Perhaps he'll go a hundred and fifty."

"What, pennies?" laughed the uncle.

"Pounds," said the child, with a surprised look at his uncle. "Bassett keeps a bigger reserve than I do."

Between wonder and amusement Uncle Oscar was silent. He pursued the matter no further, but he determined to take his nephew with him to the Lincoln races.

"Now, son," he said, "I'm putting twenty on Mirza, and I'll put five on for you on any horse you fancy. What's your pick?"

"Daffodil, uncle."

"No, not the fiver on Daffodil!"

"I should if it was my own fiver," said the child.

"Good! Good! Right you are! A fiver for me and a fiver for you on Daffodil."

The child had never been to a race-meeting before, and his eyes were blue fire. He pursed his mouth tight and watched. A Frenchman just in front had put his money on Lancelot. Wild with excitement, he flayed his arms up and down, yelling *Lancelot! Lancelot!* in his French accent.

Daffodil came in first, Lancelot second, Mirza third. The child, flushed and with eyes blazing, was curiously serene. His uncle brought him four five-pound notes, four to one.

"What am I to do with these?" he cried, waving them before the boy's eyes.

"I suppose we'll talk to Bassett," said the boy. "I expect I have fifteen hundred now; and twenty in reserve; and this twenty."

His uncle studied him for some moments.

"Look here, son!" he said. "You're not serious about Bassett and that fifteen hundred, are you?"

"Yes, I am. But it's between you and me, uncle. Honour bright?"

"Honour bright all right, son! But I must talk to Bassett."

"If you'd like to be a partner, uncle, with Bassett and me, we could all be partners. Only, you'd have to promise, honour bright, uncle, not to let it go beyond us three. Bassett and I are lucky, and you must be lucky, because it was your ten shillings I started winning with. . . ."

Uncle Oscar took both Bassett and Paul into Richmond Park for an afternoon, and there they talked.

"It's like this, you see, sir," Bassett said. "Master Paul would get me talking about racing events, spinning yarns, you know, sir. And he was always keen on knowing if I'd made or if I'd lost. It's about a year since, now, that I put five shillings on Blush of Dawn for him: and we lost. Then the luck turned, with that ten shillings he had from you: that we put on Singhalese. And since that time, it's been pretty steady, all things considering. What do you say, Master Paul?"

"We're all right when we're sure," said Paul. "It's when we're not quite sure that we go down."

"Oh, but we're careful then," said Bassett.

"But when are you *sure*?" smiled Uncle Oscar.

"It's Master Paul, sir," said Bassett in a secret, religious voice. "It's as if he had it from heaven. Like Daffodil, now, for the Lincoln. That was as sure as eggs."

"Did you put anything on Daffodil?" asked Oscar Cresswell.

"Yes, sir. I made my bit."

"And my nephew?"

Bassett was obstinately silent, looking at Paul.

"I made twelve hundred, didn't I, Bassett? I told uncle I was putting three hundred on Daffodil."

"That's right," said Bassett, nodding.

"But where's the money?" asked the uncle.

"I keep it safe locked up, sir. Master Paul he can have it any minute he likes to ask for it."

"What, fifteen hundred pounds?"

"And twenty! And *forty,* that is, with the twenty he made on the course."

"It's amazing!" said the uncle.

"If Master Paul offers you to be partners, sir, I would, if I were you: if you'll excuse me," said Bassett.

Oscar Cresswell thought about it.

"I'll see the money," he said.

They drove home again, and, sure enough, Bassett came round to the garden-house with fifteen hundred pounds in notes. The twenty pounds reserve was left with Joe Glee, in the Turf Commission deposit.

"You see, it's all right, uncle, when I'm *sure*! Then we go strong, for all we're worth. Don't we, Bassett?"

"We do that, Master Paul."

"And when are you sure?" said the uncle, laughing.

"Oh, well, sometimes I'm *absolutely* sure, like about Daffodil," said the boy; "and sometimes I have an idea; and sometimes I haven't even an idea, have I, Bassett? Then we're careful, because we mostly go down."

"You do, do you! And when you're sure, like about Daffodil, what makes you sure, sonny?"

"Oh, well, I don't know," said the boy uneasily. "I'm sure, you know, uncle; that's all."

"It's as if he had it from heaven, sir," Bassett reiterated.

"I should say so!" said the uncle.

But he became a partner. And when the Leger was coming on Paul was 'sure' about Lively Spark, which was a quite inconsiderable horse. The boy insisted on putting a thousand on the horse, Bassett went for five hundred, and Oscar Cresswell two hundred. Lively Spark came in first, and the betting had been ten to one against him. Paul had made ten thousand.

"You see," he said, "I was absolutely sure of him."

Even Oscar Cresswell had cleared two thousand.

"Look here, son," he said, "this sort of thing makes me nervous."

"It needn't uncle! Perhaps I shan't be sure again for a long time."

"But what are you going to do with your money?" asked the uncle.

"Of course," said the boy, "I started it for mother. She said she had no luck, because father is unlucky, so I thought if I was lucky, it might stop whispering."

"What might stop whispering?"

"Our house. I *hate* our house for whispering."

"What does it whisper?"

"Why—why"—the boy fidgeted—"why, I don't know. But it's always short of money, you know, uncle."

"I know it, son, I know it."

"You know people send mother writs, don't you, uncle?"

"I'm afraid I do," said the uncle.

"And then the house whispers, like people laughing at you behind your back. It's awful, that is! I thought if I was lucky—"

"You might stop it," added the uncle.

The boy watched him with big blue eyes, that had an uncanny cold fire in them, and he said never a word.

"Well, then!" said the uncle. "What are we doing?"

"I shouldn't like mother to know I was lucky," said the boy.

"Why not, son?"

"She'd stop me."

"I don't think she would."

"Oh!"—and the boy writhed in an odd way—"I *don't* want her to know, uncle."

"All right, son! We'll manage it without her knowing."

They managed it very easily. Paul, at the other's suggestion, handed over five thousand pounds to his uncle, who deposited it with the family lawyer, who was then to inform Paul's mother that a relative had put five thousand pounds into his hands, which sum was to be paid out a thousand pounds at a time, on the mother's birthday, for the next five years.

"So she'll have a birthday present of a thousand pounds for five successive years," said Uncle Oscar. "I hope it won't make it all the harder for her later."

Paul's mother had her birthday in November. The house had been 'whispering' worse than ever lately, and, even in spite of his luck, Paul could not bear up against it. He was very anxious to see the effect of the birthday letter, telling his mother about the thousand pounds.

When there were no visitors, Paul now took his meals with his parents, as he was beyond the nursery control. His mother went into town nearly every day. She had discovered that she had an odd knack of sketching furs and dress materials, so she worked secretly in the studio of a friend who was the chief 'artist' for the leading drapers. She drew the figures of ladies in furs and ladies in silk and sequins for the newspaper advertisements. This young woman artist earned several thousand pounds a year, but Paul's mother only made several hundreds, and she was again dissatisfied. She so wanted to be first in something, and she did not succeed, even in making sketches for drapery advertisements.

She was down to breakfast on the morning of her birthday. Paul watched her face as she read her letters. He knew the lawyer's letter. As his mother read it, her face hardened and became more expressionless. Then a cold, determined look came on her mouth. She hid the letter under the pile of others, and said not a word about it.

"Didn't you have anything nice in the post for your birthday, mother?" said Paul.

"Quite moderately nice," she said, her voice cold and absent.

She went away to town without saying more.

But in the afternoon Uncle Oscar appeared. He said Paul's mother had had a long interview with the lawyer, asking if the whole five thousand could not be advanced at once, as she was in debt.

"What do you think, uncle?" said the boy.

"I leave it to you, son."

"Oh, let her have it, then! We can get some more with the other," said the boy.

"A bird in the hand is worth two in the bush, laddie!" said Uncle Oscar.

"But I'm sure to *know* for the Grand National; or the Lincolnshire; or else the Derby. I'm sure to know for *one* of them," said Paul.

So Uncle Oscar signed the agreement, and Paul's mother touched the whole five thousand. Then something very curious happened. The voices in the house suddenly went mad, like a chorus of frogs on a spring evening. There were certain new furnishings, and Paul had a tutor. He was *really* going to Eton, his father's school, in the following autumn. There were flowers in the winter, and a blossoming of the luxury Paul's mother had been used to. And yet the voices in the house, behind the sprays of mimosa and almond-blossom, and from under the piles of iridescent cushions simply trilled and screamed in a sort of ectasy: "There *must* be more money! Oh-h-h; there *must* be more money. Oh, now, now-w! Now-w-w—there *must* be more money!— more than ever! More than ever!"

It frightened Paul terribly. He studied away at his Latin and Greek with his tutor. But his intense hours were spent with Bassett. The Grand National had gone by: he had not 'known', and had lost a hundred pounds. Summer was at hand. He was in agony for the Lincoln. But even for the Lincoln he didn't 'know', and he lost fifty pounds. He became wild-eyed and strange, as if something were going to explode in him.

"Let it alone, son! Don't you bother about it!" urged Uncle Oscar. But it was as if the boy couldn't really hear what his uncle was saying.

"I've got to know for the Derby! I've got to know for the Derby!" the child reiterated, his big blue eyes blazing with a sort of madness.

His mother noticed how overwrought he was.

"You'd better go to the seaside. Wouldn't you like to go now to the seaside, instead of waiting? I think you'd better," she said, looking down at him anxiously, her heart curiously heavy because of him.

But the child lifted his uncanny blue eyes.

"I couldn't possibly go before the Derby, mother!" he said. "I couldn't possibly!"

"Why not?" she said, her voice becoming heavy when she was opposed. "Why not? You can still go from the seaside to see the Derby with your Uncle Oscar, if that's what you wish. No need for you to wait here. Besides, I think you care too much about these races. It's a bad sign. My family has been a gambling family, and you won't know till you grow up how much damage it has done. But it has done damage. I shall have to send Bassett away, and ask Uncle Oscar not to talk racing to you, unless you promise to be reasonable about it: go away to the seaside and forget it. You're all nerves!"

"I'll do what you like, mother, so long as you don't send me away till after the Derby," the boy said.

"Send you away from where? Just from this house?"

"Yes," he said, gazing at her.

"Why, you curious child, what makes you care about this house so much, suddenly? I never knew you loved it."

He gazed at her without speaking. He had a secret within a secret, something he had not divulged, even to Bassett or to his Uncle Oscar.

But his mother, after standing undecided and a little bit sullen for some moments, said:

"Very well, then! Don't go to the seaside till after the Derby, if you don't wish it. But promise me you won't let your nerves go to pieces. Promise you won't think so much about horse-racing and *events*, as you call them!"

"Oh no," said the boy casually. "I won't think much about them, mother. You needn't worry. I wouldn't worry, mother, if I were you."

"If you were me and I were you," said his mother, "I wonder what we *should* do!"

"But you know you needn't worry, mother, don't you?" the boy repeated.

"I should be awfully glad to know it," she said wearily.

"Oh, well, you *can*, you know. I mean, you ought to know *you* needn't worry," he insisted.

"Ought I? Then I'll see about it," she said.

Paul's secret of secrets was his wooden horse, that which had no name. Since he was emancipated from a nurse and a nursery-governess, he had had his rocking-horse removed to his own bedroom at the top of the house.

"Surely you're too big for a rocking-horse!" his mother had remonstrated.

"Well, you see, mother, till I can have a *real* horse, I like to have some sort of animal about," had been his quaint answer.

"Do you feel he keeps you company?" she laughed.

"Oh, yes! He's very good, he always keeps me company, when I'm there," said Paul.

So the horse, rather shabby, stood in an arrested prance in the boy's bedroom.

The Derby was drawing near, and the boy grew more and more tense. He hardly heard what was spoken to him, he was very frail, and his eyes were really uncanny. His mother had sudden strange seizures of uneasiness about him. Sometimes, for half an hour, she would feel a sudden anxiety about him that was almost anguish. She wanted to rush to him at once, and know he was safe.

Two nights before the Derby, she was at a big party in town, when one of her rushes of anxiety about her boy, her first-born, gripped her heart till she could hardly speak. She fought with the feeling, might and main, for she believed in common sense. But it was too strong. She had to leave the dance and go downstairs to telephone to the country. The children's nursery-governess was terribly surprised and startled at being rung up in the night.

"Are the children all right, Miss Wilmot?"

"Oh yes, they are quite all right."

"Master Paul? Is he all right?"

"He went to bed as right as a trivet. Shall I run up and look at him?"

"No," said Paul's mother reluctantly. "No! Don't trouble. It's all right. Don't sit up. We shall be home fairly soon." She did not want her son's privacy intruded upon.

"Very good," said the governess.

It was about one o'clock when Paul's mother and father drove up to their house. All was still. Paul's mother went to her room and slipped off her white fur cloak. She had told her maid not to wait up for her. She heard her husband downstairs, mixing a whisky and soda.

And then, because of the strange anxiety at her heart, she stole upstairs to her son's room. Noiselessly she went along the upper corridor. Was there a faint noise? What was it?

She stood, with arrested muscles, outside his door, listening. There was a strange, heavy, and yet not loud noise. Her heart stood still. It was a sound-less noise, yet rushing and powerful. Something huge, in violent, hushed motion. What was it? What in God's name was it? She ought to know. She felt that she knew the noise. She knew what it was.

Yet she could not place it. She couldn't say what it was. And on and on it went, like a madness.

Softly, frozen with anxiety and fear, she turned the doorhandle.

The room was dark. Yet in the space near the window, she heard and saw something plunging to and fro. She gazed in fear and amazement.

Then suddenly she switched on the light, and saw her son, in his green pyjamas, madly surging on the rocking-horse. The blaze of light suddenly lit him up, as he urged the wooden horse, and lit her up, as she stood, blonde, in her dress of pale green and crystal, in the doorway.

"Paul!" she cried. "Whatever are you doing?"

"It's Malabar!" he screamed in a powerful, strange voice. "It's Malabar!"

His eyes blazed at her for one strange and senseless second, as he ceased urging his wooden horse. Then he fell with a crash to the ground, and she, all her tormented motherhood flooding upon her, rushed to gather him up.

But he was unconscious, and unconscious he remained, with some brain-fever. He talked and tossed, and his mother sat stonily by his side.

"Malabar! It's Malabar! Bassett, Bassett, I *know!* It's Malabar!"

So the child cried, trying to get up and urge the rocking-horse that gave him his inspiration.

"What does he mean by Malabar?" asked the heart-frozen mother.

"I don't know," said the father stonily.

"What does he mean by Malabar?" she asked her brother Oscar.

"It's one of the horses running for the Derby," was the answer.

And, in spite of himself, Oscar Cresswell spoke to Bassett, and himself put a thousand on Malabar: at fourteen to one.

The third day of the illness was critical: they were waiting for a change. The boy, with his rather long, curly hair, was tossing ceaselessly on the pillow. He neither slept nor regained consciousness, and his eyes were like blue stones. His mother sat, feeling her heart had gone, turned actually into a stone.

In the evening, Oscar Cresswell did not come, but Bassett sent a message, saying could he come up for one moment, just one moment? Paul's mother was very angry at the intrusion, but on second thoughts she agreed. The boy was the same. Perhaps Bassett might bring him to consciousness.

The gardener, a shortish fellow with a little brown moustache and sharp little brown eyes, tiptoed into the room, touched his imaginary cap to Paul's mother, and stole to the bedside, staring with glittering, smallish eyes at the tossing, dying child.

"Master Paul!" he whispered. "Master Paul! Malabar came in first all right, a clean win. I did as you told me. You've made over seventy thousand pounds, you have; you've got over eighty thousand. Malabar came in all right, Master Paul."

"Malabar! Malabar! Did I say Malabar, mother? Did I say Malabar? Do you think I'm lucky, mother? I knew Malabar, didn't I? Over eighty thousand pounds! I call that lucky, don't you, mother? Over eighty thousand pounds! I knew, didn't I know I knew? Malabar came in all right. If I ride my horse till I'm sure, then I tell you, Bassett, you can go as high as you like. Did you go for all you were worth, Bassett?"

"I went a thousand on it, Master Paul."

"I never told you, mother, that if I can ride my horse, and *get there,* then I'm absolutely sure—oh, absolutely! Mother, did I ever tell you? I *am* lucky!"

"No, you never did," said his mother.

But the boy died in the night.

And even as he lay dead, his mother heard her brother's voice saying to her: "My God, Hester, you're eighty-odd thousand to the good, and a poor devil of a son to the bad. But, poor devil, poor devil, he's best gone out of a life where he rides his rocking-horse to find a winner."

 ## Stagecoach

With *Stagecoach*, John Ford returned to the western genre for the first time in thirteen years, and his film demonstrates the potential of this form. Like other film genres, the western can function on several levels at once. Ford creates a realistic story that can also be viewed as an allegory of ideas. While Lordsburg, the destination of Ford's passengers, is no Celestial City, the journey of his passengers is as rich in allegorical and symbolic overtones as that of John Bunyan's Pilgrim. Ford and his scriptwriter, Dudley Nichols, have created a group of characters who are a microcosm of society, confronted both by internal and external threats. Their journey becomes a rite of passage for each traveler who, in the course of the trip, is revealed for what he or she is.

Although Ford has followed the basic outline of Ernest Haycox's short story, "Stage to Lordsburg," the allegoric and symbolic dimensions are largely his own. Haycox relates the story of an assortment of passengers traveling from Tonto to Lordsburg. Their stagecoach is the first to make this trip in forty-five days, and a clear threat of Indian attack exists. Yet there is no compelling reason for this group to be setting out, except perhaps for the young woman "going down to marry an infantry officer" and the "slim blond man" traveling to Lordsburg to settle a grudge. In the course of the journey, one passenger dies a natural death and another is killed during an Indian attack, but the group successfully repels the Indians, and the remaining passengers arrive in Lordsburg. This simple western tale would be forgotten today were it not for John Ford's masterly adaptation.

Ford is interested in the interaction of characters, and his passengers represent a cross section of American society, including representatives of its aristocracy, business classes, working class and outcasts. Ford retains the virtuous young woman but makes her a southern aristocrat already married to an army officer whom she is traveling to join. Like most of the passengers, Mrs. Mallory has a secret: She is pregnant and thus has a pressing reason to be joining her husband. Her increased status in Ford's film contrasts her more sharply with the only other female passenger, the town prostitute, renamed Dallas. Ford also endows his gambler with a southern background. He too has a secret: He is the errant son of southern aristocracy (Judge Greenfield of Greenfield Manor) and has served in the regiment of Mrs. Mallory's father during the Civil War. Although not a scheduled passenger, he joins the stagecoach when he sees Mrs. Mallory in order to provide protection for her. Thus, he and Mrs. Mallory form the upper classes balanced against the common folk.

The middle classes are represented by a member of the managerial class and a hard-working salesman. Mr. Gatewood, a creation of Ford's, is the town banker and one of its most distinguished citizens. He hails the stagecoach out of town with a black bag containing the $50,000 he has stolen, leaving an empty bank safe and a sullen shrew of a wife behind. Mr. Peacock is the timid whiskey drummer whose name everyone forgets. He dispenses homiletic advice to the passengers and alcohol (although none too willingly) to the doctor who accompanies them. Nearly everyone mistakes Mr. Peacock for a clergyman, pleasant but ineffectual.

Ford's other creation is the doctor, Josiah Boone, M.D., an educated self-acknowledged philosopher as well as medical doctor, who quotes Christopher Marlowe the first time we see him, and who leads an alcoholic existence among the ignorance and prejudice that characterize the town of Tonto. He is evicted by his landlady and forced to leave town. Dallas confusedly appeals to him for help as the ladies of the "Law and Order League" escort her to the stagecoach. In Haycox's story she is presumably traveling to Lordsburg in search of new clients. Ford has her and Doc traveling against their wills, having been driven out by the upright citizens of Tonto.

Unlike most of the characters, Doc and Dallas have no secrets. Dallas is identified by the soundtrack with the folk tune, "Careless Love," the story of an unwanted pregnancy, just as "I Dream of Jeannie" is associated with Mrs. Mallory, the picture of carefully cultivated refinement. Ford wants us to respond favorably to Doc and Dallas and so he does not show us the behavior that resulted in their being driven out of town. We learn by Dallas' dress and the reactions of others that she is a prostitute, but we never see her in this role, just as we never see any of the victims of Doc's alcoholism. Instead, both appear to have been persecuted by a group of self-righteous and narrow-minded women.

The final passenger to join the coach is not Malpais Bill, the "slim blond man" who rides out of town with the passengers in Haycox's story, but the Ringo Kid who, like Gatewood, stops the coach outside town. Unlike Bill, the Kid is an outlaw, having broken out of prison, and he is surprised to see the sheriff riding shotgun with Buck, the stagecoach driver. He endears himself to us by inquiring immediately about Buck's family, and we remember Buck's earlier remark to the sheriff after hearing of the Kid's escape from prison: "Busted out? Well, good for him!" This testimony to Ringo's character is corroborated by his later actions.

By making the Ringo Kid an outlaw, Ford has provided a reason for the sheriff to accompany the stagecoach. He represents the Law and presides over the group both literally (he sits on top of the stagecoach) and figuratively. The sheriff's motives, we later learn, are somewhat mixed: On the one hand, he wants Ringo in prison where he will be safe from the Plummer brothers, but there is also a reward posted for Ringo that the sheriff acknowledges he could use. It is not until the end of the film that he resolves this conflict.

Having created a microcosm of society, Ford subjects it both to external threats (the Indians) and internal dissention (unlike the story, where the group is harmonious). During the trip the travelers reveal their secrets as well as themselves. Lucy Mallory, the pillar of society, is cold, uncaring, and priggish. She softens slightly toward Dallas on the trip, but once back in civilization (Lordsburg), their relationship becomes as fixed as it was in Tonto. Lucy has her baby and is ultimately reunited with her husband, who represents that superior force of order (the cavalry) without which none of them would have survived. The gambler also divulges his secret: that he is a southern gentleman (as Lucy accurately perceived). He carries a souvenir of his former life—a silver cup from his father's estate—and still governs his life by a code of chivalrous conduct that permits him to shoot enemies in the back and revered ladies in the head. Ironically, he is killed by the Indians before he can perform his mercy killing, and his intended victim is saved by the cavalry. Gatewood is shown to be a liar, a thief, and a hypocrite, totally useless in times of crisis. He is concerned only with saving his own skin and his newly acquired fortune, yet he is incapable of doing either.

Doc and Dallas have nothing to hide; instead the trip offers them the opportunity to realize their potential for goodness. During Mrs. Mallory's childbirth, the first crisis encountered by the group, they take over and are alone responsible for the success of the delivery. Dallas is visually associated with the baby since she presents the infant to the others and protects her during the remainder of the trip, relinquishing her only when they have arrived safely in Lordsburg. Dallas is a maternal figure (as Ringo observes), contrasting rather markedly with the child's real mother who has the warmth of a desert rattler. For her kindness and her willingness to sacrifice herself for others, Dallas is amply rewarded.

Just as Dallas and Doc assist at the creation of life, so is Ringo the one primarily responsible for preserving it. He perceives the threat of Indian attack but decides not to flee when presented with an opportunity (by Dallas) because he places the well-being of the group above his own freedom. If we had any doubt about the prior testimonies of Buck and the sheriff to Ringo's innate goodness, it is dispelled when we see him demonstrate his civility and kindness to Dallas during the ride and his courage and skill in fighting during the Indian attack. We share the sheriff's certainty that Ringo will be a man of his word and return to prison after his fight with the Plummers in Lordsburg. The sheriff's final decision about Ringo's fate is complicated by Ringo's success against the Plummers: Legally, the sheriff has no choice but to lock Ringo up. In the original script, the sheriff's behavior is explained by Doc's question at the film's conclusion: "You dad-blamed fool, why didn't you tell 'em Luke confessed to killing his foreman?" In the film the sheriff breaks the law and sanctions the Kid's flight by sending him south of the border with Dallas. Ironically, the Kid preserves civilization but cannot exist within it.

Just as Ford has changed his cast of characters to create a microcosm of democracy, so has he changed the nature of the trip from a literal journey to an allegorical one. Ford has heightened the contrast of the three stagecoach stops to one another, so that the journey begins in civilization and progresses

Stagecoach. The journey into the unknown.

through increasingly primitive circumstances. As the stagecoach proceeds farther and farther from civilization, its passengers reveal themselves for what they are. The cavalry is significantly absent when the passengers undergo their testing. Each must rise—or fall—on his or her own merit. Interestingly, Haycox's passengers defeat the Indians without any outside assistance, but Ford's are not able to do so: They have exhausted their ammunition when the cavalry fortuitously arrives. The cavalry, for Ford, represents a national body clearly superior to local law enforcement figures, and it is they who lead the passengers back to civilization.

Although the stage reaches Lordsburg, that stop does not mark the end of anyone's journey, except perhaps Doc's, whose future seems no brighter than his past. The others will settle in different communities or return from whence they came. Only Dallas and Ringo are destined to live forever outside the society they have helped to preserve.

Ford has taken the simple story of a trip westward and transformed it into

Stagecoach. The outcasts as heroes: Destined to live beyond society.

an allegorical journey from civilization through the "heart of darkness" and back again to civilization. He has created a rich cast of characters who epitomize American society and who, under stress, reveal a great deal about the problems and potentials of our democratic system. *Stagecoach* demonstrates how a classic genre like the western can be exploited for allegorical purposes.

Stagecoach

Production Credits

Director	John Ford
Producers	John Ford, Walter Wanger
Screenplay by	Dudley Nichols
Based on	
"Stage to Lordsburg" by	Ernest Haycox
Director of Photography	Bert Glennon, A.S.C.
Art Director	Alexander Toluboff
Film Editors	Dorothy Spencer, Walter Reynolds
Assistant Director	Wingate Smith
Sets by	Wiard B. Ihnen
Music by	Richard Hageman, W. Franke Harling, John Leipold, Leo Shuken, Louis Gruenberg (adapted from 17 American folk tunes of the early 1880s)

USA. 1939. 105 minutes. Black & white.

Cast

The Ringo Kid	John Wayne
Dallas	Claire Trevor
Doc Boone	Thomas Mitchell
Buck	Andy Devine
Curly Wilcox	George Bancroft
Mr. Peacock	Donald Meek
Lucy Mallory	Louise Platt
Hatfield	John Carradine
Gatewood	Berton Churchill
Lt. Blanchard	Tim Holt
Chris	Chris Martin
Yakima	Elvira Rios
Billy Pickett	Francis Ford
Mrs. Pickett	Marga Daighton
Luke Plummer	Joseph Rickson
Ike Plummer	Vester Pegg
Hank Plummer	Tom Tyler

Further Reading

Anobile, Richard J., ed. *John Ford's Stagecoach*. New York: Universe Books, 1975.

Fenin, George N. and William K. Everson. *The Western: From Silents to the Seventies*. New York: Grossman, 1973.

Ford, John and Dudley Nichols. *Stagecoach* [filmscript]. New York: Frederick Ungar, 1985.

McBride, Joseph and Michael Wilmington. *John Ford*. London: Secker and Warburg, 1974.

Place, J. A. *The Western Films of John Ford*. Secaucus, N. J.: Citadel Press, 1974.

Schatz, Thomas. *Hollywood Genres: Formulas, Filmmaking, and the Studio System*. Philadelphia: Temple University Press, 1981.

Solomon, Stanley J. *Beyond Formula: American Film Genres*. New York: Harcourt Brace Jovanovich, Inc., 1976.

Wright, Will. *Six Guns and Society: A Structural Study of the Western*. Berkeley: University of California Press, 1975.

Fellini Satyricon

Following the release of his first color film, *Juliet of the Spirits* (1965), Federico Fellini found himself beset with creative difficulties. For three years he struggled with a new project, *The Voyage of G. Mastorna*. Frustrated with his work and involved in litigation over the casting of the film, Fellini fell ill and entered a hospital. His recovery was slow. When he was released he accepted an assignment for a short film, *Toby Dammit*, based on a story by Edgar Allan Poe, which was released as part of a trilogy entitled *Tales of Mystery* (1968). For his next major project he turned to another adaptation, the *Satyricon* of Petronius, a work that had been "a constant and mysterious challenge."[3] for Fellini since he first read it as a schoolboy. Although Fellini chose to adapt the work of someone else at this stage of his career, he made that work an intensely personal statement of his own predicament.

While filming the *Satyricon*, Fellini made a second short film, *Fellini: A Director's Notebook*, in which he took stock of his career and recorded his preparation for the *Satyricon*. This work sheds light on Fellini's creative process and demonstrates the personal importance of the *Satyricon* at this point in his career. For Fellini transforms the *Satyricon* into (among other things) an allegory of the artist's search for wholeness. In spite of its literary origins, the film is as personal a work as 8½.

---

[3]Federico Fellini, "Preface," in *Fellini's Satyricon*, ed. Dario Zanelli, trans. Eugene Walter and John Matthews (New York: Ballantine Books, 1970), p. 43.

One can easily see why Petronius' brilliant satyric portrait of ancient Rome appealed to Fellini, who himself had dissected modern Roman society in *La Dolce Vita* (1959). The *Satyricon* resembles a picaresque novel, with its episodic plot and emphasis on external occurrences as catalysts for change rather than any internal development of the main character. In the existing fragments of this work, we follow the sexual adventures of Encolpius, a young student, as he passes from one bizarre and fascinating situation to another, while encountering an extraordinary range of characters. Fellini has noted the parallels between Encolpius and the hippies who flocked to the Spanish Steps in Rome during the sixties, and thus, the story has contemporary relevance for him as well. Moreover, he has often used an episodic form for his own creations.

The fragmentary state of Petronius's work presents major problems for both translator and filmmaker. Episodes have been lost, and many of the remaining sections are incomplete. In his interview with Alberto Moravia, Fellini commented on the fragmentary nature of the work:

> The *Satyricon* is mysterious first and foremost because it is fragmentary. But its fragmentariness is, in a certain sense, symbolic—of the general fragmentariness of the ancient world as it appears to us today. This is the real mystery of the book and of the world represented in it. Like an unknown landscape wrapped in a thick mist that clears now here, now there, and always only for a short time.[4]

Fellini clearly values the fragmentary condition of Petronius' work, and he could easily have added that its "fragmentariness" is symbolic of the modern world as well. At the conclusion of T. S. Eliot's poem, *The Waste Land*, a work that takes as its epigraph lines from the *Satyricon*, the speaker notes: "These fragments I have shored against my ruins." *The Waste Land* is a poem composed of fragments—both personal and literary—and they aptly mirror the chaos of the contemporary world. Like Ezra Pound before and Fellini after him, T. S. Eliot respects the beauty and integrity of the fragment. Indeed, in the hands of Pound, Eliot, and others, fragmentation became a principal characteristic of modern literature.

However, a literary work in fragments can be more easily comprehended than a comparable cinematic work. To his fine translation of the *Satyricon*, William Arrowsmith adds a lengthy introduction and explanatory footnotes. In addition, to suggest continuity, Arrowsmith includes his own titles for the fragments. All this renders the text more accessible to the modern reader. Even *The Waste Land*, when published for the first time in book form, was accompanied by footnotes. But a filmmaker cannot easily present explanatory material in this way, and if the film appears to be a series of disconnected fragments, viewers will be dismayed and confused. Fellini's solutions to this dilemma are intriguing.

The world of Petronius is both historically distant and, as Fellini ob-

---

[4]Alberto Moravia and Federico Fellini, "Documentary of a Dream: A Dialogue between Alberto Moravia and Federico Fellini," in *Fellini's Satyricon*, p. 25.

served, strangely relevant. In recreating that world, Fellini has emphasized its timeless nature. Most of the film was shot within the studios of Cinecittà, and quasi-historical reconstructions coexist with futuristic science fiction sets. The combination of remote past and distant future creates an alien world with which we have no direct identification. As Fellini noted in his interview with Moravia:

> In the film everything is invented: faces, gestures, situations, surroundings, objects. To obtain this result I have entrusted myself to the inflamed and impassioned dimension of imagination. But then I have had to objectify the fruit of that imaginative operation and detach myself entirely from it in order to be able to explore it afresh both intact and unrecognizable. The same thing happens with dreams. They contain things that belong to us deeply, through which we express ourselves, but in the light of day the only cognitive relationship we can have with them is of an intellectual, conceptual kind. That is why dreams seem to our conscious selves so fugitive, alien, and incomprehensible. So in order to give this film this feeling of alienation, I have adopted a dream language, a figurative cipher which will have the allusiveness and ineffability of a dream.[5]

One experiences *Fellini Satyricon* as a dream: vague, remote, and yet clearly recognizable. The characters speak a babel of tongues, some identifiable (Latin, Italian, French, German), others mere chatter, like the speech of the woman at the villa of the suicides. Communication occurs equally through gestures whose meaning can only be inferred, and then with difficulty. Faces, encrusted with makeup, stare at the viewer like static figures on a peeling fresco, unaware of the action taking place around them. People play on musical instruments that bear no relationship to any we know, and in general perform in strange and unfamiliar ways. Transitions between scenes are abrupt and disjointed. At one point Encolpius and Eumolpus fall asleep in a field: Encolpius awakens in another place and time and looks up to see Ascyltus and Giton above him. Has he been dreaming? Or have we?

Coexisting with our feelings of estrangement and dislocation is a strange sense of unity. Fellini creates this unity through visual and aural repetitions, of which we are only dimly aware. Minor characters, differently attired and differently made up, reappear in one scene after another. Early in the film, a melody is played on an unrecognizable instrument as Encolpius and Giton enter the apartment house. Later, on board ship, Giton plays and sings this song and later still, at the villa of the suicides, the black girl sings it. The melody is again played at the end of the film. Such visual and aural motifs create a subconscious unity within the world of the film. As Fellini noted:

> Everything will be disconnected, fragmentary. And at the same time mysteriously homogenous. Every detail will stand out on its own account, isolated, dilated, absurd, monstrous—as in dreams.[6]

---

[5]Ibid., p. 26.
[6]Ibid., p. 27.

In addition to the disorientation created cinematically, the theme of fragmentation develops through a number of episodes: through the severed bodies (arms, head); through the collapse of the apartment building; through the fragmented works of art (statues, mosaics, frescos) on display throughout the film. Fragmentation functions in a larger sense as well, for Fellini has made it symbolic of the situation of Encolpius, his protagonist.

Two anecdotes are relevant here. Before making the film, Fellini visited Professor Ettore Paratore, an expert on Petronius, who explained to Fellini that "Encolpius and Eumolpus were the two faces of the author Petronius, alike even in their names."[7] And later, during the filming, Fellini's general manager, Enzo Provenzale, noted: "All these faces he [Fellini] has put in this world, he discovered himself; and in them he finds himself. They are fragments of himself."[8]

As we have seen, Fellini turned to this project at a time of artistic difficulty for him, and the fragmented state of Petronius' work is symbolic of his own predicament. The faces in the film are indeed "fragments of himself."

Fellini Satyricon. Ascyltus and Encolpius: Two aspects of single psyche?

[7]Bernardo Zapponi, "The Strange Journey," in *Fellini's Satyricon*, p. 35.
[8]Eileen Lanouette Hughes, *On the Set of Fellini Satyricon* (New York: William Morrow and Co., 1971), p. 66.

Fellini Satyricon. Eumolpus amid the fragments of the past.

Fellini identifies with Encolpius and, like Petronius, chronicles Encolpius' relationships with Giton, Ascyltus, and Eumolpus. However, Fellini differs from Petronius in making these three characters aspects of Encolpius' psyche. As he assimilates what these characters represent and then discards them, Encolpius must progress from dependence upon them to independence from them. Like the work of Petronius, Fellini's film is the story of a journey, but the journey, for Encolpius as for Fellini, is one from fragmentation to wholeness, from the darkness and confinement of the opening shots to the expansive vistas with which the film closes.

The film opens with a visual synecdoche: the shadow of Encolpius cast on a wall covered with graffiti. Encolpius declaims against Ascyltus, who has stolen Giton from him. Without Giton, Encolpius remains incomplete: "Giton. . . . I can't share you with the others, because you are part of me, you are myself, you are my soul, and my soul belongs to me. . . ."[9] Fellini cuts from a shot of the blond, feminine Encolpius to a shot of Ascyltus, who crawls into view on his hands and knees like an animal. Clearly Fellini conceives of these two as complementary types (one dark and masculine, the other light and feminine), united at this point in their mutual need for Giton.

Encolpius' search for Giton takes him to the theater of Vernaccio, where he must participate in the drama before he can regain Giton. Having done so, Encolpius and Giton turn homeward but soon become lost, and Encolpius must inquire of an old hag if she knows "where we are living." She points

[9]Federico Fellini, "The Screenplay," in *Fellini's Satyricon*, p. 94.

the way, and the doorway leads them past a blood sacrifice and through a subterranean brothel, a scene that strongly evokes Dante's Inferno. Encolpius leads Giton past the many diversions of this scene, until they finally ascend into the courtyard of a futuristic apartment house. Once inside, Encolpius makes love to Giton. The next morning they are disturbed by Ascyltus, who lures Giton away. Facing this loss, Encolpius determines to commit suicide, but the building begins to shake and is demolished by an earthquake. This incident is without basis in Petronius. In one sense, it functions as a metaphor for the state of Encolpius' world, which is collapsing around him. But more importantly, it symbolizes a violent birth for Encolpius. He is thrust out of the city and embarks upon his quest, his rivalry with Ascyltus for Giton having ended.

Fellini cuts directly from the rubble of the apartment house to an art gallery, the tranquil setting for Encolpius' encounter with Eumolpus, the poet. Here, amidst fragments of the past being lovingly preserved and restored, a new life opens up for Encolpius. In Petronius' work, this encounter follows Trimalchio's feast, which Encolpius attends with Ascyltus. Fellini, however, has the wise artist guide Encolpius to the banquet of Trimalchio, where he has his first extended social contact and where he receives exposure to various forms of pictorial art, dramatic art, and storytelling. After this banquet, he and the poet stumble across an arid plain. The poet, believing himself about to die, bequeaths the subjects of his art to Encolpius. Instead of death, sleep overtakes them.

When Encolpius awakens, he finds himself on an unknown shore. Over him stand Ascyltus and Giton. A new stage of his adventures begins, and he and the others are taken on board ship to be enslaved by Lichas. Encolpius' captivity culminates with his symbolic marriage to Lichas (another scene without basis in Petronius' work) on the open deck before what resembles a futuristic radar device. Encolpius is the bridgegroom and Lichas the bride, while Ascyltus and Giton observe with bemused interest. But the marriage is short-lived, for external turmoil (analagous to the earlier earthquake) intervenes. Civil war breaks out with the suicide/murder of the young Emperor. The soldiers of the new Emperor board the ship, behead Lichas, and seize Giton. In one of his few long dissolves, Fellini juxtaposes the head of Lichas sinking into the sea with an armed procession of the new Emperor and his soldiers.

Fellini cuts from the noise and turmoil of this procession to a scene more tranquil even than the art gallery, the villa of the cultivated patrician family. Aware of the imminent arrival of the new Emperor and his soldiers, the master and his wife liberate their slaves and send their young children to safety. Once alone, the husband slashes his wrists (in homage to Petronius, whose self-inflicted death occurred by the same means), while the wife mutters the opening lines from the Emperor Hadrian's address to his soul before taking her own life.

These simultaneous events have an important bearing on the development of Encolpius. Through his marriage, he has eliminated the need for Gi-

Fellini Satyricon. The "marriage" of Encolpius against a futuristic backdrop.

ton, who disappears at this point. Moreover, the death of the parents symbolically liberates him for his first heterosexual experience, which occurs at their villa. Significantly, he shares this experience with Ascyltus, whom he must still cast off before he can achieve wholeness.

The next crisis for Encolpius occurs in the labyrinth where he confronts the minotaur. Encolpius accepts his physical limitations and pleads for mercy, which the minotaur willingly grants him. Encolpius is acknowledged as a poet by the proconsul and given his Ariadne, with whom he unsuccessfully attempts to copulate before a large crowd of spectators. He suffers a public humiliation, similar in kind to the earlier humiliations of Vernaccio and Eumolpus. Impotency is a frequent metaphor for the condition of an artist unable to create, and the proconsul links the two in his speech to Encolpius:

> You're a cultivated young man; a poet, from what they tell me. Certainly you have shown scant ability with the sword; I suppose you show greater dexterity in maneuvering a pen; let us hope so.[10]

Among those who witness the sexual failure of Encolpius are Ascyltus and Eumolpus, whose powers he now needs. He follows them to the Garden of Delights, where Eumolpus is ruler, but the varied forms of enticement there fail to help him. Encolpius can be cured only by entering the world of myth and magic, resources without which the creative artist cannot function.

Two tales are narrated within *Fellini Satyricon*, the story of the widow of Ephesus and the story of Oenothea. A guest at Trimalchio's banquet and mock funeral tells the first of these, and as he begins his narration, Fellini cuts directly to a dramatization of the story. A beautiful young widow ceases to mourn the death of her husband and accepts a new lover in his place, finally sacrificing the corpse of her husband so that her lover can live. Her actions produce a change in her pigmentation from pallid to warm fleshy hues.[11] The meaning of this is not lost on Encolpius, for it foreshadows the conclusion of the film: his rejection of the dead weight of the past and his acceptance of the present and future. When the story concludes, we realize that it is being enacted before Trimalchio's tomb, as if to eradicate the separation of art and life and to encourage the audience to follow the widow's example.

The story of Oenothea, narrated by an old man at the Garden, more closely resembles primitive myths. Oenothea had humiliated a wizard in love with her, and as a revenge he deprived the land of fire. When the villagers ask him where fire can be found, he directs them to Oenothea's loins. In an extraordinary scene, the villagers bring bundles of faggots and place them between the outstretched legs of Oenothea, who is lying on her back. The sticks immediately ignite. Rarely has primitive magic been more convincingly depicted on the screen.

Encolpius, however, must do more than merely implement the lesson of the tale; he must actually participate in the legend. To do this, he and Ascyltus are ferried across a river by a sinister boatman, a passage with strong mythological overtones. After landing on the island of Oenothea, they witness a large imitation fish being carried aloft in a fertility ritual. Then Encolpius leaves Ascyltus to seek Oenothea.

In his own encounter with Oenothea, Encolpius observes her metamorphosis before his eyes from a beautiful seductress to a figure of death to a

---

[10]Ibid., p. 237.

[11]Stephen Snyder, "Color, Growth and Evolution in *Fellini Satyricon*," in *Federico Fellini: Essays in Criticism*, ed. Peter Bondanella (New York: Oxford University Press, 1978), p. 168.

mammoth earth mother, the figure with whom he must finally have inter-
course. Significantly, Encolpius' achievement of potency occurs at exactly
the moment when Ascyltus is wounded in combat with the boatman who had
ferried them to the island, a wound that leads to his death. At the same time,
Eumolpus dies in another location. Fellini's juxtaposition of these two deaths
with Encolpius' successful copulation suggests that his integration is complete. He has incorporated the masculine physicality of Ascyltus and the creative powers of Eumolpus, and he can now face the sea and search for the
unknown. The contrast between the aged men remaining behind, devouring
the corpse of Eumolpus, and the youthful figures moving exuberantly toward
the sea could hardly be more telling. Finally, we see nothing but the limitless
horizon, as we hear the voice of Encolpius telling of his travels:

> I decided to go with them. The ship was carrying a cargo of luxury goods
> and slaves. We anchored off ports unknown to me. . . . I heard for the
> first time the names of Keliscia . . . Rectis. . . . On an island covered by
> high sweet-scented grasses a young Greek introduced himself and told me
> that in the year. . . .[12]

Before the voice trails off, Fellini cuts to a close-up of Encolpius' face: As we
study the face, it freezes and becomes a painted fresco on a wall. Fellini pulls
back the camera and we see other figures from the film, painted on fragments
of walls and buildings, separated only by stretches of sand. Life and movement are gone: Nothing remains but a crumbling memorial of visual fragments from the past. Having achieved unity within his film, Fellini reminds
us once again that it is composed of fragments. Like the speaker at the end
of *The Waste Land*, Fellini can say: "These fragments I have shored against
my ruins."

While in the process of making his film, Fellini told an interviewer that
he wanted to:

> take all of the narrative sequences of traditional cinema out of the story,
> to give it an unremitting harshness. Its sequences should be there for one
> to contemplate: not to involve oneself with them. The meaning should
> become apparent only at the end: as it happens to whoever looks at a bas-
> relief carving, starting from any given point, at random. Only after look-
> ing at the whole sequence does he succeed in giving a meaning to the
> actions he saw sculptured in stone.[13]

It is indeed difficult for a viewer to become involved in this film, for
Fellini continually creates a sense of estrangement and alienation. As a result,
some critics have assumed that Fellini was less involved in this project than
in his earlier films. But, as we have seen, Fellini has preserved the fragmentary nature of his source and transformed it into a central theme in his work.
His film becomes an allegory of a man's search for wholeness and creativity
in stifling and chaotic times remarkably like our own.

[12]"The Screenplay," p. 274.
[13]Dario Zanelli, "From the Planet Rome," in *Fellini's Satyricon*, p. 20.

Fellini Satyricon

Production Credits

Director	Federico Fellini
Producer	Alberto Grimaldi
Screenplay by	Federico Fellini, Bernardino Zapponi
Based on ''Satyricon'' by	Petronius
Director of Photography	Giuseppe Rotunno
Film Editor	Ruggero Mastroianni
Sets by	Danilo Donati
Music by	Nino Rota

Italy. 1969. 120 minutes. Color.

Cast

Encolpius	Martin Potter
Ascyltus	Hiram Keller
Giton	Max Born
Trimalchio	Mario Romagnoli
Vernacchio	Fanfulla
Robber	Gordon Mitchell
Lichas	Alain Cuny
Suicide husband	Joseph Wheeler
Oenothea	Donyale Luna
Eumolpus	Salvo Randone
Suicide wife	Lucia Bosè
Tryphaena	Capucine
Fortunata	Magali Noël
Slave girl	Hylette Adolphe
Hermaphrodite	Pasquale Baldassarre
Minotaur	Luigi Montefiori
Ferryman	Gennaro Sabatino

Further Reading

Bondanella, Peter, ed. *Federico Fellini: Essays in Criticism.* New York: Oxford University Press, 1978.

Dick, Bernard F. "Adaptation as Archaeology." In *Modern European Filmmakers and the Art of Adaptation.* Eds. Andrew S. Horton and Joan Magretta. New York: Frederick Ungar, 1981.

Fellini, Federico. *Fellini's Satyricon* [filmscript]. Ed. Dario Zanelli; tr. Eugene Walter and John Matthews. New York: Ballantine Books, 1970.

Harcourt, Peter. *Six European Directors: Essays on the Meaning of Film Style.* Harmondsworth, England: Penguin Books, 1974.

Hughes, Eileen Lanouette. *On the Set of Fellini Satyricon: A Behind-the-Scenes Diary.* New York: William Morrow and Co., 1971.

Kauffmann, Stanley. *"Fellini Satyricon."* In *Figures of Light: Film Criticism and Comment.* New York: Harper & Row, 1971.

O'Mealy, Joseph. *"Fellini Satyricon:* A Structural Analysis." *Film Heritage,* 6, No. 4 (Summer 1971), 25–29.

Solomon, Stanley J. *The Classic Cinema: Essays in Criticism.* New York: Harcourt Brace Jovanovich, Inc., 1973.

9

Time

Introduction

Our experiences with books, plays, and films occur in time, but the measure of control we have over that time differs considerably with each medium. We usually read in private, at a rate determined by many factors (age, education, time of day, interest, and so forth). We all read at different speeds, and no two readers complete a book in the same period. A book may be put down and resumed later or perhaps laid aside permanently. Films and plays, however, are experienced in the same period of time by all viewers, unless, of course, they come late or leave early. The length of a dramatic performance may vary somewhat from one night to the next, but the length of a film remains constant. In contrast to novels and short stories, drama and film are primarily public experiences over which the individual spectator exerts little or no control.

Time is also an important element within the fictive worlds of these two media. The novel is partly defined as a genre by its sense of time, a feature that distinguishes it from the timeless worlds of fable and myth. Characters in a novel can grow, change, and mature, and even if they remain the same they do so over a period of time. This development is often presented chronologically, although it need not be. In *Tristram Shandy* (1749–67), for example, the novel concludes at a point before the birth of the hero, whose "life and adventures" the novel has related. But although *Tristram Shandy* jumps from one time period to another, the reader can deduce a rigorous time scheme underlining the events. The novelist has simply chosen not to present these events in chronological order to achieve certain effects. This method has been effectively discussed by Ford Madox Ford in his memoir of Joseph Conrad. Ford writes,

> We agreed that the general effect of a novel must be the general effect that life makes on mankind. A novel must therefore not be a narration, a report. Life does not say to you: In 1914 my next-door neighbour, Mr. Slack, erected a greenhouse and painted it with Cox's aluminum paint. . . . If you think about the matter you remember, in various unordered pictures, how one day Mr. Slack appeared in his garden and contemplated the wall of his house. You will then try to remember the year of that occurrence and you will fix it as August, 1914, because having had the foresight to bear the municipal stock of the City of Liège you were able to afford a first-class season ticket for the first time in your life. . . . [1]

Films, like works of literature, need not progress chronologically. As Ford notes, memories often consist of "various unordered pictures" connected by associations within the mind and as such can be rendered visually on film. Films can follow a sequence like that described by Ford, with jumps from one time period to another. Or, within a linear development, films can employ the literary techniques of flashback or flash-forward, where the action is narrated in chronological order but in a past or future time. Shifts in time can be indicated easily and economically in a work of literature by a temporal marker ("five years ago," "yesterday," "tomorrow") and the corresponding tense (e.g., "I ran," "I am running," and "I shall run"). These distinctions help us to situate the action and understand its temporal context. Film has none of these markers, however. A shot of a man running has no tense in itself. The shot is simply of a man running, and the tense of that action can be determined only by relationships created between this shot and the rest of the film, or by verbal means. Whereas film has greater inherent specificity than literature in terms of detail, it has no inherent specificity in terms of tense.

Another important manipulation of time is the attempt to depict simultaneity of action. In any given time period, many things are occurring at once. With depth of focus, a filmmaker can show several events taking place simultaneously within a given shot, as Orson Welles often does in *Citizen Kane*. The challenge is greater when actions are occurring in different places. Writers or directors can relate activities only sequentially, whether in words or pictures, and yet they must give the impression of simultaneity. At one point, in *Tristram Shandy*, the narrator states:

> In this attitude I am determined to let her [his mother] stand for five minutes: till I bring up the affairs in the kitchen to the same period.

[1]Ford Madox Ford, Joseph Conrad: *A Personal Remembrance* (Boston: Little, Brown and Co., 1924), pp. 192–3.

The narrator's self-conscious presentation is humorous, and we accept it as a literary convention that accomplishes its aims. Later authors, like Charles Dickens, attempt to present simultaneity more naturally, by shifting back and forth from one location to another. It is from Dickens, Sergei Eisenstein has argued, that D. W. Griffith learned the art of parallel editing in film, and he cites examples from *Oliver Twist* to support his assertion.[2] In its simplest form, parallel editing has become something of a cliché. How many times have we seen settlers under attack by Indians, with the Cavalry simultaneously riding to the besieged fort? The director cuts from one scene to the other, usually with briefer and briefer shots. This, too, is a convention, but most of us accept the illusion of simultaneity it presents because of our emotional involvement.

Such editing is frequently used in suspense and adventure films. Time appears to speed up, and we move to the edges of our seats. Here yet another sense of time is involved—the difference between clock time and our psychological sense of duration. We experience this difference constantly in our daily lives: Time spent with some people seems to pass very quickly while with others it drags on and on. Characters within a fictitious work (literature or film) also experience this phenomenon, as do readers and spectators. A skillful novelist or filmmaker can shape our psychological sense of duration so that time appears to move slowly or quickly. As the authors of *The Cinema as Art* put it:

> In the real world, our mental state determines the way time goes. In the cinema, it is the other way round: the way time goes on the screen will affect our mental state. By making time go quickly—using quick cutting, loud or lively music, dynamic composition of the images, and rapid action (comic or thrilling)—the filmmaker can induce in the audience moods of exhilaration and laughter for a comedy, excitement for an adventure film, horror and dismay for a tragedy. By making time go slowly—depicting quiet uneventful scenes, using soft, soothing music, static composition of images and slow cutting—he can induce moods of lyricism, contentment, sadness, nostalgia, or grief; the exact mood evoked will depend largely on the context and nature of the film.[3]

Narrative films also tell a story that usually covers more time than the length of the film. And here we have a situation unique to film: screen time (the actual length of the film) can be equal to narrative time (the actual time covered by the story). The narrative time of Alfred Hitchcock's *Rope* (one hour and forty-five minutes) corresponds exactly to the screen time. Moreover, the narrative time of the film begins at 7:30 P.M., so that the narrative time could have corresponded to the actual viewing time of the spectators.

[2]Sergei Eisenstein, "Dickens, Griffith, and the Film Today," *Film Form,* translated and edited by Jay Leyda (New York: The World Publishing Co., 1964), pp. 218–224.
[3]Ralph Stephenson and J. R. Debrix, *The Cinema as Art* (Maryland: Penguin Books, 1970), p. 110.

This could also be true with the stage production of a play, but never with a novel or short story, where the reading times differ from one person to another.

Filmmakers have an additional advantage: They can manipulate time mechanically. Time can be accelerated (through fast motion), decelerated (through slow motion), or stopped altogether (through a freeze frame). The combination of chronological, psychological, and mechanical manipulations of time provides the filmmaker with exhilarating challenges.

Additional Recommended Films

Don't Look Now (1972), directed by Nicholas Roeg, based on the short story by
Daphne du Maurier. The short story is available in paperback.
The Magnificent Ambersons (1942), directed by Orson Welles, based on the novel by
Booth Tarkington. The novel is available in paperback.
Little Big Man (1970), directed by Arthur Penn, based on the novel by Thomas Berger.
The novel is available in paperback.

See Also:

The Member of the Wedding (Chapter 3)
A Doll's House (Chapter 3)
Jules and Jim (Chapter 4)
The Collector (Chapter 5)
The Stranger (Chapter 6)
The Rocking-Horse Winner (Chapter 8)
Fellini Satyricon (Chapter 8)

 # An Occurrence at Owl Creek Bridge

Ambrose Bierce carefully chose the title for his short story to emphasize the insignificance and obscurity of his subject. The outlines of the story are quite simple: During the Civil War, a Southerner is caught trying to sabotage a remote bridge and is hanged for punishment. However, the event is considerably less important than the thought processes it occasions, for at the moment of his death the convicted man experiences an extended sense of time, during which he imagines himself escaping to his wife and home. So skillfully does Bierce blend his protagonist's fantasies with the actual events of the story that the absorbed reader can easily confuse the two.

The plot of Bierce's tale is much more complex than the simple story outlined above. The author has divided the story into three sections and rearranged the chronology of events in order to produce a powerful effect on the reader. Bierce employs an omniscient third-person narrator throughout, but the narrator is sometimes quite impersonal, at other times rather intrusive. These shifts from objectivity to subjectivity are often subtle; they indicate the transition from reality to fantasy in the mind of the protagonist.

The story begins in an impersonal fashion, almost like a piece of military reportage. Although details are described thoroughly, important information is deliberately withheld (such as the protagonist's name) in order to create more interest in him, to heighten our sense of detachment, and to make the presentation more objective. The scene is nearly static.

The first break in the objective presentation occurs in the second paragraph, with the personification of death. In the third paragraph the protagonist's physical appearance is described, and here too we become aware of the presence of a narrator as he creates a favorable picture of the protagonist: The protagonist has "good" features and a "kindly expression." "Evidently this was no vulgar assassin," he notes. We are gradually moving away from the objectivity of the opening.

Action is described for the first time in the next paragraph, as the final arrangements for the hanging are completed. Then, suddenly, we enter the consciousness of the protagonist: Bierce writes, "The arrangement commended itself to his judgment as simple and effective." As we continue reading, we realize that we are sharing the protagonist's perceptions. In the opening sentence of the story, the protagonist looked down into "the swift water twenty feet below"; now he lets "his gaze wander to the swirling water of the stream racing madly beneath his feet." Bierce's choice of language here reflects the shift from objective to subjective presentation. As the protagonist stares downward, a strange thing happens: His sense of time begins to change. He watches a piece of driftwood in the stream, and instead of going quickly it appears to move slowly, despite the "racing" movement of the water. He closes his eyes to think and is disturbed by a regular ticking that grows slower and slower as it increases in volume. While this occurs, he opens his eyes, looks down at the water, and then fantasizes about escaping. The reader can easily share and sympathize with his fantasy. Finally, we are told. "The Sergeant stepped aside." No more is said, but we know the results: The noose tightens as the Southern planter plunges downward.

The first part of the story raises more questions than it answers. We learn the fate of the protagonist (hanging), and we know in considerable detail how and where this occurs. But we do not know specifically who he is or why he is there. These questions are answered only in the second section of the story: We discover the protagonist's name and more details about his occupation and background. The point of view here is objective, but the diction reflects the attitudes of Peyton Farquhar: The Southern army is "gallant," they had fought a "disastrous" campaign, Farquhar "chafed under the inglorious restraint." Every attempt is made to have us identify more closely with Farquhar. Although this section does not present Farquhar's thoughts, it prepares us for the conclusion of Bierce's tale in another way: It has a surprise ending. Now we begin to understand the organization of Bierce's plot: If we reverse the first two sections (and place them in their proper chronological order), the ending ceases to be a surprise and the descriptive passages in the first part appear labored. In their present order, they engage the reader's interest and prefigure the development of the story as a whole.

Thus, the attentive reader should begin the third part prepared for the possibilities the story holds. The section takes up where the first part ended, with Farquhar's fall through the bridge. The rope tightens on his neck, and he swings "through unthinkable arcs of oscillation, like a vast pendulum." The prevalence of verbs of uncertainty in this paragraph (*seem* and *appear*), as well as the significantly large number of tropes, signal the shift to a totally subjective vision.

The subjective vision is, of course, Farquhar's fantasy of escape. Farquhar stands outside himself and observes his actions, as in a dream; he lunges up out of the water like a newborn child, his senses "preternaturally keen and alert." By the end of this section, as he wanders homeward "through so wild a region," there can be little doubt that he is living in a purely illusory world.

But Bierce gives us one final, unavoidable clue: in the penultimate paragraph, he shifts to the use of the historical present:

> He [Farquhar] stands at the gate of his own home . . . As he pushes open the gate and passes up the wide white walk, he sees a flutter of female garments . . .

Here, Farquhar's fantasy is nearly realized: His wife approaches him, and he reaches out for the safety of her arms. But darkness and silence suddenly engulf him, and the story ends with a return to the terse, objective style of the opening section.

The conclusion of Bierce's tale comes as a surprise only to the inattentive reader, for through structural and verbal means Bierce has prepared the reader for the shift from reality to illusion and back to reality. The story provides a challenge to the filmmaker, who must find visual equivalents for these clues as well as a satisfactory way of depicting Farquhar's vision.

Instead of expanding Bierce's story to the length of a feature film, Robert Enrico preserved the limitations of his source in a short film, which has been widely acclaimed.[4] The film begins in an objective manner, which captures the tone of Bierce's opening. The first shot is of a sign, nailed on an old tree:

> ORDER. Any Civilian caught interfering with the railroad bridges, tunnels, or trains will be SUMMARILY HANGED. April 4, 1862.

This is all that Enrico has retained of part two of Bierce's story: the explanation of the crime and an identification of the time period. Then Enrico cuts to a high-angle long establishing shot of the bridge and moves toward the civil-

---

[4]The film received an Academy Award in 1963.

ian about to be hanged. By the time we see the condemned man, we know his crime and his punishment but not who he is. In fact, his name is mentioned only once during the film—by the soldier whose voice and movements have been slowed down.

A number of things distinguish the realistic opening scenes of Enrico's film from the later scenes of the imagined escape: the lighting, the sound, the background, and the absence of visual and aural distortions. Like Bierce, Enrico gives his viewers ample, though subtle, indications of how to evaluate what they are viewing. The opening scenes are shot in the light of dawn, so that the bridge, setting, and soldiers appear in sharp clarity. Sounds are entirely natural but are magnified considerably to indicate the subjective (and already heightened) sense of hearing of the protagonist. There is an absence of music. The viewer is struck by the mechanical nature of the ceremony, where the "code of military etiquette" clearly prevails. As Enrico noted in an interview:

> . . . I purposefully shot all the frames in this section in a very stylized way, to be in keeping with the style of the bridge itself. The people move about on it almost like puppets. The entire hanging proceeds in the fashion of an inexorable machine impossible to deter. The passage of time is expressed solely in gestures, in the deployment of officers and soldiers, up to the moment when the order is given and the plank passes dizzyingly out of the frame into the void. All this had to be expressed mathematically and not lyrically or poetically. Poetry and lyricism were to be used in the portion of the film which followed.[5]

The bleakness of the setting is due in part to the fact that this portion of the film was shot at the end of winter. The fantasy portions were shot two weeks later, when leaves and buds had begun to appear.

Although the hanging sequence is primarily objective, there are some moments of subjectivity that prepare us for the fantasy to follow. The exaggerated natural sounds are clearly subjective. There is also some use of subjective camera (as when the protagonist views the piece of driftwood) as well as the short fantasy in which he sees his wife and home. Here, as in the story, the condemned man is disturbed by the insistent ticking of his watch. Enrico has added an effective bit of action: The protagonist's vision of wife and home is interrupted by the strident tones of the captain's voice, ordering one of the soldiers to take his watch. As the gold watch and chain are removed, the doomed man is literally and figuratively deprived of time. The viewer is also prepared for the temporal distortions that follow.

The rope breaks and the man falls into the river. His time under water seems excessively long, so that virtually all spectators are gasping for breath before he surfaces. He then stares in amazement at the forest, whose most

---

minute details appear in great clarity, down to the veins on a blade of grass. The first music in the film, the song "A Livin' Man," expresses his joy at being alive. The sequence closes ominously, with an extreme close-up of a fly caught in the web of a spider. Then the man turns and views the bridge. The soldiers move in slow motion across the bridge (as had his wife in his earlier vision). Sound, too, is initially slowed down, and then both the commands and the movements come up to normal speed. The men prepare to fire, and his flight begins.

Although the internal rhythm is rapid during the shots of the final flight, Enrico successfully conveys the feeling that his protagonist is going nowhere. He is shown swimming first in one direction, then another. At one point, Enrico employs a circular pan shot, filmed by having the man run in a circle around the panning camera. Although he appears to be moving forward, we sense that he is not. A similar effect is achieved at the conclusion, when he runs to embrace his wife. Enrico uses a telephoto lens, which compresses the space and conveys the impression that the man is running on a treadmill.

The song, "A Livin' Man," with which the fantasy sequence began, recurs at the end of the film, as the man reaches home and approaches his wife. Here, as one critic has observed, Enrico uses "the rhythm of his music to create an editing pattern for the sequence."[6] The rhythms make a hypnotic vision of repeated actions, which momentarily lull the viewer. Then, as Farquhar calls his wife's name, the music stops. The sudden shock of the hanging is abrupt. Enrico follows it with a recapitulation, in reverse order, of the opening shots of the film. The hanged man and his setting are shown with objectivity. Time has returned to normal.

Enrico succeeds in convincingly portraying the final instant of a man's life, an instant in which he seems to live out his fantasy of flight. So strongly do most viewers share the desire of the condemned man to escape that they overlook all evidence pointing to the subjective nature of this vision. The concluding shock brings us back to reality and underscores the impermanence of life and the evanescence of dreams.

An Occurrence at Owl Creek Bridge

Production Credits

Director	Robert Enrico
Producers	Marcel Ichac, Paul de Roubaix
Screenplay by	Robert Enrico
Based on the short story by	Ambrose Bierce
Director of Photography	Jean Bobbety

[6]David Coynik, *Film: Real to Reel* (Evanston, Ill.: McDougal, Littell and Co., 1976), p. 112.

Film Editors	Robert Enrico, Denise de Casabianca
Music by	Henri Lanoe

France. 1962. 27 minutes. Black and white.

Cast

Peyton Farquhar	Roger Jacquet
Abby	Anne Cornally

Further Reading

Barrett, Gerald R. and Thomas L. Erskine. *From Fiction to Film: Ambrose Bierce's "An Occurrence at Owl Creek Bridge."* Encino, California: Dickenson Publishing Co., Inc., 1973.

Coynik, David. *Film: Real to Reel*. Evanston, Ill.: McDougal, Littell and Co., 1976.

Marcus, Fred H. *Film and Literature: Contrasts in Media*. Scranton, London, Toronto: Chandler Publishing Co., 1971.

_____. *Short Story/Short Film*. Englewood Cliffs, N.J. Prentice-Hall, 1977.

Ruchti, Ulrich and Sybil Taylor. *Story Into Film*. New York: Dell Publishing Co., Inc., 1978.

Schreivogel, Paul. *An Occurrence at Owl Creek Bridge: A Visual Study*. Dayton, Ohio: Pflaum, 1969.

An Occurrence at Owl Creek Bridge

I

A man stood upon a railroad bridge in northern Alabama, looking down into the swift water twenty feet below. The man's hands were behind his back, the wrists bound with a cord. A rope closely encircled his neck. It was attached to a stout cross-timber above his head and the slack fell to the level of his knees. Some loose boards laid upon the sleepers supporting the metals of the railway supplied a footing for him and his executioners—two private soldiers of the Federal army, directed by a sergeant who in civil life may have been a deputy sheriff. At a short remove upon the same temporary platform was an officer in the uniform of his rank, armed. He was a captain. A sentinel at each end of the bridge stood with his rifle in the position known as "support," that is to say, vertical in front of the left shoulder, the hammer resting on the forearm thrown straight across the chest—a formal and unnatural position, enforcing an erect carriage of the body. It did not appear to be the duty of these two men to know what was occurring at the centre of the bridge; they merely blockaded the two ends of the foot planking that traversed it.

Beyond one of the sentinels nobody was in sight; the railroad ran straight away into a forest for a hundred yards, then, curving, was lost to view. Doubtless there was an outpost farther along. The other bank of the stream was open ground—a gentle acclivity topped with a stockade of vertical tree trunks, loopholed for rifles, with a single embrasure through which protruded the muzzle of a brass cannon commanding the bridge. Midway of the slope between bridge and fort were the spectators—a single company of infantry in line, at "parade rest," the butts of the rifles on the ground, the barrels inclining slightly backward against the right shoulder, the hands crossed upon the stock. A lieutenant stood at the right of the line, the point of his sword upon the ground, his left hand resting upon his right. Excepting the group of four at the centre of the bridge, not a man moved. The company faced the bridge, staring stonily, motionless. The sentinels, facing the banks of the stream, might have been statues to adorn the bridge. The captain stood with folded arms, silent, observing the work of his subordinates, but making no sign. Death is a dignitary who when he comes announced is to be received with formal manifestations of respect, even by those most familiar with him. In the code of military etiquette silence and fixity are forms of deference.

The man who was engaged in being hanged was apparently about thirty-five years of age. He was a civilian, if one might judge from his habit, which was that of a planter. His features were good—a straight nose, firm mouth, broad forehead, from which his long, dark hair was combed straight back, falling behind his ears to the collar of his well-fitting frock-coat. He wore a mustache and pointed beard, but no whiskers; his eyes were large and dark gray, and had a kindly expression which one would hardly have expected in one whose neck was in the hemp. Evidently this was no vulgar assassin. The liberal military code makes provision for hanging many kinds of persons, and gentlemen are not excluded.

The preparations being complete, the two private soldiers stepped aside and each drew away the plank upon which he had been standing. The sergeant turned to the captain, saluted and placed himself immediately behind that officer, who in turn moved apart one pace. These movements left the condemned man and the sergeant standing on the two ends of the same plank, which spanned three of the cross-ties of the bridge. The end upon which the civilian stood almost, but not quite, reached a fourth. This plank had been held in place by the weight of the captain; it was now held by that of the sergeant. At a signal from the former the latter would step aside, the plank would tilt and the condemned man go down between two ties. The arrangement commended itself to his judgment as simple and effective. His face had not been covered nor his eyes bandaged. He looked a moment at his "unsteadfast footing," then let his gaze wander to the swirling water of the stream racing madly beneath his feet. A piece of dancing driftwood caught his attention and his eyes followed it down the current. How slowly it appeared to move! What a sluggish stream!

He closed his eyes in order to fix his last thoughts upon his wife and children. The water, touched to gold by the early sun, the brooding mists under the banks at some distance down the stream, the fort, the soldiers, the piece of drift—all had distracted him. And now he became conscious of a new disturbance. Striking through the thought of his dear ones was a sound which he could neither ignore nor understand, a sharp, distinct, metallic percussion like the stroke of a blacksmith's hammer upon the anvil; it had the same ringing quality. He wondered what it was, and whether immeasurably distant or near by—it seemed both. Its recurrence was regular, but as slow as the tolling of a death knell. He awaited each stroke with impatience and—he knew not why—apprehension. The intervals of silence grew progressively longer; the delays became maddening. With their greater infrequency the sounds increased in strength and sharpness. They hurt his ear like the thrust of a knife; he feared he would shriek. What he heard was the ticking of his watch.

He unclosed his eyes and saw again the water below him. "If I could free my hands," he thought, "I might throw off the noose and spring into the stream. By diving I could evade the bullets and, swimming vigorously, reach the bank, take to the woods and get away home. My home, thank God, is as yet outside their lines; my wife and little ones are still beyond the invader's farthest advance."

As these thoughts, which have here to be set down in words, were flashed into the doomed man's brain rather than evolved from it the captain nodded to the sergeant. The sergeant stepped aside.

II

Peyton Farquhar was a well-to-do planter, of an old and highly respected Alabama family. Being a slave owner and like other slave owners a politician he was naturally an original secessionist and ardently devoted to the Southern cause. Circumstances of an imperious nature, which it is unnecessary to relate here, had prevented him from taking service with the gallant army that had fought the disastrous campaigns ending with the fall of Corinth, and he chafed under the inglorious restraint, longing for the release of his energies, the larger life of the soldier, the opportunity for distinction. That opportunity, he felt, would come, as it comes to all in war time. Meanwhile he did what he could. No service was too humble for him to perform in aid of the South, no adventure too perilous for him to undertake if consistent with the character of a civilian who was at heart a soldier, and who in good faith and without too much qualification assented to at least a part of the frankly villainous dictum that all is fair in love and war.

One evening while Farquhar and his wife were sitting on a rustic bench near the entrance to his grounds, a gray-clad soldier rode up to the gate and asked for a drink of water. Mrs. Farquhar was only too happy to serve him with her own white hands. While she was fetching the water her husband approached the dusty horseman and inquired eagerly for news from the front.

"The Yanks are repairing the railroads," said the man, "and are getting ready for another advance. They have reached the Owl Creek bridge, put it in order and built a stockade on the north bank. The commandant has issued an order, which is posted everywhere, declaring that any civilian caught interfering with the railroad, its bridges, tunnels or trains will be summarily hanged. I saw the order."

"How far is it to the Owl Creek bridge?" Farquhar asked.

"About thirty miles."

"Is there no force on this side the creek?"

"Only a picket post half a mile out, on the railroad, and a single sentinel at this end of the bridge."

"Suppose a man—a civilian and student of hanging—should elude the picket post and perhaps get the better of the sentinel," said Farquhar, smiling, "what could he accomplish?"

The soldier reflected. "I was there a month ago," he replied. "I observed that the flood of last winter had lodged a great quality of driftwood against the wooden pier at this end of the bridge. It is now dry and would burn like tow."

The lady had now brought the water, which the soldier drank. He thanked her ceremoniously, bowed to her husband and rode away. An hour later, after nightfall, he repassed the plantation, going northward in the direction from which he had come. He was a Federal scout.

III

As Peyton Farquhar fell straight downward through the bridge he lost consciousness and was as one already dead. From this state he was awakened—ages later, it seemed to him—by the pain of a sharp pressure upon his throat, followed by a sense of suffocation. Keen, poignant agonies seemed to shoot from his neck downward through every fibre of his body and limbs. These pains appeared to flash along well-defined lines of ramification and to beat with an inconceivably rapid periodicity. They seemed like streams of pulsating fire heating him to an intolerable temperature. As to his head, he was conscious of nothing but a feeling of fulness—of congestion. These sensations were unaccompanied by thought. The intellectual part of his nature was already effaced; he had power only to feel, and feeling was torment. He was conscious of motion. Encompassed in a luminous cloud, of which he was now merely the fiery heart, without material substance, he swung through unthinkable arcs of oscillation, like a vast pendulum. Then all at once, with terrible suddenness, the light about him shot upward with the noise of a loud plash; a frightful roaring was in his ears, and all was cold and dark. The power of thought was restored; he knew that the rope had broken and he had fallen into the stream. There was no additional strangulation; the noose about his neck was already suffocating him and kept the water from his lungs. To die of hanging at the bottom of a river!—the idea seemed to him ludicrous. He opened his eyes in the darkness and saw above him a gleam of light, but how distant, how inaccessible! He was still sinking, for the light became fainter and fainter until it was a mere glimmer. Then it began to grow and brighten, and he knew that he was rising toward the surface—knew it with reluctance, for he was now very comfortable. "To be hanged and drowned," he thought, "that is not so bad; but I do not wish to be shot. No; I will not be shot; that is not fair."

He was not conscious of an effort, but a sharp pain in his wrist apprised him that he was trying to free his hands. He gave the struggle his attention, as an idler might observe the feat of a juggler, without interest in the outcome. What splendid effort!—what magnificent, what superhuman strength! Ah, that was a fine endeavor! Bravo! The cord fell away; his arms parted and floated upward, the hands dimly seen on each side in the growing light. He watched them with a new interest as first one and then the other pounced upon the noose at his neck. They tore it away and thrust it fiercely aside, its undulations resembling those of a water-snake. "Put it back, put it back!" He thought he shouted these words to his hands, for the undoing of the noose had been succeeded by the direst pang that he had yet experienced. His neck ached horribly; his brain was on fire; his heart, which had been fluttering faintly, gave a great leap, trying to force itself out at his mouth. His whole body was racked and wrenched with an insupportable anguish! But his disobedient hands gave no heed to the command. They beat the water vigorously with quick, downward strokes, forcing him to the surface. He felt his head emerge; his eyes were blinded by the sunlight; his chest expanded convulsively, and with a supreme and drowning agony his lungs engulfed a great draught of air, which instantly he expelled in a shriek!

He was now in full possession of his physical senses. They were, indeed, preternaturally keen and alert. Something in the awful disturbance of his organic system had so exalted and refined them that they made record of things never before perceived. He felt the ripples upon his face and heard their separate sounds as they struck. He looked at the forest on the bank of the stream, saw the individual trees, the leaves and the veining of each leaf—saw the very insects upon them: the locusts, the brilliant-bodied flies, the gray spiders stretching their webs from twig to twig. He noted the prismatic colors in all the dewdrops upon a million blades of grass. The humming of the gnats that danced above the eddies of the stream, the beating of the dragon-flies' wings, the strokes of the water-spiders' legs, like oars which had lifted their boat—all these made audible music. A fish slid along beneath his eyes and he heard the rush of its body parting the water.

He had come to the surface facing down the stream; in a moment the visible world seemed to wheel slowly round, himself the pivotal point, and he saw the bridge, the fort, the soldiers upon the bridge, the captain, the sergeant, the two privates, his executioners. They were in silhouette against the blue sky. They shouted and gesticulated, pointing at him. The captain had drawn his pistol, but did not fire; the others were unarmed. Their movements were grotesque and horrible, their forms gigantic.

Suddenly he heard a sharp report and something struck the water smartly within a few inches of his head, spattering his face with spray. He heard a second report, and saw one of the sentinels with his rifle at his shoulder, a light cloud of blue smoke rising from the muzzle. The man in the water saw the eye of the man on the bridge gazing into his own through the sights of the rifle. He observed that it was a gray eye and remembered having read that gray eyes were keenest, and that all famous markmen had them. Nevertheless, this one had missed.

A counter-swirl had caught Farquhar and turned him half round; he was again looking into the forest on the bank opposite the fort. The sound of a clear, high voice in a monotonous singsong now rang out behind him and came across the water with a distinctness that pierced and subdued all other sounds, even the beating of the ripples in his ears. Although no soldier, he had frequented camps enough to know the dread significance of that deliberate, drawling, aspirated chant; the lieutenant on shore was taking a part in the morning's work. How coldly and pitilessly—with what an even, calm intonation, presaging, and enforcing tranquillity in the men—with what accurately measured intervals fell those cruel words:

"Attention, company! . . . Shoulder arms! . . . Ready! . . . Aim! . . . Fire!"

Farquhar dived—dived as deeply as he could. The water roared in his ears like the voice of Niagara, yet he heard the dulled thunder of the volley and, rising again toward the surface, met shining bits of metal, singularly flattened, oscillating slowly downward. Some of them touched him on the face and hands, then fell away, continuing their descent. One lodged between his collar and neck; it was uncomfortably warm and he snatched it out.

As he rose to the surface, gasping for breath, he saw that he had been a long time under water; he was perceptibly farther down stream—nearer to safety. The soldiers had almost finished reloading; the metal ramrods flashed all at once in the sunshine as they were drawn from the barrels, turned in the air, and thrust into their sockets. The two sentinels fired again, independently and ineffectually.

The hunted man saw all this over his shoulder; he was now swimming vigorously with the current. His brain was as energetic as his arms and legs; he thought with rapidity of lightning.

"The officer," he reasoned, "will not make that martinet's error a second time. It is as easy to dodge a volley as a single shot. He has probably already given the command to fire at will. God help me, I cannot dodge them all!"

An appalling plash within two yards of him was followed by a loud, rushing sound, *diminuendo,* which seemed to travel back through the air to the fort and died in an explosion which stirred the very river to its deeps! A rising sheet of water curved over him, fell down upon him, blinded him, strangled him! The cannon had taken a hand in the game. As he shook his head free from the commotion of the smitten water he heard the deflected shot humming through the air ahead, and in an instant it was cracking and smashing the branches in the forest beyond.

"They will not do that again," he thought; "the next time they will use a charge of grape. I must keep my eye upon the gun; the smoke will apprise me—the report arrives too late; it lags behind the missile. That is a good gun."

Suddenly he felt himself whirled round and round—spinning like a top. The water, the banks, the forests, the now distant bridge, fort and men—all were commingled and blurred. Objects were represented by their colors only; circular horizontal streaks of color—that was all he saw. He had been caught in a vortex and was being whirled on with a velocity of advance and gyration that made him giddy and sick. In a few moments he was flung upon the gravel at the foot of the left bank of the stream—the southern bank—and behind a projecting point which concealed him from his enemies. The sudden arrest of his motion, the abrasion of one of his hands on the gravel, restored him, and he wept with delight. He dug his fingers into the sand, threw it over himself in handfuls and audibly blessed it. It looked like diamonds, rubies, emeralds; he could think of nothing beautiful which it did not resemble. The trees upon the bank were giant garden plants; he noted a definite order in their arrangement, inhaled the fragrance of their blooms. A strange, roseate light shone through the spaces among their trunks and the wind made in their branches the music of æolian harps. He had no wish to perfect his escape—was content to remain in that enchanting spot until retaken.

A whiz and rattle of grapeshot among the branches high above his head roused him from his dream. The baffled cannoneer had fired him a random farewell. He sprang to his feet, rushed up the sloping bank, and plunged into the forest.

All that day he traveled, laying his course by the rounding sun. The forest seemed interminable; nowhere did he discover a break in it, not even a woodman's road. He had not known that he lived in so wild a region. There was something uncanny in the revelation.

By nightfall he was fatigued, footsore, famishing. The thought of his wife and children urged him on. At last he found a road which led him in what he knew to be the right direction. It was as wide and straight as a city street, yet it seemed untraveled. No fields bordered it, no dwelling anywhere. Not so much as the barking of a dog suggested human habitation. The black bodies of the trees formed a straight wall on both sides, terminating on the horizon in a point, like a diagram in a lesson in perspective. Overhead, as he looked up through this rift in the wood, shone great golden stars looking unfamiliar and grouped in strange constellations. He was sure they were arranged in some order which had a secret and malign significance. The wood on either side was full of singular noises, among which—once, twice, and again—he distinctly heard whispers in an unknown tongue.

His neck was in pain and lifting his hand to it he found it horribly swollen. He knew that it had a circle of black where the rope had bruised it. His eyes felt congested; he could no longer close them. His tongue was swollen with thirst; he relieved its fever by thrusting it forward from between his teeth into the cold air. How softly the turf had carpeted the untraveled avenue—he could no longer feel the roadway beneath his feet!

Doubtless, despite his suffering, he had fallen asleep while walking, for now he sees another scene—perhaps he has merely recovered from a delirium. He stands at the gate of his own home. All is as he left it, and all bright and beautiful in the morning sunshine. He must have traveled the entire night. As he pushes open the gate and passes up the wide white walk, he sees a flutter of female garments; his wife, looking fresh and cool and sweet, steps down from the veranda to meet him. At the bottom of the steps she stands waiting, with a smile of ineffable joy, an attitude of matchless grace and dignity. Ah, how beautiful she is! He springs forward with extended arms. As he is about to clasp her he feels a stunning blow upon the back of the neck; a blinding white light blazes all about him with a sound like the shock of a cannon—then all is darkness and silence!

Peyton Farquhar was dead; his body, with a broken neck, swung gently from side to side beneath the timbers of the Owl Creek bridge.

 ## Miss Julie

In *Miss Julie* (1951), Alf Sjöberg employs the limitless spatial and temporal possibilities of film to open up the one-act play by August Strindberg without violating the claustrophobic intensity of the drama. When plays are expanded in films, the result is often a dissipation of intensity; Sjöberg, has, in fact, heightened the tension by clarifying the interplay of dramatic forces.

Strindberg's play is set within the kitchen of a large Swedish manor house. Time, too, is restricted: The drama begins on Midsummer Eve in 1888 and ends the next morning. Midsummer Eve is an occasion for revelry in

Scandinavian countries, when time seems endless because of the brilliant light of the midsummer sun. Strindberg's cast of characters is limited to a triangle consisting of Miss Julie, the Count's beautiful and sexually repressed daughter; Jean, the Count's valet, a handsome, conceited man with dreams of upward mobility; and Kristin, the cook and the valet's lover and fiancée. All we learn about prior events is through the dialogue of these characters. The unrestrained merrymaking of the workers on the estate forms a counterpoint to the main action. Their presence is felt as they dance boisterously in the kitchen while Jean and Miss Julie consummate their relationship in his bedroom.

Sjöberg has opened up the setting of the play to emphasize the contrast between the worlds of Miss Julie and Jean, and to stress the pervasive sexuality of the peasants. The film begins with a shot of a caged bird; slowly the camera pulls back to reveal Miss Julie standing beside the cage, partially hidden by gauze curtains, as she furtively glances out of the window. The first shots are a perfect statement of her condition: She is a bird in a gilded cage, a thing of beauty, isolated and protected. Like many other characters in the film, she is also a voyeur, and as Sjöberg cuts to a point-of-view shot from the window, we see what she is observing; the peasants are freely erecting a maypole and frolicking gaily around it. The contrast between the two worlds could not have been made more economically.

Throughout the film, Sjöberg juxtaposes these worlds, but, with a single exception, he remains within the estate.[7] By opening up the setting, he is able to emphasize the ebullient sensuality of the peasants, which he contrasts repeatedly with the rigid deportment of Miss Julie. The spatial expansions also lay the foundations for the temporal expansions so significant in this adaptation. Sjöberg not only shows the other forces acting on Miss Julie and Jean at this particular moment: By moving into the past, Sjöberg is also able to give a greater sense of the characters' motivations. He does this through two beautifully orchestrated series of flashbacks, representing Jean's point of view and then Miss Julie's. Although the basis for Sjöberg's expansions is in the play, the treatment is entirely his own.

The first flashback occurs early in the film, when Jean is sitting in the kitchen discussing Miss Julie with Kristin. Sjöberg alters this scene by having Miss Julie arrive and overhear part of the conversation. Like many an eavesdropper, Julie is upset at what she hears. She climbs back in her cart and drives purposefully down to the pond. As she stares abjectly at the lilies, we hear the voice of Jean discussing her eccentric behavior with Kristin. It should be remembered, of course, that Jean himself has just suffered a rejection and humiliation at the hands of Miss Julie, which certainly influences the picture

---

[7]At the end of the film, we are transported to the place where the Count is spending Midsummer Eve with Miss Julie's former suitor. The Count persuades him to propose to Miss Julie once more, and they return together to the Count's estate.

of Miss Julie he presents to his own fiancée. Sjöberg cuts to Jean, with a wine glass in his hand, reminiscing to Kristin about the time he went riding with Miss Julie and her former fiancé. Sjöberg cuts back to Julie, who clutches her face in torment, while on the soundtrack we hear Jean's crude laughter. The laughter continues as we return to Jean in the kitchen and then witness his version of the events. Miss Julie, horrified at a display of sexuality between her pedigreed dog and a mutt, punishes her dog by beating him with her riding crop. When her fiancé intervenes, she humiliates him with the same crop—the visual symbol associated with her mother in the portrait that dominates so much of the film. Suddenly we realize that Miss Julie is at the very location Jean is describing, simultaneously recollecting the same events. As Jean concludes his version, Sjöberg dissolves back to the kitchen and then cuts to the pond, where Miss Julie stands in despair. Although the flashback has been related by Jean, it is in a sense a dual presentation since both he and Julie have been reliving the same event.

This treatment of time prepares us for the more innovative and thematically important flashbacks that follow. In the play Jean narrates the story of his youth, recalling the disparity he felt between his world and the world of the chateau. In the film the present literally dissolves into the past. The camera follows Jean and Miss Julie as they walk toward a lake. They pause, and the camera tracks past them, so that first Julie is excluded from the frame and then Jean. Jean's voice continues as the camera tracks toward the lake. On the other side stands a small hovel. Sjöberg dissolves, and then Jean appears as a child in the window of the hut, his chin resting on his hand, a pose we know to be characteristic of him from the view we have had of him in the kitchen. Then we see him being pursued by a menacing nun through the garden and the apple orchard of the estate. Sjöberg cuts to a high-angle shot of the nun beneath a gnarled tree; then the camera tilts up through the branches to reveal Jean and Miss Julie in the distance. For the first time in the film, past and present exist within the same frame. The importance of the past becomes increasingly apparent as it becomes spatially closer to the present.

Jean next tells Miss Julie of his admiration as a child for the Turkish pavillion. He turns his head to the right and stares out of the frame. Miss Julie looks in the same direction, and Sjöberg cuts directly to the pavillion. He cuts again to reveal the young Jean working in the onion fields and then sneaking into the pavillion. Sjöberg distorts the psychological time of the sequence through the creation of suspense by showing the nun approaching and the boy trying frantically to escape. She strides purposefully up to the pavillion and then pauses to tie her shoelace. The suspense is heightened. Then she enters and Sjöberg holds the shot on the pavillion for a relatively long time maintaining the suspense before cutting to a shot of the boy crawling out of the pavillion through the cesspool. After a brief encounter with the young Miss Julie, the chase continues. The entire estate is summoned to catch the boy. He finally plunges into the river but is fished out. His father, who had participated in the pursuit, removes his belt and gives him a sound whipping. The camera pans slowly past the workers, who are observing the beating, until the frame is filled only with foliage, although the sound of the striking belt continues; the camera then tilts down to reveal Miss Julie (as an adult, in the present) listening to Jean tell his story. Once again, Jean and Julie have become included in the physical space of the past, nearly as spectators at the event.

Sjöberg continues with Jean's story by dissolving to him as a child preparing for church. When Jean enters the chapel, he unconsciously begins to transgress the boundary of sex by advancing toward the women's section. In the section reserved for the peasants, he is not even permitted to dream of Miss Julie, for he is rudely awakened as he drops off into a romantic reverie. The young Miss Julie, however, dozes before the congregation with her mother. The discouraged boy leaves the church, and Sjöberg cuts to the mature Miss Julie, also dozing. Jean's thwarted dreams are close now to being realized.

Jean's flashbacks demonstrate his awareness of class and his persistent desire to be upwardly mobile. When he relates them to Miss Julie, he is outdoors with her, between the kitchen, which is now his home, and the mansion, which is hers. The flashbacks take place before the consummation of the affair, and, as we later learn, Jean has distorted the past to make himself appear more sympathetic in Julie's eyes.

Miss Julie's flashbacks occur only after she has slept with Jean, and they are narrated within the great hall, surrounded by portraits recalling the important figures in her past. She is seated on a chair in a position that recalls her posture as a child in Jean's flashback. As she drinks her beer, she begins to discourse on her mother. Sjöberg cuts to a shot of her mother's portrait, which hangs on the wall, and then tracks in to the picture while Julie's voice states that "she was opposed to marriage and told Father when he proposed . . ." The camera pans to the right, and we realize that the portrait is now being supported on the ground by Julie's father. We are suddenly in the past, and the Count is explaining the strange behavior of his mistress to his friends. Through a series of time lapses, Sjöberg shows us the Count's early life with Julie's mother, as he brings her home, faces the ostracism of his friends, and waits eagerly for the birth of their child. At the end of the sequence, after the birth of Julie, the Count descends once more to the portrait gallery to ponder his failed attempt to produce a male heir. A series of subjective shots of the portraits follows, concluding with a shot of an ornate full length mirror. The camera tilts down to reveal Jean standing before the mirror, staring upward. We have returned to the present, and he too has been included in the history of the family.

Sjöberg pans from Jean to reveal Julie still seated and beginning to show the signs of her drinking. Julie then explains how she was made to dress like a boy, and the camera pans past Jean to reveal the mirror, again empty. The mirror is a looking glass separating past and present; as we gaze at it, the reflection of the young Miss Julie walks into the frame from the right, dressed as a boy. The camera tilts up to show a portrait of her in very feminine attire, almost mocking the uncomfortable tomboy. Sjöberg cuts back to the reflection of Julie looking up; then as the reflection moves, the real girl enters the frame and adjusts her hat. In the background, we observe the reflection of the girl's mother and lover pass into the mirror before leaving the house. The girl's reflection runs to them, and Sjöberg dissolves to a long series of sequences depicting Julie's childhood. We see her being passed back and forth between her parents, as they struggle for power. She witnesses her mother's crazed effort to burn down the mansion and later, her father's attempt to shoot himself. The importance of this event is underlined by the remarkable series of temporal transitions it initiates.

After watching her father shoot himself, Julie collapses on the bed a short distance from the spot where he lies on the floor. Sjöberg holds the shot of Julie in close-up, dressed in white and lying on a white bed. Suddenly a black glove enters the frame to console her, and the viewer recoils with fright. The camera pulls back to reveal her mother, completely attired in black, leading the young girl away. Then Sjöberg cuts to a close-up of Miss Julie in the present, and as the camera pulls back from her, the Countess, still holding the child by the hand, passes behind her. The mother pauses, lifts her daughter in her arms, and walks out of the frame on the right. Sjöberg cuts to Jean, seated on a chair before the mirror at Julie's left, listening to her tell of her mother's influence: "Before her death," Julie explains, "I promised never to become any man's slave." While Jean sits attentively, the Countess

Miss Julie. Past and present coexist within a single frame.

enters the frame from the side, still carrying Julie. She appears first in the mirror, then passes between Jean and the mirror, and pauses in the doorway before exiting. As she stops, another figure, hitherto unnoticed, is reflected in the mirror. The figure is Miss Julie's former fiancé, who begins to rise from his chair, with a bird cage in his hand. For an instant Sjöberg balances three different temporal periods within the same frame: on the left, reflected in the mirror, the fiancé with his bird cage, representing the near past; in the middle, Jean, listening to the story in the present; and on the right, in the distant past, the mother exerting her malevolent influence on the young girl. All this happens so quickly that most viewers miss it entirely, and yet it shows how crucial the mother's influence is on Julie's relationship with her fiancé and on her relationship with Jean. The reflection of her fiancé moves into the mirror as the camera pans to meet the actual figure, who now bows and smiles at the camera. Sjöberg cuts to a reverse-angle shot, from the fiancé's point of view, as the father enters the frame. We now find ourselves at the Christmas party where Julie receives the bird cage, to which she clings tenaciously at the end of the drama. In this scene Julie is acting completely under her mother's domination: She is clothed like her, has built a shrine to her on her dressing table, and, upon entering the drawing room, raises her glass and toasts her mother's portrait. Sjöberg cuts to the portrait, then to Miss Julie drinking, then again to the portrait, with a tilt down to reveal Miss Julie drinking in the present—showing a marked contrast between her stately appearance in the flashback and her slatternly appearance with Jean.

Sjöberg manipulates time to demonstrate how decisively the past shapes the present. But he also projects into the future and shows how determined it is by present and past actions. Julie has told Jean about the suicide attempts of both her parents, and we have seen her reactions to them as a child and as an adult. It is not surprising that she is able to fantasize about her father committing suicide when Jean hears of her plight. Sjöberg shows Julie standing in the foreground before her father and a policeman, overhearing them discussing her theft of his money as she narrates the action. Unable to cope with the situation, her father leaves and shoots himself, and she then imagines his funeral. Her fantasies perfectly illustrate her state of mind. She is incapable of fantasizing a possible future life with Jean; all she can foresee is future disgrace. When she kills herself, it is in the ancestral hall, where she had sat earlier with Jean. Her father finds her sprawled on the ground, beneath the Countess's portrait. He kneels at her side and then glances upward at the picture. Sjöberg cuts to the portrait, dollies in, and fades out. The forces of the past have proved too great.

In Sjöberg's film, the burden of the past is a continuing reality, determing and shaping present and future action. His flashbacks, which begin in a rather conventional manner, become increasingly abstract and complex, until past and present, present and future, coexist in the same frames. Rarely have the temporal expansions of a play been handled with greater intelligence and subtlety.

Miss Julie. Miss Julie imagines the future, of which she is a part.

Miss Julie

Production Credits

Director	Alf Sjöberg
Screenplay by	Alf Sjöberg
Based on the play by	August Strindberg
Director of Photography	Goran Strindberg
Art Director	Bibi Lindström
Film Editor	Lennart Wallen
Music by	Dag Wiren

Sweden. 1950. 87 minutes. Black & White.

Cast

Miss Julie	Anita Björk
Jean	Ulf Palme
Miss Julie (child)	Inger Norberg
Jean (child)	Jan Hagerman

Kristin	Märta Dorff
The Count	Anders Henrikson
Berta	Lissi Alandh
Viola	Inga Gill
The Fiancé	Kurt-Olof Sundström
The Doctor	Ake Claesson
The Governess	Margaretta Krook
The Groom	Max von Sydow
The Industrialist	Ake Fridell

Further Reading

Cowie, Peter. *Swedish Cinema.* New York: A. S. Barnes & Co., 1966.

Manvell, Roger. *Theater and Film.* Rutherford, New Jersey: Fairleigh Dickinson University Press, 1979.

Rowland, Richard. "Miss Julie." In *Renaissance of the Film,* ed. Julius Bellone. New York: Collier Books, 1970.

Tyler, Parker. *Classics of the Foreign Film: A Pictorial Treasury.* New York: The Citadel Press, 1962.

Young, Vernon. "The History of *Miss Julie.*" *The Hudson Review,* 8, No. 1 (Spring 1955), 123–30.

Miss Julie
August Strindberg

Translated from the Swedish by Harry G. Carlson

Characters

MISS JULIE, 25 years old
JEAN, her father's valet, 30 years old
KRISTINE, her father's cook, 35 years old

(The action takes place in the count's kitchen on midsummer eve.)

Setting

(A large kitchen, the ceiling and side walls of which are hidden by draperies. The rear wall runs diagonally from down left to up right. On the wall down left are two shelves with copper, iron, and pewter utensils; the shelves are lined with scalloped paper. Visible to the right is most of a set of large, arched glass doors, through which can be seen a fountain with a statue of Cupid, lilac bushes in bloom, and the tops of some Lombardy poplars. At down left is the corner of a large tiled stove; a portion of its hood is showing. At right, one end of the servants' white pine dining table juts out; several chairs stand around it. The stove is decorated with birch branches; juniper twigs are strewn on the floor. On the end of the table stands a large Japanese spice jar, filled with lilac blossoms. An ice-box, a sink, and a washstand. Above the door is an old-fashioned bell on a spring; to the left of the door, the mouthpiece of a speaking tube is visible.

KRISTINE is frying something on the stove. She is wearing a light-colored cotton dress and an apron. JEAN enters. He is wearing livery and carries a pair of high riding-boots with spurs, which he puts down on the floor where they can be seen by the audience.)

JEAN. Miss Julie's crazy again tonight; absolutely crazy!

KRISTINE. So you finally came back?

JEAN. I took the Count to the station and when I returned past the barn I stopped in for a dance. Who do I see but Miss Julie leading off the dance with the gamekeeper! But as soon as she saw me she rushed over to ask me for the next waltz. And she's been waltzing ever since—I've never seen anything like it. She's crazy!

KRISTINE. She always has been, but never as bad as the last two weeks since her engagement was broken off.

JEAN. Yes, I wonder what the real story was there. He was a gentleman, even if he wasn't rich. Ah! These people have such romantic ideas. *(sits at the end of the table)* Still, it's strange, isn't it? I mean that she'd rather stay home with the servants on midsummer eve instead of going with her father to visit relatives?

KRISTINE. She's probably embarrassed after that row with her fiancé.

JEAN. Probably! He gave a good account of himself, though. Do you know how it happened, Kristine? I saw it, you know, though I didn't let on I had.

KRISTINE. No! You saw it?

JEAN. Yes, I did. —— That evening they were out near the stable, and she was "training" him—as she called it. Do you know what she did? She made him jump over her riding crop, the way you'd teach a dog to jump. He jumped twice and she hit him each time. But the third time he grabbed the crop out of her hand, hit her with it across the cheek, and broke it in pieces. Then he left.

KRISTINE. So, that's what happened! I can't believe it!

JEAN. Yes, that's the way it went! —— What have you got for me that's tasty, Kristine?

KRISTINE (*serving him from the pan*). Oh, it's only a piece of kidney I cut from the veal roast.

JEAN (*smelling the food*). Beautiful! That's my favorite *délice*. (*feeling the plate*) But you could have warmed the plate!

KRISTINE. You're fussier than the Count himself, once you start! (*She pulls his hair affectionately.*)

JEAN (*angry*). Stop it, leave my hair alone! You know I'm touchy about that.

KRISTINE. Now, now, it's only love, you know that. (JEAN *eats.* KRISTINE *opens a bottle of beer.*)

JEAN. Beer? On midsummer eve? No thank you! I can do better than that. (*opens a drawer in the table and takes out a bottle of red wine with yellow sealing wax*) See that? Yellow seal! Give me a glass! A wine glass! I'm drinking this *pur*.

KRISTINE (*returns to the stove and puts on a small saucepan*). God help the woman who gets you for a husband! What a fuss-budget.

JEAN. Nonsense! You'd be damned lucky to get a man like me. It certainly hasn't done you any harm to have people call me your sweetheart. (*tastes the wine*) Good! Very good! Just needs a little warming. (*warms the glass between his hands*) We bought this in Dijon. Four francs a liter, not counting the cost of the bottle, or the customs duty. —— What are you cooking now? It stinks like hell!

KRISTINE. Oh, some slop Miss Julie wants to give Diana.

JEAN. Watch your language, Kristine. But why should you have to cook for that damn mutt on midsummer eve? Is she sick?

KRISTINE. Yes, she's sick! She sneaked out with the gatekeeper's dog—and now there's hell to pay. Miss Julie won't have it!

JEAN. Miss Julie has too much pride about some things and not enough about others, just like her mother was. The Countess was most at home in the kitchen and the cowsheds, but a *one*-horse carriage wasn't elegant enough for her. The cuffs of her blouse were dirty, but she had to have her coat of arms on her cufflinks. —— And Miss Julie won't take proper care of herself either. If you ask me, she just isn't refined. Just now, when she was dancing in the barn, she pulled the gamekeeper away from Anna and made him dance with her. *We* wouldn't behave like that, but that's what happens when aristocrats pretend they're common people—they get *common!* —— But she is quite a woman! Magnificent! What shoulders, and what—et cetera!

KRISTINE. Oh, don't overdo it! I've heard what Clara says, and she dresses her.

JEAN. Ha, Clara! You're all jealous of each other! I've been out riding with her . . . And the way she dances!

KRISTINE. Listen, Jean! You're going to dance with me, when I'm finished here, aren't you?

JEAN. Of course, I will.

KRISTINE. Promise?

JEAN. Promise? When I say I'll do something, I do it! By the way, the kidney was very good. (*corks the bottle*)

JULIE (*in the doorway to someone outside*). I'll be right back! You go ahead for now! (JEAN *sneaks the bottle back into the table drawer and gets up respectfully.* MISS JULIE *enters and crosses to* KRISTINE *by the stove.*) Well? Is it ready? (KRISTINE *indicates that* JEAN *is present.*)

JEAN (*gallantly*). Are you ladies up to something secret?

JULIE (*flicking her handerchief in his face*). None of your business!

JEAN. Hmm! I like the smell of violets!

JULIE (*coquettishly*). Shame on you! So you know about perfumes, too? You certainly know how to dance. Ah, ah! No peeking! Go away.

JEAN (*boldly but respectfully*). Are you brewing up a magic potion for midsummer eve? Something to prophecy by under a lucky star, so you'll catch a glimpse of your future husband!

JULIE (*caustically*). You'd need sharp eyes to see him! (to KRISTINE) Pour out half a bottle and cork it well. —— Come and dance a schottische with me, Jean . . .

JEAN (*hesitating*). I don't want to be impolite to anyone, and I've already promised this dance to Kristine . . .

JULIE. Oh, she can have another one—can't you Kristine? Won't you lend me Jean?

KRISTINE. It's not up to me, ma'am. (to JEAN) If the mistress is so generous, it wouldn't do for you to say no. Go on, Jean, and thank her for the honor.

JEAN. To be honest, and no offense intended, I wonder whether it's wise for you to dance twice running with the same partner, especially since these people are quick to jump to conclusions . . .

JULIE (*flaring up*). What's that? What sort of conclusions? What do you mean?

JEAN (*submissively*). If you don't understand, ma'am, I must speak more plainly. It doesn't look good to play favorites with your servants. . . .

JULIE. Play favorites! What an idea! I'm astonished! As mistress of the house, I honor your dance with my presence. And when I dance, I want to dance with someone who can lead, so I won't look ridiculous.

JEAN. As you order, ma'am! I'm at your service!

JULIE (*gently*). Don't take it as an order! On a night like this we're all just ordinary people having fun, so we'll forget about rank. Now, take my arm! —— Don't worry, Kristine! I won't steal your sweetheart! (JEAN *offers his arm and leads* MISS JULIE *out*).

Mime

(The following should be played as if the actress playing KRISTINE *were really alone. When she has to, she turns her back to the audience. She does not look toward them, nor does she hurry as if she were afraid they would grow impatient. Schottische music played on a fiddle sounds in the distance.* KRISTINE *hums along with the music. She clears the table, washes the dishes, dries them, and puts them away. She takes off her apron. From a table drawer she removes a small mirror and leans it against the bowl of lilacs on the table. She lights a candle, heats a hairpin over the flame, and uses it to set a curl on her forehead. She crosses to the door and listens, then returns to the table. She finds the handkerchief* MISS JULIE *left behind, picks it up, and smells it. Then, preoccupied, she spreads it out, stretches it, smoothes out the wrinkles, and folds it into quarters, and so forth.)*

JEAN (*enters alone*). God, she really *is* crazy! What a way to dance! Everybody's laughing at her behind her back. What do you make of it, Kristine?

KRISTINE. Ah! It's that time of the month for her, and she always gets peculiar like that. Are you going to dance with me now?

JEAN. You're not mad at me, are you, for leaving . . .?

KRISTINE. Of course not! —— Why should I be, for a little thing like that? Besides, I know my place . . .

JEAN (*puts his arm around her waist*). You're a sensible girl, Kristine, and you'd make a good wife . . .

JULIE (*entering; uncomfortably surprised; with forced good humor*). What a charming escort—running away from his partner.

JEAN. On the contrary, Miss Julie. Don't you see how I rushed back to the partner I abandoned!

JULIE (*changing her tone*). You know, you're a superb dancer! —— But why are you wearing livery on a holiday? Take it off at once!

JEAN. Then I must ask you to go outside for a moment. You see, my black coat is hanging over here . . . (*gestures and crosses right*)

JULIE. Are you embarrassed about changing your coat in front of me? Well, go in your room then. Either that or stay and I'll turn my back.

JEAN. With your permission, ma'am! (*He crosses right. His arm is visible as he changes his jacket.*)

JULIE (*to* KRISTINE). Tell me, Kristine—you two are so close—. Is Jean your fiancé?

KRISTINE. Fiancé? Yes, if you wish. We can call him that.

JULIE. What do you mean?

KRISTINE. You had a fiancé yourself, didn't you? So . . .

JULIE. Well, we were properly engaged . . .

KRISTINE. But nothing came of it, did it? (JEAN *returns dressed in a frock coat and bowler hat.*)

JULIE. *Très gentil, monsieur Jean! Très gentil!*

JEAN. *Vous voulez plaisanter, madame!*

JULIE. *Et vous voulez parler français!* Where did you learn that?

JEAN. In Switzerland, when I was wine steward in one of the biggest hotels in Lucerne!

JULIE. You look like a real gentleman in that coat! *Charmant! (sits at the table)*

JEAN. Oh, you're flattering me!

JULIE *(offended)*. Flattering you?

JEAN. My natural modesty forbids me to believe that you would really compliment someone like me, and so I took the liberty of assuming that you were exaggerating, which polite people call flattering.

JULIE. Where did you learn to talk like that? You must have been to the theatre often.

JEAN. Of course. And I've done a lot of traveling.

JULIE. But you come from here, don't you?

JEAN. My father was a farm hand on the district attorney's estate nearby. I used to see you when you were little, but you never noticed me.

JULIE. No! Really?

JEAN. Sure. I remember one time especially . . . but I can't talk about that.

JULIE. Oh, come now! Why not? Just this once!

JEAN. No, I really couldn't, not now. Some other time, perhaps.

JULIE. Why some other time? What's so dangerous about now?

JEAN. It's not dangerous, but there are obstacles. —— Her, for example. *(indicating* KRISTINE, *who has fallen asleep in a chair by the stove)*

JULIE. What a pleasant wife she'll make! She probably snores, too.

JEAN. No, she doesn't, but she talks in her sleep.

JULIE *(cynically)*. How do *you* know?

JEAN *(audaciously)*. I've heard her! *(pause, during which they stare at each other)*

JULIE. Why don't you sit down?

JEAN. I couldn't do that in your presence.

JULIE. But if I order you to?

JEAN. Then I'd obey.

JULIE. Sit down, then. —— No, wait. Can you get me something to drink first?

JEAN. I don't know what we have in the ice box, I think there's only beer.

JULIE. Why do you say "only"? My tastes are so simple I prefer beer to wine. *(*JEAN *takes a bottle of beer from the ice box and opens it. He looks for a glass and a plate in the cupboard and serves her.)*

JEAN. Here you are, ma'am.

JULIE. Thank you. Won't you have something yourself?

JEAN. I'm not partial to beer, but if it's an order . . .

JULIE. An order? —— Surely a gentleman can keep his lady company.

JEAN. You're right, of course. *(opens a bottle and gets a glass)*

JULIE. Now, drink to my health! (He *hesitates*.) What? A man of the world—and shy?

JEAN *(In mock romantic fashion, he kneels and raises his glass.)*. Skål to my mistress!

JULIE. Bravo! —— Now kiss my shoe, to finish it properly. (JEAN *hesitates, then boldly seizes her foot and kisses it lightly.)* Perfect! You should have been an actor.

JEAN *(rising)*. That's enough now, Miss Julie! Someone might come in and see us.

JULIE. What of it?

JEAN. People talk, that's what! If you knew how their tongues were wagging just now at the dance, you'd . . .

JULIE. What were they saying? Tell me! —— Sit down!

JEAN *(sits)*. I don't want hurt you, but they were sayings things —— suggestive things, that, that . . . well, you can figure it out for yourself! You're not a child. If a woman is seen drinking alone with a man—let alone a servant—at night—then . . .

JULIE. Then what? Besides, we're not alone. Kristine is here.

JEAN. Asleep!

JULIE. Then I'll wake her up. *(rising)* Kristine! Are you asleep? (KRISTINE *mumbles in her sleep.)*

JULIE. Kristine! —— She certainly can sleep!

KRISTINE *(in her sleep)*. The Count's boots are brushed—put the coffee on—right away, right away—uh, huh—oh!

JULIE *(grabbing* KRISTINE's *nose)*. Will you wake up!

JEAN *(severely)*. Leave her alone—let her sleep!

JULIE *(sharply)*. What?

JEAN. Someone who's been standing over a stove all day has a right to be tired by now. Sleep should be respected . . .

JULIE *(changing her tone)*. What a considerate thought—it does you credit—thank you! *(offering her hand)* Come outside and pick some lilacs for me! *(During the following,* KRISTINE *awakens and shambles sleepily off right to bed.)*

JEAN. Go with you?

JULIE. With me!

JEAN. We couldn't do that! Absolutely not!

JULIE. I don't understand. Surely you don't imagine . . .

JEAN. No, I don't, but the others might.

JULIE. What? That I've fallen in love with a servant?

JEAN. I'm not a conceited man, but such things happen—and for these people, nothing is sacred.

JULIE. I do believe you're an aristocrat!

JEAN. Yes, I am.

JULIE. And I'm stepping down . . .

JEAN. Don't step down, Miss Julie, take my advice. No one'll believe you stepped down voluntarily. People will always say you fell.

JULIE. I have a higher opinion of people than you. Come and see! —— Come! *(She stares at him broodingly.)*

JEAN. You're very strange, do you know that?

JULIE. Perhaps! But so are you! —— For that matter, everything is strange. Life, people, everything. Like floating scum, drifting on and on across the water, until it sinks down and down! That reminds me of a dream I have now and then. I've climbed up on top of a pillar. I sit there and see no way of getting down. I get dizzy when I look down, and I must get down, but I don't have the courage to jump. I can't hold on firmly, and I long to be able to fall, but I don't fall. And yet I'll have no peace until I get down, no rest unless I get down, down on the ground! And if I did get down to the ground, I'd want to be under the earth . . . Have you ever felt anything like that?

JEAN. No, I dream that I'm lying under a high tree in a dark forest. I want to get up, up on top, and look out over the bright landscape, where the sun is shining, and plunder the bird's nest up there, where the golden eggs lie. And I climb and climb, but the trunk's so thick and smooth, and it's so far to the first branch. But I know if I just reached that first branch, I'd go right to the top, like up a ladder. I haven't reached it yet, but I will, even if it's only in a dream!

JULIE. Here I am chattering with you about dreams: Come, let's go out! Just into the park! *(She offers him her arm, and they start to leave)*.

JEAN. We'll have to sleep on nine midsummer flowers, Miss Julie, to make our dreams come true! *(They turn at the door.* JEAN *puts his hand to his eye.)*

JULIE. Did you get something in your eye?

JEAN. It's nothing—just a speck—it'll be gone in a minute.

JULIE. My sleeve must have brushed against you. Sit down and let me help you. *(She takes him by the arm and seats him. She tilts his head back and with the tip of a handkerchief tries to remove the speck.)* Sit still, absolutely still! *(She slaps his hand.)* Didn't you hear me? —— Why, you're trembling; the big, strong man is trembling! *(feels his biceps)* What muscles you have!

JEAN *(warning)*. Miss Julie!

JULIE. Yes, *monsieur* Jean.

JEAN. Attention! Je ne suis qu'un homme!

JULIE. Will you sit still —— There! Now it's gone! Kiss my hand and thank me.

JEAN *(rising)*. Miss Julie, listen to me! —— Kristine has gone to bed! —— Will you listen to me!

JULIE. Kiss my hand first!

JEAN. Listen to me!

JULIE. Kiss my hand first!

JEAN. All right, but you've only yourself to blame!

JULIE. For what?

JEAN. For what? Are you still a child at twenty-five? Don't you know that's it's dangerous to play with fire?

JULIE. Not for me. I'm insured.

JEAN *(boldly)*. No, you're not! But even if you were, there's combustible material close by.

JULIE. Meaning you?

JEAN. Yes! Not because it's me, but because I'm young ——

JULIE. And handsome—what incredible conceit! A Don Juan perhaps! Or a Joseph! Yes, that's it, I do believe you're a Joseph!

JEAN. Do you?

JULIE. I'm almost afraid so. (JEAN *boldly tries to put his arm around her waist and kiss her. She slaps his face.*) How dare you?

JEAN. Are you serious or joking?

JULIE. Serious.

JEAN. Then so was what just happened. You play games too seriously, and that's dangerous. Well, I'm tired of games. You'll excuse me if I get back to work. I haven't done the Count's boots yet and it's long past midnight.

JULIE. Put the boots down!

JEAN. No! It's the work I have to do. I never agreed to be your playmate, and never will. It's beneath me.

JULIE. You're proud.

JEAN. In certain ways, but not in others.

JULIE. Have you ever been in love?

JEAN. We don't use that word, but I've been fond of many girls, and once I was sick because I couldn't have the one I wanted. That's right, sick, like those princes in the Arabian Nights—who couldn't eat or drink because of love.

JULIE. Who was she? (JEAN *is silent*). Who was she?

JEAN. You can't force me to tell you that.

JULIE. But if I ask you as an equal, as a—friend? Who was she?

JEAN. You!

JULIE *(sits)*. How amusing . . .

JEAN. Yes, if you like! It was ridiculous! —— You see, that was the story I didn't want to tell you earlier. Maybe I will now. Do you know how the world looks from down below? —— Of course you don't. Neither do hawks and falcons, whose backs we can't see because they're usually soaring up there above us. I grew up in a shack with seven brothers and sisters and a pig, in the middle of a wasteland, where there wasn't a single tree. But from our window I could see the tops of apple trees above the wall of your father's garden. That was the Garden of Eden, guarded by angry angels with flaming swords. All the same, the other boys and I managed to find our way to the Tree of Life. —— Now you think I'm contemptible, I suppose.

JULIE. Oh, all boys steal apples.

JEAN. You say that, but you think I'm contemptible anyway. Oh well! One day I went into the Garden of Eden with my mother, to weed the onion beds. Near the vegetable garden was a small Turkish pavilion in the shadow of jasmine bushes and overgrown with honeysuckle. I had no idea what it was used for, but I'd never seen such a beautiful building. People went in and came out again, and one day the door was left open. I sneaked close and saw walls covered with pictures of kings and emperors, and red curtains with fringes at the windows—now you know the place I mean. I —— *(breaks off a sprig of lilac and holds it in front of* MISS JULIE's *nose)* —— I'd never been inside the manor house, never seen anything except the church—but this was more beautiful. From then on, no matter where my thoughts wandered, they returned—there. And gradually I got a longing to experience, just once, the full pleasure of—*enfin,* I sneaked in, saw, and marveled! But then I heard someone coming! There was only one exit for ladies and gentlemen, but for me there was another, and I had no choice but to take it! (MISS JULIE, *who has taken the lilac sprig, lets it fall on the table.)* Afterwards, I started running. I crashed through a raspberry bush, flew over a strawberry patch, and came up onto the rose terrace. There I caught sight of a pink dress and a pair of white stockings—it was you. I crawled under a pile of weeds, and I mean under—under thistles that pricked me and wet dirt that stank. And I looked at you as you walked among the roses, and I thought: if it's true that a thief can enter heaven and be with the angels, then why can't a farmhand's son here on God's earth enter the manor house garden and play with the Count's daughter?

JULIE *(romantically).* Do you think all poor children would have thought the way you did?

JEAN *(at first hesitant, then with conviction).* If *all* poor—yes—of course. Of course!

JULIE. It must be terrible to be poor!

JEAN *(with exaggerated suffering).* Oh, Miss Julie! Oh! —— A dog can lie on the Countess's sofa, a horse can have his nose patted by a young lady's hand, but a servant —— *(changing his tone)* —— oh, I know—now and then you find one with enough stuff in him to get ahead in the world, but how often? —— Anyhow, do you know what I did then? —— I jumped in the mill stream with my clothes on, was pulled out, and got a beating. But the following Sunday, when my father and all the others went to my grandmother's, I arranged to stay home. I scrubbed myself with soap and water, put on my best clothes, and went to church so that I could see you! I saw you and returned home, determined to die. But I wanted to die beautifully and pleasantly, without pain. And then I remembered that it was dangerous to sleep under an elder bush. We had a big one, and it was in full flower. I plundered its treasures and bedded down under them in the oat bin. Have you ever noticed how smooth oats are?—and soft to the touch, like human skin . . . ! Well, I shut the lid and closed my eyes. I fell asleep and woke up feeling very sick. But I didn't die, as you can see. What was I after? —— I don't know. There was no hope of winning you, of course. —— You were a symbol of the hopelessness of ever rising out of the class in which I was born.

JULIE. You're a charming storyteller. Did you ever go to school?

JEAN. A bit, but I've read lots of novels and been to the theatre often. And then I've listened to people like you talk—that's where I learned most.

JULIE. Do you listen to what we say?

JEAN. Naturally! And I've heard plenty, too, driving the carriage or rowing the boat. Once I heard you and a friend . . .

JULIE. Oh?——What did you hear?

JEAN. I'd better not say. But I was surprised a little. I couldn't imagine where you learned such words. Maybe at bottom there isn't such a great difference between people as we think.

JULIE. Shame on you! We don't act like you when we're engaged.

JEAN *(staring at her)*. Is that true?——You don't have to play innocent with me, Miss . . .

JULIE. The man I gave my love to was a swine.

JEAN. That's what you all say—afterwards

JULIE. All?

JEAN. I think so. I know I've heard that phrase before, on similar occasions.

JULIE. What occasions?

JEAN. Like the one I'm talking about. The last time . . .

JULIE *(rising)*. Quiet! I don't want to hear any more!

JEAN. That's interesting—that's what *she* said, too. Well, if you'll excuse me, I'm going to bed.

JULIE *(gently)*. To bed? On midsummer eve?

JEAN. Yes! Dancing with the rabble out there doesn't amuse me much.

JULIE. Get the key to the boat and row me out on the lake. I want to see the sun come up.

JEAN. I that wise?

JULIE. Are you worried about your reputation?

JEAN. Why not? Why should I risk looking ridiculous and getting fired without a reference, just when I'm trying to establish myself. Besides, I think I owe something to Kristine.

JULIE. So, now it's Kristine . . .

JEAN. Yes, but you, too.——Take my advice, go up and go to bed!

JULIE. Am I to obey you?

JEAN. Just this once—for your own good! Please! It's very late. Drowsiness makes people giddy and liable to lose their heads! Go to bed! Besides— unless I'm mistaken—I hear the others coming to look for me. And if they find us together, you'll be lost! *(The* CHORUS *approaches, singing:)*

The swineherd found his true love
a pretty girl so fair,

The swineherd found his true love
but let the girl beware.

For then he saw the princess
the princess on the golden hill,
but then saw the princess,
so much fairer still.

So the swineherd and the princess
they danced the whole night through,
and he forgot his first love,
to her he was untrue.

And when the long night ended,
and in the light of day, of day,
the dancing too was ended,
and the princess could not stay.

Then the swineherd lost his true love,
and the princess grieves him still,
and never more she'll wander
from atop the golden hill.

JULIE. I know all these people and I love them, just as they love me. Let them
  come in and you'll see.
JEAN. No, Miss Julie, they don't love you. They take your food, but they spit
  on it! Believe me! Listen to them, listen to what they're singing!——No,
  don't listen to them!
JULIE *(listening)*. What are they singing?
JEAN. It's a dirty song! About you and me!
JULIE. Disgusting! Oh! How deceitful!——
JEAN. The rabble is always cowardly! And in a battle like this, you don't fight;
  you can only run away!
JULIE. Run away? But where? We can't go out—or into Kristine's room.
JEAN. True. But there's my room. Necessity knows no rules. Besides, you can
  trust me. I'm your friend and I respect you.
JULIE. But suppose—suppose they look for you in there?
JEAN. I'll bolt the door, and if anyone tries to break in, I'll shoot!——
  Come!*(on his knees)* Come!
JULIE *(urgently)*. Promise me . . .?
JEAN. I swear! (MISS JULIE *runs off right.* JEAN *hastens after her.*)

Ballet

*(Led by a fiddler, the servants and farm people enter, dressed festively, with flowers
in their hats. On the table they place a small barrel of beer and a keg of schnapps,
both garlanded. Glasses are brought out, and the drinking starts. A dance circle is*

formed and "The Swineherd and the Princess" is sung. When the dance is finished, everyone leaves, singing.)

(MISS JULIE *enters alone. She notices the mess in the kitchen, wrings her hands, then takes out her powder puff and powders her nose.)*

JEAN *(enters, agitated).* There, you see? And you heard them. We can't possibly stay here now, you know that.

JULIE. Yes, I know. But what can we do?

JEAN. Leave, travel, far away from here.

JULIE. Travel? Yes, but where?

JEAN. To Switzerland, to the Italian lakes. Have you ever been there?

JULIE. No. Is it beautiful?

JEAN. Oh, an eternal summer—oranges growing everywhere, laurel trees, always green . . .

JULIE. But what'll we do there?

JEAN. I'll open a hotel—with first-class service for first-class people.

JULIE. Hotel?

JEAN. That's the life, you know. Always new faces, new languages. No time to worry or be nervous. No hunting for something to do—there's always work to be done: bells ringing night and day, train whistles blowing, carriages coming and going, and all the while gold rolling into the till! That's the life!

JULIE. Yes, it sounds wonderful. But what'll I do?

JEAN. You'll be mistress of the house: the jewel in our crown! With your looks . . . and your manner—oh—success is guaranteed! It'll be wonderful! You'll sit in your office like a queen and push an electric button to set your slaves in motion. The guests will file past your throne and timidly lay their treasures before you.——You have no idea how people tremble when they get their bill.——I'll salt the bills and you'll sweeten them with your prettiest smile.——Let's get away from here——*(takes a timetable out of his pocket)*——Right away, on the next train!——We'll be in Malmö six-thirty tomorrow morning, Hamburg at eight-forty; from Frankfort to Basel will take a day, then on to Como by way of the St. Gotthard Tunnel, in, let's see, three days. Three days!

JULIE. That's all very well! But Jean—you must give me courage!——Tell me you love me! Put your arms around me!

JEAN *(hesitating).* I want to—but I don't dare. Not in this house, not again. I love you—never doubt that—you don't doubt it, do you, Miss Julie?

JULIE *(shy, very feminine).* "Miss!"——Call me Julie! There are no barriers between us any more. Call me Julie!

JEAN *(tormented).* I can't! There'll always be barriers between us as long as we stay in this house.——There's the past and there's the Count. I've never met anyone I had such respect for.——When I see his gloves lying on a chair, I feel small.——When I hear that bell up there ring, I jump like a skittish horse.——And when I look at his boots standing there so stiff

and proud, I feel like bowing! *(kicking the boots)* Superstitions and preju-
dices we learned as children—but they can easily be forgotten. If I can
just get to another country, a republic, people will bow and scrape when
they see my livery—*they'll* bow and scrape, you hear, not me! I wasn't
born to cringe. I've got stuff in me, I've got character, and if I can only
grab onto that first branch, you watch me climb! I'm a servant today, but
next year I'll own my own hotel. In ten years I'll have enough to retire.
Then I'll go to Rumania and be decorated. I could—mind you I said
could—end up a count!

JULIE. Wonderful, wonderful!

JEAN. Ah, in Rumania you just buy your title, and so you'll be a countess after
all. My countess!

JULIE. But I don't care about that—that's what I'm putting behind me! Show
me you love me, otherwise—otherwise, what am I?

JEAN. I'll show you a thousand times—afterwards! Not here! And whatever
you do, no emotional outbursts, or we'll both be lost! We must think this
through coolly, like sensible people. *(He takes out a cigar, snips the end,
and lights it.)* You sit there, and I'll sit here. We'll talk as if nothing
happened.

JULIE *(desperately)*. Oh, my God! Have you no feelings?

JEAN. Me? No one has more feelings than I do, but I know how to control
them.

JULIE. A little while ago you could kiss my shoe—and now!

JEAN *(harshly)*. Yes, but that was before. Now we have other things to think
about.

JULIE. Don't speak harshly to me!

JEAN. I'm not—just sensibly! We've already done one foolish thing, let's not
have any more. The Count could return any minute, and by then we've
got to decide what to do with our lives. What do you think of my plans
for the future? Do you approve?

JULIE. They sound reasonable enough. I have only one question: for such a
big undertaking you need capital—do you have it?

JEAN *(chewing on the cigar)*. Me? Certainly! I have my professional expertise,
my wide experience, and my knowledge of languages. That's capital
enough, I should think!

JULIE. But all that won't even buy a train ticket.

JEAN. That's true. That's why I'm looking for a partner to advance me the
money.

JULIE. Where will you find one quickly enough?

JEAN. That's up to you, if you want to come with me.

JULIE. But I can't; I have no money of my own. *(pause)*

JEAN. Then it's all off . . .

JULIE. And . . .

JEAN. Things stay as they are.

JULIE. Do you think I'm going to stay in this house as your lover? With all the servants pointing their fingers at me? Do you imagine I can face my father after this? No! Take me away from here, away from shame and dishonor——Oh, what have I done! My God, my God! *(She cries.)*

JEAN. Now, don't start that old song!——What have you done? The same as many others before you.

JULIE *(screaming convulsively)*. And now you think I'm contemptible!——I'm falling, I'm falling!

JEAN. Fall down to my level and I'll lift you up again.

JULIE. What terrible power drew me to you? The attraction of the weak to the strong? The falling to the rising? Or was it love? Was this love? Do you know what love is?

JEAN. Me? What do you take me for? You don't think this was my first time, do you?

JULIE. The things you say, the thoughts you think!

JEAN. That's the way I was taught, and that's the way I am! Now don't get excited and don't play the grand lady, because we're in the same boat now!——Come on, Julie, I'll pour you a glass of something special! *(He opens a drawer in the table, takes out a wine bottle, and fills two glasses already used.)*

JULIE. Where did you get that wine?

JEAN. From the cellar.

JULIE. My father's burgundy!

JEAN. That'll do for his son-in-law, won't it?

JULIE. And I drink beer! Beer!

JEAN. That only shows I have better taste.

JULIE. Thief!

JEAN. Planning to tell?

JULIE. Oh, oh! Accomplice of a common thief! Was I drunk? Have I been walking in a dream the whole evening? Midsummer eve! A time of innocent fun!

JEAN. Innocent, eh?

JULIE *(pacing back and forth)*. Is there anyone on earth more miserable than I am at this moment?

JEAN. Why should you be? After such a conquest? Think of Kristine in there. Don't you think she has feelings, too?

JULIE. I thought so awhile ago, but not any more. No, a servant is a servant . . .

JEAN. And a whore is a whore!

JULIE *(on her knees, her hands clasped)*. Oh, God in Heaven, end my wretched life! Take me away from the filth I'm sinking into! Save me! Save me!

JEAN. I can't deny I feel sorry for you. When I lay in that onion bed and saw you in the rose garden, well . . . I'll be frank . . . I had the same dirty thoughts all boys have.

JULIE. And you wanted to die for me!

JEAN. In the oat bin? That was just talk.

JULIE. A lie, in other words!

JEAN. *(beginning to feel sleepy).* More or less! I got the idea from a newspaper story about a chimney sweep who curled up in a firewood bin full of lilacs because he got a summons for not supporting his illegitimate child . . .

JULIE. So, that's what you're like . . .

JEAN. I had to think of something. And that's the kind of story women always go for.

JULIE. Swine!

JEAN. *Merde!*

JULIE. And now you've seen the hawk's back . . .

JEAN. Not exactly its *back* . . .

JULIE. And I was to be the first branch . . .

JEAN. But the branch was rotten . . .

JULIE. I was to be the sign on the hotel . . .

JEAN. And I the hotel . . .

JULIE. Sit at your desk, entice your customers, pad their bills . . .

JEAN. That I'd do myself . . .

JULIE. How can anyone be so thoroughly filthy?

JEAN. Better clean up then!

JULIE. You lackey, you menial, stand up, when I speak to you!

JEAN. Menial's strumpet, lackey's whore, shut up and get out of here! Who are you to lecture me on coarseness? None of my kind is ever as coarse as you were tonight. Do you think one of your maids would throw herself at a man the way you did? Have you ever seen any girl of my class offer herself like that? I've only seen it among animals and streetwalkers.

JULIE *(crushed).* You're right. Hit me, trample on me. I don't deserve any better. I'm worthless. But help me! If you see any way out of this, help me, Jean, please!

JEAN *(more gently).* I'd be lying if I didn't admit to a sense of triumph in all this, but do you think that a person like me would have dared even to look at someone like you if you hadn't invited it? I'm still amazed . . .

JULIE. And proud . . .

JEAN. Why not? Though I must say it was too easy to be really exciting.

JULIE. Go on, hit me, hit me harder!

JEAN *(rising).* No! Forgive me for what I've said! I don't hit a man when he's down, let alone a woman. I can't deny though, that I'm pleased to find out that what looked so dazzling to us from below was only tinsel, that the hawk's back was only gray, after all, that the lovely complexion was only powder, that those polished fingernails had black edges, and that a dirty handkerchief is still dirty, even if it smells of perfume . . .! On the other hand, it hurts me to find out that what I was striving for wasn't finer, more substantial. It hurts me to see you sunk so low that you're inferior to your own cook. It hurts like watching flowers beaten down by autumn rains and turned into mud.

JULIE. You talk as if you were already above me.

JEAN. I am. You see, I could make you a countess, but you could. never make me a count.

JULIE. But I'm the child of a count—something you could never be!

JEAN. That's true. But I could be the father of counts—if . . .

JULIE. But you're a thief. I'm not.

JEAN. There are worse things than being a thief! Besides, when I'm working in a house, I consider myself sort of a member of the family, like one of the children. And you don't call it stealing when a child snatches a berry off a full bush. *(His passion is aroused again.)* Miss Julie, you're a glorious woman, much too good for someone like me! You were drinking and you lost your head. Now you want to cover up your mistake by telling yourself that you love me! You don't. Maybe there was a physical attraction— but then your love is no better than mine.——I could never be satisfied to be no more than an animal to you, and I could never arouse real love in you.

JULIE. Are you sure of that?

JEAN. You're suggesting it's possible——Oh, I could fall in love with you, no doubt about it. You're beautiful, you're refined——*(approaching and taking her hand)*——cultured, lovable when you want to be, and once you start a fire in a man, it never goes out. *(putting his arm around her waist)* You're like hot, spicy wine, and one kiss from you . . . *(He tries to lead her out, but she slowly frees herself.)*

JULIE. Let me go!?——You'll never win me like that.

JEAN. *How* then?——Not like that? Not with caresses and pretty speeches. Not with plans about the future or rescue from disgrace! *How* then?

JULIE. How? How? I don't know!——I have no idea!——I detest you as I detest rats, but I can't escape from you.

JEAN. Escape with me!

JULIE *(pulling herself together)*. Escape? Yes, we must escape!——But I'm so tired. Give me a glass of wine? (JEAN *pours the wine. She looks at her watch.*) But we must talk first. We still have a little time. *(She drains the glass, then holds it out for more.)*

JEAN. Don't drink so fast. It'll go to your head.

JULIE. What does it matter?

JEAN. What does it matter? It's vulgar to get drunk! What did you want to tell me?

JULIE. We must escape! But first we must talk, I mean I must talk. You've done all the talking up to now. You told about your life, now I want to tell about mine, so we'll know all about each other before we go off together.

JEAN. Just a minute! Forgive me! If you don't want to regret it afterwards, you'd better think twice before revealing any secrets about yourself.

JULIE. Aren't you my friend?

JEAN. Yes, sometimes! But don't rely on me.

JULIE. You're only saying that.——Besides, everyone already knows my secrets.——You see, my mother was a commoner—very humble background. She was brought up believing in social equality, women's rights, and all that. The idea of marriage repelled her. So, when my father proposed, she replied that she would never become his wife, but he could be her lover. He insisted that he didn't want the woman he loved to be less respected than he. But his passion ruled him, and when she explained that the world's respect meant nothing to her, he accepted her conditions.

But now his friends avoided him and his life was restricted to taking care of the estate, which couldn't satisfy him. I came into the world—against my mother's wishes, as far as I can understand. She wanted to bring me up as a child of nature, and, what's more, to learn everything a boy had to learn, so that I might be an example of how a woman can be as good as a man. I had to wear boy's clothes and learn to take care of horses, but I was never allowed in the cowshed. I had to groom and harness the horses and go hunting—and even had to watch them slaughter animals—that was disgusting! On the estate men were put on women's jobs and women on men's jobs—with the result that the property became run down and we became the laughing stock of the district. Finally, my father must have awakened from his trance because he rebelled and changed everything his way. My parents were then married quietly. Mother became ill—I don't know what illness it was—but she often had convulsions, hid in the attic and in the garden, and sometimes stayed out all night. Then came the great fire, which you've heard about. The house, the stables, and the cowshed all burned down, under very curious circumstances, suggesting arson, because the accident happened the day after the insurance had expired. The quarterly premium my father sent in was delayed because of a messenger's carelessness and didn't arrive in time. *(She fills her glass and drinks.)*

JEAN. Don't drink any more!

JULIE. Oh, what does it matter.——We were left penniless and had to sleep in the carriages. My father had no idea where to find money to rebuild the house because he had so slighted his old friends that they had forgotten him. Then my mother suggested that he borrow from a childhood friend of hers, a brick manufacturer who lived nearby. Father got the loan without having to pay interest, which surprised him. And that's how the estate was rebuilt.——*(drinks again)* Do you know who started the fire?

JEAN. The Countess, your mother.

JULIE. Do you know who the brick manufacturer was?

JEAN. Your mother's lover?

JULIE. Do you know whose money it was?

JEAN. Wait a moment—no, I don't.

JULIE. It was my mother's.

JEAN. You mean the Count's, unless they didn't sign an agreement when they were married.

JULIE. They didn't.——My mother had a small inheritance which she didn't want under my father's control, so she entrusted it to her—friend.

JEAN. Who stole it!

JULIE. Exactly! He kept it.——All this my father found out, but he couldn't bring it to court, couldn't repay his wife's lover, couldn't prove it was his wife's money! It was my mother's revenge for being forced into marriage against her will. It nearly drove him to suicide—there was a rumor that he tried with a pistol, but failed. So, he managed to live through it and my mother had to suffer for what she'd done. You can imagine that those were a terrible five years for me. I loved my father, but I sided with my mother because I didn't know the circumstances. I learned from her to hate men—you've heard how she hated the whole male sex—and I swore to her I'd never be a slave to any man.

JEAN. But you got engaged to that lawyer.

JULIE. In order to make him my slave.

JEAN. And he wasn't willing?

JULIE. He was willing, all right, but I wouldn't let him. I got tired of him.

JEAN. I saw it—out near the stable.

JULIE. What did you see?

JEAN. I saw—how he broke off the engagement.

JULIE. That's a lie! I was the one who broke it off. Has he said that he did? That swine . . .

JEAN. He was no swine. I'm sure. So, you hate men, Miss Julie?

JULIE. Yes!——Most of the time! But sometimes—when the weakness comes, when passion burns! Oh, God, will the fire never die out?

JEAN. Do you hate me, too?

JULIE. Immeasurably! I'd like to have you put to death, like an animal . . .

JEAN. I see—the penalty for bestiality—the woman gets two years at hard labor and the animal is put to death. Right?

JULIE. Exactly!

JEAN. But there's no prosecutor here—and no animal. So, what'll we do?

JULIE. Go away!

JEAN. To torment each other to death?

JULIE. No! To be happy for—two days, a week, as long as we can be happy, and then—die . . .

JEAN. Die? That's stupid! It's better to open a hotel!

JULIE *(without listening).*——on the shore of Lake Como, where the sun always shines, where the laurels are green at Christmas and the oranges glow.

JEAN. Lake Como is a rainy hole, and I never saw any oranges outside the stores. But tourists are attracted there because there are plenty of villas to be rented out to lovers, and that's a profitable business.——Do you know why? Because they sign a lease for six months—and then leave after three weeks!

JULIE *(naively).* Why after three weeks?

JEAN. They quarrel, of course! But they still have to pay the rent in full! And so you rent the villas out again. And that's the way it goes, time after time. There's never a shortage of love—even if it doesn't last long!

JULIE. You don't want to die with me?

JEAN. I don't want to die at all! For one thing, I like living, and for another, I think suicide is a crime against the Providence which gave us life.

JULIE. You believe in God? *You?*

JEAN. Of course I do. And I go to church every other Sunday.——To be honest, I'm tired of all this, and I'm going to bed.

JULIE. Are you? And do you think I can let it go at that? A man owes something to the woman he's shamed.

JEAN *(taking out his purse and throwing a silver coin on the table)*. Here, I don't like owing anything to anybody.

JULIE *(pretending not to notice the insult)*. Do you know what the law states . . .

JEAN. Unfortunately the law doesn't state any punishment for the woman who seduces a man!

JULIE *(as before)*. Do you see any way out but to leave, get married, and then separate?

JEAN. Suppose I refuse such a *mésalliance?*

JULIE. *Mésalliance* . . .

JEAN. Yes, for me! You see, I come from better stock than you. There's no arsonist in my family.

JULIE. How do you know?

JEAN. You can't prove otherwise. We don't keep charts on our ancestors—there's just the police records! But I've read about your family. Do you know who the founder was? He was a miller who let the king sleep with his wife one night during the Danish War. I don't have any noble ancestors like that. I don't have any noble ancestors at all, but I could become one myself.

JULIE. This is what I get for opening my heart to someone unworthy, for giving my family's honor . . .

JEAN. Dishonor!——Well, I told you so: when people drink, they talk, and talk is dangerous!

JULIE. Oh, how I regret it!——How I regret it!——if you at least loved me.

JEAN. For the last time—what do you want? Shall I cry; shall I jump over your riding crop? Shall I kiss you and lure you off to Lake Como for three weeks, and then God knows what . . .? What shall I do? What do you want? This is getting painfully embarrassing! But that's what happens when you stick your nose in women's business. Miss Julie! I see that you're unhappy. I know you're suffering, but I can't understand you. We don't have such romantic ideas; there's not this kind of hate between us. Love is a game we play when we get time off from work, but we don't have all day and night, like you. I think you're sick, really sick. Your mother was crazy, and her ideas have poisoned your life.

JULIE. Be kind to me. At least now you're talking like a human being.

JEAN. Be human yourself, then. You spit on me, and you won't let me wipe myself off——

JULIE. Help me! Help Me! Just tell me what to do, where to go!

JEAN. In God's name, if I only knew myself!

JULIE. I've been crazy, out of my mind, but isn't there any way out?

JEAN. Stay here and keep calm! No one knows anything!

JULIE. Impossible! The others know and Kristine knows.

JEAN. No they don't, and they'd never believe a thing like that!

JULIE. *(hesitantly)*. But—it could happen again!

JEAN. That's true!

JULIE. And then?

JEAN *(frightened)*. Then?——Why didn't I think about that? Yes, there is only one thing to do—get away from here! Right away! I can't come with you, then we'd be finished, so you'll have to go alone—away—anywhere!

JULIE. Alone?——Where?——I can't do that!

JEAN. You must! And before the Count gets back! If you stay, you know what'll happen. Once you make a mistake like this, you want to continue because the damage has already been done . . . Then you get bolder and bolder—until finally you're caught! So leave! Later you can write to the Count and confess everything—except that it was me! He'll never guess who it was, and he's not going to be eager to find out, anyway.

JULIE. I'll go if you come with me.

JEAN. Are you out of your head? Miss Julie runs away with her servant! In two days it would be in the newspapers, and that's something you father would never live through.

JULIE. I can't go and I can't stay! Help me! I'm so tired, so terribly tired. ——Order me! Set me in motion—I can't think or act on my own . . .

JEAN. What miserable creatures you people are! You strut around with your noses in the air as if you were the lords of creation! All right, I'll order you. Go upstairs and get dressed! Get some money for the trip, and then come back down!

JULIE. *(in a half-whisper)*: Come up with me!

JEAN. To your room?——Now you're crazy again! *(hesitates for a moment)* No! Go, at once! *(takes her hand to lead her out)*

JEAN. *(as she leaves)*: Speak kindly to me, Jean!

JEAN. An order always sounds unkind—now you know how it feels. (JEAN, *alone, sighs with relief. He sits at the table, takes out a notebook and pencil, and begins adding up figures, counting aloud as he works. He continues in dumb show until* KRISTINE *enters, dressed for church. She is carrying a white tie and shirt front.)*

KRISTINE. Lord Jesus, what a mess! What have you been up to?

JEAN. Oh, Miss Julie dragged everybody in here. You mean you didn't hear anything? You must have been sleeping soundly.

KRISTINE. Like a log.

JEAN. And dressed for church already?

KRISTINE. Of course! You remember you promised to come with me to communion today!

JEAN. Oh, yes, that's right.——And you brought my things. Come on, then! *(He sits down.* KRISTINE *starts to put on his shirt front and tie. Pause.* JEAN *begins sleepily)* What's the gospel text for today?

KRISTINE. On St. John's Day?—the beheading of John the Baptist, I should think!

JEAN. Ah, that'll be a long one, for sure.——Hey, you're choking me!——Oh, I'm sleepy, so sleepy!

KRISTINE. Yes, what have you been doing, up all night? Your face is absolutely green.

JEAN. I've been sitting here gabbing with Miss Julie.

KRISTINE. She has no idea what's proper, that one! *(pause)*

JEAN. You know, Kristine . . .

KRISTINE. What?

JEAN. It's really strange when you think about it.——Her!

KRISTINE. What's so strange?

JEAN. Everything! *(pause)*

KRISTINE *(looking at the half-empty glasses standing on the table)*. Have you been drinking together, too?

JEAN. Yes.

KRISTINE. Shame on you!——Look me in the eye!

JEAN. Well?

KRISTINE. Is it possible? Is it possible?

JEAN *(thinking it over for a moment)*. Yes, it is.

KRISTINE. Ugh! I never would have believed it! No, shame on you, shame!

JEAN. You're not jealous of her, are you?

KRISTINE. No, not of her! If it had been Clara or Sofie I'd have scratched your eyes out!——I don't know why, but that's the way I feel.——Oh, it's disgusting!

JEAN. Are you angry at her, then?

KRISTINE. No, at you! That was an awful thing to do, awful! Poor girl!—— No, I don't care who knows it—I won't stay in a house where we can't respect the people we work for.

JEAN. Why should we respect them?

KRISTINE. You're so clever, you tell me! Do you want to wait on people who can't behave decently? Do you? You disgrace yourself that way, if you ask me.

JEAN. But it's a comfort to know they aren't any better than us.

KRISTINE. Not for me. If they're no better, what do we have to strive for to better ourselves.——And think of the Count! Think of him! As if he hasn't had enough misery in his life! Lord Jesus! No, I won't stay in this house any longer!——And it had to be with someone like you! If it had been that lawyer, if it had been a real gentleman . . .

JEAN. What do you mean?

KRISTINE. Oh, you're all right for what you are, but there are men and gentlemen, after all!——No, this business with Miss Julie I can never forget. She was so proud, so arrogant with men, you wouldn't have believed she could just go and give herself—and to someone like you! And she was going to have poor Diana shot for running after the gatekeepers' mutt!—

—Yes, I'm giving my notice, I mean it—I won't stay here any longer. On the twenty-fourth of October, I leave!

JEAN. And then?

KRISTINE. Well, since the subject has come up, it's about time you looked around for something since we're going to get married, in any case.

JEAN. Where am I going to look? I couldn't find a job like this if I was married.

KRISTINE. No, that's true. But you can find work as a porter or as a caretaker in some government office. The state doesn't pay much, I know, but it's secure, and there's a pension for the wife and children . . .

JEAN (*grimacing*). That's all very well, but it's a bit early for me to think about dying for a wife and children. My ambitions are a little higher than that.

KRISTINE. Your ambitions, yes! Well, you have obligations, too! Think about them!

JEAN. Don't start nagging me about obligations, I know what I have to do! (*listening for something outside*) Besides, this is something we have plenty of time to think over. Go and get ready for church.

KRISTINE. Who's that walking around up there?

JEAN. I don't know, unless it's Clara.

KRISTINE (*going*). You don't suppose it's the Count, who came home without us hearing him?

JEAN (*frightened*). The Count? No, I don't think so. He'd have rung.

KRISTINE (*going*). Well, God help us! I've never seen anything like this before. (*The sun has risen and shines through the treetops in the park. The light shifts gradually until it slants in through the windows.* JEAN *goes to the door and signals.* MISS JULIE *enters, dressed in travel clothes and carrying a small birdcage, covered with a cloth, which she places on a chair.*)

JULIE. I'm ready now.

JEAN. Shh! Kristine is awake.

JULIE (*very nervous during the following*). Does she suspect something?

JEAN. She doesn't know anything. But my God, you look awful!

JULIE. Why? How do I look?

JEAN. You're pale as a ghost and—excuse me, but your face is dirty.

JULIE. Let me wash up then.——(*She goes to the basin and washes her hands and face.*) Give me a towel!——Oh—the sun's coming up.

JEAN. Then the goblins will disappear.

JULIE. Yes, there must have been goblins out last night!——Jean, listen, come with me! I have some money now.

JEAN (*hesitantly*). Enough?

JULIE. Enough to start with. Come with me! I just can't travel alone on a day like this—midsummer day on a stuffy train—jammed in among crowds of people staring at me. Eternal delays at every station, while I'd wish I had wings. No, I can't, I can't! And then there'll be memories, memories of midsummer days when I was little. The church—decorated with birch leaves and lilacs; dinner at the big table with relatives and friends; the afternoons in the park, dancing, music, flowers, and games. Oh, no matter how far we travel, the memories will follow in the baggage car, with remorse and guilt!

JEAN. I'll go with you—but right away, before it's too late. Right this minute!

JULIE. Get dressed, then! *(picking up the bird cage)*

JEAN. But no baggage! It would give us away!

JULIE. No, nothing! Only what we can have in the compartment with us.

JEAN *(has taken his hat)*. What've you got there? What is it?

JULIE. It's only my greenfinch. I couldn't leave her behind.

JEAN. What? Bring a birdcage with us? You're out of your head! Put it down!

JULIE. It's the only thing I'm taking from my home—the only living being that loves me, since Diana was unfaithful. Don't be cruel! Let me take her!

JEAN. Put the cage down, I said!——And don't talk so loudly—Kristine will hear us!

JULIE. No, I won't leave her in the hands of strangers! I'd rather you killed her.

JEAN. Bring the thing here, then, I'll cut its head off!

JULIE. Oh, But don't hurt her! Don't . . . no, I can't.

JEAN. Bring it here! I can!

JULIE *(taking the bird out of the cage and kissing it)*. Oh, my little Serena, must you die and leave your mistress?

JEAN. Please don't make a scene! Your whole future is at stake! Hurry up! *(He snatches the bird from her, carries it over to the chopping block, and picks up a meat cleaver.* MISS JULIE *turns away.)* You should have learned how to slaughter chickens instead of how to fire pistols. *(He chops off the bird's head.)* Then you wouldn't feel faint at the sight of blood.

JULIE *(screaming)*. Kill me, too! Kill me! You, who can slaughter an innocent animal without blinking an eye! Oh, how I hate, how I detest you! There's blood between us now! I curse the moment I set eyes on you! I curse the moment I was conceived in my mother's womb!

JEAN. What good does cursing do? Let's go!

JULIE *(approaching the chopping block, as if drawn against her will)*. No, I don't want to go yet. I can't . . . until I see . . . Shh! I hear a carriage——*(She listens, but her eyes never leave the cleaver and the chopping block.)* Do you think I can't stand the sight of blood? You think I'm so weak . . . Oh,— I'd like to see your blood and your brains on a chopping block!——I'd like to see your whole sex swimming in a sea of blood, like my little bird . . . I think I could drink from your skull! I'd like to bathe my feet in your open chest and eat your heart roasted whole!——You think I'm weak. You think I love you because my womb craved your seed. You think I want to carry your spawn under my heart and nourish it with my blood— bear your child and take your name! By the way, what is your family name? I've never heard it.——Do you have one? I was to be Mrs. Bootblack—or Madame Pigsty.——You dog, who wears my collar, you lackey, who bears my coat of arms on your buttons—do I have to share you with my cook, compete with my own servant? Oh! Oh! Oh!——You think I'm a coward who wants to run away! No, now I'm staying—and let the storm break! My father will come home . . . to find his desk broken open . . . and his money gone! Then he'll ring—that bell . . . twice for his valet—and then he'll send for the police . . . and then I'll tell everything! Everything! Oh, what a relief it'll be to have it all end—if only it will end!——And then he'll have a stroke and die . . . That'll be the end of all of us—and there'll be peace . . . quiet . . . eternal rest!——And then our coat of arms will be broken against his coffin—the family title extinct— but the valet's line will go on in an orphanage . . . win laurels in the gut- ter, and end in jail!

JEAN. There's the blue blood talking! Very good, Miss Julie! Just don't let that miller out of the closet! (KRISTINE *enters, dressed for church, with a psalm- book in her hand.*)

JULIE *rushing to* KRISTINE *and falling into her arms, as if seeking protection).* Help me, Kristine! Help me against this man!

KRISTINE *(unmoved and cold).* What a fine way to behave on a Sunday morn- ing! *(sees the chopping block)* And look at this mess!——What does all this mean? Why all this screaming and carrying on?

JULIE. Kristine! You're a woman and my friend! Beware of this swine!

JEAN *(uncomfortable).* While you ladies discuss this, I'll go in and shave. *(slips off right)*

JULIE. You must listen to me so you'll understand!

KRISTINE. No, I could never understand such disgusting behavior! Where are you off to in your traveling clothes?——And he had his hat on.—— Well?——Well?——

JULIE. Listen to me, Kristine! Listen, and I'll tell you everything——

KRISTINE. I don't want to hear it . . .

JULIE. But you must listen to me . . .

KRISTINE. What about! If it's about this silliness with Jean, I'm not interested, because it's none of my business. But if you're thinking of tricking him into running out, we'll soon put a stop to that!

JULIE *(extremely nervous).* Try to be calm now, Kristine, and listen to me! I can't stay here, and neither can Jean—so we must go away . . .

KRISTINE. Hm, hm!

JULIE *(brightening).* You see, I just had an idea——What if all three of us go— abroad—to Switzerland and start a hotel together?——I have money, you see—and Jean and I could run it—and I thought you, you could take care of the kitchen . . . Wouldn't that be wonderful?——Say yes! And come with us, and then everything will be settled!——Oh, do say yes! *(embrac- ing* KRISTINE *and patting her warmly)*

KRISTINE *(coolly, thoughtfully).* Hm, hm!

JULIE *(presto tempo).* You've never traveled, Kristine.——You must get out and see the world. You can't imagine how much fun it is to travel by train—

always new faces—new countries.——And when we get to Hamburg, we'll stop off at the zoo—you'll like that.——and then we'll go to the theatre and the opera—and when we get to Munich, dear, there we have museums, with Rubens and Raphael, the great painters, as you know.———You've heard of Munich, where King Ludwig lived—the king who went mad.——And then we'll see his castles—they're still there and they're like castles in fairy tales.——And from there it isn't far to Switzerland—and the Alps.——Imagine—the Alps have snow on them even in the middle of summer!——And oranges grow there and laurel trees that are green all year round——(JEAN *can be seen in the wings right, sharpening his razor on a strop which he holds with his teeth and his left hand. He listens to the conversation, with satisfaction, nodding now and then in approval.* MISS JULIE *continues tempo prestissimo.*) And then we'll start a hotel—and I'll be at the desk, while Jean greets the guests . . . does the shopping . . . writes letters.——You have no idea what a life it'll be—the train whistles blowing and the carriages arriving and the bells ringing in the rooms and down in the restaurant.——And I'll make out the bills—and I know how to salt them! . . . You'll never believe how timid travelers are when they have to pay their bills!——And you—you'll be in charge of the kitchen. ——Naturally, you won't have to stand over the stove yourself.——And since you're going to be seen by people, you'll have to wear beautiful clothes.——And you, with your looks—no, I'm not flattering you—one fine day you'll grab yourself a husband!——You'll see!——A rich Englishman—they're so easy to——(*slowing down*)——catch—and then we'll get rich—and build ourselves a villa on Lake Como.——It's true it rains there a little now and then, but——(*dully*)——the sun has to shine sometimes—although it looks dark—and then . . . of course we could always come back home again——(*pause*)——here—or somewhere else——

KRISTINE. Listen, Miss Julie, do you believe all this?

JULIE (*crushed*). Do I believe it?

KRISTINE. Yes!

JULIE (*wearily*). I don't know. I don't believe in anything any more. (*She sinks down on the bench and cradles her head in her arms on the table.*) Nothing! Nothing at all!

KRISTINE (*turning right to where* JEAN *is standing*). So, you thought you'd run out!

JEAN (*embarrassed; puts the razor on the table*). Run out? That's no way to put it. You hear Miss Julie's plan, and even if she is tired after being up all night, it's still a practical plan.

KRISTINE. Now you listen to me! Did you think I'd work as a cook for that . . .

JEAN. (*sharply*). You watch what you say in front of your mistress! Do you understand?

KRISTINE. Mistress!

JEAN. Yes!

KRISTINE. Listen to him! Listen to him!

JEAN. Yes, you listen! It'd do you good to listen more and talk less! Miss Julie is your mistress. If you despise her, you have to despise yourself for the same reason!

KRISTINE. I've always had enough self-respect——

JEAN. ——to be able to despise other people!

KRISTINE. ——to stop me from doing anything that's beneath me. You can't say that the Count's cook has been up to something with the groom or the swineherd! Can you?

JEAN. No, you were lucky enough to get hold of a gentleman!

KRISTINE. Yes, a gentleman who sells the Count's oats from the stable.

JEAN. You should talk—taking a commission from the grocer and bribes from the butcher.

KRISTINE. What?

JEAN. And you say you can't respect your employers any longer. You, you, you!

KRISTINE. Are you coming to church with me, now? You could use a good sermon after your fine deed!

JEAN. No, I'm not going to church today. You'll have to go alone and confess what you've been up to.

KRISTINE. Yes, I'll do that, and I'll bring back enough forgiveness for you, too. The Savior suffered and died on the Cross for all our sins, and if we go to Him with faith and a penitent heart, He takes all our sins on Himself.

JEAN. Even grocery sins?

JULIE. And do you believe that, Kristine?

KRISTINE. It's my living faith, as sure as I stand here. It's the faith I learned as a child, Miss Julie, and kept ever since. "Where sin abounded, grace did much more abound!"

JULIE. Oh, if I only had your faith. If only . . .

KRISTINE. Well, you see, we can't have it without God's special grace, and that isn't given to everyone——

JULIE. Who is it given to then?

KRISTINE. That's the great secret of the working of grace, Miss Julie, and God is no respecter of persons, for the last shall be the first . . .

JULIE. Then He does respect the last.

KRISTINE (*continuing*). . . . and it is easier for a camel to go through the eye of a needle, than for a rich man to enter the Kingdom of God. That's how it is, Miss Julie! Anyhow, I'm going now—alone, and on the way I'm going to tell the groom not to let any horses out, in case anyone wants to leave before the Count gets back!——Goodbye! (*leaves*)

JEAN. What a witch!——And all this because of a greenfinch!——

JULIE (*dully*). Never mind the greenfinch!——Can you see any way out of this? Any end to it?

JEAN *(thinking)*. No!

JULIE. What would you do in my place?

JEAN. In your place? Let's see—as a person of position, as a woman who had—fallen. I don't know—wait, now I know.

JULIE *(taking the razor and making a gesture)*. You mean like this?

JEAN. Yes! But—understand—*I* wouldn't do it! That's the difference between us!

JULIE. Because you're a man and I'm a woman? What sort of difference is that?

JEAN. The usual difference—between a man and a woman.

JULIE *(with the razor in her hand)*. I want to, but I can't!——My father couldn't either, the time he should have done it.

JEAN. No, he shouldn't have! He had to revenge himself first.

JULIE. And now my mother is revenged again, through me.

JEAN. Didn't you ever love your father, Miss Julie?

JULIE. Oh yes, deeply, but I've hated him, too. I must have done so without realizing it! It was he who brought me up to despise my own sex, making me half woman, half man. Whose fault is what's happened? My father's, my mother's, my own? My own? I don't have anything that's my own, I don't have a single thought that I didn't get from my father, not an emotion that I didn't get from my mother, and this last idea—that all people are equal—I got that from my fiancé.——That's why I called him a swine! How can it be my fault? Shall I let Jesus take on the flame, the way Kristine does?——No, I'm too proud to do that and too sensible—thanks to my father's teachings.——And as for someone rich not going to heaven, that's a lie. But Kristine won't get in—how will she explain the money she has in the savings bank? Whose fault is it?——What does it matter whose fault it is? I'm still the one who has to bear the blame, face the consequences . . .

JEAN. Yes, but . . . *(the bell rings sharply twice.* MISS JULIE *jumps up.* JEAN *changes his coat.)* The Count is back! Do you suppose Kristine—*(He goes to the speaking tube, taps the lid, and listens.)*

JULIE. He's been to his desk!

JEAN. It's Jean, sir! *(listening; the audience cannot hear the Count's voice.)* Yes, sir! *(listening)* Yes, sir! Right away! *(listening)* At once, sir! *(listening)* I see, in half an hour!

JULIE *(desperately frightened)*. What did he say? Dear Lord, what did he say?

JEAN. He wants his boots and his coffee in half an hour!

JULIE. So, in half an hour! Oh, I'm so tired. I'm not able to do anything, I can't repent, can't run away, can't stay, can't live—can't die! Help me now! Order me, and I'll obey like a dog! Do me this last service, save my honor, save his name! You know what I *should* do, but don't have the will to . . . You will it, you order me to do it!

JEAN. I don't know why——but now I can't either——I don't understand ——It's as if this coat made it impossible for me to order you to do anything.——And now, since the Count spoke to me—I—I can't really explain it—but—ah, it's the damn lackey in me!——I think if the Count came down here now—and ordered me to cut my throat, I'd do it on the spot.

JULIE. Then pretend you're he, and I'm you!——You gave such a good performance before when you knelt at my feet. ——You were a real nobleman.——Or—have you ever seen a hypnotist in the theatre? (JEAN *nods*.) He says to his subject: "Take the broom," and he takes it. He says: "Sweep," and he sweeps——

JEAN. But the subject has to be asleep.

JULIE *(ecstatically)*. I'm already asleep.——The whole room is like smoke around me—and you look like an iron stove—shaped like a man in black, with a tall hat—and your eyes glow like coals when the fire is dying—and your face is a white patch, like ashes——(*The sunlight has reached the floor and now shines on* JEAN.)——it's so warm and good——(*She rubs her hands as if warming them before a fire.*)——and bright—and so peaceful!

JEAN *(taking the razor and putting it in her hand)*. Here's the broom! Go now while it's bright—out to the barn—and . . . *(whispers in her ear)*

JULIE *(awake)*. Thank you. I'm going now to rest! But just tell me—that those who are first can also receive the gift of grace. Say it, even if you don't believe it.

JEAN. The first? No, I can't!——But wait—Miss Julie—now I know! You're no longer among the first—you're now among—the last!

JULIE. That's true.——I'm among the very last. I'm the last one of all. Oh! ——But now I can't go!——Tell me once more to go!

JEAN. No, now I can't either! I can't!

JULIE. And the first shall be the last!

JEAN. Don't think, don't think! You're taking all my strength from me, making me a coward.——What was that! I thought the bell moved!——No! Shall we stuff paper in it?——To be so afraid of a bell!——But it isn't just a bell.——There's someone behind it—a hand sets it in motion—and something else sets the hand in motion.——Maybe if you cover your ears— cover your ears— But then it rings even louder! rings until someone answers.——And then it's too late! And then the police come—and— then——(*The bell rings twice loudly.* JEAN *flinches, then straightens up.*) It's horrible! But there's no other way!——Go! (MISS JULIE *walks firmly out through the door.*)

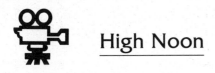

High Noon

Between the appearance of John Cunningham's short story, "The Tin Star," in *Colliers* (December 6, 1947) and the release of *High Noon* (1952), Fred Zinnemann's adaptation of Cunningham's story, the political climate in the United States altered significantly. The determined optimism of "The Tin Star" had been replaced by a spirit of fearful conformity. Zinnemann and his writer Carl Foreman retain the outlines of Cunningham's story but create a political allegory illuminating the dynamics of the McCarthy era in America as do few other contemporary works. "The Tin Star" shows a system of values being passed on from one generation to the next, as a dying sheriff bequeaths his badge to his younger deputy. There is no apostolic succession in *High Noon*: At the end of the film the tin star is cast into the dirt by a man who has been betrayed by those who once called themselves his friends. The town has succumbed to cowardice and conformity. Will Kane has fought for the town and lived; the town, by refusing to fight, has died.

Fred Zinnemann has made a suspenseful drama from Cunningham's story. In both works the sheriff awaits the return of a killer for whose earlier conviction he was responsible. Zinnemann has changed the time of the train's arrival from 4:10 to noon. By beginning his drama at 10:30 a.m., he makes the viewers experience the passage of time in as nearly a realistic manner as possible. Narrative time (roughly one hour and forty minutes) and screen time (eighty-four minutes) are close—but the differences are very significant.

From the opening minutes of the film, we know that a confrontation will occur at noon, with only the outcome remaining in doubt. Because Zinnemann establishes the time of the encounter, he involves the viewer emotionally in his drama. Suspense is created immediately, and the viewer watches helplessly as the hands of all the clocks in Hadleyville move irrevocably toward noon. Time is limited and Will Kane, the sheriff, must organize a posse to match the force of the returning outlaws. The situation is quite different in the story.

Cunningham's sheriff is a widower whose gunfighting days are past. Arthritis afflicts him, and the mayor wants him to resign and leave town while he can. One of his deputies has just quit and the other wants to quit. But the sheriff remains because it is his town and because of the memory of his wife, whose grave he visits on the day of the encounter. One gunman, already in town, follows him to the graveyard and taunts him by shooting several times into the air. His deputy hears the shots, sees the sheriff's horse running loose, and attacks the gunman when he returns to town. Both the two principal protagonists—the sheriff and the convicted killer—are absent when the fight begins. The sheriff realizes what has happened and hastens back to town, arriving shortly before the 4:10 train pulls in. The wounded deputy tells the sheriff he still has time to leave, but in the end it is the sheriff who sacrifices himself to save the life of his deputy. As the sheriff lies dying on the dusty street, he learns that his deputy has decided to remain and carry on for him.

Zinnemann's film opens with three of the killers assembling outside town. The soundtrack carries the plaintive lament sung by Tex Ritter: "Do not forsake me, oh my darling./On this our wedding day . . . " This song, which recurs at crucial moments in the film to heighten the suspense, expresses the sheriff's fears at the moment he is being married. Before his wedding day is out, he will have been betrayed by everyone but his wife, and very nearly by her as well.

As the three gunmen ride into Hadleyville, the church bells are tolling loudly, presumably at 10:30. After this, clocks will appear in nearly every scene. In the judge's chambers, where Will and Amy are being married, the clock on the wall reads 10:33. This is the first indication that the sheriff is outside the community—he is not being married in church. Kane, we learn, has resigned as sheriff, although his replacement is not expected until the following day. Shortly after the ceremony a telegram is delivered announcing the pardon of Frank Miller. The depot agent, who has brought the telegram, reports that Frank Miller is expected on the noon train. Time has begun to play a crucial role in the film. Watches are consulted (it is 10:40), and Kane is urged by his close friends to leave town. He is no longer marshal, and this is the simplest way to avoid trouble. Leaving his gun behind, he embarks on a new life with his Quaker bride, but his sense of responsibility forces him to return and defend his town. His decision, as he slowly learns, causes nothing but pain for himself and others. No one is willing to support him, except for the town drunk and an adolescent boy. When the noon train arrives, he stands alone on the empty streets of Hadleyville.

The actual time elapsed between 10:30 and noon (screen time) is one and one-quarter hours, but time appears to be moving faster because we are aware of actions occurring simultaneously (the gunmen ride into town as the wedding is taking place) and because of the rapid rhythm of the scenes. Time is allowed to slow down when the sheriff is not present (notably in those scenes between Harvey, his deputy, and Helen Ramirez, his former girl friend), but as soon as we return to Kane the pace picks up again. Because we identify with Kane, we experience the passage of time as he does. (The gunmen, by contrast, seek to overcome their boredom by alcohol and music.) We are continually made aware of time by the presence of clocks and watches, even when we cannot read their faces; by references to time ("Be back in ten minutes," one eager townsman tells Kane, "loaded for bear"); and by a rhythmic ticking of a clock on the soundtrack, often used as a transitional device. Some locations, such as Fuller's home, the saloon, and Helen Ramirez's bedroom, have two clocks, so that a clock can be included in virtually every shot. A wooden sign in the shape of a clock swings over the side-

High Noon. The ubiquitous clock brings together the sheriff and his former lover.

walk before a watch repair shop. Each indication of time reminds us of the inevitable confrontation at noon.

The rhythm of the film becomes slightly slower in the final minutes before noon, as Kane, believing his wife has left him, becomes resigned to facing the gunmen alone. Just before noon, the pace quickens with a montage of short shots recapitulating the film so far, and showing the townspeople in their postures of impotent conformity. The townspeople also function as surrogates for the audience; like them, we anxiously wait for something to happen. The montage represents Kane's thoughts as he sees those in his mind who have deserted him. He has approached everyone and his rejection has been total: by his wife, who plans to leave on the noon train; by the judge, who delivers a cynical lesson in civics as he rolls up his American flag and prepares to depart; by his deputy, who quits in anger because he has not been named Kane's successor; by the locals in the bar, who miss the excitement of the old days and dislike Kane; by his good friend Fuller, who hides inside his house when Kane approaches; by the entire congregation, who are swayed into apathy by the testimony of Jonas Henderson, who has just served as best man at Kane's wedding; and even by Kane's childhood idol, the old sheriff, who had gotten him the job. The sequence culminates with the piercing cry of the train whistle and a shot of the engine pulling into the station. The moment we have been awaiting has finally arrived and time, which had been propelling us, suddenly stands still. Kane remains at his desk, writing his will. By making time now appear to move slowly, Zinnemann heightens the anxiety of his audience. Our response is just the opposite of what it was earlier: Now we want time to pass quickly so that the encounter can be over. Clocks are conspicuously absent until the very end of the shootout, when Frank Miller enters the marshal's office and seizes Amy Kane. The clock on the wall reads 12:10. From high noon to 12:10, narrative time has been slower than screen time (thirteen minutes), a reversal of the relationship in the first part of the film. By making time appear to pass slowly, Zinnemann has heightened the tension on the streets of Hadleyville and emphasized the brutality of the wasteful carnage. In the final two minutes of the film, screen time and narrative time are exactly the same.

The narrative time of *High Noon* runs roughly from 10:25 to 12:15, while the screen time is eighty-four minutes. Most viewers (and many early critics of the film) assumed the times to be identical. By manipulating the time scheme to create suspense, Zinnemann has involved his otherwise supine spectators in a striking political allegory of conformity and passivity.

High Noon

Production Credits

Director	Fred Zinnemann
Producer	Stanley Kramer
Screenplay by	Carl Foreman
Based on "The Tin Star" by	John M. Cunningham
Director of Photography	Floyd Crosby
Art Director	Rudolph Sternad
Film Editor	Elmo Williams
Music by	Dimitri Tiomkin

USA. 1952. 84 minutes. Black & white.

Cast

Will Kane	Gary Cooper
Jonas Henderson	Thomas Mitchell
Harvey Pell	Lloyd Bridges
Helen Ramirez	Katy Jurado

Amy Kane
Percy Mettrick
Martin Howe
Sam Fuller
Mildred Fuller
Ben Miller
Frank Miller
Colby
Pierce

Grace Kelly
Otto Kruger
Lon Chaney
Harry Morgan
Eve McVeagh
Sheb Woolley
Ian MacDonald
Lee Van Cleef
Bob Wilke

Further Reading

Burton, Howard. "High Noon: Everyman Rides Again." *The Quarterly of Film, Radio and Television*, 8, No. 1 (Fall 1953), 80–86.

Fenin, George N. and William K. Everson. *The Western: From Silents to the Seventies*. New York: Grossman, 1973.

French, Philip. *Westerns: Aspects of a Movie Genre*. Oxford University Press, 1977.

Garrett, George P., O. B. Hardison, Jr., and Jane R. Gelfman, Eds. *Film Scripts Two*. New York: Appleton-Century Crofts, 1971.

Giannetti, Louis D. *Masters of the American Cinema*. Englewood Cliffs, N.J.: Prentice-Hall, 1981.

Phillips, Gene D. "Fred Zinnemann: An Interview." *Journal of Popular Film and Television*, 7 (1978), 56–66.

————. *The Movie-Makers: Artists in an Industry*. Chicago: Nelson-Hall Co., 1973.

Wright, Will. *Six Guns and Society: A Structural Study of the Western*. Berkeley: University of California Press, 1975.

The Tin Star
John M. Cunningham

Sheriff Doane looked at his deputy and then down at the daisies he had picked for his weekly visit, lying wrapped in newspaper on his desk. "I'm sorry to hear you say that, Toby. I was kind of counting on you to take over after me."

"Don't get me wrong, Doane," Toby said, looking through the front window. "I'm not afraid, I'll see you through this shindig. I'm not afraid of Jordan or young Jordan or any of them. But I want to tell you now. I'll wait till Jordan's train gets in. I'll wait to see what he does. I'll see you through whatever happens. After that, I'm quitting."

Doane began kneading his knuckles, his face set against the pain as he gently rubbed the arthritic, twisted bones. He said nothing.

Toby looked around, his brown eyes troubled in his round, olive-skinned face. "What's the use of holding down a job like this? Look at you. What'd you ever get out of it? Enough to keep you eating. And what for?"

Doane stopped kneading his arthritic hands and looked down at the star on his shirt front. He looked from it to the smaller one on Toby's. "That's right," he said. "They don't even hang the right ones. You risk your life catching somebody, and the damned juries let them go so they can come back and shoot at you. You're poor all your life, you got to do everything twice, and in the end they pay you off in lead. So you can wear a tin star. It's a job for a dog, son."

Toby's voice did not rise, but his eyes were a little wider in his round, gentle face. "Then why keep on with it? What for? I been working for you for two years—trying to keep the law so sharp-nosed money-grabbers can get rich, while we piddle along on what the county pays us. I've seen men I used to bust playing marbles going up and down this street on four-hundred-dollar-saddles, and what've I got? Nothing. Not a damned thing."

There was a little smile around Doane's wide mouth. "That's right, Toby. It's all for free. The headaches, the bullets and everything, all for free. I found that out long ago." The mock-grave look vanished. "But somebody's got to be around and take care of things." He looked out of the window at the people walking up and down the crazy boardwalks. "I like it free. You know what I mean? You don't get a thing for it. You've got to risk everything. And you're free inside. Like the larks. You know the larks? How they get up in the sky and sing when they want to? A pretty bird. A very pretty bird. That's the way I like to feel inside."

Toby looked at him without expression. "That's the way you look at it. I don't see it. I've only got one life. You talk about doing it all for nothing, and that gives you something. What? What've you got now, waiting for Jordan to come?"

"I don't know yet. We'll have to wait and see.

Toby turned back to the window. "All right, but I'm through. I don't see any sense in risking your neck for nothing."

"Maybe you will," Doane said, beginning to work on his hands again.

"Here comes Mettrick. I guess he don't give up so easy. He's still got that resignation in his hand."

"I guess he doesn't," Doane said. "But I'm through listening. Has young Jordan come out of the saloon yet?"

"No," Toby said, and stepped aside as the door opened. Mettrick came in. "Now listen, Doane," he burst out, "for the last time—"

"Shut up, Percy," Doane said. "Sit down over there and shut up or get out."

The flare went out of the mayor's eyes. "Doane," he moaned, "you are the biggest—"

"Shut up," Doane said. "Toby, has he come out yet?"

Toby stood a little back from the window, where the slant of golden sunlight, swarming with dust, wouldn't strike his white shirt.

"Yes. He's got a chair. He's looking this way, Doane. He's still drinking. I can see a bottle on the porch beside him."

"I expected that. Not that it makes much difference." He looked down at the bunch of flowers.

Mettrick, in the straight chair against the wall, looked up at him, his black eyes scornful in his long, hopeless face.

"Don't make much difference? Who the hell do you think you are, Doane? God? It just means he'll start the trouble without waiting for his stinking brother, that's all it means." His hand was shaking, and the white paper hanging listlessly from his fingers fluttered slightly. He looked at it angrily and stuck it out at Doane. "I gave it to you. I did the best I could. Whatever happens, don't be blaming me, Doane. I gave you a chance to resign, and if—" He left off and sat looking at the paper in his hand as though it were a dead puppy of his that somebody had run a buggy over.

Doane, standing with the square, almost chisel-pointed tips of his fingers just touching the flowers, turned slowly, with the care of movement he would have used around a crazy horse. "I know you're my friend, Percy. Just take it easy, Percy. If I don't resign, it's not because I'm ungrateful."

"Here comes Staley with the news," Toby said from the window. "He looks like somebody just shot his grandma."

Percy Mettrick laid his paper on the desk and began smoothing it out ruefully. "It's not as though it were dishonorable, Doane. You should have quit two years ago, when your hands went bad. It's not dishonorable now. You've still got time."

He glanced up at the wall clock. "It's only three. You've got an hour before he gets in you can take your horse . . ." As he talked to himself, Doane looking slantwise at him with his little smile, he grew more cheerful. "Here." He jabbed a pen out at Doane. "Sign it and get out of town."

The smile left Doane's mouth. "This is an elective office. I don't have to take orders, even if you are the mayor." His face softened. "It's simpler than you think, Percy. When they didn't hang Jordan, I knew this day would come. Five years ago, I knew it was coming, when they gave him that silly sentence. I've been waiting for it."

"But not to commit suicide," Mettrick said in a low voice, his eyes going down to Doane's gouty hands. Doane's knobby, twisted fingers closed slowly into fists, as though hiding themselves; his face flushed slightly. "I may be slow, but I can still shoot."

The mayor stood up and went slowly over to the door.

"Goodby, Doane."

"I'm not saying goodby, Percy. Not yet."

"Goodby," Mettrick repeated, and went out of the door.

Toby turned from the window. His face was tight around the mouth. "You should have resigned like he said, Doane. You ain't a match for one of them alone, much less two of them together. And if Pierce and Frank Colby come, too, like they was all together before—"

"Shut up, shut up," Doane said. "For God's sake, shut up." He sat down suddenly at the desk and covered his face with his hands. "Maybe the pen changes a man." He was sitting stiff, hardly breathing.

"What are you going to do, Doane?"

"Nothing. I can't do anything until they start something. I can't do a thing. . . . Maybe the pen changes a man. Sometimes it does. I remember—"

"Listen, Doane," Toby said, his voice, for the first time, urgent. "It maybe changes some men, but not Jordan. It's already planned, what they're going to do. Why else would young Jordan be over there, watching? He's come three hundred miles for this."

"I've seen men go in the pen hard as rock and come out peaceful and settle down. Maybe Jordan—"

Toby's face relapsed into dullness. He turned back to the window listlessly. Doane's hands dropped.

"You don't think that's true, Toby?"

Toby sighed. "You know it isn't so, Doane. He swore he'd get you. That's the truth."

Doane's hands came up again in front of his face, but this time he was looking at them, his big gray eyes going quickly from one to the other, almost as though he were afraid of them. He curled his fingers slowly into fists, and uncurled them slowly, pulling with all his might, yet slowly. A thin sheen on his face reflected the sunlight from the floor. He got up.

"Is he still there?" he asked.

"Sure, he's still there."

"Maybe he'll get drunk. Dead drunk."

"You can't get a Jordan that drunk."

Doane stood with feet apart, looking at the floor, staring back and forth along one of the cracks. "Why didn't they hang him?" he asked the silence in the room.

"Why didn't they hang him?" he repeated, his voice louder.

Toby kept his post by the window, not moving a muscle in his face, staring out at the man across the street. "I don't know," he said. "For murder, they should. I guess they should; but they didn't."

Doane's eyes came again to the flowers, and some of the strain went out of his face. Then suddenly his eyes closed and he gave a long sigh, and then, luxuriously, stretched his arms. "Good God!" he said, his voice easy again. "It's funny how it comes over you like that." He shook his head violently. "I don't know why it should. It's not the first time. But it always does."

"I know," Toby said.

"It just builds up and then it busts."

"I know."

"The train may be late."

Toby said nothing.

"You never can tell," Doane said, buckling on his gun belt. "Things may have changed with Jordan. Maybe won't even come. You never can tell. I'm going up to the cemetery as soon as we hear from Staley."

"I wouldn't. You'd just tempt young Jordan to start something."

"I've been going up there every Sunday since she died."

"We'd best both just stay in here. Let them make the first move."

Feet sounded on the steps outside and Doane stopped breathing for a second. Staley came in, his face pinched, tight and dead, his eyes on the floor. Doane looked him over carefully.

"Is it on time?" he asked steadily.

Staley looked up, his faded blue eyes distant, pointed somewhere over Doane's head. "Mr. Doane, you ain't handled this thing right. You should of drove young Jordan out of town." His hand went to his chest and he took off the deputy's badge.

"What are you doing?" Doane asked sharply.

"If you'd of handled it right, we could have beat this," Staley said, his voice louder.

"You know nobody's done nothing yet," Toby said softly, his gentle brown eyes on Staley. "There's nothing we can do until they start something."

"I'm quitting, Mr. Doane," Staley said. He looked around for someplace to put the star. He started for the desk, hesitated, and then awkwardly, with a peculiar diffidence, laid the star gently on the window sill.

Doane's jaw began to jut a little. "You still haven't answered my question. Is the train on time?"

"Yes. Four ten. Just on time." Staley stood staring at Doane, then swallowed. "I saw Frank Colby. He was in the livery putting up his horse. He'd had a long ride on that horse. I asked him what he was doing in town—friendly like." He ducked his head and swallowed again. "He didn't know I was a deputy, I had my star off." He looked up again. "They're all meeting together, Mr. Doane. Young Jordan, and Colby and Pierce. They're going to meet Jordan when he comes in. The same four."

"So you're quitting," Doane said.

"Yes, sir. It ain't been handled right."

Toby stood looking at him, his gentle eyes dull. "Get out," he said, his voice low and tight.

Staley looked at him, nodded and tried to smile, which was too weak to last. "Sure."

Toby took a step toward him. Staley's eyes were wild as he stood against the door. He tried to back out of Toby's way.

"Get out," Toby said again, and his small brown fist flashed out. Staley stepped backward and fell down the steps in a sprawling heap, scrambled to his feet and hobbled away. Toby closed the door slowly. He stood rubbing his knuckles, his face red and tight.

"That didn't do any good," Doane said softly.

Toby turned on him. "It couldn't do no harm," he said acidly, throwing the words into Doane's face.

"You want to quit, too?" Doane asked, smiling.

"Sure, I want to quit," Toby shot out. "Sure. Go on to your blasted cemetery, go on with your flowers, old man—" He sat down suddenly on the straight chair. "Put a flower up there for me, too."

Doane went to the door. "Put some water on the heater, Toby. Set out the liniment that the vet gave me. I'll try it again when I get back. It might do some good yet."

He let himself out and stood in the sunlight on the porch, the flowers drooping in his hand, looking against the sun across the street at the dim figure under the shaded porch.

Then he saw the two other shapes hunkered against the front of the saloon in the shade of the porch, one on each side of young Jordan, who sat tilted back in a chair. Colby and Pierce. The glare of the sun beat back from the blinding white dust and fought shimmering in the air.

Doane pulled the brim of his hat farther down in front and stepped slowly down to the board sidewalk, observing carefully from squinted eyes, and just as carefully avoiding any pause which might be interpreted as a challenge.

Young Jordan had the bottle to his lips as Doane came out. He held it there for a moment motionless, and then, as Doane reached the walk, he passed the bottle slowly sideward to Colby and leaned forward, away from the wall, so that the chair came down softly. He sat there, leaning foward slightly, watching while Doane untied his horse. As Doane mounted, Jordan got up. Colby's hand grabbed one of his arms. He shook it off and untied his own horse from the rail.

Doane's mouth tightened and his eyes looked a little sad. He turned his horse, and holding the flowers so the jog would not rattle off the petals, headed up the street, looking straight ahead.

The hoofs of his horse made soft, almost inaudible little plops in the deep dust. Behind him he heard a sudden stamping of hoofs and then the harsh splitting and crash of wood. He looked back. Young Jordan's horse was up on the sidewalk, wild-eyed and snorting, with young Jordan leaning forward half out of the saddle, pushing himself back from the horse's neck, back off the horn into the saddle, swaying insecurely. And as Jordan managed the horse off the sidewalk Doane looked quickly forward again, his eyes fixed distantly ahead and blank.

He passed men he knew, and out of the corner of his eye he saw their glances slowly follow him, calm, or gloomy, or shrewdly speculative. As he passed, he knew their glances were shifting to the man whose horse was softly coming behind him. It was like that all the way up the street. The flowers were drooping markedly now.

The town petered out with a few Mexican shacks, the road dwindled to broad ruts, and the sage was suddenly on all sides of him, stretching away toward the heat-obscured mountains like an infinite multitude of gray-green sheep. He turned off the road and began the slight ascent up the little hill whereon the cemetery lay. Grasshoppers shrilled invisibly in the sparse, dried grass along the track, silent as he came by, and shrill again as he passed, only to become silent again as the other rider came.

He swung off at the rusty barbed wire Missouri gate and slipped the loop from the post, and the shadow of the other slid tall across his path and stopped. Doane licked his lips quickly and looked up, his grasp tightening on the now sweat-wilted newspaper. Young Jordan was sitting his horse, openmouthed, leaning forward with his hands on the pommel to support himself, his eyes vague and dull. His lips were wet and red, and hung in a slight smile.

A lark made the air sweet over to the left, and then Doane saw it, rising into the air. It hung in the sun, over the cemetery. Moving steadily and avoiding all suddenness, Doane hung his reins over the post.

"You don't like me, do you?" young Jordan said. A long thread of saliva descended from the corner of his slackly smiling mouth.

Doane's face set into a sort of blank preparedness. He turned and started slowly through the gate, his shoulders hunched up and pulled backward.

Jordan got down from the saddle, and Doane turned toward him slowly. Jordan came forward straight enough, with his feet apart, braced against staggering. He stopped three feet from Doane, bent forward, his mouth slightly open.

"You got any objections to me being in town?"

"No," Doane said, and stood still.

Jordan thought that over, his eyes drifting idly sideways for a moment. Then they came back, to a finer focus this time, and he said, "Why not?" hunching forward again, his hands open and held away from the holsters at his hips.

Doane looked at the point of his nose. "You haven't done anything, Jordan. Except get drunk. Nothing to break the law."

"I haven't done nothing," Jordan said, his eyes squinting away at one of the small, tilting tombstones. "By God, I'll do something. Whadda I got to do?" He drew his head back, as though he were farsighted, and squinted. "Whadda I got to do to make you fight, huh?"

"Don't do anything," Doane said quietly, keeping his voice even. "Just go back and have another drink. Have a good time."

"You think I ain't sober enough to fight?" Jordan slipped his right gun out of its holster, turning away from Doane. Doane stiffened. "Wait, mister," Jordan said.

He cocked the gun. "See that bird?" He raised the gun into the air, squinting along the barrel. The bright nickel of its finish gleamed in the sun. The lark wheeled and fluttered. Jordan's arm swung unsteadily in a small circle.

He pulled the trigger and the gun blasted. The lark jumped in the air, flew away about twenty feet, and began circling again, catching insects.

"Missed 'im," Jordan mumbled, lowering his arm and wiping sweat off his forehead. "Damn it, I can't see!" He raised his arm again. Again the heavy blast cracked Doane's ears. Down in the town, near the Mexican huts, he could see tiny figures run out into the street.

The bird didn't jump this time, but darted away out of sight over the hill.

"Got him," Jordan said, scanning the sky. His eyes wandered over the graveyard for a moment, looking for the bird's body. "Now you see?" he said, turning to Doane, his eyes blurred and watering with the sun's glare. "I'm going down and shoot up the damned town. Come down and stop me, you old—"

He turned and lurched sideways a step, straightened himself out and walked more steadily toward his horse, laughing to himself. Doane turned away, his face sick, and trudged slowly up the hill, his eyes on the ground.

He stopped at one of the newer graves. The headstone was straight on this one. He looked at it, his face changing expression. "Here lies Cecelia Doane, born 1837, died 1885, the loyal wife . . ."

He stopped and pulled a weed from the side of the grave, then pulled a bunch of withered stems from a small green funnel by the headstone, and awkwardly took the fresh flowers out of the newspaper. He put the flowers into the funnel, wedging them firmly down into the bottom, and set it down again. He stood up and moved back, wiping sweat from his eyes.

A sudden shout came from the gate, and the sharp crack of a quirt. Doane turned with a befuddled look.

Jordan was back on his horse, beating Doane's. He had looped the reins over its neck so that it would run free. It was tearing away down the slope headed back for town.

Doane stood with his hat in his hand, his face suddenly beet red. He took a step after Jordan, and then stood still, shaking a little. He stared fixedly after him, watching him turn into the main road and toward the main street again. Then, sighing deeply, he turned back to the grave. Folding the newspaper, he began dusting off the heavy slab, whispering to himself. "No, Cissie. I could have gone. But, you know—it's my town."

He straightened up, his face flushed, put on his hat, and slapping the folded paper against his knee, started down the path. He got to the Missouri gate, closed it, and started down the ruts again.

A shot came from the town, and he stopped. Then there were two more, sharp spurts of sound coming clear and definite across the sage. He made out a tiny figure in a blue shirt running along a sidewalk.

He stood stock-still, the grasshoppers singing in a contented chorus all around him in the bright yellow glare. A train whistle came faint from off the plain, and he looked far across it. He made out the tiny trailed plume of smoke.

His knees began to quiver very slightly and he began to walk, very slowly, down the road.

Then suddenly there was a splatter of shots from below. The train whistle came again, louder, a crying wail of despair in the burning, brilliant, dancing air.

He began to hurry, stumbling a little in the ruts. And then he stopped short, his face open in fear. "My God, my empty horse, those shots—Toby, no!" He began to run, shambling, awkward and stumbling, his face ashen.

From the end of the street, as he hobbled panting past the tightshut Mexican shanties, he could see a blue patch in the dust in front of the saloon, and shambled to a halt. It wasn't Toby, whoever it was, lying there face down: face buried in the deep, pillowing dust, feet still on the board sidewalk where the man had been standing.

The street was empty. None of the faces he knew looked at him now. He drew one of his guns and cocked it and walked fast up the walk, on the saloon side.

A shot smashed ahead of him and he stopped, shrinking against a store front. Inside, through the glass door, he could see two pale faces in the murk. Blue powder smoke curled out from under the saloon porch ahead of him.

Another shot smashed, this time from his office. The spurt of smoke, almost invisible in the sunlight, was low down in the doorway. Two horses were loose in the street now, his own, standing alert up past the saloon, and young Jordan's, half up on the boardwalk under one of the porches.

He walked forward, past young Jordan's horse, to the corner of the saloon building. Another shot slammed out of his office door, the bullet smacking the window ahead of him. A small, slow smile grew on his mouth. He looked sideways at the body in the street. Young Jordan lay with the back of his open to the sun, crimson and brilliant, his bright nickel gun still in his right hand, its hammer still cocked, unfired.

The train whistle moaned again, closer.

"Doane," Toby called from the office door, invisible. "Get out of town." There was a surge of effort in the voice, a strain that made it almost a squeal. "I'm shot in the leg. Get out before they get together."

A door slammed somewhere. Doane glanced down between the saloon and the store beside it. Then he saw, fifty yards down the street, a figure come out of another side alley and hurry away down the walk toward the station. From the saloon door another shot slammed across the street. Toby held his fire.

Doane peered after the running figure, his eyes squinting thoughtfully. The train's whistle shrieked again like the ultimatum of an approaching conqueror at the edge of town, and in a moment the ground under his feet began to vibrate slightly and the hoarse roar of braking wheels came up the street.

He turned back to the young Jordan's horse, petted it around the head a moment and then took it by the reins close to the bit. He guided it across the street, keeping its body between him and the front of the saloon, without drawing fire, and went on down the alley beside his office. At the rear door he hitched the horse and went inside.

Toby was on the floor, a gun in his hand, his hat beside him, peering out across the sill. Doane kept low, beneath the level of the window, and crawled up to him. Toby's left leg was twisted peculiarly and blood leaked steadily out from the boot top onto the floor. His face was sweating and very pale, and his lips were tight.

"I thought he got you," Toby said, keeping his eyes on the saloon across the street. "I heard those shots and then your horse came bucketing back down the street. I got Jordan. Colby got me in the leg before I got back inside."

"Never mind about that. Come on, get on your feet if you can and I'll help you on the horse in back. You can get out of town and I'll shift for myself."

"I think I'm going to pass out. I don't want to move. It won't hurt no worse getting killed than it does now. The hell with the horse! Take it yourself."

Doane looked across the street, his eyes moving over the door and the windows carefully, inch by inch.

"I'm sorry I shot him," Toby said. "It's my fault. And it's my fight now, Doane. Clear out."

Doane turned and scuttled out of the back. He mounted the horse and rode down behind four stores. He turned up another alley, dashed across the main street, down another alley, then back up behind the saloon.

He dismounted, his gun cocked in his hand. The back door of the place was open and he got through it quickly, the sound of his boot heels dimmed under the blast of a shot from the front of the saloon. From the dark rear of the room, he could see Pierce, crouched behind the bar, squinting through a bullet hole in the stained-glass bottom half of the front window.

There was a bottle of whisky standing on the bar beside Pierce; he reached out a hand and tilted the bottle up to his mouth, half turning toward Doane as he did so. Pierce kept the bottle to his lips, pretending to drink, and, with his right hand invisible behind the bar, brought his gun into line with Doane.

The tip of Pierce's gun came over the edge of the bar, the rest of him not moving a hair, and Doane, gritting his teeth, squeezed slowly and painfully on his gun trigger. The gun flamed and bucked in his hand, and he dropped it, his face twisting in agony. The bottle fell out of Pierce's hand and spun slowly on the bar. Pierce sat there for a moment before his head fell forward and he crashed against the edge of the bar and slipped down out of sight.

Doane picked up his gun with his left hand and walked forward to the bar, holding his right hand like a crippled paw in front of him. The bottle had stopped revolving. Whisky inside it, moving back and forth, rocked it gently. He righted it and took a short pull at the neck, and in a moment the pain lines relaxed in his face. He went to the bat-wing doors and pushed one of them partly open.

"Toby!" he called.

There was no answer from across the street, and then he saw the barrel of a revolver sticking out of his office door, lying flat, and behind it one hand, curled loosely and uselessly around the butt.

He looked down the street. The train stood across it. A brakeman moved along the cars slowly, his head down. There was nobody else in sight.

He started to step out, and saw then two men coming up the opposite walk, running fast. Suddenly one of them stopped, grabbing the other by the arm, and pointed at him. He stared back for a moment, seeing Jordan clearly now, the square, hard face unchanged except for its pallor, bleak and bony as before.

Doane let the door swing to and continued to watch them over the top of it. They talked for a moment. Then Colby ran back down the street—well out of effective range—sprinted across it and disappeared. Down the street the engine, hidden by some building, chuffed angrily, and the cars began to move again. Jordan stood still, leaning against the front of a building, fully exposed, a hard smile on his face.

Doane turned and hurried to the back door. It opened outward. He slammed and bolted it, then hurried back to the front and waited, his gun ready. He smiled as the back door rattled, turned, fired a shot at it and listened. For a moment there was no sound. Then something solid hit it, bumped a couple of times and silence came again.

From the side of the building, just beyond the corner where Pierce's body lay, a shot crashed. The gun in the office door jumped out of the hand and spun wildly. The hand lay still.

He heard Jordan's voice from down the street, calling, the words formed slowly, slightly spaced.

"Is he dead?"

"Passed out," Colby called back.

"I'm going around back to get him. Keep Doane inside." Jordan turned and disappeared down an alley.

Doane leaned across the bar, knocked bottles off the shelves of the back bar and held his pistol on the corner of the wall, about a foot above the floor.

"Pierce," he said.

"Throw out your guns," Pierce answered.

Doane squinted at the corner, moved his gun slightly and fired. He heard a cry of pain, then curses; saw the bat-wing doors swing slightly. Then he turned and ran for the back door. He threw back the bolt and pushed on the door. It wouldn't give. He threw himself against it. It gave a little at the bottom. Colby had thrown a stake up against it to keep him locked in.

He ran back to the front.

Across the street, he could see somebody moving in his office, dimly, beyond the window. Suddenly the hand on the floor disappeared.

"Come on out, you old——" Pierce said, panting. "You only skinned me." His voice was closer than before, somewhere between the door and the corner of the building, below the level of the stained glass.

Then Doane saw Toby's white shirt beyond the window opposite. Jordan was holding him up, and moving toward the door. Jordan came out on the porch, hugging Toby around the chest, protecting himself with the limp body. With a heave he sent Toby flying down the steps, and jumped back out of sight. Toby rolled across the sidewalk and fell into the street, where he lay motionless.

Doane looked stupidly at Toby, then at young Jordan, still lying with his feet cocked up on the sidewalk.

"He ain't dead, Doane," Jordan called. "Come and get him if you want him alive." He fired through the window. Dust jumped six inches from Toby's head. "Come on out, Doane, and shoot it out. You got a chance to save him." The gun roared again, and dust jumped a second time beside Toby's head, almost in the same spot.

"Leave the kid alone," Doane called. "This fight's between you and me."

"The next shot kills him, Doane."

Doane's face sagged white and he leaned against the side of the door. He could hear Pierce breathing heavily in silence, just outside. He pushed himself away from the door and drew a breath through clenched teeth. He cocked his pistol and strode out, swinging around. Pierce fired from the sidewalk, and Doane aimed straight into the blast and pulled as he felt himself flung violently around by Pierce's bullet.

Pierce came up from the sidewalk and took two steps toward him, opening and shutting a mouth that was suddenly full of blood, his eyes wide and wild, and then pitched down at his feet.

Doane's right arm hung useless, his gun at his feet. With his left hand he drew his other gun and stepped out from the walk, his mouth wide open, as though he were gasping for breath or were about to scream, and took two steps toward Toby as Jordan came out of the office door, firing. The slug caught Doane along the side of his neck, cutting the shoulder muscle, and his head fell over to one side. He staggered on, firing. He saw Toby trying to get up, saw Jordan fall back against the building, red running down the front of his shirt, and the smile gone.

Jordan stood braced against the building, holding his gun in both hands, firing as he slid slowly down. One bullet took Doane in the stomach, another in the knee. He went down, flopped forward and dragged himself up to where Toby lay trying to prop himself up on one elbow. Doane knelt there like a dog, puking blood into the dust, blood running out of his nose, but his gray eyes almost indifferent, as though there were one man dying and another watching.

He saw Jordan lift his gun with both hands and aim it toward Toby, and as the hammer fell, he threw himself across Toby's head and took it in the back. He rolled off onto his back and lay staring into the sky.

Upside down, he saw Toby take his gun and get up on one elbow, level it at Jordan and fire, and then saw Toby's face, over his, looking down at him as the deputy knelt in the street.

They stayed that way for a long moment, while Doane's eyes grew more and more dull and the dark of his blood in the white dust grew broader. His breath was coming hard, in small sharp gasps.

"There's nothing in it, kid," he whispered. "Only a tin star. They don't hang the right ones. You got to fight everything twice. It's a job for a dog."

"Thank you, Doane."

"It's all for free. You going to quit, Toby?"

Toby looked down at the gray face, his mouth and chin and neck crimson, the gray eyes dull. Toby shook his head. His face was hard as a rock.

Doane's face suddenly looked a little surprised, his eyes went past Toby to the sky. Toby looked up. A lark was high above them, circling and fluttering, directly overhead. "A pretty bird," Doane mumbled. "A very pretty bird."

His head turned slowly to one side, and Toby looked down at him and saw him as though fast asleep.

He took Doane's gun in his hand, and took off Doane's star, and sat there in the street while men slowly came out of stores and circled about them. He sat there unmoving, looking at Doane's half-averted face, holding the two things tightly, one in each hand, like a child with a broken toy, his face soft and blurred, his eyes unwet.

After a while the lark went away. He looked up at the men, and saw Mettrick.

"I told him he should have resigned," Mettrick said, his voice high. "He could have taken his horse—"

"Shut up," Toby said. "Shut up or get out." His eyes were sharp and his face placid and set. He turned to another of the men. "Get the doc," he said. "I've got a busted leg. And I've got a lot to do."

The man looked at him, a little startled, and then ran.

GLOSSARY

Vocabularies of Literature and Film

Aerial shot. A shot using a moving camera, usually mounted on a helicopter.

Allegory. A work in which the characters, events, and sometimes the setting function on several discrete levels at once, so that the surface story illustrates and parallels another story, often religious or political.

Allusion. A reference within a text or film to another source, usually religious, literary, cinematic, or historical.

Angle. The position from which the camera is directed toward the subject. (See *high-angle shot; low-angle shot; eye-level shot.*)

Aperture. The opening that controls the amount of light entering the camera.

Asynchronous sound. Any sound not synchronized with the accompanying visuals (also called *nonsynchronous* sound).

Auteur theory. A theory developed in France that attributes the authorship of a film to its director.

Available light. See *natural light.*

Background music. Any music accompanying a film, sometimes used to create a mood, to provide continuity, or to reinforce—or undercut—the action.

Back light. Light directed toward a subject from the rear, so that the face is somewhat in shadows.

Back projection shot. A *shot* for which the actors perform within a studio before a translucent screen, onto which a movie is projected from the rear. When filmed from the front, the actors appear to be in a projected scene. (Also called a *rear projection shot*.)

Bird's eye view. A *shot* taken from directly above the subject, which usually creates a measure of detachment in the viewer.

Boom shot. A shot using a moving camera fixed on a boom or crane (also called a *crane shot*).

Bottom lighting. Lighting subjects from below, to make them appear menacing and sinister.

Circular pan. A shot in which the camera moves in a complete circle (also called *three hundred and sixty-degree pan*).

Climax. The culminating action of a narrative.

Close-up (CU). A *shot* taken so that the character's head fills the screen.

Commentator. An objective *narrator* who is usually unseen and personally uninvolved in the material, as in the newsreel sequence of *Citizen Kane*.

Composition. The placement and movement of persons and objects within the *frame*. Persons and objects assume different degrees of importance depending on their position within a frame, and relationships can be suggested by these means. For example, a character's significance can be emphasized by placing him in the foreground, so that he dominates characters and objects in the background; or he can be placed on the right side of the frame that, because we tend to "read" a picture from left to right, is a more dominant position.

Conclusion. The result or outcome of the action of a drama or story.

Continuity editing. Assembling the individual *shots* so that they follow one another in the proper temporal and spatial order. (See *montage*.)

Crane shot. See *boom shot*.

Credits. A listing of the most important participants in the making of a film. This would include the director, producer, actors, technicians, etc.

Cross cutting. The repeated cutting between two distinctly different locations to suggest simultaneity of action (also called *parallel cutting*).

Cut. The simplest and most common transition. One shot is literally cut and spliced to the next. Cuts can be smooth and unobtrusive or abrupt and shocking, depending on the effect the director wishes to create. (See *match cut; jump cut; cross cutting; transition; cutaway shot*.)

Cutaway shot. A shot that cuts away from the main action to a reaction shot, a parallel action, or a subordinate action.

Decelerated motion. See *slow motion*.

Deep focus. A photographic technique that permits a clarity of focus from *close-up* range to infinity.

Denouement. The resolution of a drama.

Depth of field. The distance between which objects remain in focus, determined by the size of the *aperture*.

Dialogue. Conversation between two or more characters.

Director. The person with responsibility for how the script is filmed.

Dissolve. A slow *transition*, in which one image *fades out* while the other *fades in*. As one image overlaps the other, there is a *superimposition*, which can be as short or as long as the filmmaker desires.

Dolly shot. A *shot* using a moving camera fixed on a dolly. A camera may dolly in or dolly out, or dolly with a subject. (See *tracking shot; trucking shot*.)

Double exposure. The *superimposition* on film of one image upon another.

Dramatic irony. A situation in which the reader or viewer understands that the truth is very different from what it appears to be to the fictional characters.

Dubbing. The addition of sound after the film has been photographed. Or the substitution of a soundtrack in one language for the original, as when a foreign film is dubbed into English.

Dutch-angle shot. See *oblique-angle shot.*

Dynamic editing. See *montage.*

Editor. The person with responsibility for assembling the film.

Establishing shot. A shot at the beginning of a film that enables the viewer to determine time, locale, or mood.

Exciting force. A single action that propels the dramatic action.

Exposition. The introductory scene(s) of a play or novel in which the time and place are established and the principal characters are introduced.

Exterior. The representation of an outside scene.

External rhythm. The speed with which one *shot* succeeds another in a film. *Citizen Kane* contains 563 shots in two hours; Hitchcock's *The Birds* has 1360 shots in the same time period, and thus is considered a very rapidly *paced* film.

Extreme close-up (ECU). A *shot* taken from close proximity, so that a small detail fills the screen.

Extreme long shot (ELS). A *shot* taken from a great distance, so that the image appears small (a figure, for example, walking on the distant horizon).

Eye-level shot. A *shot* taken from eye level, to suggest neutrality, objectivity, or equality. (Contrast with *high-* and *low-angle shots.*)

Fade in / Fade out. A transition that conveys a sense of finality, as with the end of a chapter or the lowering of the curtain at a play. With a fade out, the image on the screen gradually becomes dark. A fade in begins with a dark screen and the image gradually becomes visible.

Falling action. The actions that follow the turning point or climax and lead to the conclusion.

Fast motion. The result of filming the action at slower than normal speed. When projected on the screen, action appears to be accelerated, often producing a comic effect.

Fill light. A source of light to supplement the *key light* and produce secondary illumination, as well as to control shadows.

Filter. A piece of glass or plastic, mounted in a rim, which fits over the camera lens. A filter is used to alter the quality of light entering the camera, in order to create lighter, darker, or differently colored composition.

First-person point of view. A mode of storytelling in which the narrator speaks in the first person, as "I."

Fish-eye lens. A lens with an extremely wide angle that distorts the image.

Flashback. A sudden shift to a time before the fictional present of the work.

Flash-forward. A sudden shift into the future.

Flash pan. See *swish pan.*

Flip. A *transition* in which the image appears to flip over, by revolving on a horizontal axis, to reveal an image on the other side.

Focal length. The distance from the optical center of a lens to the plane of principal focus.

Frame. The smallest unit of film, the rectangular still photograph which, by being projected on the screen twenty-four times a second, gives the illusion of motion.

Frame can also refer to the perimeter of the image on the screen, a usage similar to "picture frame."

Frame enlargement. A *still* made by blowing up a shot from a finished film.

Frame narration. A narration that includes one or more other stories within it.

Freeze frame. The repetition of a single frame to give the impression of a still photograph. It often suggests the immobility or stasis of a character.

Front light. Light directed toward a subject from the front, so that the face is fully illuminated.

Front projection shot. Similar to *back projection,* except that the actors perform within a studio before a translucent screen on which a movie is projected from the front.

Full shot. A *long shot* in which the human body fills the frame from top to bottom.

Genre. In film criticism, a recognizable type of film with well-defined thematic features (e.g., the western, the gangster film, etc.). In literary criticism, a categorization by literary species—the traditional categories being tragedy, comedy, epic, satire, and lyric, to which the novel, essay, and biography have been more recently added.

High-angle shot. A shot in which the camera views the subject from above, making the subject appear vulnerable and/or insignificant.

High contrast. A style of lighting that emphasizes extremes of contrast.

High-key lighting. Bright illumination that produces a set with few shadows.

Homage. A *shot* that pays tribute to another film or filmmaker.

Indirect discourse. A version of a speaker's utterance transformed for inclusion in a larger sentence (e.g., She told me she was tired).

Interior. Representation of an inside scene.

Internal monologue. The ordered presentation of a character's thoughts.

Internal rhythm. The speed of movement within an individual *shot.*

Iris. A *transition* common in silent films that is used principally to evoke a past era (as in the newsreel sequence of *Citizen Kane*). In an iris out, a dark circle begins at the center of the frame and increases in size until the screen is entirely dark. An iris in begins with a tiny circle of light in a dark screen that expands until a scene is revealed and fills the screen.

Jump cut. A *cut* that transcends space and is often used to condense time or action. For example, a character enters a taxi and a jump cut reveals the taxi arriving at a train station.

Key light. The principal source of artificial light within a scene.

Lap dissolve. Short for "overlap dissolve," which has become shortened to *dissolve.* (See *dissolve.*)

Leitmotif. A recurrent image or musical passage associated with a character or theme.

Light. See *natural light, key light, bottom lighting, top lighting, front light, back light, side light, fill light, high key lighting, low key lighting, high contrast.*

Local music. Music that has its source within the visual and rarely has a neutral value. The jazz song "It Can't Be Love" sung during the outing in the Everglades in *Citizen Kane* is a realistic part of the scene, but it clearly comments on the action as well.

Location. An actual environment used for a film production, as opposed to a studio set.

Long lens. See *telephoto lens.*

Long shot (LS). A *shot* taken from a distance so a single person fills the frame from head to toe. (See *full shot*.)

Long take. A *take* of lengthy duration.

Loose framing. Shooting so that the frame loosely encloses the actor or actors, leaving an abundance of empty space around them. It often connotes freedom.

Low-angle shot. A *shot* in which the camera views the subject from below, making the subject appear larger than life and in a dominant position. Many of the shots of Kane as a young man are taken from low angle, so that he seems to tower over his surroundings.

Low-key lighting. Lighting that produces a dark set with heavy shadow.

Masking. A technique whereby part of the image is blocked out.

Match cut. A *cut* in which the two adjacent *shots* are similar in size and composition.

Match dissolve. A *dissolve* in which the two adjacent *shots* are similar in size and composition. In *Citizen Kane,* Welles employs a match dissolve to go from Susan Alexander's parlor on the night Kane meets her to the more elaborate setting he establishes her in.

Matte shot. A process for combining two separate *shots* on one print. The setting for the picnic sequence near the end of *Citizen Kane* is taken from an earlier movie, *Son of Kong;* Welles has matted out an ape and matted in footage of Kane and his second wife to make it appear as if they were filmed in the Everglades.

Medium shot (MS). A *shot* taken at such a distance that a person is shown from head to waist.

Metaphor. A *trope* or figurative use of language in which two distinctly different things are compared or identified directly.

Metonymy. A *trope* or figurative use of language in which a term is substituted for something with which it is closely associated.

Mise-en-scène. A French theatrical term (literally translated as ''placing on the stage'') used to indicate the total visual effect created by everything we see within the *frame:* the setting, costume, makeup, props—in short, all the visual constituents of the image. The mise-en-scène may be realistic or highly stylized, depending on the intentions of the *director.*

Monologue. The speech of a character when no one else is present.

Montage. An arrangement of *shots* that distorts time and space; creating a montage is also called *dynamic editing.* The meaning of the sequence is produced by the juxtaposition of shots rather than by the content of any individual shot. Preceding Susan Alexander's suicide attempt in *Citizen Kane* is a montage that encapsulates her career and her increasing sense of desperation. (See *continuity editing.*)

Moviola. A piece of editing equipment that permits one to examine a film *frame* by frame.

Moving shot. Any *shot* produced with a camera that moves through space, either physically or optically. (See *dolly shot, boom shot, tracking shot, trucking shot, zoom shot.*)

Multiple exposure. A special optical effect whereby several images are superimposed.

Narrative time. The length of time covered by the story.

Narrator. The one who tells the story. The narrator may be an actual character in the fictive work (e.g., Meursault is the first-person narrator of Albert Camus's novel *The Stranger*) or may be an omniscient voice in either novel or film (as in *Jules and Jim*).

Natural light. Light for a scene that comes from real sources within the film—for example, the sun, a candle, a street lamp.

Natural sounds. Sounds that have a source within the scene and make the scene more realistic. But natural sounds can also be used for dramatic intensification, as with the ticking of the clock in *High Noon*.

Nonsynchronous sound. See *synchronous sound*.

Objective shot. A *shot* not identified with the *point of view* of any character.

Objective time. The chronological presentation of events.

Oblique-angle shot. A *shot* in which the camera is tilted slightly at an oblique angle, usually to convey discord or lack of balance (also called a *Dutch-angle shot*).

Omniscient narrator. A narrator with total knowledge of the characters, events, and actions of the story.

Out take. Any part of a *take* that ends on the cutting-room floor.

Over-the-shoulder shot. A *shot* taken from behind one of the characters (over the shoulder) and including the back of the head and the front of the person or object that character is facing.

Pace. The tempo of a film, determined by the *internal* and *external rhythm* of the *shots*.

Pan. The horizontal movement of a camera on a stationary axis; short for "panorama shot."

Parallel editing. See *cross cutting*.

Picaresque. An episodic form of prose fiction in which the adventures of the hero are chronicled.

Plot. The organization of the actions and events of a story.

Point of view. The perspective or perspectives employed by an author to determine how the story is narrated.

Point-of-view shot. See *subjective shot*.

Process shot. A special effects *shot*, combining two or more images by *back projection* or *front projection*.

Producer. The person with responsibility for the business aspects of a film.

Prologue. An introductory act or event.

Psychological time. Our perception of duration—how quickly or slowly time seems to pass.

Rack focus shot. A *shot* in which movement is created optically by shifting the focus from one plane to another. For example, an actor in the foreground of the shot can go out of focus as someone in the background comes into focus.

Reaction shot. A *shot* (usually medium to close-up) that captures the response of a character to an unexpected action or comment.

Rear projection shot. See *back projection shot*.

Reverse-angle shot. A *shot* taken 180 degrees from the previous shot, thus revealing more of the scene.

Reverse motion. The projection of images backward to create a magical or supernatural effect.

Rhythm. See *internal rhythm; external rhythm*.

Rising action. The development of conflicts and complications that precedes the *turning point* or *climax*.

Scene. A group of *shots* with a unity of location.

Screen time. The actual length of the movie when projected on the screen.

Script. The written form of the film. The amount of detail (camera angle, etc.) varies from writer to writer.

Sequence. A group of interrelated scenes usually building toward a climax.

Shooting ratio. The ratio in a finished film between the number of feet of film actually shot and the number of feet used.

Shot. An uninterrupted series of frames projected on the screen.

Side light. Light directed toward a subject from the side, so that half the face is partially in shadows.

Simile. A *trope,* or figurative use of language, in which two distinctly different things are compared using *like* or *as.*

Slow motion. The result of filming the action at faster than normal speed. When projected on the screen, the action appears to move slowly, which gives the *sequence* a dancelike quality.

Soft focus. The use of a special lens to make the image appear slightly hazy and thereby romanticized.

Soliloquy. In drama, the thoughts of a character as uttered before the audience.

Sound. Can be divided into three categories:

- The spoken voice (see *dialogue; monologue; voice-over; narrator; commentator; dubbing*).
- sound effects (see *natural sounds*).
- music (see *local music; leitmotif; background music*).

(See also *synchronous sound, asynchronous sound.*)

Silent speed. The speed (between 16 and 18 frames per second) at which a silent film is projected.

Sound speed. The speed (24 frames per second) at which sound film is projected.

Still. A still photograph taken during production and generally used for publicity. (See *frame enlargement.*)

Stream of consciousness. An attempt to represent random mental processes verbally.

Structure. The relationship of the parts of a work to the whole.

Subjective shot. A *shot* that shows a character or setting as though through the eyes of another character (also called *point-of-view* shot).

Subjective sound. Sound used to indicate the psychological state of the protagonist.

Superimposition. The simultaneous occurrence of two different visual images, one on top of the other, as in a *dissolve.*

Swish pan. A very rapid pan (also called a *flash pan*), sometimes used as a *transition,* as in the breakfast sequence in *Citizen Kane.*

Symbol. An action, object, person, or name that signifies more than its literal meaning. A flag is a piece of cloth; it is also a symbol of its country.

Synchronous sound. Any sound that has an obvious source in the accompanying visuals and is synchronized with the action or, in the case of a person, with the lips.

Synecdoche. A *trope* or figurative use of language in which a part is substituted for the whole, or the whole for a part.

Take. A strip of film resulting from one continuous shooting of the camera. A take may be edited into one or more shots.

Telephoto lens. A lens (also called a *long lens*) that magnifies the image but flattens it as well, thus creating a sense of foreshortened perspective.

Three hundred and sixty-degree pan. See *circular pan.*

Three-shot. A shot containing three characters.

Tight framing. Shooting a scene so that the actor or actors appear to be tightly enclosed by the perimeters of the *frame.* Tight framing often suggests entrapment.

Tilt shot. A *shot* taken from a camera moving vertically on a stationary axis.

Time. See *screen time; narrative time; psychological time; objective time; flashback; flash-forward.*

Top lighting. Lighting a subject from above to create an angelic or ethereal effect.

Tracking shot. Historically, a *shot* using a moving camera fixed on tracks. A camera may track in, track out, or track with a subject. (See *dolly shot; trucking shot.*)

Transition. Passage from one shot to another. Transitions may be used to indicate a change of scene; they can condense action and time; or they may suggest relationships between the objects or persons they connect. (See *dissolve; fade in / fade out; cut; match cut; jump cut; iris; wipe; flip.*)

Trope. The figurative use of a word or expression. For examples of tropes, see *simile; metaphor; metonymy; synecdoche.*

Trucking shot. Historically, a shot using a moving camera fixed on a truck; now used interchangeably with *tracking shot.* (See also *dolly shot.*)

Turning point. See *climax.*

Two-shot. A *shot* containing two characters.

Verbal irony. A statement with two opposed meanings. For example, the comment "That is nice" could be used ironically to mean the opposite.

Voice-over. A form of narration in which a character's lips remain closed while the voice is heard, expressing his or her thoughts. Voice-over has a more subjective effect than *monologue.*

Wide-angle lens. A lens that includes more in the width of the composition than a normal lens but that has a shallower focal length.

Wipe. A *transition* that gives the impression of a vertical line moving across the screen and pushing off one image as another succeeds it. A series of wipes may suggest a succession of temporal periods, as in the early sequence in *The Throne of Blood,* where the king and his counselors await the news of the battle, or a succession of objects, as in the newsreel sequence of *Citizen Kane.*

Zoom shot. A *shot* creating a sense of movement through space by optic means. Whereas the *dolly* shot appears to move through three-dimensional space, the zoom shot flattens space.

INDEX